Crane Operations

Richard Skiba

Copyright © 2024 by Richard Skiba

All rights reserved.

No portion of this book may be reproduced in any form without written permission from the publisher or author, except as permitted by copyright law.

This publication is designed to provide accurate and authoritative information in regard to the subject matter covered. While the publisher and author have used their best efforts in preparing this book, they make no representations or warranties with respect to the accuracy or completeness of the contents of this book and specifically disclaim any implied warranties of merchantability or fitness for a particular purpose. No warranty may be created or extended by sales representatives or written sales materials. The advice and strategies contained herein may not be suitable for your situation. You should consult with a professional when appropriate. Neither the publisher nor the author shall be liable for any loss of profit or any other commercial damages, including but not limited to special, incidental, consequential, personal, or other damages.

Skiba, Richard (author)

Crane Operations

ISBN 978-0-9756552-6-9 (paperback) 978-0-9756552-7-6 (eBook)

Non-fiction

Contents

Preface	1
1. Introduction	4
2. Cranes Defined	21
3. Static Cranes – Tower Cranes	45
4. Derrick and Portal Boom Cranes	176
5. Bridge Cranes	275
6. Personnel and Materials Hoist	302
7. Slewing Mobile Cranes	324
8. Truck Mounted/Vehicle Loading Crane	400
9. Non-Slewing Mobile Cranes	421
10. Crane Hooks and Lifting Gear	444
11. Load Calculations	471
12. References	493
Index	495

Preface

This book provides a comprehensive guide to crane operation, covering various types of cranes and associated tasks involved in operating them safely and efficiently. It begins with an introduction, followed by chapters dedicated to defining different types of cranes, including static cranes like tower cranes, derrick and portal boom cranes, bridge and gantry cranes, personnel and materials hoists, slewing mobile cranes, truck-mounted/vehicle loading cranes, and non-slewing mobile cranes. Each chapter delves into the specific features, functions, and operational considerations of the respective crane types.

The book also discusses essential tasks and procedures involved in crane operation, such as planning work tasks, preparing for tasks, performing tasks, and packing up after completing tasks. For each crane type, it outlines steps for planning and preparing work tasks, including identifying task requirements, assessing work area conditions, establishing lifting capacities, and implementing hazard identification and risk control measures. Additionally, it covers pre-start crane checks, setting up cranes correctly, conducting operational checks, and assessing weather and environmental conditions.

Furthermore, the book details procedures for performing work tasks, including determining safe lifts within crane capacity, positioning crane components over loads, connecting lifting equipment and gear, and monitoring load and crane movements. It emphasizes the importance of constant communication, adherence to safe work procedures, and vigilant monitoring during crane operation to ensure safety and efficiency.

Finally, the book provides guidance on packing up after completing work tasks, including stowing and securing crane components, applying motion locks and brakes, shutting down the crane, and conducting post-operational checks for compliance with legislative responsibilities and manufacturer requirements. Overall, the book serves as a comprehensive resource for crane operators, covering all aspects of crane operation and safety procedures.

The crane information provided within this book is intended to be general in nature and may not encompass all aspects of crane operation. It is important to note that each item of crane plant has its own specific characteristics and operational requirements that may vary. Crane operators are strongly advised to consult the manufacturer's guides and manuals prior to the operation of any crane to ensure compliance with safety standards and operational procedures.

Furthermore, it is crucial to acknowledge that crane operations and terminology can differ across jurisdictions. Crane operators should be aware that regulations and guidelines pertaining to crane usage may vary depending on the location. Therefore, it is essential for crane operators to familiarize themselves with the applicable laws, regulations, and standards in their respective jurisdictions.

Additionally, crane operators are urged to review workplace policies and procedures before operating any crane. Workplace-specific protocols may exist to address unique hazards and safety considerations, which must be adhered to for safe crane operation.

Moreover, it is important to recognize that in many jurisdictions, crane licensing requirements apply. Crane operators are responsible for ensuring that they meet all jurisdictional legislative requirements relevant to their sites of practice. This may include obtaining appropriate licenses, certifications, or permits to operate cranes legally and safely within their jurisdiction.

Sample load charts, specifications, interpretations and calculations are used throughout this book for demonstration purposes only and should not be taken to be sued in any other manner. Every crane model is accompanied by its own distinct load chart, which may vary depending on the crane's configurations and is supplied by the crane's manufacturer. They are not portable from one model to another, and operators must always ensure they are referring to documentation relevant to the plant they are operating.

While efforts have been made to provide accurate and informative crane information, users are reminded of the need for due diligence and compliance with applicable regulations, manufacturer guidelines, workplace policies, and licensing requirements to ensure safe and lawful crane operations.

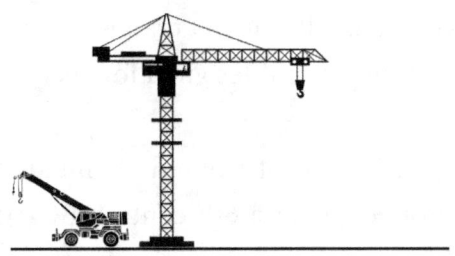

Chapter One

Introduction

A crane is a type of heavy machinery used for lifting and moving large and heavy objects. It typically consists of a hoist, wire ropes or chains, and sheaves, all mounted on a horizontal boom, which is often connected to a vertical mast. Cranes are commonly used in construction sites, manufacturing facilities, shipping yards, and other industrial settings to lift and transport materials, equipment, and goods. They come in various types, including tower cranes, mobile cranes, overhead cranes, and gantry cranes, each designed for specific applications and site conditions.

The invention of cranes is attributed to the ancient Greeks, who developed them around the late 6th century BC. Archaeological evidence suggests that these early cranes were powered by humans or animals, such as donkeys, walking inside a wheel to lift weights. They were predominantly used in the construction of buildings and in the loading and unloading of ships (Chant & Goodman, 2005).

The Industrial Revolution marked a significant turning point for crane technology, with the introduction of steam engines, electric motors, and internal combustion engines powering these machines. Today's cranes often incorporate simple machines with sophisticated technologies, including computer systems, to enhance lifting capabilities and safety measures (Talbott, 2007).

Crane operators are responsible for operating stationary or mobile cranes to lift, move, and position heavy objects, often found at various locations such as wharves, shipyards, and construction sites. Given the potential consequences of errors in crane operation, this role entails a significant level of responsibility.

Key tasks and duties include operating cranes to lift and relocate items as directed, conducting inspections and maintenance on equipment, ensuring ground conditions are suitable for crane setup, placing support materials under outrigger pads when necessary, positioning the crane accurately, and attaching loads securely. Additionally, crane operators monitor cabin instruments to ensure loads remain within safe limits and follow ground team signals for load placement.

Successful crane operators possess a range of skills, both technical and interpersonal. These include strong communication skills to understand and follow instructions, mechanical aptitude for conducting inspections and maintenance, coordination for precise load movement, teamwork for effective collaboration with ground personnel, mathematical and physics knowledge for load management and stability assessment, physical fitness for performing tasks efficiently, and a thorough understanding of safety protocols to ensure a safe working environment.

Working as a crane operator offers various benefits, including competitive wages and high demand for skilled operators in the construction industry. Crane operators typically work in outdoor environments such as construction sites, mines, and shipyards, often exposed to various weather conditions. Despite the challenges, the role provides opportunities for meaningful contributions to large-scale projects and a supportive work environment characterized by teamwork and camaraderie.

Individuals may opt to pursue a career as crane operators for several compelling reasons. Firstly, the field offers a high earning potential.

Crane operators typically command competitive salaries, particularly as they gain experience and develop specialized skills. For individuals seeking stable and lucrative employment opportunities, the financial rewards associated with this profession can be highly appealing.

In terms of renumeration or financial rewards associated with the role of Crane Operator, in Australia in 2024, the typical gross salary for a tower crane operator averages $99,001 per year, corresponding to an hourly rate of $48. Additionally, they may receive an average bonus of $1,960 (Salary Expert, 2024). These salary figures are derived from data obtained directly from employers and anonymous employees through salary surveys. For those with entry-level experience (1-3 years), the average salary stands at $72,532, while more experienced senior-level operators (8+ years) command an average salary of $121,358 (Salary Expert, 2024). The typical annual salary for a Mobile Crane Operator amounts to $97,709, translating to an hourly rate of $ 47. The salary range typically falls between $70,253 and $ 117,544 for professionals in this field.

In Canada, the average annual salary for a Mobile Crane Operator is $74,423, with an hourly rate of $36. The salary range typically falls between $53,510 and $89,531 for Mobile Crane Operators (Economic Research Institute, 2024).

In Germany, the average annual salary for a Mobile Crane Operator is €59,456, with an hourly rate of €29. The salary range typically falls between €42,749 and €71,526 (Economic Research Institute, 2024).

In Japan, the average annual salary for a Mobile Crane Operator is JPY 5,544,659, equating to JPY 2,666 per hour. The salary range typically spans between JPY 3,986,610 and JPY 6,670,225 for Mobile Crane Operators (Economic Research Institute, 2024).

In Poland, the average gross salary for a construction crane operator is 90,871 zł annually, with an equivalent hourly rate of 44 zł. Additionally, they typically receive an average bonus of 1,745 zł. These salary estimates are derived from data collected directly from employers and anonymous employees. For those entering the field with 1-3 years of experience, the average salary for a construction crane operator is 66,579 zł, while senior-level operators with 8 or more years of experience earn an average of 111,150 zł annually (Salary Expert, 2024).

The average pay for a Mobile Crane Operator is £42,109 a year and £20 an hour in the United Kingdom (Economic Research Institute, 2024). The average salary range for a Mobile Crane Operator is between £30,277 and £50,657. The average crane operator salary in the United Kingdom is £38,925 per year or £19.96 per hour. Entry level positions start at £27,300 per year while most experienced workers make up to £50,700 per year (talent.com, 2024).

In the USA, the average annual salary for crane operators is $46,122, which equates to $22.17 per hour (Economic Research Institute, 2024). Entry-level roles typically begin at $37,043 annually, while seasoned professionals can earn $71,224 per year. In the United States, the average annual salary for a Mobile Crane Operator is $66,630, with an hourly rate of $32. The salary range typically falls between $47,907 and $80,156 for Mobile Crane Operators (Economic Research Institute, 2024).

Moreover, there is a consistent demand for crane operators across various industries, including construction, shipping, manufacturing, and logistics. This perpetual need for skilled professionals in the field ensures job security and creates opportunities for career advancement.

One of the attractive aspects of this profession is the diverse array of work environments it offers. Crane operators may find themselves working in dynamic settings such as construction sites, ports, warehouses, and industrial facilities. For those who enjoy working outdoors and thrive in varied work environments, this diversity can be particularly enticing.

Operating a crane necessitates the acquisition of technical skills, spatial awareness, and the ability to perform under pressure. As such, individuals who relish the opportunity to learn new skills and master complex machinery may find the profession intellectually stimulating and fulfilling.

Crane operators play a pivotal role in numerous construction and industrial projects, contributing to the completion of tasks such as erecting buildings and safely manoeuvring heavy machinery. Witnessing tangible outcomes of their work can instil a sense of accomplishment and job satisfaction among crane operators.

Additionally, the profession may offer opportunities for travel, especially for those engaged in large-scale construction projects or industries with operations in diverse locations. This prospect of experiencing new places and cultures can be appealing to individuals with a sense of adventure.

Finally, operating a crane presents both physical and mental challenges. Successfully manoeuvring heavy loads requires physical stamina, while maintaining focus and attention to detail is essential for safe and efficient operation. For individuals who thrive on challenges and enjoy hands-on work, the profession provides a fulfilling blend of physical and mental activity.

Becoming a crane operator presents a rewarding career path for individuals seeking financial stability, job security, skill development, and the opportunity to make a tangible impact across various industries.

Local Variations in Definitions and Terms

In the context of crane operation, "dogging" refers to the role of a worker who assists the crane operator by providing guidance and communication during lifting operations. The term "dogman" or "dogger" is often used interchangeably with this role.

The primary responsibilities of a dogger include:

1. Load Position Reporting: The dogger observes and monitors the position of the load being lifted. They communicate this information to the crane operator, especially when the load is out of the operator's direct line of sight or obscured by obstacles.

2. Signal Communication: Doggers use predetermined hand signals or verbal commands to direct the crane operator regarding load movement, positioning, and any necessary adjustments. Clear and effective communication between the dogger and the operator is crucial for safe and precise crane operations.

3. Safety Oversight: Doggers play a key role in ensuring that lifting operations are conducted safely. They assess the surrounding environment for potential hazards, such as overhead obstacles, power lines, or uneven terrain, and communicate any safety concerns to the crane operator.

4. Assistance with Rigging: In some cases, doggers may assist with the rigging and attachment of loads to the crane's hook. They ensure that the load is properly secured and balanced before signalling the crane operator to lift.

Overall, the role of a dogger is essential for maintaining safety and efficiency during crane operations. By providing clear communication, monitoring load movements, and assessing safety risks, doggers help minimize the risk of accidents and ensure that lifting tasks are carried out smoothly and effectively.

In some contexts, "dogger" and "swamper" may refer to similar roles, particularly in industries involving heavy equipment and machinery like construction, logging, or crane operation. However, there are also differences in the specific tasks and responsibilities associated with each role.

A "dogger" typically refers to a worker who assists the crane operator during lifting operations, providing guidance, communication, and safety oversight as described in the previous explanation. Doggers focus on ensuring that loads are lifted, moved, and positioned safely and accurately.

On the other hand, a "swamper" often refers to a worker who assists with various tasks related to equipment operation and maintenance, including loading and unloading materials, cleaning equipment, and performing minor repairs. While a swamper may also assist with rigging and signalling during crane operations, their responsibilities may be broader and encompass a range of support duties beyond just crane operation.

The terminology can vary depending on the industry and region, so while there may be overlap in the tasks performed by doggers and swampers, the specific duties and titles can differ based on the context of the work environment.

The usage of terms like "dogger" and "swamper" can vary depending on the region and industry. Here's a breakdown of where these terms are commonly used and some other variations of the role:

1. **Dogger:**

    - **Australia and New Zealand**: The term "dogger" is commonly used in Australia and New Zealand, particularly in industries such as construction, mining, and maritime.

    - **United Kingdom**: The term "dogger" is also used in the UK, primarily in the context of maritime operations, referring to a worker responsible for handling mooring lines on ships or assisting with cargo handling.

2. **Swamper:**

    - **North America (United States and Canada)**: The term

"swamper" is commonly used in North America, particularly in industries like logging, trucking, and heavy equipment operation. A swamper typically assists with various tasks related to equipment operation and maintenance.

- **United Kingdom**: In the UK, "swamper" can also be used in the context of trucking or transportation to refer to an assistant who helps with loading and unloading cargo or assisting the driver with various tasks.

Other variations or similar roles may include:

- **Rigger**: A rigger is responsible for setting up and securing rigging equipment for lifting operations. They ensure that loads are properly attached and balanced for safe lifting and movement.

- **Signalperson or Signaller**: A signalperson, also known as a signaller in some regions, is responsible for communicating with the crane operator using standardized hand signals or radio communication to guide the lifting and movement of loads.

- **Ground Crew**: This term is more general and may encompass various support roles on the ground, including doggers, swampers, riggers, signalpersons, and others involved in crane operations and equipment handling.

- **Spotter**: In some contexts, particularly in industries like construction or warehouse operations, a spotter may be responsible for guiding equipment operators to ensure safe movement and positioning in tight or hazardous areas.

These roles and terms may have regional variations and can be influenced by the specific industry practices and terminology used in different countries or regions.

Throughout this book, references to dogging encompasses the various essential functions on a construction site, with the primary responsibility being skilled in the safe use of slinging techniques to secure loads. An individual appropriately trained in dogging is referred to as a dogman or dogger, holding a crucial role across construction, demolition, heavy vehicle industries, shipping, freight, and related sectors.

The dogger assumes the principal responsibility for meticulously selecting and inspecting lifting equipment to securely sling a load, highlighting their significant role in ensuring site safety. Failure to properly secure loads with slings, hooks, and chains can pose significant safety risks, underscoring the necessity for thorough training and licensing of doggers.

Additionally, doggers are proficient in guiding plant operators to manoeuvre loads safely around the site. In addition to securing and slinging loads, they assist crane, telehandler, and excavator operators in navigating challenging visibility conditions. Through the use of hand signals, whistles, and two-way radios for communication, doggers effectively direct plant operators to safely deposit their loads.

In the US, the equivalent role to a dogger would typically be referred to as a rigger or a signal person. These individuals are responsible for rigging and signalling during lifting operations, ensuring that loads are properly secured and guiding equipment operators to manoeuvre loads safely. They play a crucial role in maintaining safety on construction sites, similar to doggers in other parts of the world.

In the UK and around Europe, the equivalent role to a dogger would typically be referred to as a slinger or a banksman. These individuals are responsible for slinging loads and providing guidance to equipment operators during lifting operations, ensuring safety and efficiency on construction sites. They perform tasks similar to doggers, including selecting and inspecting lifting equipment, guiding equipment operators, and communicating effectively using signals and radios.

References to swamper, slinger, signal person, banksman throughout this book are take to be that of a dogger as defined above.

The terms "tons" and "tonnes" both refer to units of mass or weight, but they are used differently in various regions and contexts.

1. Tons: In the United States and some other English-speaking countries, "tons" typically refers to short tons or US tons. A short ton is equivalent to 2,000 pounds or approximately 907.185 kilograms. This unit is commonly used in industries such as construction, transportation, and manufacturing in these regions.

2. Tonnes: In many other parts of the world, including most English-speaking countries outside of the United States, "tonnes" is used. A tonne, also known as a metric ton, is a unit of mass in the metric system. It is equivalent to 1,000 kilograms or approximately 2,204.623 pounds. The metric tonne is the preferred unit of measurement in most scientific, engineering, and international trade contexts worldwide.

While both "tons" and "tonnes" are units of mass or weight, "tons" typically refers to the short ton used in the United States, while "tonnes" refers to the metric ton used in most other parts of the world. It's important to clarify which unit is being used in a specific context to avoid confusion when working with lifting plant.

Crane Operator Licensing and Training

Crane operating licenses, also known as certifications or qualifications, are regulatory requirements or voluntary credentials that individuals must obtain to operate cranes safely and legally in various jurisdictions worldwide. These licenses typically demonstrate that the operator has received appropriate training, possesses the necessary skills, and understands the safety protocols associated with crane operation.

Legislative frameworks for Crane Operator Certification exist in numerous countries to ensure the safe operation of cranes. For instance, in the United States, OSHA regulations implemented in April 2019 aim to enhance crane operators' knowledge and training to minimize accidents. These regulations shift the responsibility for operator readiness onto the employer and encompass various construction equipment, including mobile cranes, tower cranes, and digger derricks (Skiba, 2020). Compliance with these regulations mandates that crane operators must be certified or licensed and receive continuous training to operate new equipment.

Similarly, in Australia, crane operators must obtain a high-risk work license to operate a range of cranes. Before obtaining a national license for high-risk work, individuals must undergo assessment by a registered training organization (RTO) to evaluate their training, skills, and knowledge under realistic workplace conditions (Skiba, 2020).

In Singapore, becoming a Registered Crane Operator entails passing a relevant crane operator course conducted by an accredited training provider (ATP) and obtaining certification within six months before applying for registration. The Singaporean government, through the Ministry of Manpower (MOM), is actively advocating for higher standards in crane operator competence to mitigate accidents. Initiatives include biennial health checks for crane operators over the age of 50 and stricter regulations for mini crane usage (Skiba, 2020).

In Europe, the certification of crane operators varies among Member States, ranging from compulsory to optional regulations. Efforts are underway to develop a European Operator Licensing System (ECOL) aimed at mobile crane operators. This system requires participants to be at least 18 years old and hold a valid EU class-C driving license.

In the United Kingdom, the Construction Plant Competence Scheme (CPCS) issues skills cards for crane operators, indicating their competency to operate specific types of cranes safely. While participation in the scheme is not mandatory, it provides employers with assurance of an individual's competence and skills (Skiba, 2020).

The following is an overview of crane operating licenses in different parts of the world:

1. United States: In the United States, crane operators must comply with Occupational Safety and Health Administration (OSHA) regulations. OSHA's crane standard requires operators to be certified or licensed, and it outlines specific training, evaluation, and certification requirements. Certification programs are offered by accredited organizations, and operators may need additional endorsements for specific crane types or tasks.

2. Canada: Canada has provincial regulations governing crane operator certification. Certification requirements vary by province but generally involve completing a training program, passing written and practical exams, and obtaining a license from the appropriate provincial regulatory authority.

3. Australia: In Australia, crane operators are required to hold a high-risk work license issued by the relevant state or territory regulatory authority. To obtain this license, operators must complete formal training and assessment conducted by registered training organizations (RTOs) and demonstrate competency in operating specific types of cranes.

4. United Kingdom: The United Kingdom's construction industry operates under the Construction Plant Competence Scheme (CPCS). Crane operators can obtain certification through accredited training providers by passing both theoretical and practical assessments. The CPCS issues competence cards indicat-

ing the operator's qualifications.

5. European Union: European Union member states may have their own regulations regarding crane operator certification. However, efforts are underway to establish a European Operator Licensing System (ECOL) to standardize certification requirements and promote mobility within the EU. Training institutes offer ECOL training, and participants must meet age and licensing prerequisites.

6. Singapore: In Singapore, crane operators must complete relevant training courses conducted by accredited training providers (ATPs) and obtain certification. The Ministry of Manpower (MOM) oversees crane operator registration and sets competency standards to enhance safety and reduce accidents.

7. Japan: Japan has certification programs for crane operators administered by industry associations and government agencies. Operators must undergo training and pass examinations to obtain certification. The Japanese government regulates crane operation to ensure compliance with safety standards.

8. Other Countries: Many other countries have their own regulations or industry standards for crane operator licensing and certification. These may include training requirements, competency assessments, and periodic renewal processes to ensure continued compliance with safety standards.

Overall, crane operator licensing and certification requirements vary by country, but they generally aim to ensure that operators have the necessary skills, knowledge, and training to perform their duties safely and effectively, thereby reducing the risk of accidents and promoting workplace safety.

Globally, there is a lack of uniformity in training approaches and requirements for crane operators. Training methods vary widely and may be integrated into national systems, mandated by regulatory bodies, aligned with specific competency standards, endorsed by industry organizations, or conducted independently of formal training structures (Skiba, 2020).

Internationally, numerous crane operation training programs exist outside of national or obligatory frameworks. These programs are offered by various entities such as industry associations, employers, professional bodies, vocational education providers, and equipment suppliers. In some countries, particularly on the international stage, there are comprehensive and well-established competency frameworks tailored for crane operation.

Crane operators require comprehensive knowledge and skills to ensure the safe and efficient operation of cranes. Here are the key aspects they need to be familiar with (Skiba, 2020):

1. **Preparation for Crane Operations:**

    - Conduct pre-start and start-up checks for equipment.
    - Identify and rectify or report faults or defects.
    - Confirm attachment of lifting gear according to workplace procedures.
    - Ensure the work area is clear and safe.
    - Assess ground suitability for crane operation.
    - Determine appropriate paths for crane operation and load placement.
    - Identify and address hazards using risk control measures.

2. **Commencing Crane Operations:**

- Position, stabilize, and level the crane before lift operations.
- Interpret load charts accurately.
- Confirm load weight within crane capacity and operating radius.
- Configure crane for the specified lift.
- Prepare loads for lift in accordance with crane limitations and rigging requirements.
- Access crane safely according to manufacturer specifications.

3. **Operating Within Equipment Capacities:**
   - Perform pre-operation checks.
   - Utilize crane controls to lift and position loads safely.
   - Monitor equipment performance using indicators and alarms.
   - Manage hazards and risks during operations to ensure safety.

4. **Crane Travel (where relevant):**
   - Plan a suitable route for crane travel.
   - Monitor and manage hazards along the route.
   - Follow relevant standards, guidelines, and organizational procedures during crane travel.

5. **Completing Crane Operations:**
   - Shut down crane following correct procedures.

- Park, secure, and conduct post-operational inspection according to workplace procedures.

6. **Housekeeping Activities:**

    - Clear work area and dispose/recycle materials appropriately.

    - Manage or report hazards to maintain a safe environment.

    - Complete required record-keeping and distribution as necessary.

Additionally, crane operators must be knowledgeable about various aspects related to crane operations, including:

- Relevant legislation, regulations, and standards.

- Crane and hoisting terminology and systems.

- Causes of crane incidents and accident prevention.

- Site hazard recognition.

- Equipment performance and limitations.

- Load charts and capacity calculations.

- Safety procedures for working near power lines and assembling/disassembling crane components.

- Proper use of lifting accessories, wire ropes, and chains.

- Environmental conditions affecting crane operations.

- Crane operator's authority to halt operations.

This comprehensive understanding ensures that crane operators can safely and effectively carry out their responsibilities.

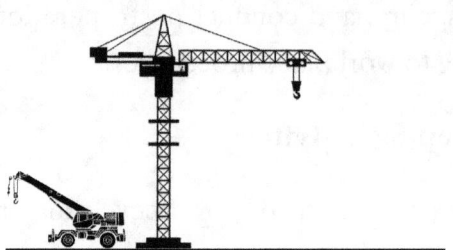

Chapter Two
Cranes Defined

There are two primary crane categories: static and mobile. A static crane is fixed, lifting loads along a set path. See Figure 1 for an example. Conversely, a mobile crane is mounted on wheels or treads, allowing mobility between job sites, an example shown as Figure 2.. Unlike static cranes, mobile cranes can perform "pick and carry" operations, moving loads to different locations using their wheels or treads. Depending on the model, some mobile cranes may require outriggers, counterweights, or on-site assembly.

Figure 1: A tower crane on the Alexan Waterloo apartment tower under construction at 700 East 11th Street, Austin, Texas, United States. Larry D. Moore, CC BY-SA 4.0, via Wikimedia Commons.

The primary difference between a static crane and a mobile crane lies in their mobility and setup process:

1. Static Crane:

    - Static cranes, also known as stationary cranes or tower cranes, are fixed to a specific location during operation.

    - They are typically installed on-site using a large base or foundation and a vertical mast, which provides stability.

    - Static cranes are commonly used for lifting heavy loads over relatively short distances, such as in construction projects where materials need to be moved vertically within a confined area.

    - While static cranes offer high lifting capacity and stability, they lack mobility and must be disassembled and reassembled at each new location, which can be time-consuming.

2. Mobile Crane:

    - Mobile cranes are designed for mobility and can be easily transported to different worksites.

    - They are mounted on wheels or tracks, allowing them to move around the worksite and access various areas where lifting is required.

    - Mobile cranes come in various configurations, including truck-mounted cranes, rough terrain cranes, and all-terrain cranes, each suited for different terrain and lifting requirements.

    - Mobile cranes are often preferred for projects that require flexibility and rapid setup, as they can be quickly deployed and repositioned as needed.

- While mobile cranes offer versatility and convenience, they may have lower lifting capacities compared to static cranes, particularly for very heavy loads or when lifting at great heights.

The main distinction between static and mobile cranes is their mobility and setup process: static cranes are stationary and require on-site assembly, while mobile cranes can be easily transported and quickly set up at different locations (Al-Hussein et al., 2001).

Figure 2: Liebherr mobile crane in Munich. High Contrast, CC BY 3.0 DE, via Wikimedia Commons.

Ship's cranes are a little different. A ship's crane, as shown in Figure 3 and Figure 4, is not typically considered a static crane. While some ship cranes may have fixed components or be permanently installed on a vessel, they are designed to be mobile and adaptable to various maritime operations. Ship cranes are used for loading and unloading cargo, handling containers, and performing other tasks aboard ships and at ports.

Figure 3: Crane onboard the heavy-lift ship La Paimpolaise, lifting a hatch cover. Hervé Cozanet, CC BY-SA 3.0, via Wikimedia Commons.

Ship cranes often have features that allow them to rotate and extend their reach, providing flexibility in accessing cargo holds and reaching different areas of the ship. They may be mounted on rails or tracks on the deck of the vessel, allowing them to move along the ship's length or from side to side.

Figure 4: Sormec Marine Cranes on board of vessel. MiriamGagliardo, CC BY-SA 3.0, via Wikimedia Commons.

Overall, ship cranes are more akin to mobile cranes in terms of their functionality and mobility, as they are designed to operate in dynamic maritime environments and are capable of moving and adjusting to different tasks and conditions.

Selecting the appropriate crane for a specific site involves considering various factors such as the type of loads requiring lifting, the height and horizontal distances involved, the swing radius, duration of lifting operations, utilization factor, degree of mobility needed, and compatibility with other equipment like concreting plants. Each of these factors plays a crucial role in determining the most suitable crane model to optimize efficiency and safety in lifting operations.

While static, mobile, and ship's cranes serve different purposes and operate in distinct environments, they share some common similarities:

1. Lifting Capability: All three types of cranes are designed to lift heavy loads, whether it's construction materials on a building site (static and mobile cranes), or cargo on a ship (ship's crane). They utilize various mechanisms such as hoists, cables, and winches to perform lifting operations.

2. Mechanical Components: Static, mobile, and ship's cranes all consist of similar mechanical components, including booms, jibs, hoists, and control systems. These components enable them to manipulate loads and perform lifting tasks efficiently.

3. Safety Considerations: Safety is paramount in the operation of all types of cranes. Static, mobile, and ship's cranes must adhere to safety regulations and standards to ensure the well-being of workers and prevent accidents. This includes proper maintenance, regular inspections, and adherence to load capacity limits.

4. Operator Training: Operating any type of crane requires specialized training and certification. Whether it's controlling a static crane on a construction site, manoeuvring a mobile crane at different job sites, or operating a ship's crane on a vessel, crane operators must undergo comprehensive training to safely and effectively handle the equipment.

5. Load Handling Techniques: Regardless of the type of crane, operators use similar load handling techniques to lift, lower, and position loads. This includes proper rigging techniques, load balancing, and coordination with ground personnel or crew members to ensure safe and efficient operations.

6. Application Flexibility: While each type of crane is optimized for specific applications and environments, they all offer some degree of flexibility in terms of their capabilities. For example, mobile cranes can be outfitted with different attachments or accessories to adapt to various lifting tasks, while ship's cranes may have features such as telescopic booms or cargo grabs to accommodate different types of cargo handling operations.

Overall, while there are distinct differences between static, mobile, and ship's cranes, they share commonalities in terms of their function, mechanical components, safety considerations, operator training, load handling techniques, and application flexibility.

Lifting capability is a fundamental aspect shared by static, mobile, and ship's cranes. These specialized machines are engineered to hoist and transport heavy loads efficiently and safely across a range of settings. Whether it's lifting construction materials at a construction site or handling cargo aboard a ship, cranes serve as indispensable tools in a range of industries. Their lifting prowess enables them to manoeuvre loads that would otherwise be impractical or impossible for manual labour alone.

Each crane type employs a variety of mechanisms to achieve lifting tasks. Hoists, cables, and winches are among the essential components utilized to lift and manipulate heavy loads with precision and control. These mechanisms are meticulously engineered to withstand significant weight and stress, ensuring reliable performance even under demanding conditions. Whether it's raising materials to towering heights on a construction site or loading and unloading cargo on a vessel, the lifting mechanisms of cranes enable seamless operation and efficient workflow.

Hoists, cables, and winches are essential components of cranes and other lifting equipment. Here's an overview of each and how they work:

1. Hoists: Hoists, as shown in Figure 5 are mechanical devices used to lift and lower heavy loads vertically. They consist of a motorized drum or pulley system around which a cable or chain is wrapped. When activated, the motor turns the drum or pulley, causing the cable or chain to either lift or lower the load. Hoists are commonly used in conjunction with cranes, overhead lifting systems, and elevators.

2. Cables: Cables are strong, flexible strands typically made of steel

wire ropes used to transmit force in lifting applications. In crane systems, cables are attached to the load being lifted on one end and to the hoist or winch on the other end. As the hoist or winch activates, the cable winds around a drum or pulley, lifting or lowering the load. Cables are designed to withstand heavy loads and provide reliable lifting capabilities.

3. Winches: Winches, as shown in are mechanical devices used to pull or hoist heavy loads horizontally or at an angle. They consist of a drum around which a cable or rope is wound, as well as a motor or manual crank mechanism to rotate the drum. When the winch is activated, the drum rotates, winding the cable or rope onto the drum and pulling the load attached to the other end. Winches are commonly used in applications such as vehicle recovery, marine operations, and construction.

Hoists, cables, and winches work together to lift, lower, and move heavy loads in crane and lifting applications. The hoist provides vertical lifting motion, while cables transmit force and winches provide horizontal pulling or hoisting capabilities. Together, these components form the essential machinery for a wide range of lifting tasks in various industries.

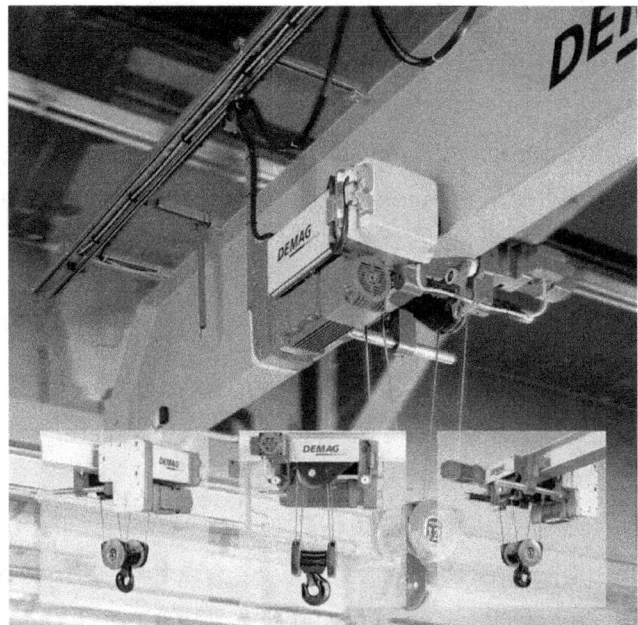

Figure 5: Bridge Crane with Wire Rope Hoist. Rvancopp, CC BY 3.0 US, via Wikimedia Commons.

Figure 6: Winch, crane mounted on a Tatra truck. Horst74, CC BY 3.0, via Wikimedia Commons.

The versatility of cranes in their lifting capabilities extends to their ability to adapt to diverse load types and environments. From lifting steel beams and concrete blocks on a construction site to handling containers and equipment on a ship's deck, cranes are designed to accommodate a wide range of loads. Their lifting capacity, combined with the flexibility to operate in various settings, makes cranes indispensable assets in industries where heavy lifting is a routine requirement.

Mechanical components are integral parts of static, mobile, and ship's cranes, facilitating their ability to manipulate heavy loads and conduct lifting operations effectively. These cranes share several common mechanical elements:

1. Booms: Booms, see Figure 7, are structural arms that extend from the crane's base and provide reach for lifting operations. They can be fixed or adjustable in length and angle, depending on the crane type and application. Booms are essential for reaching loads at various heights and distances.

2. Jibs: Jibs, see Figure 7, are additional arms or extensions mounted at the end of the main boom, providing additional reach and flexibility for lifting and manoeuvring loads. They can rotate or pivot independently of the main boom, allowing for precise positioning of the load.

3. Hoists: Hoists are mechanical devices used for lifting and lowering loads vertically. They typically consist of a motorized drum or pulley system around which a cable or chain is wrapped. Hoists provide the primary lifting motion for cranes, enabling them to raise and lower heavy loads safely and efficiently.

4. Control Systems: Control systems regulate the operation of the crane, including the movement of the boom, jib, hoist, and other functions. They may include manual controls operated by a crane operator or automated systems controlled by comput-

erized interfaces. Control systems ensure precise and smooth operation of the crane during lifting tasks.

These mechanical components work together, as shown in the diagram in Figure 8, seamlessly to enable static, mobile, and ship's cranes to manipulate loads with precision and control. Whether lifting materials on a construction site, handling cargo on a ship, or performing maintenance tasks in an industrial setting, these components play a critical role in the functionality and efficiency of cranes across various applications.

Figure 7: Boom and Jib working in Nijswijk, the Netherlands. zoetnet, CC BY 2.0, via Wikimedia Commons.

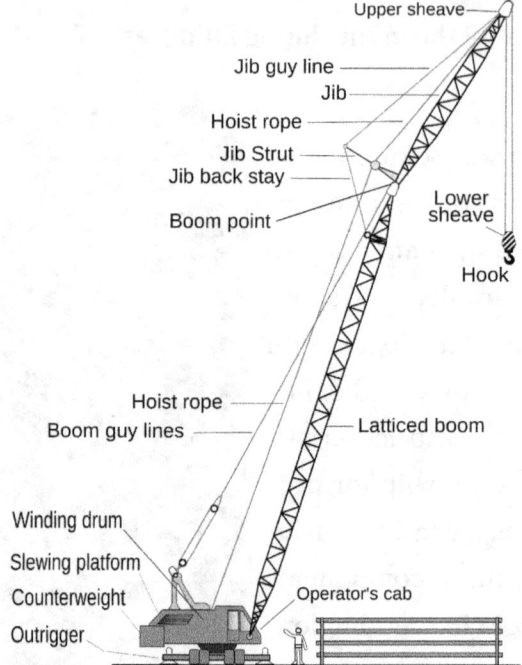

Figure 8: Crawler type derrick crane. Wilfredo R. Rodriguez H. edited by Gregory David Harington, CC BY-SA 3.0, via Wikimedia Commons.

Understanding industrial crane terminologies can greatly enhance efficiency and convenience in your work. These include:

Counterweights: Counterweights, as shown in Figure 9, play a crucial role in maintaining the balance of a crane, preventing tipping and ensuring stability while lifting heavy loads.

CRANE OPERATIONS 33

Figure 9: Crawler crane with counterweights. Cjp24, CC BY-SA 4.0, via Wikimedia Commons.

In crane operations, a counterweight, commonly composed of metal or concrete, is positioned opposite the crane's fulcrum to ensure balance and stability while lifting. Crucial components of crane design, counterweights maintain equilibrium, preventing tipping due to heavy loads. By counteracting the load's weight, they ensure safe and efficient crane operation. Counterweights are integral to both crawler and mobile cranes, serving to counterbalance the weight beneath the hook and prevent potential toppling. Given their significance, counterweights may require periodic exchange. Some mobile cranes feature detachable counterweights, essential for preventing forward tipping during operation. Positioned typically at the rear end of the crane, opposite the jib or working arm, counterweights strategically balance the crane by offsetting the load on the jib side. This configuration enhances stability during lifting. Adjusting counterweights is essential to achieve the desired lifting capacity for various loads, accomplished by adding or removing counterweight slabs or blocks to meet project specifications.

Boom: The boom serves as the arm of the crane, facilitating the lifting and adjustment of loads by extending or retracting. It acts like a telescopic or fixed arm, allowing for precise movement of objects closer to or farther away from the crane.

Figure 10: Liebherr mobile crane 450T, Brisbane, with telescopic boom. Kgbo, CC BY-SA 4.0, via Wikimedia Commons.

Load Block: The load block, or hook block, encompasses all crane accessories, including hooks, swivels, bearings, pins, frames, and sheaves, connected by hoisting ropes. This assembly ensures safe and efficient load handling. An example is shown as Figure 11.

CRANE OPERATIONS

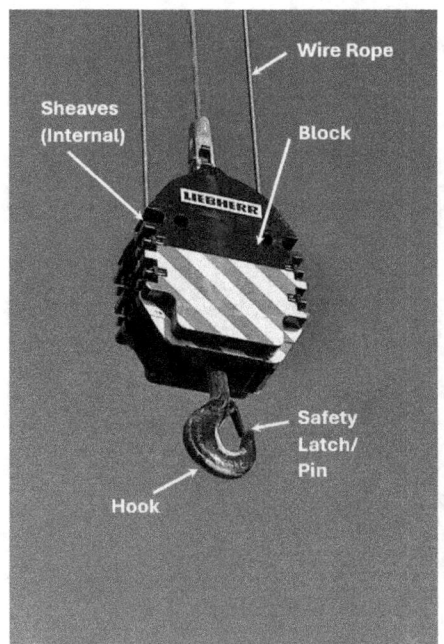

Figure 11: A Liebherr 50 t lifting hook and block. © 2010 K. Krallis SV1XV, CC BY-SA 3.0, via Wikimedia Commons.

Sheaves are components of a load block used in crane operations. They are pulley wheels with grooves designed to hold wire cables or ropes (lines). These grooved wheels spin on axles inside the frame of the block, allowing the line to move freely with minimal friction and wear on the cable. Sheaves serve various purposes in crane operations, including redirecting cables or ropes, lifting loads, and transmitting power. They play a crucial role in facilitating smooth and efficient lifting operations by ensuring the proper movement and distribution of loads.

Slings: Slings, as shown in Figure 12, act as the support system for the crane's hook, providing stability when lifting heavy loads. They are constructed from various materials, including wire rope, chain rope, and synthetic materials.

Figure 12: Slings and Spreader Bar. © Raimond Spekking / CC BY-SA 4.0 (via Wikimedia Commons).

Note a spreader bar is also shown in Figure 12. When it comes to overhead lifting, both lifting beams and spreader bars serve as essential devices for stabilizing and supporting heavy loads safely and efficiently. However, distinguishing between these two hoisting bars and understanding their respective applications can be crucial. While they share many similarities, recognizing their differences is key to selecting the most suitable hoisting bar for your specific needs.

Lifting beams typically consist of a long I-beam structure with a single attachment link centred on the top side, which connects to the hook of the crane or lifting machine (Breitsprecher, 2022). On the underside of the beam, there are two or more connection points evenly spaced out, allowing attachment to the load via hooks or slings. Lifting beams excel in general-purpose lifting tasks that don't require significant headroom, making them ideal for confined spaces like warehouses and sheds.

They can also handle multiple loads simultaneously and are particularly effective with lighter and flexible loads. The design of lifting beams enables them to correct for lifting multiple unbalanced loads, reducing the need for multiple load trips (Breitsprecher, 2022).

On the other hand, spreader bars share a similar I-beam design with lifting beams but have two lifting points positioned on opposite sides of the beam instead of a centred single lifting point. Spreader bars are intended to be used with lifting slings, connecting the crane or lifting machine to the ends of the beam (Breitsprecher, 2022). They can feature two or more attachment points underneath the beam for hooking to the cargo during lifting operations. Spreader bars prioritize control in lifting tasks, enhancing load stability and enabling the lifting of heavy-duty cargo that might otherwise break under a singular connection point.

In terms of design, lifting beams are typically heavier and more durable than spreader bars. The singular attachment point at the top of the lifting beam concentrates pressure, making it more susceptible to shearing and bending under heavy loads. Spreader bars, by contrast, are designed to distribute weight more evenly, with the two lifting points compressing the load inward rather than stressing the lifting point and connection points underneath (Breitsprecher, 2022). Additionally, spreader bars work with lifting slings to evenly distribute the load weight, while lifting beams can directly connect to the hook of the lifting equipment without requiring lifting slings.

Outriggers and Stabilizers: Outriggers enhance crane stability by increasing its footprint, allowing for level operation even on uneven surfaces. Proper planning for outrigger space is essential when installing or hiring a crane to ensure safe and efficient operation.

Figure 13: Extended outriggers to level and stabilize the crane. Source: Canva.

Stabilizers and outriggers come in various configurations, tailored to different crane types, aiming to mitigate rollover risks when the vehicle's combined load and centre of gravity extend beyond its support base. Outriggers elevate the vehicle's wheels from the ground, while stabilizers are predominantly utilized with vehicle loading cranes and do not lift the vehicle's wheels (Safe Work Australia, 2020). Figure 13 shows extended outriggers. Employing outriggers with mobile cranes enhances stability during lifting operations. Regardless of ground conditions, materials like timbers should be positioned beneath the outriggers to distribute the load, except in cases where engineering specifies direct outrigger pad application. Outriggers must be deployed as per the manufacturer's guidelines for the specific mobile crane type, also serving to level the crane. These outriggers should be clearly marked for the operator to identify partial or full extension positions. Crane lifting with partially extended outriggers should only be conducted using cranes approved by the manufacturer and equipped with suitable overload interlocks. For lifts with partially extended outriggers, the appropriate outrigger configuration outlined in the relevant load chart must be adhered to.

Jibs: A jib is a type of boom accessory that extends the length of the crane's boom. It includes variations such as the fly jib, fixed jib, and luffing jib.

A fly jib attaches to the main boom using pin connectors, serving as a lightweight extension with limited capacity. Its angle can be adjusted during setup but remains fixed during operation.

The fixed jib, a higher capacity version of the fly jib, connects to the main boom tip via a hinge. Fixed pendant lines are then used to adjust its angle, making it capable of handling heavier loads. Unlike the fly jib, the fixed jib operates as an axially loaded member, offering greater adjustability in length.

Similarly, the luffing jib utilizes a hinge connection for attachment, with pendant lines connected to a winch line to vary its angle independently from the boom. While sturdy and high-capacity, luffing jibs require skilled operators and additional drums for line management.

The term "fixed pendant lines" refers to the lines or cables attached to a fixed jib on a crane. These lines are utilized to adjust the angle of the fixed jib, which in turn affects how the crane handles heavy loads. Unlike the fly jib, where adjustments may be limited and the jib operates as a moment arm, the fixed jib functions as an axially loaded member.

As an axially loaded member, the fixed jib is designed to bear the load along its axis, distributing the weight evenly and minimizing stress concentration. This design allows for greater adjustability in length, providing more flexibility in adapting to various lifting scenarios and load requirements.

Fly jibs are typically found on small to medium telescoping boom cranes, stowed on the side of the boom for easy deployment. They are limited by the line pull capacity of a single line part.

Fixed jibs, including fly jibs, can be mounted on crawler cranes of various capacities, from 100t to the largest models available. Their typical maximum design capacity is determined by the line pull capacity multiplied by up to three line parts for a single sheave block.

Luffing jibs necessitate cranes equipped with extra drums to manage multiple lines, with lattice boom configurations requiring at least three drums for main boom, luffing boom, and whip operations. Telescoping cranes, requiring only two drums, can manage luffing boom and whip operations efficiently. While specific crane sizes vary, luffer capacities can reach substantial levels, particularly in larger crane models.

Slewing and Non-slewing: In terms of crane movement, a slewing crane lifts and suspends its load before rotating it using a boom rotating mechanism. Conversely, non-slewing cranes lack a rotating base section. Understanding this key difference is crucial as it impacts the design and operation of both slewing and non-slewing mobile cranes.

Mobile non-slewing cranes, as shown in Figure 14 do not feature rotating joints, which aligns with their typically compact profile. These cranes utilize a permanent articulation joint to lift and relocate loads, relying on the mobile truck's drive section for movement. While they lack slewing capabilities, these cranes boast high manoeuvrability due to their four-wheeled chassis. Their crane section is robust, primarily focusing on lifting and lowering payloads.

Figure 14: Non-Slewing mobile articulated crane.

On the other hand, slewing lifters incorporate a rotating turntable section, providing them with greater site versatility and z-axis capability. While the mobile chassis transports the lifter to its destination, outriggers can be deployed to anchor it in place. This allows the arcing boom to operate effectively in crowded construction areas, covering every point on a full 360° circle. As a result, loads located behind the crane can be accessed without the need for complex manoeuvring or reversing the truck.

Figure 15: Slewing Mobile Crane. Antti Leppänen, CC BY-SA 3.0, via Wikimedia Commons.

A crane is a complex piece of machinery consisting of the components outlined above working together seamlessly to lift heavy loads safely and efficiently. At the heart of the crane is the boom, a long, extendable arm that supports the load. The boom can be fixed or telescopic, allowing it to reach varying heights and distances. It is typically mounted on a rotating platform, enabling it to rotate horizontally to position the load precisely.

Attached to the end of the boom is the hoist, a mechanism used to lift and lower the load. The hoist consists of a motorized drum, see Figure 16, or winch around which the lifting cables are wound. As the drum rotates, the cables either spool in to lift the load or spool out to lower it.

CRANE OPERATIONS

Figure 16: Winch drums for multilayer wire rope spooling. Alfons Kifmann, CC BY-SA 3.0 DE, via Wikimedia Commons.

The lifting cables are a critical component of the crane, providing the means to support the load. These cables are made of high-strength steel and are designed to withstand the weight of the load while maintaining stability. The cables run from the hoist to a hook or other attachment point on the load.

Counterweights play a crucial role in balancing the crane and preventing it from tipping over. These weights are typically located near the base of the crane and are adjusted based on the weight of the load being lifted. By offsetting the weight of the load, counterweights ensure that the crane remains stable throughout the lifting operation.

Finally, the crane's controls allow the operator to manoeuvre the crane and control the lifting process. These controls may include joysticks, levers, or buttons that operate the hoist, boom, and rotation mechanisms. The operator uses these controls to position the crane, raise or lower the load, and adjust the boom as needed.

In operation, the crane operator uses the controls to position the boom and hoist over the load. The hoist is then activated, and the lifting cables spool in, raising the load off the ground. The operator carefully monitors the lifting process, adjusting the controls as necessary to ensure the load remains stable and balanced. Once the load is in the desired position, the hoist is activated in reverse to lower the load safely to the ground.

Overall, the various components of a crane work together in a coordinated manner to lift heavy loads safely and efficiently, making cranes essential tools in construction, manufacturing, and other industries.

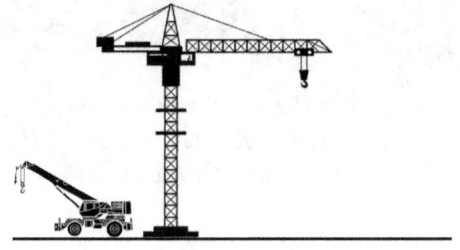

Chapter Three

Static Cranes – Tower Cranes

A static crane, also known as a stationary crane or fixed crane, is a type of crane that remains in a fixed position during operation and does not move from one location to another. Unlike mobile cranes, which are mounted on trucks or crawlers and can be transported to different job sites, static cranes are permanently installed at a specific location, such as a construction site or industrial facility.

The primary characteristic of a static crane is its immobility. These cranes are typically anchored to a concrete foundation or other stable structure, ensuring that they remain securely in place while lifting heavy loads. This stability is essential for safely lifting and manoeuvring heavy materials in construction and other industries.

Static cranes come in various configurations and designs to suit different applications and lifting requirements. Common types of static cranes include tower cranes, overhead cranes, gantry cranes, and jib cranes. Each type of static crane has its own unique features and capabilities, making them suitable for specific tasks and environments. Tower cranes are considered within this chapter and derrick and portal boom cranes in the next chapter. Bridge cranes are discussed in chapter 5.

Figure 17: Tower cranes London. sludgegulper, CC BY-SA 2.0, via Wikimedia Commons.

Tower cranes, for example, are tall, freestanding structures with a vertical mast and horizontal boom that can be raised or lowered as needed. These cranes are commonly used in high-rise construction projects to lift materials to upper floors.

Overhead cranes, on the other hand, are typically mounted on rails or beams attached to the ceiling of a building or structure. They feature a movable bridge with a hoist that can traverse along the length of the crane, allowing for precise positioning of the load.

Gantry cranes are similar to overhead cranes but are supported by upright legs or gantries instead of being suspended from the ceiling.

This design provides greater flexibility in terms of the crane's location and movement within a facility.

Jib cranes consist of a horizontal boom or jib that is attached to a vertical mast or wall-mounted bracket. These cranes are often used in workshops, warehouses, and manufacturing plants for lifting and moving materials in a specific area.

Overall, static cranes are essential tools in construction, manufacturing, and other industries where heavy lifting is required. Their stationary design and robust construction make them reliable and efficient for handling a wide range of materials and loads.

Tower Cranes

Tower cranes are easily recognizable fixtures on construction sites due to their towering structures, which consist of a vertical mast and an extended horizontal jib. The jib, which protrudes from the mast, can rotate a full 360 degrees around the mast, aided by a trolley that moves along the jib's length to position the load precisely. Typically used for long-term construction projects or in permanent installations, static cranes like tower cranes excel in lifting and moving heavy loads along predetermined paths, offering stability and safety on-site. There are several types of tower cranes, including hammerhead, luffing, and self-erecting cranes, each serving different construction needs.

Figure 18: Tower Crane (Canberra). D0a5l0e6, CC BY-SA 4.0, via Wikimedia Commons.

Tower cranes are unparalleled in their lifting capacity and height capabilities, making them indispensable for lifting heavy materials to considerable heights. Despite their immense power, tower cranes have limited mobility, as they are fixed to a single area and cannot travel to different locations easily. They offer excellent stability and precision but lack the flexibility of mobile cranes. Tower cranes are particularly beneficial for industrial construction projects due to their unmatched lifting capabilities and stability, but their high cost, maintenance requirements, and labour-intensive installation process make hiring them a more practical option in many cases.

Operating a tower crane is not a solo endeavour. The process of lifting materials involves a collaborative effort among an operator, a swamper or lift director or dogger, and a rigging crew.

The operator, stationed in the crane's cab, oversees its movements and lifting operations. Despite the use of cameras, the operator's direct line of sight is often obstructed during lifting tasks, necessitating reliance on the swamper or lift director or dogger for guidance.

The swamper or lift director or dogger supervises the lifting process from the ground, maintaining direct communication with the operator via radio. Their role encompasses ensuring the safe attachment of the load and verifying that it falls within the crane's capacity. Additionally, they are responsible for clearing the path of travel for the operator.

The rigging crew is tasked with attaching the load to the crane's hook. Their responsibilities include securely tethering the load and ensuring its safe attachment to the crane's lifting apparatus. Together, these individuals form a cohesive team essential to the smooth operation of the construction site's lifting activities.

Tower cranes are classified into three general types: luffing, hammerhead (including topless), and self-erecting cranes (Safe Work Australia, 2015). Hammerhead, luffing, and self-erecting tower cranes are three distinct types of tower cranes, each with unique features and capabilities.

1. **Hammerhead Tower Cranes:**

    - Hammerhead tower cranes are characterized by their distinctive shape, resembling a hammerhead, hence the name.

    - They have a horizontal jib that extends from the mast, and the load is typically suspended from the end of the jib.

    - These cranes have a fixed horizontal jib angle, meaning they cannot adjust the angle of the jib during operation.

    - Hammerhead cranes are commonly used in construction projects where a fixed jib angle is sufficient, such as high-rise buildings and large infrastructure projects.

- They offer high lifting capacities and are well-suited for lifting heavy loads to great heights.

2. **Luffing Tower Cranes**:

    - Luffing tower cranes are designed with a luffing jib, which allows for variable jib angles during operation.

    - Unlike hammerhead cranes, luffing cranes can adjust the angle of the jib to accommodate varying site conditions and lift requirements.

    - The ability to luff the jib enables these cranes to work in confined spaces or areas with overhead obstacles, making them ideal for urban construction sites.

    - Luffing cranes are often used in projects where precise load positioning is required, such as in densely populated areas or near existing structures.

3. **Self-Erecting Tower Cranes**:

    - Self-erecting tower cranes are unique in that they can be assembled and disassembled on-site without the need for additional equipment or external assistance.

    - These cranes are mounted on a wheeled chassis, allowing them to be easily transported and maneuvered around the construction site.

    - Self-erecting cranes offer versatility and efficiency, as they can be quickly set up and dismantled, making them suitable for short-term or temporary projects.

    - They are commonly used in residential construction, renovation projects, and smaller-scale developments where mobility and ease of setup are essential.

In summary, hammerhead tower cranes have a fixed jib angle and high lifting capacities, luffing cranes feature adjustable jib angles for precise load positioning, and self-erecting cranes offer mobility and ease of setup for temporary construction projects. Each type of tower crane has its advantages and is selected based on the specific requirements of the construction site and project.

Hammerhead Tower Cranes

The distinctive feature of the hammerhead tower crane, as shown in Figure 19, is its vertical mast (tower), accompanied by a horizontal jib that supports the cab. A trolley moves horizontally along the mast, carrying the cable and hook, thereby enabling the hook to be positioned at any location along the mast.

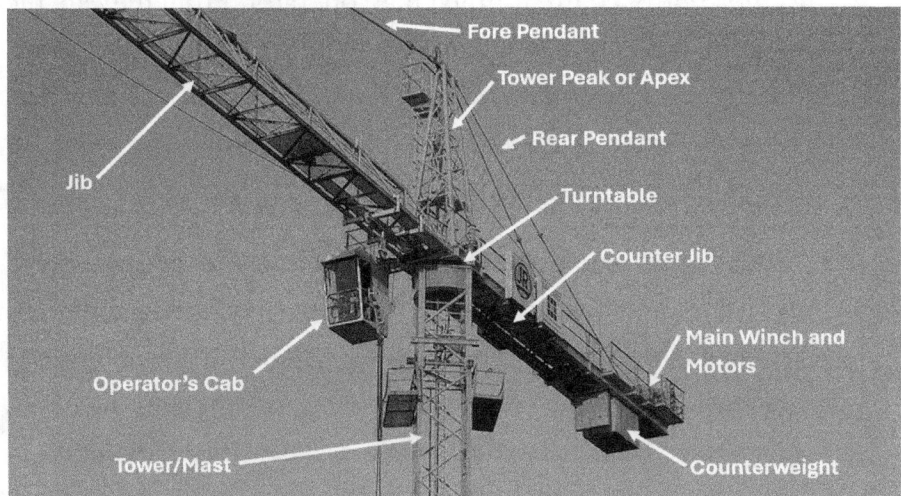

Figure 19: Hammerhead Tower Crane. High Contrast, CC BY 3.0 DE, via Wikimedia Commons.

The key components and functions of hammerhead cranes:

1. Vertical Mast (Tower): The vertical mast serves as the primary support structure of the crane, providing stability and elevation. Constructed from sturdy steel sections, the mast is anchored to a concrete foundation to ensure stability during lifting operations. The height of the mast varies depending on the specific requirements of the construction project, with taller masts typically used for high-rise buildings.

2. Horizontal Jib: Attached to the mast is the horizontal jib, which extends outward from the mast and carries the load. The jib can vary in length, with longer jibs allowing the crane to reach farther distances on the construction site. The jib is equipped with a trolley mechanism that enables the load to be moved horizontally along its length, providing flexibility in positioning materials.

3. Cab: Positioned at the end of the horizontal jib, the cab serves as the control centre for the crane operator. From the cab, the operator has a clear view of the construction site and can control the crane's movements using a series of levers and controls. The cab is equipped with safety features to protect the operator during lifting operations.

4. Trolley and Hook: A trolley runs along the length of the mast horizontally, carrying the cable and hook assembly. This arrangement allows the hook to be positioned at any point along the mast, facilitating precise lifting and placement of materials. The hook is attached to the load via a cable, which is wound and unwound using a winch system controlled by the operator.

5. Counterweights: To maintain stability and balance while lifting heavy loads, hammerhead cranes are equipped with counterweights located near the top of the mast. These counterweights

offset the weight of the load being lifted, preventing the crane from tipping over.

6. Slewing Mechanism: Hammerhead cranes feature a slewing mechanism that allows the entire crane to rotate horizontally. This rotation capability enables the crane operator to position the jib and the load precisely over the desired location on the construction site, maximizing efficiency and productivity.

7. Safety Features: Like all construction equipment, hammerhead cranes are equipped with various safety features to protect workers and property on the construction site. These may include overload protection systems, emergency stop mechanisms, and anti-collision devices to prevent accidents and ensure safe operation.

Luffing Tower Cranes

The luffing jib type of tower crane, as shown in Figure 20, shares a structural similarity with the hammerhead variant but distinguishes itself with a significant capability: the capacity to raise and lower the jib. This innovative design imparts enhanced flexibility to luffing cranes, enabling them to lift heavier loads with precision. Despite their higher cost compared to hammerhead cranes, luffing cranes offer superior efficiency, characterized by a smaller rotation radius that facilitates navigation in tighter construction sites. Moreover, they excel in scenarios where multiple cranes operate concurrently, further enhancing their versatility.

A luffing tower crane is a specialized construction apparatus tailored for projects in spatially constrained or obstacle-laden environments. Unlike conventional tower cranes featuring fixed horizontal jibs, luffing cranes incorporate a jib that can be adjusted at an angle relative to the mast. This unique configuration empowers the crane to operate amidst confined spaces or adjacent to towering structures without impeding neighbouring buildings or structures.

The primary components and functionalities of a luffing tower crane include:

1. Vertical Mast (Tower): Analogous to other tower cranes, a luffing tower crane comprises a vertical mast, serving as the primary support structure for the crane. Fabricated from interconnected steel sections and anchored to a concrete foundation, the mast ensures stability during lifting operations.

2. Luffing Jib: The hallmark feature of a luffing tower crane is its luffing jib, deviating from the fixed horizontal jib prevalent in conventional tower cranes. Affixed to the mast via a hinge mechanism, the luffing jib can be raised or lowered at an angle, endowing the crane with unparalleled manoeuvrability in tight spaces or proximity to obstacles while reaching substantial elevations.

3. Counterweights: Essential for maintaining equilibrium and stability during lifting tasks, luffing tower cranes are outfitted with counterweights positioned near the mast's apex. These counterweights counterbalance the load being hoisted, mitigating the risk of the crane tipping over.

4. Slewing Mechanism: Similar to conventional tower cranes, luffing cranes feature a slewing mechanism facilitating horizontal rotation of the entire crane. This rotational capability empowers the crane operator to precisely position the jib and load over designated locations on the construction site, optimizing operational efficiency.

5. Luffing Mechanism: In addition to the slewing mechanism, luffing tower cranes incorporate a luffing mechanism governing the jib's angle. By adjusting the luffing angle, the crane operator can raise or lower the jib to varying heights or navigate around obstructions present on the construction site.

6. Cab: Positioned at the jib's end, the cab serves as the nerve centre for crane operations, affording the operator an unobstructed view of the construction site. Equipped with an array of levers and controls, the operator can seamlessly manipulate the crane's movements, ensuring precise execution of lifting tasks.

7. Safety Features: Compliant with stringent safety standards, luffing tower cranes incorporate an array of safety features to safeguard personnel and property on the construction site. These may include overload protection systems, emergency stop mechanisms, and anti-collision devices, enhancing operational safety and minimizing the risk of accidents.

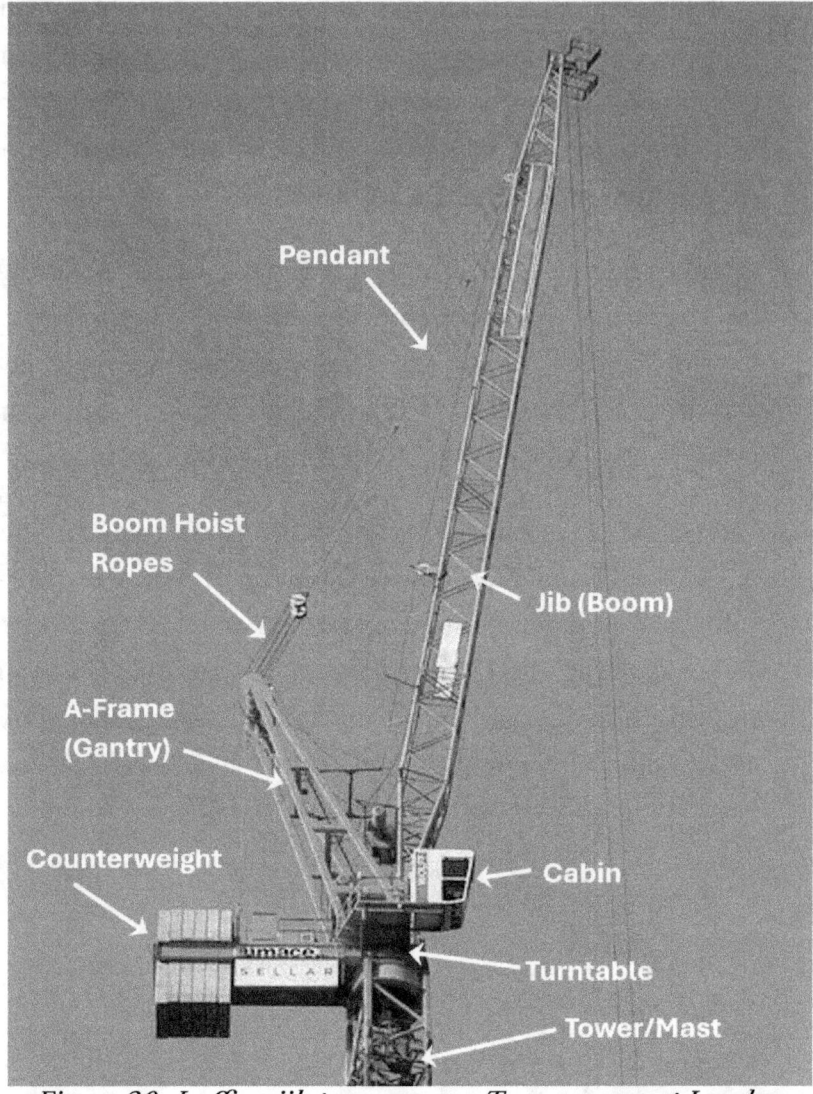

Figure 20: Luffing jib tower crane. Tower crane at London Bridge by Stephen McKay, CC BY-SA 2.0, via Wikimedia Commons.

Luffing tower cranes represent an indispensable asset in construction ventures encountering spatial constraints or obstructive elements. With their ability to adjust the jib angle, these cranes navigate confined spaces without impeding neighbouring structures, rendering them invaluable in urban construction endeavours and densely populated locales. Additionally, their adaptability and versatility make them a preferred choice for construction projects requiring precision lifting operations amidst challenging environments.

A level-luffing crane maintains a consistent hook level during luffing, achieved by vertically adjusting the crane jib to move the hook inward or outward relative to the base (Technomax, 2021). This feature is crucial for precise load handling in tasks such as construction or shipbuilding where careful movement near ground level is essential. Particularly suited for construction projects with limited space and a high priority on safety, a luffing tower crane offers versatile functionality.

The operation of a level luffing tower crane is unique. The horse-head jib pivots converge and flex upward or downward to facilitate load passage during luffing, with horizontal swinging maintaining the hook position. Various operational methods exist, with the mechanical approach being the simplest, resembling a parallelogram in structure for intuitive understanding. Alternatively, rope manipulation, either electronically or hydraulically, can achieve luffing motion.

Manual adjustments are made at ground level, where fixed offsets are set, requiring lowering of the boom and removal of vertical movement pins before gradually raising the boom to the desired angle and securing it with pins (Technomax, 2021). This process, although effective, is labour-intensive and time-consuming, particularly when adjusting extreme offset angles or with long extensions touching the boom head. Hydraulic jibs eliminate the need for such manual tasks.

If equipped, the operator can luff the jib with a load from the cab, with some models offering a luffing range from 5° to 40°, enhancing operational flexibility and efficiency (Technomax, 2021). The crane's versatility allows for mid-lift adjustments without setup time, enabling the operator to focus on executing lifts accurately and safely.

Self-Erecting Tower Cranes

Self-erecting cranes, comparatively lighter within the static crane category, are engineered for swift setup and disassembly, making them optimal for confined spaces or shorter construction projects. While they excel in manoeuvrability and rapid deployment, their lifting capacity falls short of other tower crane types. A self-erector, tailored for swift transportation and assembly, comes in various models, each with different load capacities, see Figure 21.

Self-erecting tower cranes offer a multitude of applications on construction sites, presenting a novel approach to material handling and hoisting tasks. Consequently, they introduce innovative uses beyond conventional methods, with customers continuously discovering new applications almost daily.

Here are some examples:

- Placing various jobsite materials such as lumber, engineered floor joists, trusses, and masonry.

- Erecting complete wall sections, whether on the first level, lower levels, upper levels, or for interior and exterior purposes.

- Hoisting, positioning, and setting trusses, roof rafters, steel beams, and interior structural and decorative timbers.

- Facilitating the movement of materials to designated staging/assembly areas, including exterior and interior wall sections, roof sections, gables, dormers, and beam sections.

- Handling tasks like picking up and emptying trash receptacles directly into jobsite dumpsters, placing roof sheeting and shingle bundles, and positioning workers using a "man basket" for various tasks like window installation, siding installation, and painting.

- Accessing hard-to-reach areas for the placement or work on assemblies such as chimney tops, cupolas, high eaves, and gutters.

- Facilitating the placement of concrete via a concrete skip.

These examples merely scratch the surface of the versatility of self-erecting tower cranes. Continual innovation and exploration of new uses are key to enhancing jobsite efficiency and safety.

The primary benefit of employing self-erecting tower cranes boils down to value—a balance where the savings in construction costs outweigh the expenses associated with renting/owning and operating the crane.

Reports from crane owners and users commonly highlight several advantages:

- Reduction in manual labour hours equivalent to four or more persons.

- Shortened job completion times, particularly during the framing cycle, by 15% or more.

- Decreased reliance on multiple pieces of material handling equipment.

- Environmental friendliness compared to traditional alternatives.

These benefits stem from the features and applications of the crane:
Enhanced Efficiency and Productivity

- Reduction of manual labour performed by carpenters, allowing them to focus on core tasks and improving overall productivity and morale.

- Streamlined assembly of construction components through

- dedicated staging areas, minimizing disruptions and facilitating efficient material distribution.

- Single-person operation for various tasks, enabled by remote control functionality, reducing the need for additional personnel.

- Maximized jobsite space due to the crane's minimal footprint, allowing for optimized material storage and staging.

- Minimization of material handling, with items delivered to a central location and dispersed only when needed, reducing redundancy.

Reduced Equipment and Labor Costs
- Elimination of the need for multiple material handling equipment, leading to cost savings and reduced fuel consumption.

- Applicability in constrained or challenging terrain, where manual labour might be the only viable option.

- Consistent and reliable performance, without the limitations or risks associated with human labour.

- Reduced dependence on dedicated labourers due to the crane's versatility in various tasks.

- Enhanced jobsite safety by minimizing manual tasks and mitigating workers' compensation claims.

Overall, the utilization of self-erecting tower cranes not only improves operational efficiency but also contributes to cost savings and enhanced safety measures on construction sites.

Figure 21: Self-erecting tower crane arriving at a construction yard as a truck trailer. User:EPO, Attribution, via Wikimedia Commons.

In the realm of cranes, self-erectors generally cater to residential and commercial projects of six stories or fewer, with jib radii spanning from 80 to 160 feet (24 to 48 metres), hook heights from 55 to 120 feet (16 to 36 metres), tip loads ranging between 1,000 and 3,000 pounds (453 kilograms and 1,360 kilograms), and maximum loads varying from 2,000 to 11,000 pounds (907 to 4,989 kilograms. These cranes fold into manageable sections, usually four or more, for transport, with the tower and jib collapsing into multiple segments, rendering them ready for legal road transport via mounted axles or flatbed trailers.

The setup process typically takes between fifteen to thirty minutes from erection initiation to full extension. Calibration and testing follow erection before operational use, completing the setup in a matter of hours, typically within two to three. Smaller self-erectors come with permanent ballast attached, while larger ones often require additional ballast, set separately. Those with full ballast attached are termed "self-contained."

Figure 22: A partially raised self-erecting tower crane. User:EPO, Attribution, via Wikimedia Commons.

Self-erecting tower cranes, also known as self-assembling or self-erecting cranes, are a specialized crane breed designed for expedient deployment, mobility, and operational efficiency, particularly in construction sites with spatial constraints or limited access. Featuring a vertical mast, a rotating upper structure, and a jib with a lifting mechanism, these cranes are typically mounted on wheeled or tracked chassis, facilitating easy transportation and assembly without auxiliary equipment.

Self-erecting tower cranes integrate hydraulic or electric mechanisms for self-assembly and disassembly, eliminating reliance on other cranes. Versatile and adaptable, they fulfill a spectrum of lifting tasks on construction sites, boasting lifting capacities ranging from 1 to 8 tons and jib lengths spanning 20 to 40 meters. Equipped with various safety features, these cranes ensure accident prevention and secure operation, contributing to their growing popularity in the construction industry.

Figure 23: Self-erecting tower crane Potain IGO 36, Building Fairs Brno 2011. Pavel Ševela, CC BY-SA 3.0, via Wikimedia Commons.

Key features of self-erecting tower cranes:
1. **Design and Structure**:
    - Self-erecting tower cranes consist of a vertical mast, a rotating upper structure, and a jib (horizontal boom) with a lifting mechanism at the end.

- These cranes are typically mounted on a wheeled or tracked chassis for mobility.
- The design allows the crane to be easily transported to the site and assembled without the need for additional equipment like mobile cranes.

2. **Setup and Assembly**:

- Self-erecting tower cranes feature hydraulic or electric mechanisms that allow them to assemble and disassemble themselves without assistance from other cranes.
- During assembly, the crane's sections are unfolded and extended hydraulically until it reaches its full height.
- The process is controlled by an operator from a remote console or control panel.

3. **Mobility**:

- Self-erecting tower cranes are designed for easy transportation between job sites. They can often be towed behind a truck or carried on a trailer.
- Some models are equipped with outriggers for stabilization during operation.

4. **Versatility**:

- These cranes are versatile and can be used for a variety of lifting tasks on construction sites, including lifting steel beams, concrete panels, and other heavy materials.
- They are particularly useful in urban areas or sites with limited space where larger cranes may not be practical.

5. **Capacity and Reach**:

- While self-erecting tower cranes generally have a smaller lifting capacity compared to larger tower cranes, they still offer significant lifting capabilities, typically ranging from 1 ton to 8 tons.

- The jib length (horizontal reach) can vary depending on the model but usually ranges from 20 meters to 40 meters.

6. **Safety Features**:

- Self-erecting tower cranes are equipped with various safety features to prevent accidents and ensure safe operation.

- These features may include overload protection, emergency stop buttons, safety interlocks, and alarms.

7. **Cost and Efficiency**:

- While self-erecting tower cranes may have a higher initial cost compared to traditional mobile cranes, they can offer cost savings over the long term due to their efficiency and ease of use.

- Their quick setup and dismantling times can reduce labour costs and downtime on the construction site.

8. **Maintenance**:

- Like any heavy machinery, self-erecting tower cranes require regular maintenance to ensure safe and reliable operation.

- Maintenance tasks may include inspections, lubrication, and repairs as needed.

9. **Popular Manufacturers**:

    ◦ Several manufacturers produce self-erecting tower cranes, including Potain (a brand of Manitowoc), Liebherr, Terex, and Comansa, among others.

Self-climbing tower cranes pose a significant risk of severe or fatal injury in the event of crane collapse during climbing operations. The climbing frame must withstand substantial static and dynamic forces associated with the climbing process.

To minimize the risk of injury from crane collapse during climbing operations, the following measures should be implemented:

- Scheduling climbing operations to minimize potential risks to personnel.

- Restricting unnecessary personnel from the worksite during climbing operations.

- Establishing an exclusion zone of sufficient size to contain structural failure.

- Prohibiting individuals from entering the area directly behind the tower crane beneath the counterweights during climbing operations.

- Avoiding slew operations while climbing.

- Conducting a comprehensive physical inspection of the counterweight trolleys, including side plates, bolts, pins, safety gear, ropes, and turnbuckles, before commencing climbing operations.

Personnel involved in climbing operations must undergo training and receive instructions on the climbing procedure specific to the model and type of crane involved in the climbing sequence. The climbing sequence should strictly adhere to the crane manufacturer's instructions.

Climbing operations should not be attempted when wind speeds exceed 36 km/hour. However, the crane rigging crew retains the discretion to cease work if they deem it unsafe, even at lower wind speeds. Climbing operations should not commence if either the recommended maximum wind speed or the actual wind speed is unknown.

Tower Crane Siting

Tower crane siting refers to the process of strategically selecting and positioning tower cranes on construction sites to optimize their efficiency, safety, and functionality. Proper siting is crucial for ensuring smooth operations and minimizing risks. Here's an overview of considerations for tower crane siting:

1. Site Layout and Accessibility: Evaluate the layout of the construction site to identify suitable locations for tower cranes. Consider factors such as the size and shape of the site, existing structures, access roads, and proximity to material storage areas. Ensure that crane placement allows for easy access and manoeuvrability without obstructing traffic flow.

2. Height and Reach Requirements: Determine the height and reach needed for the tower crane to effectively serve the construction project. Consider the height of the buildings or structures being erected, as well as the crane's lifting capacity and jib length. Position the crane in a location that provides adequate coverage of the entire worksite while minimizing potential obstructions.

3. Ground Conditions and Foundation: Assess the ground condi-

tions to ensure stability and support for the tower crane. Conduct soil tests to determine the bearing capacity and suitability of the ground for crane foundations. Install proper foundations, such as concrete footings or base anchors, to securely anchor the crane and distribute loads safely.

4. Clearance and Safety Zones: Maintain sufficient clearance around the tower crane to prevent collisions with nearby structures, equipment, or personnel. Follow safety regulations and manufacturer guidelines regarding minimum clearance distances for overhead power lines, buildings, and other obstructions. Establish safety zones or barricaded areas around the crane to restrict unauthorized access and ensure worker safety.

5. Wind and Weather Conditions: Consider the impact of wind and weather conditions on crane operations and stability. Position the crane to minimize exposure to strong winds and adverse weather conditions, such as storms or lightning. Install wind monitoring devices and implement procedures for crane shutdown or securing in high wind situations.

6. Communication and Visibility: Ensure clear lines of communication between crane operators, signallers, and other personnel on the construction site. Position the crane where operators have optimal visibility of the work area and surrounding hazards. Use signalling devices, such as radios or hand signals, to coordinate crane movements and ensure safe operation.

7. Environmental and Regulatory Compliance: Adhere to environmental regulations and local zoning ordinances when siting tower cranes. Obtain necessary permits and approvals from regulatory authorities before installing cranes on the construction site. Consider environmental factors, such as noise and emissions,

and implement mitigation measures as required.

By carefully evaluating these factors and following best practices for tower crane siting, construction project managers can ensure efficient operations, minimize risks, and maintain a safe working environment on the job site.

When determining the placement of a tower crane or self-erecting tower crane, it is essential to assess its working radius in relation to various factors:

- Nearby permanent or temporary structures and equipment

- Common access points used by workers and others in the vicinity

- Public access areas such as sidewalks, roads, and railways.

The size and configuration of the crane's base should adhere to the manufacturer's guidelines and consider multiple factors including tower height, tie spacing, wind speed, terrain characteristics, ground conditions, boom length, and lifting capacity.

To mitigate the risk of accidents, a documented procedure should be developed. This procedure should cover the following aspects:

- Positioning the crane to minimize the need for other equipment to operate within its working radius

- Ensuring that cranes and other equipment with counterweights are situated in a manner that prevents collisions during slewing operations

- Establishing clear communication protocols between the crane crew and operators of other equipment

- Scheduling work activities to minimize overlap between crane operations and other equipment, reducing the likelihood of conflicts at the same height or location

- Implementing a tower crane climbing procedure that ensures the crane remains at a safe distance above nearby structures or equipment, such as jump forms, to prevent collisions.

In situations where multiple cranes share airspace but are located on adjacent worksites, it is crucial for the principal contractors of each site to collaborate. They must coordinate to maintain adequate clearance between cranes, minimizing the risk of collision. This coordination should include identifying responsible individuals from each worksite, establishing scheduling requirements for crane operations, and implementing effective communication channels between the sites.

Erecting a Tower Crane

Tower cranes are transported to construction sites using 10 to 12 tractor-trailer rigs. Upon arrival, the crew utilizes a mobile crane to assemble the jib and machinery section, which are then positioned horizontally onto a 40-foot (12-meter) mast composed of two sections. Subsequently, the mobile crane affixes the counterweights.

The mast, firmly anchored, serves as the foundation for the crane's ascent. It consists of a sizable triangulated lattice structure, typically measuring 10 feet (3.2 meters) square, providing the necessary structural integrity to support the crane upright.

To reach its maximum height, the crane incrementally extends itself, adding one mast section at a time. This process involves the use of a top climber or climbing frame positioned between the slewing unit and the mast's apex. The sequential steps are as follows:

- The crew balances the counterweight by suspending a weight on the jib.

- The slewing unit is detached from the mast's top. Hydraulic rams within the top climber propel the slewing unit upward by 20 feet (6 meters).

- Using the crane itself, the crane operator lifts another 20-foot mast section into the gap created by the climbing frame. Once securely fastened, the crane extends by an additional 20 feet.

Upon completion of the building and the need for crane removal, the process is reversed: the crane disassembles its mast autonomously, with smaller cranes subsequently dismantling the remaining components.

The erection of tower cranes constitutes high-risk construction work, as failure to adhere to the crane designer's or manufacturer's instructions can lead to injury and property damage, including crane collapse, falls from heights, and falling objects. To mitigate these risks, a Safe Work Method Statement tailored for high-risk construction work must be developed for tower crane erection, taking into account various factors:

- Compliance with crane designer's or manufacturer's instructions.

- Ensuring crane stability.

- Consideration of adverse effects on other equipment, structures, or work processes.

- Utilization of specialized tools, jigs, and appliances to minimize injury risks.

- Implementation of control measures for securing crane components.

- Assessment of environmental conditions, such as wet or windy weather, and adherence to relevant electrical installation standards.

Tower crane components must undergo thorough inspection and testing before delivery to the workplace, as outlined in the Guide to inspecting and maintaining cranes. Erecting and dismantling activities should be supervised by a competent person and carried out according to manufacturer's instructions or those prepared by a qualified individual, such as an engineer.

Written instructions for erection and dismantling activities should be readily accessible on-site, with tower sections clearly and permanently labelled with their model type and serial number. It is imperative that tower sections match those specified in the engineer's crane base drawing to ensure safety. Additionally, crane manufacturers may stipulate sequential installation or removal of counter-jib, counterweights, and boom components.

Environmental conditions must align with the crane manufacturer's specifications before erecting or dismantling a tower crane, ensuring components remain controllable when suspended. Only parts meeting manufacturer specifications or those verified by a competent person should be used during erection.

Precautions should be taken regarding tower bolts or pins, ensuring correct type, grade, compatibility with crane components, and proper torque to prevent loosening or fatigue. Footings and foundations for tower crane installations must adhere to engineering principles and undergo certification by a competent person, considering geotechnical inspections specific to the site.

Crane ties, securing the crane to supporting structures, must be installed at designated intervals according to manufacturer and installation designer instructions. Similarly, counterweights play a crucial role in crane stability and should be affixed as per manufacturer specifications to prevent overturning or falling.

A sequence for erecting a tower crane is outlined as (Forest, 2024):

1. Familiarize yourself with the configuration. Before commencing work on-site, erection teams should have a clear understanding of the tower crane's hook height and jib length. This knowledge is crucial for calculating the necessary number of ballast blocks required for the base and counter jib. Deviations from the correct configuration midway through assembly can lead to unnecessary delays, expenses, and customer dissatisfaction. Establishing the correct configuration enables the erection team to plan the task sequence effectively and ensure each crew member is adequately prepared for smooth on-site operations.

2. Select the appropriate assist crane. By comprehending the specifications of the tower crane, teams can select the most suitable mobile crane for the job. The size of the mobile crane must match the requirements of the tower crane assembly. Grove all-terrain cranes are preferred for tower crane assembly due to their compact dimensions, extended boom, and high capacity.

3. Determine the optimal crane placement. It is crucial to position the tower crane correctly from the outset, as relocating it post-assembly is challenging. Selecting the ideal location for the mobile crane also saves time and streamlines site preparation.

4. Prepare the site meticulously. The site's ground must be level and capable of supporting the tower crane's weight to ensure stability post-setup. This is particularly critical for larger cranes with heavier components. The customer is responsible for leveling the ground before erection, with verification conducted by Crane Care teams through a two-step process using laser lenses and rulers. Understanding ground pressure is essential, and any soft or uneven ground should be compacted or filled with steel reinforced concrete. Additionally, the site owner must provide necessary amenities such as power, site access, and, in

some cases, permission for street closure. These aspects must be addressed prior to commencing work.

5. Coordinate logistics efficiently. Many urban areas impose restrictions on road closures and heavy vehicle movement, necessitating careful coordination of arrival times for both the tower and mobile cranes. This minimizes wastage and waiting times. The erection team and customer must collaborate to plan the transportation sequence and installation in advance.

6. Monitor weather conditions closely. Erection teams must monitor weather forecasts and schedule work for calm days, as tower cranes cannot be assembled in winds exceeding 50 km/hour (31 mph). Work should not commence if wind speeds are unknown or exceed safety thresholds. Grove mobile cranes are equipped with anemometers to ensure operators are constantly aware of wind conditions.

7. Adhere strictly to the technical manual. Tower crane erection involves heavy components, intricate procedures, and inherent risks, necessitating strict adherence to procedure. Erection teams undergo training to meticulously follow technical manuals, prioritizing safety and efficiency. Assembly tasks are designed to minimize aerial work, reducing risks associated with working at heights.

8. Maintain a safety perimeter. Ground crew members must maintain a safe distance of at least 6 m (19.7 ft) from the mast during erection. This precaution, emphasized during training, mitigates the risk of accidents caused by falling objects. Ground crew should step back as soon as pin installation signals the start of the process.

9. Utilize designated slinging points effectively. Potain tower cranes feature slinging points on every lift component, facilitating faster and more efficient assembly. These points, integrated into the tower crane structure, allow mobile crane lifting chains to hook onto them securely. Proper utilization of slinging points is especially critical for jib erection, ensuring the horizontal positioning of heavy components. Erection teams should pre-calculate the appropriate slinging points for jib erection to streamline the process.

10. Maintain composure and professionalism. All personnel involved in erection activities must receive adequate training and possess appropriate tools and Personal Protective Equipment (PPE). Despite challenges and pressure on large job sites, maintaining a calm demeanour is essential for safety. Stress or pressure can compromise risk assessment and decision-making. If any concerns arise regarding ground conditions or weather, erection activities should be halted, and the situation communicated clearly to the customer. Safety remains the foremost priority, and no compromises should be made to expedite the job at the expense of safety.

Rated capacity limiters

When an overload is detected, a rated capacity limiter intervenes to prevent further overloading of the crane by halting any crane functions that could exacerbate the overload (Safe Work Australia, 2015). Rated capacity refers to the maximum load permissible for attachment and handling by the crane in its present configuration, excluding the weight of accessories such as the hook block, falls of rope, slings, and rigging hardware. Additionally, the load to be lifted encompasses the weight of all lifting apparatus not permanently affixed to the crane. Guidance on deductions to be made can be found in the crane's load chart.

A crane load chart is a graphical representation or table provided by the crane manufacturer that outlines the crane's lifting capacities and operating parameters under various conditions. It typically includes information such as boom length, load radius, and maximum lifting capacity for different configurations of the crane, such as boom angle and counterweight settings. Load charts are essential for crane operators to determine the safe working load limits for specific lifting tasks, considering factors such as the distance from the crane's centre, the angle of the boom, and the weight of the load being lifted. By consulting the load chart, operators can ensure that they operate the crane within its safe working limits to prevent overloading and potential accidents.

Load charts, alternatively referred to as rated capacity charts, delineate the safe lifting capabilities of the crane. Load charts should be available for the crane operator to verify the crane is not being overloaded. Operating tower cranes within their rated capacity is paramount for safety.

Regardless of the crane's age, rated capacity limiters should be installed on tower cranes. These limiters are designed to prohibit hoisting a load (Safe Work Australia, 2015):

- Beyond 100% capacity (noting that 100% of the maximum rated capacity is typically utilized only during commissioning).

- When the load surpasses 100% of the specified radius.

If a tower crane is equipped with a load indicator as per its design and manufacture, it should be maintained in a serviceable condition. In cases where a self-erecting tower crane lacks a load indicator, the crane owner is responsible for ensuring the implementation of a system to routinely test the reliability and accuracy of the rated capacity limiter.

Working radius indicator

Tower cranes should be equipped with a radius indicator, which showcases the radius of the suspended load, typically measured from the centre of the slew ring. The displayed working radius should be in meters and provide accuracy within a range of +10 percent to -3 percent of the actual radius (Safe Work Australia, 2015). In cases where the crane is remotely operated, and the jib is horizontally positioned and fully visible to the operator, the indicator may comprise 1-meter graduations marked on the jib, with numbers inscribed at intervals that are appropriate, such as every 5 meters (Safe Work Australia, 2015).

Dual braking systems

Two braking systems, known as dual braking systems, must be installed on the luff function of rope luffing tower cranes, as well as other functions designated by the crane manufacturer. These systems should be utilized in accordance with applicable technical design standards.

The luff function refers to the vertical movement of the jib or boom of the crane. Having dual braking systems ensures redundancy and enhances safety. If one braking system were to fail, the second braking system would act as a backup, preventing uncontrolled movement of the luffing mechanism. This redundancy is critical in high-risk environments such as construction sites, where the failure of essential crane components could lead to accidents, injuries, or damage to property.

The dual braking system in rope luffing tower cranes typically consists of two separate braking mechanisms, each serving as a backup to the other. Here's how it generally works:

    1. Primary Brake: The primary brake is the main braking system

responsible for controlling the movement of the luffing mechanism. It is engaged during normal crane operation to slow down or stop the luffing motion when required. This brake is typically hydraulic or electrically actuated and is directly controlled by the crane operator.

2. Secondary Brake: The secondary brake acts as a backup to the primary brake. It is designed to automatically engage in the event of a failure or malfunction in the primary brake system. This backup brake provides an additional layer of safety by preventing uncontrolled movement of the luffing mechanism even if the primary brake fails.

3. Monitoring and Control: The operation of the dual braking system is often monitored by the crane's control system or safety devices. Sensors may be installed to detect any abnormalities or malfunctions in the braking systems. In the event of a detected issue with the primary brake, the control system triggers the engagement of the secondary brake to prevent accidents.

4. Maintenance and Testing: Regular maintenance and testing of both braking systems are essential to ensure their proper functioning. Crane operators and maintenance personnel must follow manufacturer guidelines and industry standards for inspecting, lubricating, and adjusting the brakes to maintain optimal performance and safety.

Commissioning

Commissioning involves conducting essential inspections, tests, and adjustments to ensure that tower cranes and self-erecting cranes meet specified requirements and are safe to operate before being utilized (Safe Work Australia, 2015). This process should be carried out by a competent individual once the crane has been erected and before it is put into service.

During commissioning, test weights or load cells are employed to validate the accurate calibration of both the maximum load capacity and the load moment for each tower crane installation.

Written instructions detailing the commissioning procedure for tower cranes should be readily available to relevant personnel in the workplace. It is crucial to adhere to these written instructions when commissioning a crane.

In cases where rated capacity limiters, overload cut-outs, or motion switches have been bypassed or disconnected during erection, they must be reconnected and tested according to a written procedure before the crane is put into operation (Safe Work Australia, 2015).

Wind Conditions

The primary concern regarding crane safety during high winds is the impact of wind pressure on the load carried by the tower crane. Understanding wind pressure begins with measuring wind speed, which can be accomplished using tools such as wireless anemometers. Wind pressure is directly proportional to the square of the wind speed; thus, a doubling of wind speed results in a fourfold increase in wind pressure. For instance, if the wind speed doubles from 14 mph to 28 mph, the pressure exerted on the crane increases by a factor of four (Sacarlet Tech, 2022).

This underscores the importance of monitoring wind speed conditions when operating a tower crane, as even minor increases in wind speed can significantly affect crane safety. The standard practice for measuring wind speed involves installing a wireless anemometer, or wind speed sensor, typically on the highest part of the crane, such as the jib for tower cranes.

While traditional crane safety protocols often rely on weather forecasts, these forecasts provide only a general overview of expected wind conditions and cannot predict wind gusts accurately. Relying solely on forecasts may lead to suboptimal efficiency, increased costs, and extended project deadlines. Therefore, it is crucial to utilize on-site weather monitoring tools to detect potentially hazardous winds accurately.

In conclusion, the best practice for operating tower cranes involves continuous monitoring of wind conditions and accounting for wind speed variations to ensure safe crane operations.

Wind conditions can have a significant impact on crane operations and the crane's rated capacity. Crane load charts typically provide information on allowable wind speeds. Strong winds can impose additional loads on a crane and potentially affect its stability.

While a maximum permissible operational wind speed is typically incorporated into the design of tower cranes, this limit may not always be applicable during actual operations, such as when a crane operator is actively lifting a load. Tower crane installations are often designed to withstand maximum operational wind speeds, as outlined in relevant technical standards, such as 72 km/hour or 20 meters/second (Safe Work Australia, 2015), as specified in Australia in as specified in AS 1418.4: Cranes, hoists and winches – Tower cranes.

In the United States, OSHA has delineated "high-wind" conditions as winds surpassing 64.4 kilometres per hour (40 miles per hour), or 48.3 kilometres per hour (30 miles per hour) (Sacarlet Tech, 2022). To adhere to safety regulations set forth by OSHA, HSE, and other governing bodies, the implementation of on-site wind monitoring tools, such as anemometers, on cranes is mandated.

Anemometers serve as crucial instruments for ensuring crane safety. By continuously monitoring wind conditions and alerting crane operators to potential hazards, they play a pivotal role in preventing crane accidents. Typically used to gauge wind speed and direction, an anemometer typically comprises components such as cups or propellers that rotate in response to wind exposure. The rotation of these components generates an electrical signal, which the device then processes to furnish wind speed and direction readings.

Various types of anemometers exist, including cup anemometers, propeller anemometers, and ultrasonic anemometers. Cup anemometers, which feature three or four rotating cups, are the most prevalent variant. Similarly, propeller anemometers, also referred to as vane anemometers, employ a rotating propeller to measure wind characteristics. In contrast, ultrasonic anemometers utilize sound waves to assess wind speed and direction. Anemometers can be affixed to cranes or utilized as handheld devices. Crane operators frequently employ handheld anemometers to assess wind conditions before lifting loads as a precautionary measure.

Widely employed across various sectors, including weather forecasting, aviation, marine navigation, and industrial operations, anemometers play a vital role in crane safety by furnishing real-time wind data to crane operators and other personnel on site. This data aids in identifying unsafe wind conditions for crane operations, enabling pre-emptive measures to mitigate wind-related risks. Additionally, anemometers can detect wind shear and gusts, highlighting potential hazards and assisting in accident prevention efforts.

Wireless anemometers, such as the Scarlet Tech WL-21 Wireless Anemometer, represent an effective solution for monitoring wind conditions during crane operations. Equipped with advanced technology, these devices offer comprehensive wind speed, direction, temperature, and pressure data in real-time, empowering crane operators to make informed decisions and avoid operating cranes in adverse weather conditions.

Although the tower crane base and ties may be engineered to handle higher operational wind speeds, crane operators should adhere to the manufacturer's specifications and exercise caution when wind speeds exceed safe limits.

To accurately measure wind speed, an anemometer, or wind gauge, should be installed on each tower crane. The positioning of the anemometer should allow for an unobstructed reading and may vary depending on the crane type. For instance, on luffing tower cranes, the anemometer should be fixed at the top of the A-frame, while on non-luffing tower cranes, it can be installed on either the A-frame or machine deck hand-rail (Safe Work Australia, 2015).

It's important to note that wind gusts can have a different impact on the crane compared to constant winds. Crane operators should make lift decisions based on guidance provided by the crane manufacturer and their own experience. If an operator deems a crane operation to be hazardous, they have the discretion to refrain from operating the crane. In such cases, seeking information from the crane manufacturer or a competent person regarding safe lift conditions is recommended.

In terms of priority, considering the utmost importance first and then moving to subsequent essential factors beyond wind conditions, three fundamental safety precautions should be observed for tower crane lifting operations (Sacarlet Tech, 2022):

3. Load Considerations:

Several variables influence the load, including wind resistance, the dimensions and shape of the load, as well as wind speed and direction. It is imperative to ensure that lifting operations are conducted within the safe working load capacity of the crane.

2. Manufacturer's Specifications:

Each type and model of crane is accompanied by specific limitations established by the manufacturer, which are based on the crane's design and setup. These limitations must never be surpassed. A typical maximum wind speed allowance for tower cranes is 20 m/s (45 mph / 72 kph).

3. Crane Operator Expertise:

The crane operator holds the highest level of expertise among the personnel involved in crane operations. They must possess comprehensive knowledge of the crane being operated, encompassing its configuration, as well as the procedures for lifting and handling materials, in addition to being well-versed in wind conditions and their effects.

In situations where ladders are utilized, the choice of ladder access method may be dictated by the available space within the tower. Incorporating landings between ladder segments, along with alterations in ladder direction, should be implemented wherever feasible within the tower structure. This approach serves to alleviate worker fatigue by facilitating rest intervals and diminishes the likelihood of worker injuries, particularly in the event of a fall from the ladder.

Figure 24: Tower crane access ladders. Joe Mabel, CC BY-SA 4.0, via Wikimedia Commons.

The vertical span between landings should not surpass 6 meters. It's noteworthy that crane manufacturers may design longer tower sections, thus permitting the initial ladder closest to the ground in the tower to extend up to 12.5 meters, with subsequent ladders potentially spanning up to 10 meters (Safe Work Australia, 2015).

While providing rest platforms adjacent to a vertical ladder is an option, it alone does not suffice as a viable measure to mitigate potential fall distances. Similarly, utilizing fold-down platforms is discouraged due to their potential hindrance to rescue operations and increased risk of falls while descending the ladder.

The implementation of internal guardrails on tower landings serves to mitigate the risk of individuals falling either internally within or off the tower structure. Certain tower cranes come equipped with internal guardrails installed on tower landings to safeguard against falls down the access aperture. This may involve installing a guardrail on the internal side of the access hole or a rail that extends around the rear of the access opening. However, installing an internal guardrail on the top tower landing may pose challenges, as the slewing motion of the crane could potentially cause damage to the guardrail's lower end and lead to entrapment of individuals on the top tower landing.

An enclosure, commonly referred to as a ladder cage, must be installed on the A-frame to prevent individuals from falling off the ladder. This ensures that in the event of a fall, the person remains confined within the cage and lands onto the machine deck rather than falling off the tower crane. The bottommost part of the ladder cage should be positioned between 2 meters and 2.2 meters above the lower deck (Safe Work Australia, 2015). Moreover, the horizontal gap between the vertical bars of the ladder cage should not surpass 150 millimetres. Alternatively, mesh infill can be utilized in place of vertical bars.

Perimeter edge protection encompassing the machine deck of tower cranes is essential to safeguard the crane operator and maintenance personnel against falls. This protective measure should include a top rail, a mid-rail, and a kickboard.

Figure 25: Tower Cranes with guard rails fitted. Tower Cranes at St James' Centre by M J Richardson, CC BY-SA 2.0, via Wikimedia Commons.

Platforms attached to saddle bags, known as saddle bag platforms, might be necessary on tower cranes equipped with mobile counterweights to facilitate riggers' access during crane erection and for maintenance personnel. Safe access to these platforms can be ensured by incorporating a trapdoor in the machine deck or installing a ladder cage on the saddle bag ladder. It's imperative that these platforms feature a top rail, mid-rail, and kickboard for safety measures. It's advised against climbing over the guardrail of the machine deck and descending via a ladder onto the platform.

Access to crane jibs on tower cranes that are not self-erecting necessitates the installation of rigger's runs and static lines along the entire length of the jib for riggers and crane operators during erection, inspection, and maintenance tasks. Individuals should utilize the static line along with two lanyards or a lanyard equipped with a 'pigtail' at one end to ensure continuous attachment to the crane throughout the process.

Signs on tower cranes

It is not advisable to affix signs onto tower crane structures due to potential interference with crane operation during windy conditions. Signs that are not securely fastened to the structure may become detached during crane operations, posing a risk of injury to individuals in the vicinity of the crane.

Prior to attaching signs to the tower crane structure, careful consideration must be given to the potential wind loading of the sign and its impact on the design of various crane components such as the crane base, tower sections, crane ties, and rated capacity. Manufacturer and designer confirmation should be sought to ensure that the design of the sign and its attachments to the crane are suitable for the intended purpose. It should be verified that maintenance on the sign will not be required for the duration of the crane's presence on site.

Flexible signs should be constructed from UV-resistant materials to ensure longevity and should be securely fastened to the crane boom using a tying system capable of withstanding potential wind loads. Solid signs, on the other hand, should be affixed to the crane structure using bolted connections that clamp around the outside of the chords or lacings of the structure.

When attaching solid signs, it is important to refrain from drilling holes into the crane structure, welding joints onto the crane structure, or using strapping and cable ties for securing the signs.

Self-Erecting Tower Crane Considerations

Self-erecting tower cranes are commonly utilized, especially on small to medium-sized construction sites, due to their self-contained nature, eliminating the need for additional cranes for assembly. Typically, self-erecting tower cranes feature a horizontal boom that unfolds during erection, often accompanied by a telescopic tower, with the counterweight typically positioned at the crane's base.

In contrast to traditional tower cranes, self-erecting variants do not necessitate attachment to a crane base. Moreover, they typically lack a cabin, instead being operated remotely. While this remote operation offers flexibility by allowing the operator to manoeuvre within the crane's operating vicinity, it has also resulted in instances where the crane inadvertently collided with overhead power lines or other obstructions.

Operating self-erecting tower cranes requires adherence to specific protocols. The crane should be operated from a designated area, with the operator maintaining close proximity to the crane during lifting operations to ensure clear visibility of the load. In cases where maintaining sight of the load is challenging, a dogger should assist by reporting the load's position to the operator, ensuring safe operation.

Remote operation is also a viable option for self-erecting tower cranes and some traditional tower cranes, utilizing either hard-wired pendant controls or wireless controls. The reliability of control circuits, particularly in wireless remotes, should mirror that of controls in a conventional cabin. Wireless remotes should possess unique coding to prevent signal corruption and interference from external devices.

For remotely operated tower cranes, including self-erecting variants, a dedicated operator should be available to manage crane operations. Additionally, a team of competent individuals should be on hand to oversee lifts, especially in scenarios involving multiple drop-off points hidden from the operator's view. Effective communication between the crane operator and other personnel is essential, particularly if the operator is also fulfilling roles such as dogging or undertaking additional tasks. During operations, the crane operator should remain stationary while the load is in motion, and if relocation is necessary, the crane should not be operated until the travel path is clear of obstacles and hazards. To prevent unintended activation of remote functions or unauthorized use, the remote control should be securely turned off and communication maintained among all involved parties.

Installing a barricade around self-erecting tower cranes is crucial for safety measures. The counterweights of these cranes are situated at their base, posing a significant risk to individuals who inadvertently enter the slewing arc of these counterweights.

To mitigate this risk, it's recommended to erect a barricade around the crane's base, typically consisting of 1800 mm high mesh fencing (Safe Work Australia, 2015). This barricade acts as a protective barrier, preventing unauthorized access to the area where the counterweights operate. Additionally, the barricade should be strategically positioned to allow ample space, ensuring individuals are not inadvertently trapped between the barricade and the moving counterweights.

Maintenance access for self-erecting tower cranes is typically facilitated without the need for climbing the towers during operational phases. Instead, maintenance tasks are usually performed by folding the crane. However, certain self-erecting tower cranes may feature ladders on their towers to enable maintenance access. If a vertical maintenance ladder is provided, the necessity for a permanent vertical rail or rope is obviated. However, individuals ascending the ladder must be equipped with a fall-arrest system for safety measures. Additionally, the utilization of work platforms, such as elevating work platforms, should be contemplated for conducting maintenance activities.

Planning for Tower Crane Operation

The initial phase of ensuring the safe utilization of a tower crane involves meticulous planning, encompassing several key aspects:

- Developing a comprehensive scope of work.

- Carefully selecting an appropriate crane for the intended tasks.

- Establishing a robust and secure system of work.

Commencing the planning process for tower crane operations at the earliest opportunity is paramount, and it necessitates collaboration and consultation with all relevant stakeholders. This may entail engaging with various parties such as the principal contractor, crane owner, supplier, electricity supply authority, project designer, managers, crane operators and crew, as well as other personnel involved in the project.

Thorough planning endeavours to identify strategies for safeguarding individuals engaged in diverse activities within and around the tower crane's vicinity. These activities include erection, climbing, commissioning, inspection, and dismantling of the crane, as well as direct involvement in lifting operations by personnel like crane operators and doggers. Furthermore, it aims to ensure the safety of individuals conducting other work tasks at the worksite and those situated in adjacent areas, encompassing public spaces or private properties.

CRANE OPERATIONS

Figure 26: Tower crane under construction. Tower crane under construction by Thomas Nugent, CC BY-SA 2.0, via Wikimedia Commons.

Integration of dedicated dates and times for inspection and maintenance activities into the construction project schedule is imperative. These schedules should align seamlessly with the recommendations provided by the crane manufacturer, facilitating timely and proactive maintenance interventions to uphold the crane's operational integrity and safety standards.

Planning tower crane operations as such, includes a number of tasks to be performed. These include:

1. **Reviewing Task Instructions and Obtaining Relevant Information:**

    ○ Begin by thoroughly reviewing task instructions provided by supervisors or project managers.

- Consult with relevant personnel, such as supervisors, engineers, or safety officers, to seek clarification on any aspects of the task instructions that are unclear.

- Obtain relevant workplace information, including site layout, existing hazards, and any specific requirements or restrictions related to the task at hand.

2. **Interpreting Information and Safe Work Method Statements (SWMSs):**

    - Obtain and interpret information from Safe Work Method Statements (SWMSs) to ensure activities align with workplace-specific safety requirements.

    - Ensure that all activities are performed in compliance with SWMSs, which outline safe work procedures for specific tasks.

3. **Equipment Inspection, Use, Maintenance, and Storage:**

    - Obtain and interpret manufacturer requirements regarding equipment inspection, use, maintenance, and storage.

    - Ensure that equipment inspections are conducted according to manufacturer guidelines to maintain safety and operational integrity.

4. **Identifying Hazards and Determining Risk Controls:**

    - Identify workplace and task-specific hazards, particularly those associated with working at heights.

    - Determine required risk controls and safety measures, including fall prevention and fall arrest equipment, to mitigate identified hazards.

- Ensure appropriate personal protective equipment (PPE) is selected and utilized based on identified hazards and risk controls.

5. **Minimizing Risk of Falling Objects:**

   - Identify methods for moving and placing tools, equipment, and materials to minimize the risk of falling objects.

   - Implement measures such as securing tools and materials, using barriers or containment systems, and providing adequate signage to prevent objects from falling.

6. **Calculating Load Weight and Consultation with Licensed Dogger:**

   - Calculate load weight based on the type and quantity of materials being lifted.

   - Consult with a licensed dogger to confirm load weight calculations and ensure they are within the rated capacity of the crane and the working load limit (WLL) of the lifting gear.

7. **Inspecting Crane and Load Movement Paths:**

   - Determine and inspect crane and load movement paths to identify any obstructions, hazards, or potential risks.

   - Ensure that movement paths are clear and free from obstacles to prevent accidents during crane operations.

8. **Confirming Implementation of Traffic Management Plan:**

- Confirm the implementation of a traffic management plan to manage vehicle and pedestrian traffic around the crane and lifting area.

- Ensure that all personnel are aware of traffic management procedures and adhere to designated traffic routes and safety zones.

9. **Establishing Communication Methods**:

- Establish required communication methods with relevant personnel, including crane operators, signal persons, spotters, and ground crew.

- Ensure that communication devices such as two-way radios or hand signals are readily available and functional.

10. **Maintaining Communication for Clear Communication of Lift Plan and Risk Controls**:

- Establish and maintain communication with relevant personnel to ensure the lift plan and risk controls are communicated clearly.

- Communicate any changes or updates to the lift plan or risk controls promptly to all involved parties to maintain safety and coordination throughout the task.

Reviewing task instructions and obtaining relevant information is a crucial step in ensuring the successful completion of any job within a construction site or industrial setting. It begins with a comprehensive review of task instructions provided by supervisors or project managers. These instructions serve as the foundation for understanding the scope, requirements, and objectives of the task at hand. By thoroughly examining the instructions, workers can gain clarity on what needs to be accomplished and how to proceed effectively.

However, task instructions may not always provide all the necessary details or clarification, especially in complex or unfamiliar situations. Therefore, it is essential to consult with relevant personnel, such as supervisors, engineers, or safety officers, to seek clarification on any aspects of the instructions that are unclear. These individuals possess valuable knowledge and expertise that can help fill in any gaps or address any uncertainties regarding the task requirements.

In addition to seeking clarification, obtaining relevant workplace information is essential for proper task planning and execution. This includes understanding the site layout, existing hazards, and any specific requirements or restrictions related to the task. By gathering this information, workers can assess potential risks, identify safety measures, and determine the best approach to carry out the task safely and efficiently. Whether it's understanding the layout of the work area or being aware of potential hazards, having access to relevant workplace information is critical for making informed decisions and ensuring overall workplace safety. Therefore, thorough review and consultation with relevant personnel are essential steps in preparing for task execution and mitigating potential risks.

Interpreting information, particularly from Safe Work Method Statements (SWMSs), is paramount for ensuring that workplace activities align with safety requirements specific to the site. SWMSs serve as comprehensive documents that outline the necessary steps, precautions, and procedures to carry out various tasks safely and effectively. To begin, it's crucial to obtain the relevant SWMSs pertinent to the task at hand. These documents provide detailed guidance on the safest practices and protocols for specific activities within the workplace.

Once obtained, it's essential to thoroughly interpret the information outlined in the SWMSs. This involves carefully reviewing each section to understand the recommended procedures, hazard controls, and safety measures relevant to the task. By comprehensively interpreting the SWMSs, workers can gain insight into the potential risks associated with the task and identify the necessary precautions to mitigate those risks effectively.

Furthermore, ensuring that all activities are performed in compliance with the SWMSs is imperative for maintaining workplace safety standards. These documents serve as a blueprint for safe work practices, and adherence to their guidelines is essential to minimize the risk of accidents or injuries. Therefore, it's essential to strictly follow the procedures outlined in the SWMSs, as they are designed to promote safe work practices and prevent workplace incidents.

Overall, interpreting information from SWMSs plays a vital role in ensuring that activities are conducted in compliance with workplace-specific safety requirements. By obtaining and comprehensively reviewing these documents, workers can effectively identify potential hazards, implement appropriate control measures, and carry out tasks safely and efficiently, ultimately contributing to a safer work environment for all personnel involved.

Ensuring the proper inspection, use, maintenance, and storage of equipment is paramount for maintaining safety standards and operational efficiency on a construction site. The first step in this process involves obtaining and carefully interpreting the manufacturer's requirements pertaining to equipment inspection, use, maintenance, and storage. These requirements typically encompass detailed guidelines and recommendations provided by the equipment manufacturer to ensure safe and effective operation.

Once the manufacturer's requirements have been obtained and understood, it is imperative to adhere strictly to these guidelines during equipment inspections. Regular inspections should be conducted according to the specified intervals outlined by the manufacturer. These inspections aim to identify any potential defects, wear and tear, or malfunctions that may compromise the safety or performance of the equipment.

During equipment inspections, personnel should meticulously examine all critical components and mechanisms, checking for signs of damage, corrosion, or mechanical issues. Any discrepancies or anomalies discovered during the inspection process should be promptly addressed and rectified to maintain the equipment's operational integrity and mitigate potential safety risks.

In addition to conducting routine inspections, it is essential to ensure that equipment is used in accordance with the manufacturer's recommendations and specifications. This includes adhering to load capacity limits, operational guidelines, and safety protocols outlined in the manufacturer's documentation. Proper training and supervision of personnel operating the equipment are also essential to minimize the risk of accidents or misuse.

Furthermore, regular maintenance activities should be carried out as per the manufacturer's guidelines to prevent premature wear and tear and ensure the longevity of the equipment. This may include lubrication, adjustment, calibration, or replacement of components as necessary. By adhering to the manufacturer's maintenance recommendations, potential issues can be identified and addressed proactively, reducing the likelihood of unexpected equipment failures or breakdowns.

Finally, proper storage practices should be observed to protect the equipment from environmental factors such as moisture, corrosion, or extreme temperatures that could compromise its integrity. Equipment should be stored in designated areas that are clean, dry, and free from potential hazards. Additionally, measures should be taken to secure equipment against theft or unauthorized access when not in use.

Adherence to manufacturer requirements regarding equipment inspection, use, maintenance, and storage is essential for ensuring safety, reliability, and longevity in construction operations. By following these guidelines diligently, construction professionals can minimize risks, maximize efficiency, and uphold the highest standards of workplace safety.

Identifying hazards and determining risk controls is a critical aspect of maintaining safety in construction environments, particularly when operating tower cranes where working at heights presents significant risks. The first step in this process involves conducting a comprehensive assessment to identify workplace and task-specific hazards. This includes evaluating various factors such as the physical work environment, equipment used, work tasks performed, and overall work design and management.

Of particular concern in tower crane operations are hazards associated with working at heights. This includes risks such as falls from elevated positions, which can result in serious injuries or fatalities. By carefully assessing the work environment and tasks involved, potential hazards related to working at heights, such as unstable surfaces, unsecured materials, or inadequate fall protection measures, can be identified.

Once hazards have been identified, the next step is to determine the required risk controls and safety measures to mitigate these risks effectively. This may involve implementing fall prevention measures, such as installing guardrails, toe boards, or safety nets to prevent falls from elevated areas. Additionally, fall arrest systems, including harnesses, lanyards, and anchor points, should be employed to safely arrest a fall should one occur.

It is essential to ensure that appropriate personal protective equipment (PPE) is selected and utilized based on the identified hazards and risk controls. This may include providing workers with suitable safety helmets, high-visibility clothing, safety footwear, and, most importantly, fall protection equipment such as harnesses and lanyards. Proper training and instruction on the correct use of PPE are also essential to ensure its effectiveness in mitigating risks.

Furthermore, regular inspections and maintenance of fall protection equipment are crucial to ensuring its reliability and effectiveness in the event of a fall. Equipment should be inspected before each use to detect any signs of damage or wear and promptly replaced or repaired as necessary. By consistently monitoring and maintaining fall protection equipment, the likelihood of equipment failure or malfunction during use can be minimized, thereby enhancing worker safety.

Identifying hazards and determining risk controls are essential steps in ensuring the safety of tower crane operations. By conducting thorough assessments, implementing appropriate safety measures, and providing adequate training and equipment, construction professionals can effectively mitigate risks associated with working at heights and create a safer working environment for all personnel involved.

Figure 27: Many hazards can exist in sites where tower cranes are used. Ventilation structure Olbrachtova - a Prague metro D line construction site in Na Strži street. Joker Island, CC0, via Wikimedia Commons.

The initial step in the risk management process involves the comprehensive identification of all hazards associated with a tower crane within a workplace setting. This process necessitates a thorough examination aimed at identifying potential sources of harm to individuals. Hazards commonly emerge from various aspects of work and their interactions, encompassing the physical work environment, equipment, materials, work tasks, and work design and management practices.

A range of typical hazards linked with tower cranes must be acknowledged, including structural or mechanical failures, collisions with personnel or structures, adverse weather conditions such as high winds, falling objects during loading or unloading operations, and the risk of individuals falling from height. Identifying hazards entails inspecting the workplace and analysing various activities associated with the lifecycle of the tower crane, from installation to decommissioning, to ascertain potential risks and dangers that may arise.

Additionally, ensuring safe design practices and incorporating principles of good work design during the design phase can significantly contribute to hazard elimination and risk mitigation. Design considerations should encompass all stages of the tower crane's lifecycle, addressing aspects such as manufacture, transportation, installation, maintenance, and disposal. Tower crane designers, including engineers and industrial designers, play a crucial role in integrating safety measures into the design process.

Conducting regular inspections of tower cranes within the workplace is essential for identifying potential hazards and ensuring compliance with safety standards. Responsible individuals with management or control of the plant must review pertinent safety information and observe how tower cranes are utilized in practice. Consulting with workers, reviewing manufacturer instructions, and considering factors such as the crane's condition, location, and suitability are integral aspects of the inspection process.

Moreover, reviewing safety information from various sources, including manufacturers, maintenance technicians, regulators, and industry standards, provides valuable insights into tower crane hazards and risk control measures. Analysing incident records, workplace injury reports, maintenance logs, and other relevant data enables the identification of recurring faults, incidents, or misuse patterns, aiding in root cause analysis and risk mitigation strategies. Implementing data logging and remote monitoring systems further enhances understanding of crane usage patterns, incidents, and component lifespans, facilitating proactive maintenance and risk management efforts.

Minimizing the risk of falling objects is paramount in tower crane operations to ensure the safety of workers and bystanders on the construction site. The first step in this process involves identifying effective methods for moving and placing tools, equipment, and materials to minimize the risk of objects falling from elevated positions. This may include utilizing mechanical lifting devices, such as hoists or cranes, to transport heavy or bulky items safely to their intended locations. Additionally, establishing designated areas for storing tools and materials at ground level can help minimize the need for overhead storage and reduce the risk of objects being dropped or knocked over.

Once methods for moving and placing objects have been identified, it is essential to implement appropriate measures to prevent objects from falling. This may involve securing tools and materials using lanyards, tethers, or other forms of restraints to prevent them from becoming dislodged or falling from elevated work areas. Additionally, barriers or containment systems, such as guardrails, toe boards, or debris nets, can be installed around work areas to contain falling objects and prevent them from reaching lower levels.

Providing adequate signage and communication is another essential aspect of minimizing the risk of falling objects. Clear signage should be displayed in areas where overhead work is being performed to alert workers and bystanders to the potential hazards of falling objects. Furthermore, establishing effective communication protocols, such as using hand signals or verbal warnings, can help ensure that workers are aware of potential risks and take appropriate precautions to prevent accidents.

Regular inspections of work areas should also be conducted to identify any potential hazards or risks associated with falling objects. This includes inspecting tools, equipment, and materials for signs of damage or wear that could compromise their integrity and lead to accidents. Any defective or damaged items should be promptly repaired or replaced to maintain a safe working environment.

Minimizing the risk of falling objects in tower crane operations requires a proactive approach that involves identifying effective methods for moving and placing objects, implementing appropriate preventive measures, providing clear signage and communication, and conducting regular inspections. By taking these steps, construction professionals can create a safer working environment and reduce the likelihood of accidents caused by falling objects.

Calculating the load weight is a critical aspect of tower crane operation, as it directly impacts the crane's stability and safety during lifting operations. This process begins with a thorough assessment of the type and quantity of materials to be lifted, taking into account factors such as density, volume, and weight distribution. Precise calculations are essential to prevent overloading the crane, which can lead to structural failure or collapse, posing significant risks to personnel and property.

Consultation with a dogger is essential to verify load weight calculations and ensure compliance with safety regulations and manufacturer specifications. Doggers possess specialized knowledge and training in crane operations, including load dynamics and weight distribution. By collaborating with a licensed professional, crane operators can confirm that load weight remains within the rated capacity of the crane and the working load limit (WLL) of the lifting gear, mitigating the risk of equipment failure and accidents.

Furthermore, consultation with a dogger provides an additional layer of safety assurance, as these experts can offer insights and recommendations to optimize lifting operations and minimize risks. Their expertise enables them to assess various factors, such as environmental conditions, rigging configurations, and load handling techniques, to ensure safe and efficient crane operation. Effective communication between crane operators and licensed doggers is essential to address any concerns or uncertainties regarding load weight calculations and implement appropriate risk mitigation measures.

Calculating load weight and consulting with a dogger are integral steps in ensuring the safe and efficient operation of tower cranes. By accurately assessing load requirements and seeking expert guidance, crane operators can minimize the risk of accidents and ensure compliance with safety standards, ultimately promoting a safe working environment for all personnel involved in lifting operations.

Inspecting crane and load movement paths is a critical aspect of ensuring safe crane operations on a construction site. This process begins by meticulously determining the routes that the crane and loads will traverse during lifting operations. By conducting a thorough inspection, potential obstructions, hazards, or risks along these paths can be identified proactively.

During the inspection, attention should be given to various factors that could impede the movement of the crane or pose risks to personnel and property. These may include overhead obstacles such as power lines, trees, building structures, or protruding equipment. Additionally, ground-level hazards such as uneven terrain, debris, or temporary construction materials must be carefully noted.

Efforts should be made to ensure that crane and load movement paths remain clear and unobstructed throughout the duration of crane operations. This involves promptly removing any identified obstructions or hazards that could interfere with the safe movement of the crane or jeopardize the safety of workers and bystanders. Clear communication and coordination among site personnel are essential to maintain the integrity of movement paths.

Regular monitoring and inspection of movement paths should be integrated into the site's safety protocols to address any changes or developments that may occur during construction activities. By consistently assessing and maintaining clear pathways for crane operations, the risk of accidents and incidents can be significantly mitigated, promoting a safer working environment for all individuals involved in the construction process.

Confirming the implementation of a traffic management plan is crucial for ensuring the safe movement of vehicles and pedestrians around the crane and its lifting area on a construction site. This process involves verifying that the traffic management plan, which outlines procedures for controlling and directing traffic flow, has been effectively put into action.

Firstly, it's essential to review the details of the traffic management plan to understand designated traffic routes, safety zones, and any specific protocols related to crane operations. This includes identifying areas where vehicle and pedestrian traffic may intersect with crane activities, such as material delivery zones or loading areas.

Once the traffic management plan is understood, efforts should be made to confirm its implementation on the ground. This may involve conducting site inspections to ensure that traffic control measures, such as signage, barriers, or designated pathways, are in place and clearly visible. Additionally, coordination with site personnel, including crane operators, flaggers, and site supervisors, can provide valuable insights into the effectiveness of traffic management procedures.

Figure 28: Traffic management applied. Crane at site 33W. Atomic Taco from Seattle, WA, USA, CC BY-SA 2.0, via Wikimedia Commons.

Personnel involved in crane operations and other construction activities must be briefed on traffic management protocols and instructed to adhere to designated traffic routes and safety zones. This includes raising awareness about the potential hazards associated with vehicular and pedestrian traffic in proximity to crane operations and emphasizing the importance of following established safety measures at all times.

Regular monitoring and enforcement of traffic management procedures are essential to maintain safe working conditions around the crane and lifting area. By confirming the implementation of the traffic management plan and ensuring compliance with established protocols, the risk of accidents and collisions involving vehicles and pedestrians can be minimized, contributing to a safer work environment on the construction site.

Establishing effective communication methods is paramount for ensuring smooth and safe operations involving tower cranes and associated personnel on construction sites. The first step in this process involves determining the necessary communication methods required to facilitate seamless coordination among relevant personnel. This may include crane operators, signal persons, spotters, ground crew, supervisors, and other workers involved in crane operations.

Once the communication needs are identified, efforts should be made to ensure that the necessary communication devices are readily available and functional. This may involve providing personnel with two-way radios, hand signals, or other communication tools that enable real-time communication and coordination. It is essential to verify that these devices are in good working condition and adequately charged to maintain communication reliability throughout the operation.

Additionally, clear protocols should be established regarding the use of communication methods to ensure consistent and effective communication among team members. This includes defining signal codes, hand signals, or verbal commands that will be used to convey instructions and information during crane operations. Personnel should be trained on the proper use of communication devices and protocols to minimize the risk of miscommunication or errors.

Regular communication checks and drills can help ensure that communication methods are functioning correctly and that personnel are familiar with their use. By establishing reliable communication methods and promoting clear communication protocols, construction teams can enhance safety, efficiency, and coordination during tower crane operations, reducing the risk of accidents and improving overall project performance.

Figure 29: Tower Crane Operator. Ian Barber, CC BY 3.0 , via Wikimedia Commons

Preparing for Tower Crane Operation

In operating a tower crane, several crucial steps must be taken to ensure safe and efficient operation. Here's a breakdown of each step:
1. Check Signs and Labels: Before operating the crane, it's essential to inspect all signs and labels on the crane for visibility and legibility. This includes checking warning signs, load capacity labels, and any other safety instructions. Clear and visible sig-

nage ensures that operators and other personnel are aware of important safety information while working with the crane.

2. Assess Weather Conditions: Prior to operating the crane, it's necessary to assess weather conditions, especially wind and adverse weather factors. Operators should determine whether these conditions fall within the manufacturer's requirements for safe crane operation. If conditions exceed safe limits, operations may need to be postponed or adjusted to ensure safety.

3. Access Crane Safely: Safe access to the crane is essential for operators and maintenance personnel. Before climbing or accessing the crane, individuals should ensure that proper access routes are available and free from obstructions. Using designated access points and following established safety protocols helps minimize the risk of accidents or injuries during access.

4. Test Crane Safety Devices: Before starting crane operations, it's important to test all safety devices and systems in accordance with workplace requirements. This includes testing emergency stop buttons, limit switches, overload protection systems, and any other safety features installed on the crane. Testing ensures that these devices are functioning correctly and can respond effectively in case of emergencies.

5. Carry Out Pre-Start Checks: Prior to starting the crane, operators should conduct pre-start checks to inspect the crane for any damage or defects. This includes visually inspecting structural components, mechanical parts, electrical systems, and hydraulic systems for signs of wear, damage, or malfunction. Any identified issues should be reported, recorded, and addressed promptly in accordance with safe work practices and manufacturer requirements.

6. Check Crane Logbook: Operators should verify that the crane logbook has been completed and signed, confirming that it contains accurate and up-to-date information relevant to the crane's type and current compliance status. Additionally, any rectifications or maintenance activities should be documented and signed off accordingly to ensure comprehensive record-keeping and compliance with workplace procedures.

7. Start Crane and Perform Operational Checks: After completing pre-start checks and ensuring all safety measures are in place, operators can start the crane and perform operational checks. This involves testing crane functions such as hoisting, slewing, and trolley movement to ensure smooth and safe operation. During operation, operators should remain vigilant for any abnormal noises, smoke, or fumes, which may indicate potential issues requiring further investigation or maintenance. If abnormalities are detected, the crane should be shut down, tagged out, reported, and recorded as per established procedures and manufacturer requirements.

Ensuring the visibility and legibility of signs and labels on a tower crane is a fundamental aspect of crane safety. Before initiating crane operations, operators must conduct a thorough inspection of all signage affixed to the crane structure. This includes examining warning signs that highlight potential hazards, load capacity labels that specify weight limits, and any other safety instructions or guidelines displayed prominently on the crane.

CRANE OPERATIONS 111

Figure 30: Signage on a tower crane at a building construction site in Taichung. , Attribution, via Wikimedia Commons.

Clear and visible signage serves as a crucial communication tool, conveying vital safety information to crane operators and other personnel working in the vicinity. By inspecting signs and labels for visibility, operators can ensure that essential safety messages are easily readable, even from a distance or under varying lighting conditions. This proactive approach helps minimize the risk of misinterpretation or oversight of critical safety protocols during crane operations.

In addition to checking the visibility of signs and labels, operators should also assess their legibility to confirm that the information provided is clear and comprehensible. Illegible or faded signage may hinder operators' ability to quickly access important safety information, potentially compromising the safety of crane operations. By verifying the legibility of signage, operators can address any issues promptly, such as replacing worn-out labels or improving lighting conditions to enhance readability.

Overall, the process of checking signs and labels on a tower crane underscores the importance of proactive safety measures in crane operations. By ensuring that all safety instructions and warnings are clearly visible and legible, operators contribute to a safer work environment, reducing the risk of accidents and injuries associated with crane operations. This proactive approach aligns with industry best practices and regulatory requirements, emphasizing the paramount importance of effective communication and hazard awareness in crane safety protocols.

Assessing weather conditions, particularly wind and adverse weather factors, is a critical step in ensuring the safe operation of a tower crane. Before initiating crane operations, operators must conduct a thorough evaluation of current weather conditions at the worksite. This assessment involves monitoring weather forecasts and observing on-site conditions to determine if they comply with the manufacturer's specified requirements for safe crane operation.

One of the primary weather factors that operators must assess is wind speed. Tower cranes are particularly susceptible to wind-related risks, as strong winds can exert significant forces on the crane structure and loads, potentially compromising stability and safety. Operators should reference the crane manufacturer's guidelines to identify the maximum allowable wind speeds for safe operation. If current wind speeds exceed these limits, operators may need to suspend crane operations until conditions improve or implement additional safety measures, such as reducing crane height or adjusting load capacities.

In addition to wind speed, operators should also consider other adverse weather conditions that could impact crane safety, such as heavy rain, lightning, or extreme temperatures. Adverse weather factors can pose various risks to crane operations, including reduced visibility, slippery surfaces, and electrical hazards. Operators should assess whether these conditions pose a threat to crane stability, equipment integrity, or the safety of personnel working in the vicinity.

Ultimately, the goal of assessing weather conditions is to prioritize safety and mitigate risks associated with adverse weather factors during crane operations. By proactively monitoring and evaluating weather conditions, operators can make informed decisions to ensure the safety of crane operations and minimize the risk of accidents or damage. This proactive approach aligns with industry best practices and regulatory requirements, emphasizing the importance of vigilance and adherence to safety protocols in response to changing weather conditions.

Ensuring safe access to the tower crane is paramount to the well-being of operators and maintenance personnel. Before attempting to climb or access the crane, individuals must conduct a thorough assessment of the access route to ensure its safety and suitability for use. This assessment includes checking for any potential obstructions, hazards, or obstacles along the access path that could impede safe passage.

Operators and maintenance personnel should utilize designated access points established for accessing the crane safely. These access points are typically equipped with appropriate safety features, such as ladders, stairs, or platforms, designed to facilitate safe and efficient entry to the crane structure. It's imperative that individuals strictly adhere to these designated access points and refrain from improvising alternative routes, as doing so may pose unnecessary risks and compromise safety.

Before initiating the ascent, individuals should also ensure that they are equipped with the necessary personal protective equipment (PPE), such as harnesses, helmets, and sturdy footwear, to mitigate the risk of falls or other accidents during the climb. Additionally, individuals should be trained in proper climbing techniques and safety procedures to minimize the likelihood of accidents or injuries while accessing the crane.

Throughout the ascent, individuals should maintain a vigilant awareness of their surroundings and exercise caution when navigating potentially hazardous areas, such as narrow passages or uneven surfaces. Clear communication among team members is essential to coordinate safe access and alert others to any potential hazards or obstacles encountered along the way.

By prioritizing safety and adhering to established access procedures, individuals can minimize the risk of accidents or injuries during crane access operations. Regular inspection and maintenance of access routes, coupled with ongoing training and adherence to safety protocols, are essential components of a comprehensive safety program aimed at promoting safe crane access practices.

Testing crane safety devices is a crucial step in ensuring the safe operation of the equipment. Before commencing crane operations, operators and maintenance personnel must systematically test all safety devices and systems installed on the crane to verify their proper functioning and effectiveness in emergency situations.

The testing process typically involves inspecting and evaluating various safety features, including emergency stop buttons, limit switches, overload protection systems, and any other safety mechanisms incorporated into the crane's design. Operators should follow established procedures outlined by workplace requirements and manufacturer guidelines when conducting these tests.

To begin the testing process, operators should activate each safety device individually and observe its response to ensure it functions as intended. This may involve simulating emergency scenarios or applying controlled loads to trigger the activation of safety mechanisms, such as overload protection systems or limit switches.

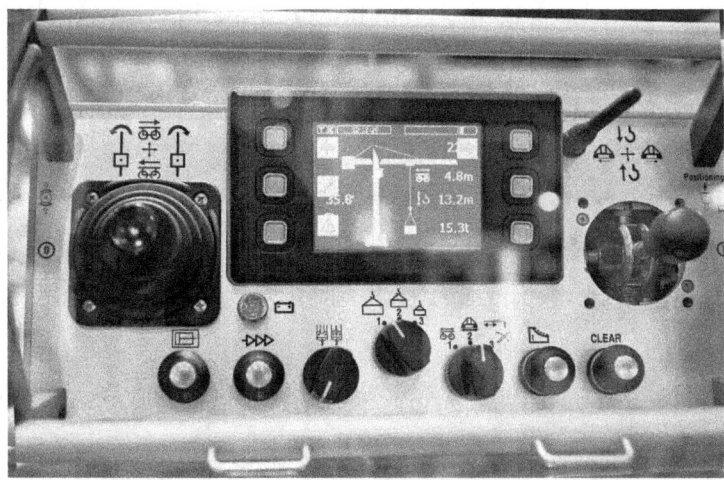

Figure 31: Tower crane controls. Source: Canva.

During the testing process, operators should pay close attention to any signs of malfunction or irregular behaviour exhibited by the safety devices. Any discrepancies or abnormalities detected during testing should be promptly addressed and rectified to ensure the crane's safety systems are fully operational and reliable.

Upon completion of the testing procedure, operators should document the results and maintain detailed records of the testing process for compliance and auditing purposes. These records serve as evidence of the crane's safety compliance and can be referenced in the event of inspections or audits by regulatory authorities or workplace safety inspectors.

Regular testing and maintenance of crane safety devices are essential to uphold safety standards and prevent accidents or injuries during crane operations. By conducting thorough and systematic testing of safety systems, operators can ensure the continued safe and reliable performance of the crane while minimizing the risk of equipment failures or malfunctions.

Before commencing work each shift, the crane operator must perform a comprehensive pre-start visual inspection and operational test of the crane, adhering to the guidelines outlined in the manufacturer's operations manual. This inspection covers a range of critical components and systems, ensuring that the crane is in optimal working condition and meets safety standards.

During the pre-start check, the operator should visually inspect various aspects of the crane's condition and setup, including but not limited to the structure, crane access points, and logbooks. Additionally, key components such as counterweights, wire ropes, rope winch drums, anchorages, splices, and lifting hooks should be examined for any signs of damage or wear.

The inspection should also encompass power systems, including the power supply, electrical cabinet, and main isolation switch, as well as fluid systems such as fuel, coolant, oils, hydraulics, lubrication, and any potential spillages. Furthermore, brake mechanisms, emergency load lowering equipment, load radius indicators, load charts, rated capacity, manufacturer's data plates, warning lights, devices, and firefighting equipment should be thoroughly inspected for functionality and compliance.

Following the visual inspection, the operator must conduct an operational check, which involves starting the crane in accordance with workplace procedures and manufacturer specifications. During this process, all limits, governors, controls, gauges, mechanisms, warning devices, indicators, switches, fixtures, brakes, locks, and pins should be tested and inspected where practical.

Moreover, the operator should verify that rated capacity and radii measurements align with the load moment indicator to ensure accurate load handling capabilities. By diligently performing these pre-start checks and operational tests, the crane operator can help mitigate the risk of equipment failure, enhance workplace safety, and ensure efficient crane operations throughout the shift.

Carrying out pre-start checks is a fundamental practice to ensure the safe and efficient operation of a crane. Before initiating any crane operations, operators must meticulously inspect various components and systems of the crane to identify any potential damage, defects, or malfunctions that could compromise its safety or performance.

The pre-start check process involves a comprehensive visual inspection of key structural, mechanical, electrical, and hydraulic components of the crane. Operators should carefully examine critical elements such as the boom, mast, jib, hook, cables, sheaves, and wire ropes for signs of wear, corrosion, cracks, or other forms of damage.

Additionally, operators should inspect electrical systems, including control panels, switches, cables, and connectors, to ensure they are in good condition and free from damage or exposed wiring that could pose electrical hazards.

Hydraulic systems, including hoses, cylinders, valves, and fittings, should also be inspected for leaks, wear, or damage that could affect the crane's hydraulic performance or stability during operation.

During the pre-start checks, operators should pay particular attention to safety devices and features such as emergency stop buttons, limit switches, overload protection systems, and safety guards. These safety mechanisms must be inspected to verify their proper functioning and ensure they can effectively mitigate risks during crane operations.

Any identified issues or abnormalities observed during the pre-start checks should be promptly reported, recorded, and addressed in accordance with established safe work practices, workplace-specific procedures, and manufacturer requirements. Operators should follow designated protocols for reporting defects or damage, which may involve notifying supervisors, maintenance personnel, or safety officers and taking appropriate corrective actions to rectify the issues.

To check the crane logbook effectively, operators should first ensure that it has been accurately filled out and signed, indicating compliance with regulatory standards and workplace protocols. The logbook should contain detailed information pertinent to the specific type of crane being operated and its current compliance status.

Operators should carefully review the entries in the logbook to confirm that all required information has been documented. This includes details such as previous maintenance activities, inspections, repairs, and any modifications made to the crane. Each entry should be dated and signed by the individual responsible for the respective task or activity.

In addition to verifying the completeness of the logbook entries, operators should also ensure that any rectifications or maintenance activities noted in the logbook have been addressed and signed off as required. This step is crucial for maintaining an accurate record of the crane's maintenance history and ensuring that all necessary repairs or adjustments have been properly documented and completed.

Furthermore, operators should cross-reference the information in the logbook with workplace procedures and manufacturer requirements to confirm compliance with relevant guidelines and standards. Any discrepancies or inconsistencies should be promptly addressed and rectified to maintain the integrity of the logbook and uphold safety standards.

To start the crane and perform operational checks, operators should follow a systematic procedure to ensure safe and efficient operation. Firstly, after completing pre-start checks and confirming that all safety measures are in place, operators should initiate the crane's start-up sequence according to workplace procedures and manufacturer guidelines.

Once the crane is started, operators should conduct operational checks to verify that all crane functions are functioning as intended. This includes testing the hoisting mechanism, slewing motion, trolley movement, and any other relevant functions specific to the crane model being operated. Operators should pay close attention to the smoothness and responsiveness of these operations, as any irregularities may indicate potential issues that need to be addressed.

During the operational checks, operators should remain vigilant for any abnormal signs such as unusual noises, smoke, or fumes emanating from the crane. These abnormalities could be indicative of mechanical problems, electrical faults, or other issues that may compromise safety or performance. If any abnormalities are detected, operators should promptly shut down the crane, tag it out of service, report the issue to appropriate personnel, and record the incident in accordance with established procedures and manufacturer requirements.

Additionally, operators should ensure that all operational controls, gauges, indicators, and warning devices are functioning properly and accurately reflect the crane's status. This includes verifying the accuracy of load indicators, rated capacity displays, and any other safety-critical components that provide vital information during crane operation.

By starting the crane and performing thorough operational checks, operators can verify the crane's functionality and readiness for use while proactively identifying any issues that may require attention. This proactive approach helps ensure safe and efficient crane operation, minimizes the risk of accidents or malfunctions, and contributes to overall workplace safety and productivity.

The following provides an example of a tower crane's startup sequence:

1. Power On: Ensure that the main power switch, typically located in the crane's control cabin or control panel, is in the off position before starting. Switch on the main power supply to the crane.

2. Control System Initialization: Depending on the crane's design and control system, initialize the control console or panel. This may involve entering access codes, activating control interfaces, and initializing computerized systems.

3. System Diagnostics: Many modern tower cranes are equipped with diagnostic systems that perform self-checks upon startup. Monitor the diagnostic display or indicators for any error codes or warnings that may require attention.

4. Safety Checks: Verify that all safety devices and systems are functional. Test emergency stop buttons, limit switches, overload protection systems, and any other safety features installed on the crane.

5. Engine Start (if applicable): If the crane is equipped with an engine, start the engine according to the manufacturer's instructions. This may involve turning the ignition key or pressing a start button while monitoring engine gauges for proper operation.

6. Control Panel Check: Ensure that all control panels and interfaces are responsive and functional. Test joystick controls, buttons, switches, and touchscreens to ensure they are correctly configured and calibrated.

7. Hoisting and Slewing Checks: Test the hoisting mechanism and slewing motion to verify smooth operation. Raise and lower the crane hook (or load) and rotate the crane turret to check for any abnormal noises or vibrations.

8. Trolley Movement: If the crane is equipped with a trolley mechanism, test the trolley movement along the jib or boom. Ensure that the trolley moves smoothly and accurately along the designated path.

9. Safety Device Activation: Activate safety devices such as load moment indicators, anti-collision systems, and obstacle detection sensors. Ensure that these devices are functioning correctly and can respond effectively in case of emergencies.

10. Final Checks: Perform a final visual inspection of the crane and its surroundings to ensure everything is in order. Verify that all warning lights, alarms, and indicators are functioning properly.

11. Confirmation: Once all checks have been completed satisfactorily and no issues are detected, confirm that the crane is ready for use. Communicate with relevant personnel to ensure everyone is aware of the crane's operational status.

Transferring Loads

Tower crane movements include:

1. Luffing: Luffing refers to the vertical movement of the jib or boom of a tower crane. It allows the crane operator to adjust the angle of the jib, either raising or lowering it relative to the horizontal position. This movement is essential for positioning the load at various heights and distances from the crane's base. Luffing is typically controlled using a motorized mechanism located within the crane's jib, which adjusts the angle of the jib in response to the operator's commands.

2. Slewing: Slewing involves the rotation of the entire crane structure around its vertical axis. This movement enables the crane to swing or pivot horizontally, allowing the load to be moved to different positions around the crane's operating radius. Slewing is controlled by a motorized mechanism located at the base of the crane, which rotates the entire upper structure, including the jib, cabin, and counterweights. The operator uses controls in the cabin to initiate and control the slewing motion, carefully positioning the load as required.

3. Hoisting and Lowering: Hoisting and lowering refer to the vertical movement of the load, typically using a hook or lifting attachment attached to the crane's hoist rope. Hoisting involves lifting the load from the ground or a lower position to a higher elevation, while lowering involves the reverse process of lowering the load back down. These movements are controlled by the crane operator using controls in the cabin, which regulate the speed and direction of the hoist motor. The hoist rope is wound around a drum connected to the hoist motor, allowing the load to be raised or lowered with precision.

4. Trolleying: Trolleying, also known as traveling or traversing, refers to the horizontal movement of the load along the length of the jib or boom. This movement allows the crane operator to position the load closer to or farther away from the crane's base, adjusting its horizontal position as needed. Trolleying is typically achieved using a motorized mechanism located on the jib, which moves the trolley carriage along a track or rail mounted on the jib. The operator controls the trolleying motion using controls in the cabin, ensuring precise positioning of the load.

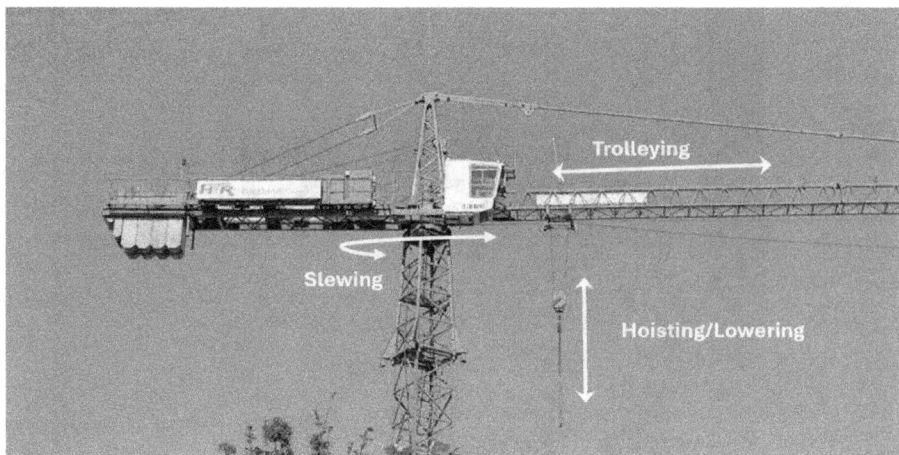

Figure 32: Crane movements. High Contrast, CC BY 3.0 DE, via Wikimedia Commons.

These movements are fundamental to the operation of a tower crane and are carefully coordinated by the operator to ensure safe and efficient lifting operations. Each movement requires skill and precision to manoeuvre the load into the desired position while maintaining stability and safety throughout the lifting process.

To position the boom or jib and hook block over the load as directed by a dogger, the crane operator must first receive clear instructions from the dogger regarding the precise positioning required. This typically involves manipulating the crane's controls to extend, retract, raise, or lower the boom or jib until the hook block is directly above the load. The operator must carefully coordinate with the dogger, ensuring that the crane movements are executed accurately and safely to align the hook block with the designated load area.

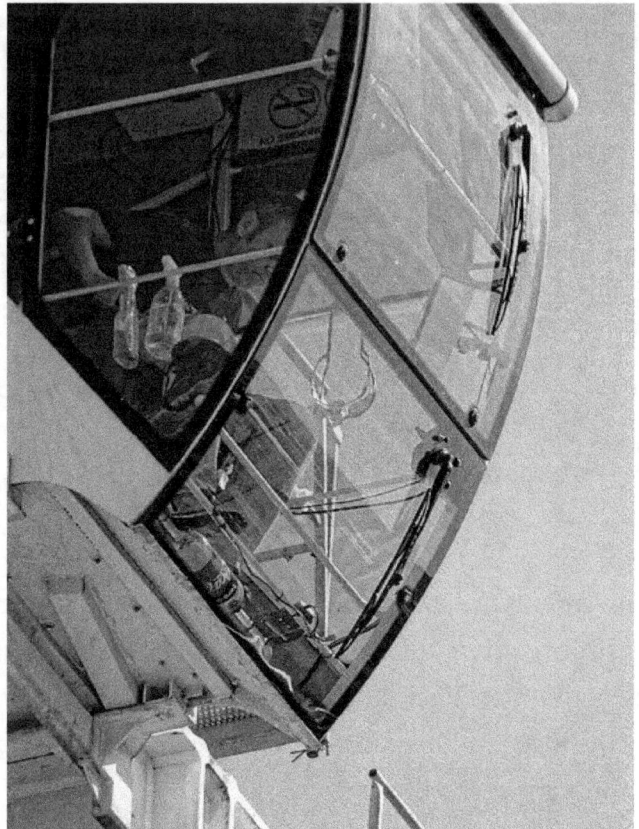

Figure 33: Operator in the control cabin of a tower crane positioning the jib and hook block over the load. Acabashi, CC BY-SA 4.0, via Wikimedia Commons.

Once the boom or jib and hook block are correctly positioned, the operator will carry out a test lift under the supervision of the licensed dogger. This test lift allows for checks and adjustments to be made to the slinging arrangement as directed by the dogger. The operator will lift the load a short distance off the ground to verify that the slings are properly secured and that the load is stable. Any necessary adjustments to the slinging arrangement will be communicated by the dogger, and the operator will make the required changes before proceeding with the lift.

Under the direction of the licensed dogger, the crane operator will then transfer the load using appropriate crane movements. This involves smoothly and precisely lifting the load from its initial position and carefully manoeuvring it to its destination. The operator must follow the dogger's instructions closely, adjusting crane movements as necessary to ensure safe and controlled transfer of the load. This may include raising, lowering, slewing, or trolleying the load as directed by the dogger to navigate obstacles or position the load accurately.

Communication between the crane operator and licensed dogger is essential throughout the lifting operation. The operator will use radio communication and interpret hand and whistle signals from the dogger to coordinate crane movements effectively. Clear and concise communication is critical to ensure that the operator understands the dogger's instructions and can execute them accurately. The operator must remain attentive to signals from the dogger and respond promptly to ensure the safe and efficient transfer of the load.

Figure 34: Transferring a load. Globetrotter19, CC BY-SA 3.0, via Wikimedia Commons.

Once the load has been successfully transferred to its destination, the crane operator will lower and land the load in accordance with the dogger's instructions. This involves carefully lowering the load to the ground or designated landing area using controlled crane movements. Once the load is safely positioned, the lifting gear, such as slings or chains, will be disconnected from the load. The operator will follow the dogger's guidance to ensure that the disconnection process is carried out safely and efficiently, minimizing the risk of accidents or injuries during this final phase of the operation.

Shutting Down and Securing a Tower Crane

To apply hoist, luffing, trolley, and travel brakes on a tower crane, the operator must first ensure that the crane is in a stable position and that there are no loads suspended. The operator will engage the hoist brake by activating the control mechanism that controls the hoisting motion, locking the hoist drum in place. Similarly, the luffing brake, which controls the raising and lowering of the jib or boom, will be engaged using the designated control mechanism. The trolley brake, responsible for moving the load horizontally along the jib, and the travel brake, used for moving the entire crane on its tracks or wheels, will also be activated as needed. These brakes are typically engaged using control levers or switches located in the crane's operator cabin.

When shutting down the crane, the operator will follow the manufacturer's requirements to place the crane in the weather-vane position. This involves positioning the crane's boom or jib perpendicular to the prevailing wind direction to minimize wind resistance and reduce the risk of damage during idle periods. The operator will use the crane's controls to rotate the boom or jib to the correct orientation, ensuring that it is securely locked in place.

After shutting down the crane, the operator will carry out routine shutdown checks to ensure that all systems are functioning correctly and that the crane is secure. This includes visually inspecting components such as brakes, cables, and structural elements for signs of damage or wear. The operator will also ensure that all access points, including the cabin and any maintenance hatches, are securely closed and locked to prevent unauthorized access.

To exit the crane safely, the operator will follow established procedures, which may include securely stowing personal belongings, powering down electrical systems, and descending from the operator cabin using the designated access ladder or platform. The operator will exercise caution when exiting the crane, ensuring that all steps and surfaces are clear and free from obstruction.

Finally, any damage or defects observed during shutdown or exit procedures will be promptly reported and recorded by the operator. This information will be documented in the crane's maintenance logbook or other relevant records, and appropriate action will be taken to address the issues identified. By promptly reporting and recording damage or defects, operators contribute to the maintenance and safety of the crane, helping to prevent accidents and ensure continued reliable operation.

Self-Erecting Tower Crane Operation

Setting up a self-erecting tower crane involves a series of precise steps to ensure stability, safety, and proper functioning. Here's a detailed explanation of each stage of the setup process:

1. **Site Preparation**:
    - Before setting up the crane, the construction site must be adequately prepared. This involves clearing the area where the crane will be positioned, ensuring the ground is level and stable, and removing any obstacles or debris that could interfere with the crane's operation.

2. **Transport and Unloading**:
    - The self-erecting tower crane is transported to the site on a truck or trailer. Once it arrives, the crane is unloaded using a crane or other lifting equipment. Care must be taken during unloading to ensure the crane components are not damaged.

3. **Assembly of Base and Mast**:
    - The assembly process begins with erecting the crane's base and mast sections. The base is typically anchored to a con-

crete foundation or supported by concrete blocks or pads. The mast sections, which form the vertical structure of the crane, are then assembled and attached to the base.

4. **Hydraulic System Setup**:

- Self-erecting tower cranes rely on hydraulic systems for the erection and folding of the boom or jib. The hydraulic system must be set up and connected to the crane's control panel. This involves connecting hydraulic hoses, checking fluid levels, and ensuring all components are functioning properly.

5. **Boom or Jib Installation**:

- Once the base and mast are in place, the crane's boom or jib is installed. This involves unfolding or extending the boom to its full length and securing it to the mast. Care must be taken to ensure the boom is properly aligned and supported to prevent instability.

6. **Counterweight Installation**:

- Counterweights are essential for stabilizing the crane and balancing the load during lifting operations. The counterweights are typically attached to the rear of the crane's base or mast using bolts or pins. The weight and distribution of the counterweights must be carefully calculated to ensure the crane remains stable under load.

7. **Electrical and Control Setup**:

- The crane's electrical system and control panel must be set up and connected to a power source. This involves installing wiring, switches, and control panels, as well as testing the electrical components to ensure they are functioning correctly.

8. **Safety Checks and Testing**:

    - Before putting the crane into operation, thorough safety checks and testing are essential. This includes inspecting all components for damage or defects, testing the hydraulic and electrical systems, and conducting load tests to ensure the crane can handle its maximum rated capacity safely.

9. **Final Adjustments and Calibration**:

    - Once the crane is fully assembled and tested, final adjustments and calibration may be necessary to ensure optimal performance. This includes adjusting tension in cables or hydraulic hoses, calibrating the crane's sensors and control systems, and verifying that all safety features are functioning as intended.

10. **Safety Briefing and Documentation**:

    - Before operating the crane, all personnel involved should receive a safety briefing covering the crane's operation, safety procedures, and emergency protocols. Additionally, all setup and testing activities should be documented for compliance and record-keeping purposes.

Transporting and unloading a self-erecting tower crane is a critical stage in its deployment at a construction site. Typically, the crane arrives at the site pre-assembled on a truck or trailer, ready for installation. When the crane reaches its destination, it's essential to proceed with caution during the unloading process to prevent any damage to its components.

Firstly, the transportation vehicle carrying the crane is positioned at a designated unloading area, preferably close to the installation site. The unloading area should be clear of obstacles and debris, providing ample space for manoeuvring the crane components.

Next, the crane is unloaded from the truck or trailer using another crane or lifting equipment capable of handling its weight and size. Careful coordination is required during this process to ensure smooth and safe unloading. The lifting equipment carefully hoists the crane components, maintaining balance and stability throughout the operation.

As the crane is lifted from the transportation vehicle, operators must monitor and guide the process to prevent any swinging or sudden movements that could lead to accidents or damage. Additionally, communication between the crane operator and ground personnel is crucial to ensure a safe and coordinated unloading process.

Once the crane is successfully lifted off the transportation vehicle, it is carefully lowered to the ground and positioned in the designated assembly area. Special attention is paid to ensure that all crane components are securely placed and aligned, minimizing the risk of damage or misalignment.

Throughout the unloading process, safety protocols must be strictly followed to protect both personnel and equipment. This includes wearing appropriate personal protective equipment, adhering to established lifting procedures, and conducting thorough pre-operational checks on all equipment involved.

By adhering to these guidelines and exercising caution and precision during the transport and unloading of a self-erecting tower crane, construction crews can ensure that the crane arrives safely and ready for assembly at the construction site, minimizing the risk of delays or damage to equipment.

The assembly of the base and mast of a self-erecting tower crane marks a pivotal stage in the setup process, laying the foundation for the crane's vertical structure. It begins with careful planning and preparation to ensure a smooth and efficient assembly process.

Initially, the crane's base is positioned and secured onto the designated foundation or support structure. This may involve anchoring the base to a concrete foundation using anchor bolts or securing it onto concrete blocks or pads. Ensuring the stability and alignment of the base is paramount to the overall structural integrity of the crane.

Once the base is securely in place, the mast sections are assembled and installed vertically on top of the base. These mast sections form the core vertical structure of the crane, providing the framework for the subsequent assembly of the jib and other components.

The assembly of the mast sections requires precision and attention to detail to ensure proper alignment and connection between each section. Typically, mast sections are bolted or pinned together, with careful consideration given to the structural integrity and load-bearing capacity of each connection.

Throughout the assembly process, safety measures are paramount to protect workers and equipment. This includes using appropriate personal protective equipment, such as helmets and harnesses, adhering to established safety protocols, and conducting regular inspections to identify and address any potential hazards or risks.

Setting up the hydraulic system is a critical step in preparing a self-erecting tower crane for operation. These cranes depend on hydraulic systems for the smooth and efficient erection and folding of the boom or jib, making it essential to ensure that the hydraulic components are properly installed and functioning.

The first task in hydraulic system setup involves connecting hydraulic hoses to the crane's control panel. These hoses serve as the conduits through which hydraulic fluid flows to power various crane functions.

Careful attention must be paid to ensure that hoses are securely connected and free from leaks or damage that could compromise the system's performance.

Once the hoses are connected, it's essential to check the hydraulic fluid levels in the reservoir. Proper fluid levels are crucial for maintaining optimal hydraulic system performance and preventing damage to hydraulic components. Any discrepancies in fluid levels should be addressed promptly by adding or draining fluid as needed.

After verifying fluid levels, a comprehensive inspection of the hydraulic system should be conducted to ensure that all components are functioning correctly. This includes checking hydraulic pumps, cylinders, valves, and other components for signs of wear, damage, or malfunction. Any issues identified during the inspection should be addressed immediately to prevent operational problems or safety hazards.

Throughout the hydraulic system setup process, adherence to safety protocols is paramount to protect personnel and equipment from potential hazards. This includes following manufacturer guidelines and recommendations, using appropriate personal protective equipment, and conducting regular safety checks to identify and mitigate risks.

After the base and mast of the self-erecting tower crane are securely assembled, the next step is to install the crane's boom or jib. This process is essential for extending the reach of the crane and enabling it to lift loads to the desired height and distance.

To install the boom or jib, the crane operator typically utilizes hydraulic mechanisms to unfold or extend the boom to its full length. This may involve activating controls from the crane's control panel or using a remote control device to manoeuvre the boom into position. During this process, it's crucial to ensure that the boom unfolds smoothly and without any obstructions to prevent damage to the crane components.

Once the boom is extended to its full length, it is securely attached to the mast using bolts, pins, or other fastening mechanisms. Careful attention must be paid to ensure that the boom is properly aligned and supported to maintain stability during crane operation. Any misalignment or instability could compromise the safety and effectiveness of the crane and pose a risk to personnel and property in the vicinity.

Throughout the boom installation process, communication between the crane operator and ground personnel is essential to coordinate the movement and positioning of the boom accurately. Clear and effective communication ensures that all parties involved are aware of their roles and responsibilities, minimizing the risk of accidents or errors during the installation process.

Once the boom or jib is securely installed and aligned, a thorough inspection should be conducted to verify that all connections are properly tightened, and the boom is structurally sound. Any issues or discrepancies should be addressed promptly to ensure the safe and efficient operation of the crane. With the boom successfully installed, the self-erecting tower crane is now ready for use in lifting and moving loads on the construction site.

Once the base and mast of the self-erecting tower crane are assembled, the installation of counterweights becomes crucial for maintaining stability and balance during lifting operations. Counterweights are designed to offset the weight of the load being lifted, ensuring that the crane remains steady and secure throughout the lifting process.

The installation of counterweights typically involves attaching them to the rear of the crane's base or mast. This can be done using bolts, pins, or other fastening mechanisms to securely hold the counterweights in place. Care must be taken to ensure that the counterweights are properly aligned and evenly distributed to achieve optimal balance and stability.

CRANE OPERATIONS

Figure 35: Counterweights being delivered to site and unloaded. User:EPO, Attribution, via Wikimedia Commons.

Before installing the counterweights, it's essential to calculate the precise weight and distribution required based on the anticipated load capacity and operating conditions of the crane. This calculation considers factors such as the length of the boom, the height of the lift, and the weight of the materials being lifted. By accurately calculating the counterweight requirements, operators can ensure that the crane remains safe and stable under various load conditions.

During the installation process, operators should follow manufacturer guidelines and safety protocols to minimize the risk of accidents or injuries. This may involve using lifting equipment or machinery to position the counterweights safely and securely onto the crane. Additionally, regular inspections should be conducted to verify that the counterweights are properly installed and in good condition, with any issues addressed promptly to maintain crane safety.

Once the counterweights are securely installed, a final inspection should be carried out to confirm that they are properly aligned and balanced. Any adjustments or corrections should be made as needed to ensure the crane's stability and safety during lifting operations. With the counterweights successfully installed, the self-erecting tower crane is now ready for use in lifting and moving loads on the construction site.

Setting up the electrical system and control panel of a self-erecting tower crane is a critical step in preparing the crane for operation. This process involves several key tasks to ensure that the crane's electrical components are properly installed, connected, and functioning safely and efficiently.

Firstly, the electrical wiring and components must be installed according to manufacturer specifications and electrical codes. This includes routing and connecting wires, cables, and conduits to the control panel, motor, sensors, and other electrical devices throughout the crane's structure. Care must be taken to properly secure and insulate wiring to prevent damage or electrical hazards during operation.

Once the wiring is in place, the control panel is installed and connected to the crane's electrical system. The control panel houses switches, buttons, joysticks, and other controls that enable the operator to manoeuvre the crane's boom, jib, trolley, and hoist. It also contains safety features such as emergency stop buttons and overload protection systems to ensure safe crane operation.

After the control panel is connected, thorough testing of the electrical components is essential to verify proper functionality and safety. This includes testing switches, controls, sensors, and safety systems to ensure they respond correctly to input and operate within specified parameters. Any issues or malfunctions discovered during testing should be addressed promptly to prevent safety hazards or operational disruptions.

Additionally, the electrical system must be connected to a reliable power source, such as a generator or electrical grid, to supply power to the crane's motors, lights, and other electrical devices. Proper grounding and electrical protection measures should be implemented to safeguard against electrical faults, surges, or other hazards that could pose a risk to personnel or equipment.

Throughout the setup process, adherence to safety protocols and electrical codes is paramount to prevent accidents, injuries, or damage to the crane or surrounding infrastructure. Operators and technicians should be properly trained in electrical safety practices and procedures to minimize risks and ensure the safe and efficient operation of the self-erecting tower crane.

Before commencing operations with a self-erecting tower crane, comprehensive safety checks and testing procedures are imperative to guarantee the crane's reliability and operational integrity. These checks encompass a meticulous examination of all components, systems, and mechanisms to detect any signs of damage, wear, or malfunction that could compromise safety during operation.

The inspection process involves scrutinizing structural components, such as the base, mast, boom, and counterweights, for any visible signs of cracks, corrosion, or deformation. Additionally, hydraulic and electrical systems must undergo thorough evaluation to ensure proper functionality and adherence to manufacturer specifications. Hydraulic hoses, fittings, and cylinders are inspected for leaks, damage, or improper connections, while electrical wiring, controls, and safety devices are tested to verify correct operation and responsiveness.

Load tests are a crucial aspect of safety checks, involving the lifting and lowering of loads to assess the crane's capacity and stability under varying conditions. These tests validate that the crane can safely handle its maximum rated capacity without exceeding load limits or experiencing structural strain. Load tests also help identify any deficiencies in the crane's performance, allowing for adjustments or corrective actions to be taken before actual operations commence.

Throughout the safety checks and testing process, adherence to safety protocols and standards is paramount to mitigate risks and ensure the safety of personnel and equipment. Qualified personnel, such as certified crane inspectors or technicians, should conduct the inspections and tests in accordance with established procedures and guidelines. Any identified issues or anomalies should be promptly addressed and resolved before the crane is cleared for operation.

Regular safety checks and testing should be incorporated into the crane's maintenance schedule to ensure ongoing safety and compliance with regulatory requirements. By prioritizing safety and vigilance in the inspection and testing process, operators can mitigate potential hazards and ensure the safe and efficient operation of the self-erecting tower crane throughout its service life.

After completing the initial setup and testing of the self-erecting tower crane, it's essential to perform final adjustments and calibration to fine-tune the crane's performance and ensure its optimal operation. This phase involves meticulously reviewing all aspects of the crane's functionality and making any necessary adjustments to enhance its efficiency and safety.

One crucial aspect of final adjustments involves tensioning cables or hydraulic hoses to achieve the appropriate level of tautness. Proper tensioning ensures smooth and precise movement of crane components, minimizing the risk of slack or excessive strain during operation. Hydraulic systems, in particular, require careful adjustment to optimize fluid flow and pressure, enhancing the crane's lifting capabilities and responsiveness.

Calibration of sensors and control systems is another critical step in the final adjustment process. Sensors responsible for monitoring load weight, boom position, and other vital parameters must be calibrated to provide accurate readings and feedback to the crane's control panel.

This ensures that the crane operates within safe limits and responds accurately to operator commands.

Verifying the functionality of all safety features is paramount during final adjustments. Safety devices such as limit switches, emergency stop buttons, and overload protection systems must be thoroughly tested to confirm their reliability in detecting and mitigating potential hazards. Any discrepancies or malfunctions discovered during testing should be promptly addressed to maintain the crane's safety and compliance with regulatory standards.

Throughout the final adjustments and calibration process, close attention should be paid to manufacturer specifications and guidelines. Adhering to recommended procedures ensures that adjustments are made within safe operating parameters and minimizes the risk of overloading or damaging crane components. Qualified personnel with expertise in crane assembly and maintenance should oversee these tasks to ensure proper execution and compliance with safety standards.

By conducting thorough final adjustments and calibration, operators can optimize the performance and safety of the self-erecting tower crane, ensuring its readiness for reliable and efficient operation on the construction site. This meticulous approach helps mitigate risks, enhance productivity, and prolong the service life of the crane, contributing to overall project success and safety.

Prior to commencing crane operations, it is imperative to conduct a comprehensive safety briefing for all personnel involved in the operation. This briefing serves as a crucial step in ensuring that everyone understands the crane's operation, safety protocols, and emergency procedures, thereby minimizing the risk of accidents or injuries on the worksite. During the safety briefing, key topics such as safe operating practices, hazard identification, and the use of personal protective equipment (PPE) should be addressed to promote a culture of safety among the team.

Furthermore, documentation plays a vital role in maintaining compliance with regulatory requirements and facilitating effective record-keeping throughout the setup process. All setup activities, including assembly, testing, and safety checks, should be meticulously documented to provide a clear record of the crane's installation and preparation for operation. This documentation serves as valuable evidence of compliance with safety standards and can be invaluable in the event of an inspection or audit by regulatory authorities.

The safety briefing should be conducted by qualified personnel with expertise in crane operation and safety procedures. This ensures that all relevant information is communicated clearly and effectively to personnel at all levels of the organization. Emphasis should be placed on the importance of adhering to safety protocols and reporting any concerns or hazards promptly to prevent accidents and ensure a safe working environment.

In addition to verbal communication during the safety briefing, written documentation such as safety manuals, operating procedures, and emergency contact information should be provided to all personnel for reference. This allows individuals to review important safety information as needed and reinforces key concepts covered during the briefing. Documentation should be easily accessible and prominently displayed in areas where it can be readily accessed by personnel.

Operating a self-erecting tower crane involves precise coordination between the crane operator and the licensed dogger to ensure safe and efficient lifting operations. This includes:

1. Position Boom or Jib and Hook Block Over Load: The first step is to position the boom or jib and hook block directly over the load to be lifted. This is typically done based on the instructions provided by the licensed dogger, who assesses the load and determines the optimal position for lifting. The crane operator carefully manoeuvres the crane's boom or jib using the crane's

controls, adjusting the angle and position as directed by the dogger to ensure proper alignment with the load.

2. Carry Out Test Lift: Before lifting the load, a test lift is often conducted to ensure that the load is properly secured and balanced and that the crane can handle the weight without issues. The test lift allows the licensed dogger to check the slinging arrangements and make any necessary adjustments to ensure that the load is stable and secure. The crane operator slowly raises the load a short distance off the ground, allowing the dogger to inspect the lifting gear and confirm that everything is in order before proceeding with the full lift.

3. Transfer Loads Using Appropriate Crane Movements: Once the test lift is successful and the load is deemed ready for transfer, the crane operator, under the direction of the licensed dogger, begins the transfer process using appropriate crane movements. This may involve hoisting the load vertically, slewing or rotating the crane to position the load at the desired destination, and possibly trolleying or traversing the load horizontally along the crane's jib or boom. The operator carefully follows the instructions provided by the dogger to ensure precise and controlled movements throughout the transfer process.

4. Use Radio and Interpret Signals: Communication between the crane operator and the licensed dogger is critical during lifting operations. The operator typically uses a two-way radio to communicate with the dogger, who may be positioned near the load or at a vantage point where they have a clear view of the lifting area. In addition to verbal communication over the radio, the dogger may also use hand signals or whistle signals to provide instructions to the crane operator. The operator must be proficient in interpreting these signals and responding accordingly

to ensure safe and efficient lifting operations.

5. **Lower and Land Load**: Once the load has been successfully transferred to its destination, the crane operator, again under the direction of the licensed dogger, begins the process of lowering the load to the ground. The operator carefully controls the descent speed to ensure a smooth and controlled landing, allowing the load to be safely placed at the desired location. After the load has been landed, the lifting gear is disconnected from the load, and the crane is prepared for the next lifting operation.

By following these steps and maintaining clear communication with the dogger, the crane operator can safely and effectively perform lifting operations using a self-erecting tower crane.

Using the operator controls on a self-erecting tower crane requires familiarity with the various control functions and their corresponding actions. Here's an explanation of how to use these controls, along with examples:

1. **Hoist Control**: The hoist control is used to raise and lower the load. Typically, it consists of a lever or buttons that allow the operator to control the speed and direction of the hoist motor. For example:

    - Pushing the lever or button forward raises the load.
    - Pulling the lever or button backward lowers the load.
    - The operator can adjust the speed of lifting by controlling the pressure or position of the lever.

2. **Trolley Control**: The trolley control is used to move the load horizontally along the jib or boom of the crane. It may consist of a joystick or buttons for precise control of trolley movement.

For example:

- Pushing the joystick or pressing the buttons in one direction moves the load along the jib to the desired position.

- Releasing the joystick or buttons stops the trolley movement, and the load remains in its current position.

3. **Slewing Control**: The slewing control is used to rotate the crane's upper structure (slewing ring) and boom assembly horizontally. It allows the operator to position the load accurately. For example:

    - Rotating the control lever or turning the control dial in one direction causes the crane to rotate clockwise.

    - Rotating the control lever or dial in the opposite direction causes the crane to rotate counterclockwise.

    - The operator can adjust the slewing speed to suit the requirements of the lifting task.

4. **Travel Control**: The travel control is used to move the entire crane along its rail tracks or wheels on the job site. It enables the crane to be positioned for optimal lifting operations. For example:

    - Pressing the forward or backward buttons on the travel control panel moves the crane in the corresponding direction.

    - Releasing the buttons stops the crane's movement, and it remains stationary at the desired location.

5. **Emergency Stop Button**: The emergency stop button is a critical safety feature that immediately halts all crane movements in case of an emergency. It is typically prominently located on the

control panel for quick access by the operator. For example:

- Pressing the emergency stop button instantly stops all crane functions, including hoisting, trolleying, slewing, and travel.

- The emergency stop button should only be used in emergency situations to prevent accidents or injuries.

6. **Radio Remote Control**: Some self-erecting tower cranes may be equipped with a radio remote control system that allows the operator to control the crane from a distance. The remote control unit typically replicates the functions of the operator controls on the crane's control panel.

Operators should receive thorough training on the use of these controls and familiarize themselves with their operation before operating the crane to ensure safe and efficient lifting operations. Regular maintenance and inspection of the control systems are also essential to ensure they remain in proper working condition.

Hammerhead Tower Crane Operating Radius and Rated Capacity

Operators using Hammerhead Tower Cranes must interpret load charts for several crucial reasons.

Firstly, ensuring safety is paramount in crane operations. Interpreting load charts is fundamental to prevent exceeding the crane's rated lifting capacity, which could lead to equipment failure, structural damage, or catastrophic accidents such as collapses. By providing operators with critical information, load charts help maintain safe operating conditions.

Secondly, understanding stability is essential for safe crane operation. Load charts enable operators to grasp the crane's capacity and limitations across different configurations, including boom length and load radius. Adhering to load chart guidelines prevents compromising the crane's stability, which could result in tipping over or loss of control, ultimately preventing accidents.

Moreover, compliance with regulations and industry standards is imperative. Many jurisdictions and regulatory bodies mandate crane operators to adhere to manufacturer specifications and guidelines, including load capacities. Following load charts ensures compliance with these regulations, mitigating liability risks.

In addition, interpreting load charts facilitates optimal performance. Operators can make informed decisions to optimize crane performance by selecting the appropriate boom length, load radius, and configuration based on the load chart. This maximizes lifting efficiency and productivity while upholding safety standards.

Furthermore, load chart interpretation plays a crucial role in risk management. By accurately assessing load capacities and operating within safe limits, operators can mitigate the risk of accidents, injuries, and property damage. Load charts provide valuable data to assess potential hazards and make informed decisions to minimize risks.

Lastly, demonstrating professionalism and competence is expected of crane operators. Proficiency in interpreting load charts reflects professionalism and competence in crane operation. It instils confidence in clients, employers, and regulatory authorities regarding the operator's ability to perform tasks safely and efficiently.

In summary, interpreting load charts is indispensable for crane operators using Hammerhead Tower Cranes to ensure safety, stability, compliance, optimal performance, risk management, and professionalism in their operations.

To read and interpret these charts:

1. **Understand the Basics:**

   - The load chart is usually found in the crane's operator manual or on a placard inside the crane cabin.

   - It displays the maximum load that the crane can lift under various conditions.

2. **Main Components of a Load Chart:**

   - **Boom Length:** The distance from the pivot point of the crane to the tip of the boom.

   - **Radius:** The horizontal distance from the crane's centre of rotation to the centre of the load.

   - **Lifting Capacity:** The maximum weight the crane can lift at a specific radius and boom length.

   - **Boom Angle:** The angle between the boom and the horizontal plane.

   - **Counterweights:** The amount of counterweight used, as this affects lifting capacity.

   - **Outriggers:** Indicates whether the outriggers are extended or retracted, which impacts the crane's stability and lifting capacity.

3. **Reading the Chart:**

   - Locate the desired boom length and follow the row across to find the corresponding lifting capacities at various radii.

   - Note that as the radius increases (the load is further from the crane's centre), the lifting capacity generally decreases.

- Check for any footnotes or symbols that may indicate specific conditions or limitations, such as reduced capacity with side loads, wind restrictions, or requirements for outrigger deployment.

4. **Consider Operational Factors:**

    - **Wind Speed:** High winds can reduce lifting capacity and operational safety.

    - **Ground Conditions:** Ensure the ground is capable of supporting the crane and load without excessive settling or shifting.

    - **Side Loads:** Avoid side loading the boom as it significantly reduces capacity and can cause structural damage.

    - **Operational Speeds:** High speeds in hoisting, slewing, or trolley movements can affect the crane's stability.

5. **Safety Margins:**

    - Always factor in a safety margin. Never operate right at the crane's maximum capacity.

    - Be aware of dynamic loading effects which can occur from rapid movements or stopping, potentially increasing the load on the crane.

6. **Certification and Local Regulations:**

    - Ensure compliance with local safety regulations and standards.

    - Operators must be certified and trained to interpret and use load charts effectively.

7. **Use of Load Indicators:**

    ○ Modern cranes are equipped with load moment indicators (LMIs) that provide real-time information about the load being lifted and the crane's current capacity. Ensure this system is operational and understood by the crane operator.

Understanding and respecting the load chart is vital for the safety of crane operations. Misinterpretation or ignorance of these charts can lead to accidents, including tip-overs, structural failures, or dropped loads, leading to property damage, injury, or even fatalities. Always consult with a qualified crane operator or engineer if there is any doubt about the crane's lifting capacity or operational conditions. Figure 36**Error! Reference source not found.** shows an example of a hammerhead tower crane. Figure 37 shows the jib configuration to correspond to the sample load chart.

Jib m	Fall	Radius (max) m	Capacity (max) t	15	20	25	30	35	40	45	50	55	60
60	4	3~12.24	8.0	6.44	4.72	3.68	2.99	2.50	2.13	1.84	1.61	1.43	1.27
	2	3~23.38	4.0	4.00	4.00	3.71	3.02	2.53	2.16	1.87	1.64	1.46	1.3
55	4	3~13.17	8.0	6.97	5.11	4.00	3.26	2.73	2.33	2.02	1.77	1.57	
	2	3~25.16	4.0	4.00	4.00	4.00	3.29	2.78	2.36	2.05	1.80	1.60	
50	4	3~14.34	8.0	7.63	5.61	4.39	3.59	3.01	2.58	2.24	1.97		
	2	3~27.4	4.0	4.00	4.00	4.00	3.62	3.04	2.61	2.27	2.00		
45	4	3~15.03	8.0	8.00	5.90	4.63	3.78	3.18	2.72	2.37			
	2	3~28.73	4.0	4.00	4.00	4.00	3.81	3.21	2.75	2.40			
40	4	3~15.25	8.0	8.00	5.90	4.70	3.84	3.23	2.77				
	2	3~29.15	4.0	4.00	4.00	4.00	3.87	3.26	2.80				
35	4	3~15.42	8.0	8.00	6.06	4.79	3.89	3.27					
	2	3~29.46	4.0	4.00	4.00	4.00	3.92	3.30					
30	4	3~15.7	8.0	8.00	6.18	4.85	3.97						
	2	3~30.00	4.0	4.00	4.00	4.00	4.00						

Figure 36: Example of a load chart for a hammerhead tower crane.

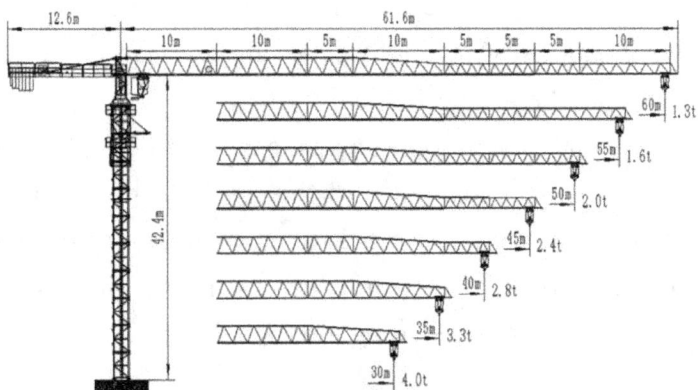

Figure 37: Jib configurations for sample hammerhead tower crane.

This load chart provides information on the crane's lifting capacity at different jib lengths. Here's how to interpret it:

1. **Jib (m)**: This column lists the different lengths of the jib (also known as the boom or arm) of the crane.

2. **Fall**: This column may indicate the number of falls in the hoist rope system, which can affect the crane's lifting capacity. More falls typically result in increased lifting capacity.

3. **Radius (max) (m)**: This column specifies the maximum radius at which the crane can operate with the corresponding jib length.

4. **Capacity (max) (t)**: This column indicates the maximum lifting capacity of the crane at the specified jib length and radius. The values represent the maximum weight in metric tons (t) that the crane can lift at each combination of jib length and radius.

A fall is a term used to describe the number of parts that the hoist rope is reeved through. For instance, if a rope is reeved through the system twice, it is referred to as having "two falls."

The number of falls in the hoist rope system can indeed affect the crane's lifting capacity. More falls generally result in increased lifting capacity for several reasons:

1. Mechanical Advantage: Increasing the number of falls increases the mechanical advantage of the system. This means that the load is distributed over more ropes, reducing the strain on each individual rope. As a result, the crane can lift heavier loads without risking overloading the ropes.

2. Greater Stability: More falls also typically provide greater stability to the load. With multiple ropes supporting the load, there is less chance of the load swinging or becoming unbalanced during lifting, which can improve safety and control.

3. Redundancy and Safety: Having multiple falls adds redundancy to the system. If one rope were to fail, the others can still support the load, reducing the risk of accidents or catastrophic failures.

However, it's essential to note that while more falls generally increase lifting capacity, they may also affect the crane's speed and efficiency. With more rope to pull through the system, the crane's lifting and lowering speeds may decrease. Crane operators must consider these factors and balance them based on the specific requirements of the lifting task.

Reeving, integral to crane and hoisting systems, involves the threading or passing of a rope or cable through a series of pulleys, sheaves, or blocks. This process is essential for creating a mechanical advantage necessary for lifting heavy loads efficiently and safely.

In a typical reeving setup, a crane's hoisting mechanism comprises a set of pulleys or sheaves mounted at various points along the crane's boom or mast. These pulleys are strategically arranged to facilitate the passage of the rope through them.

The rope, often constructed from steel wire or synthetic materials, is then threaded or passed through the pulleys in a specific configuration. This configuration varies based on the crane's design and the intended lifting capacity required for the task at hand.

As the rope is reeved through the system, it may pass through multiple times, resulting in what is known as "falls." Each passage through the system constitutes one fall, and the number of falls directly influences the mechanical advantage of the system and, consequently, the crane's lifting capacity.

Both ends of the rope are typically anchored—one end to the drum of the crane's hoist mechanism and the other end to the load being lifted. This ensures stability and control during the lifting process.

By reeving the rope through the pulleys or sheaves, the crane operator can achieve a mechanical advantage, enabling the crane to lift heavier loads than would be possible with a single line. The mechanical advantage is determined by factors such as the number of falls and the specific configuration of the reeving system.

Overall, reeving plays a fundamental role in crane operation, allowing for the safe and efficient lifting of heavy loads by leveraging mechanical advantage. Proper reeving practices are essential to ensure smooth and secure lifting operations, thereby minimizing the risk of accidents or equipment damage.

Now, let's interpret an example entry from the load chart:
- At a jib length of 30 meters:

  - The crane has a maximum lifting capacity of 8.0 tons at a radius of 15 meters.
  - This means that with a jib length of 30 meters and a radius of 15 meters, the crane can safely lift loads weighing up to 8.0 tons.

- At a jib length of 60 meters:

- The crane has a maximum lifting capacity of 1.27 tons at a radius of 15 meters.

- This means that with a jib length of 60 meters and a radius of 15 meters, the crane can safely lift loads weighing up to 1.27 tons.

These values provide crucial information for crane operators to determine the appropriate jib length and radius for their specific lifting tasks, ensuring safe and efficient lifting operations.

This load chart illustrates the relationship between the jib length and the crane's lift capacity at various radii. Here's what we can understand from it:

1. Decreasing Lift Capacity with Increasing Jib Length: As the jib length increases, the crane's maximum lifting capacity generally decreases at any given radius. This is evident from the decreasing values in the "Capacity (max)" column as the jib length increases.

2. Impact of Radius on Lift Capacity: The lift capacity also varies with the radius at which the load is being lifted. Generally, the farther the load is from the crane (larger radius), the lower the lift capacity. This is noticeable by comparing the lift capacities at different radii for each jib length.

3. Effect of Number of Falls: The number of falls in the hoist rope system (indicated in the "Fall" column) may affect the crane's lifting capacity. Typically, a higher number of falls can increase the lifting capacity, as more falls distribute the load over multiple ropes.

4. Optimal Jib Length-Radius Combination: Crane operators need to consider the optimal combination of jib length and radius

based on the weight of the load to be lifted. For example, for heavier loads, a shorter jib length and smaller radius might be preferable to maximize the crane's lift capacity.

5. Trade-off between Reach and Capacity: There's often a trade-off between reach (jib length) and lifting capacity. While a longer jib provides greater reach, it usually comes at the expense of reduced lifting capacity, especially at longer radii.

Overall, this load chart provides valuable information for crane operators to make informed decisions regarding the selection of jib length and radius to safely and efficiently lift loads of varying weights and at different distances from the crane.

As an example of using the load chart, let's say you were asked to lift a load of 9.5 tonnes. To determine if it would be safe to lift a load of 9.5 tonnes using the provided load chart, we need to identify the appropriate row based on the closest radius to the intended lifting point and the fall configuration.

Let's assume we're using a 4-fall configuration, and we're lifting the load at a radius of 30 meters. From the load chart:

- For a 4-fall configuration at a radius of 30 meters, the maximum capacity is 8.00 tons.

Since the load we intend to lift is 9.5 tonnes, which exceeds the maximum capacity of 8.00 tonnes at the specified radius and fall configuration, it would not be safe to lift the load.

In this scenario, we would need to either reduce the weight of the load or consider repositioning the crane to a closer radius where the lifting capacity meets or exceeds the load requirement. Alternatively, if feasible, using a different fall configuration or crane setup that can accommodate the desired load weight may also be considered.

As another example, let's say we wanted to determine the minimum jib size to place a 3 tonne load to a 30 m radius using the load chart shown in Figure 36, for a 30-metre jib, the maximum capacity at a 30-metre radius is provided. Under a 4-fall configuration, the capacity is 3.97 tonnes, and under a 2-fall configuration, it's 4 tonnes.

Given this information, a 30-metre jib can indeed handle a 3-ton load at a 30-metre radius, making it the minimum jib size required for this operation. The capacities at this length and radius under both fall configurations are more than sufficient for a 3-tonne load.

Likewise, if we ask can a weight of 6.25 tonnes be lifted with a 55m jib at a 25m radius and with 2 parts of line? For a 55-metre jib at a 25-meter radius with a 2-fall line configuration, the maximum capacity is listed as 4 tonnes. Therefore, a weight of 6.25 tons cannot be lifted under these conditions, as it exceeds the maximum capacity provided in the load chart.

If on the other hand we ask, with the crane configured using 2 parts of line and using a 45m jib, what is the maximum weight that can be lifted at a 35m radius? According to the load chart, for a 45-metre jib at a 35-metre radius with a 2-fall line configuration, the maximum lifting capacity is explicitly listed as 3.78 tonnes. Therefore, with the crane configured using 2 parts of line and a 45-metre jib, the maximum weight that can be lifted at a 35-metre radius is 3.78 tonnes. Thank you for pointing out the correct information.

Luffing Jib Tower Crane Operating Radius and Rated Capacity

In the context of luffing jib tower cranes, the operational radius refers to the horizontal distance from the crane's slew axis (centre of rotation) to the point where the load is being lifted or lowered. It indicates how far the crane can reach horizontally to perform lifting operations. The operational radius is a crucial parameter that determines the crane's ability to access and manoeuvre loads within a specific area on the job site.

The operational radius is determined by the combination of the crane's boom length and luffing angle. As the luffing jib crane's jib is raised or lowered (luffed), it affects the horizontal reach of the crane. The operational radius varies depending on the specific configuration of the crane, including the boom length, luffing angle, and counterweight setup. Crane manufacturers provide specifications detailing the operational radius for different boom lengths and luffing angles, allowing operators to plan lifting operations effectively within the crane's reach.

Load charts, on the other hand, provide essential information regarding the crane's lifting capacities at various operational radii and boom angles. They typically consist of a graphical representation of the crane's lifting capacity plotted against the operational radius and boom angle. Load charts are essential tools for crane operators to determine the maximum weight that the crane can lift safely at different working radii and boom configurations.

Load charts provide critical information about the crane's lifting capacities under various conditions. They typically include:
- Boom Length: Load charts often feature different sections corresponding to different boom lengths available on the crane. Each section of the chart represents the crane's lifting capacities at specific boom lengths.

- Luffing Angle: Load charts may also include variations in lifting capacities based on the luffing angle of the crane's jib. The lifting capacity changes as the luffing angle is adjusted, affecting the crane's operational radius and load-handling capabilities.

- Load Radius: Load charts display the crane's lifting capacities at different operational radii, indicating the maximum allowable load weight that the crane can lift safely at each radius.

- Outrigger Configuration: Load charts may also take into account the crane's outrigger configuration, as deploying outriggers can enhance the crane's stability and lifting capacity.

By referencing the load chart corresponding to the crane's boom length, luffing angle, and operational radius, operators can determine the maximum allowable load weight for a given lifting scenario. It is essential for crane operators to consult the load chart before performing any lifting operation to ensure compliance with safety regulations and prevent overloading situations that could compromise crane stability and safety. Regular training on load chart interpretation is crucial for crane operators to make informed decisions and conduct lifting operations safely and efficiently.

Reading a luffing boom tower crane load chart requires understanding various parameters such as boom length, luffing angle, operational radius, and lifting capacity. Here's an example of how to interpret and read a luffing boom tower crane load chart:

1. **Identify Boom Length and Luffing Angle**: The load chart will typically have sections corresponding to different boom lengths and luffing angles. For example, the chart may include sections for boom lengths of 50 meters, 60 meters, and 70 meters, and luffing angles ranging from 0 degrees to 80 degrees.

2. **Select the Appropriate Section**: Determine the boom length and luffing angle applicable to your lifting scenario. Locate the section of the load chart that corresponds to these parameters.

3. **Find the Load Radius**: The load chart will have a grid or table indicating the operational radius or load radius. This represents the horizontal distance from the crane's slew axis to the load. Find the specific load radius relevant to your lifting operation.

CRANE OPERATIONS

4. **Read the Lifting Capacities**: Once you've located the correct section and load radius, look for the lifting capacities displayed in the chart. The lifting capacities are typically shown in metric tons (or other applicable units) and are organized by boom angle and load radius.

5. **Interpret the Values**: The values in the load chart represent the maximum allowable load weight that the crane can lift safely under the specified conditions. For example, at a particular load radius and luffing angle, the load chart might indicate that the crane can lift a maximum of 10 metric tons.

6. **Consider Other Factors**: In addition to boom length, luffing angle, and load radius, consider other factors that may affect lifting capacities, such as wind speed, crane configuration, and ground conditions. Ensure that the lifting operation complies with all safety regulations and manufacturer recommendations.

Here's a simplified example of how a luffing boom tower crane load chart might appear (Figure 38):

Luffing Angle (deg)	Boom Length: 60 metres	
	Load Radius (meters)	Lifting Capacity (metric tons)
0		
20	10	12
40	15	10
60	20	5
80	25	6

Figure 38: Simplified example of luffing boom load chart.

In this example:
- The load chart section corresponds to a 60-metre boom length.
- Luffing angles range from 0 degrees to 80 degrees.
- The lifting capacities are provided for different load radii (10, 15, 20, and 25 meters) at each luffing angle.

- For instance, at a luffing angle of 20 degrees and a load radius of 10 meters, the crane can safely lift a maximum of 12 metric tons. As a further example, let us consider a hypothetical luffing boom tower crane load chart as shown in Figure 39.

Hook Reach	Maximum Capacity-Radius		Ft m	13* 4*	66 20	98 30	107 32.5	115 35	123 37.5	131 40	139 42.5	148 45	156 47.5	164 50	172 52.5	180 55	189 57.5	197 60	205 62.5	213 65
213 ft 65m	26,460 lbs – 127 ft	lbs		26,460	26,460	26,460	26,460	26,460	26,460	25,245	22,155	20,945	19,160	17,550	16,115	14,795	13,625	12,520	11,530	10,580
	12 000 kg – 38.8m	kg		12 000	12 000	12 000	12 000	12 000	12 000	11 450	10 410	9 500	8 690	7 960	7 310	6 710	6 180	5 680	5 230	4 800
197 ft 60m	26,460 lbs – 136 ft	lbs		26,460	26,460	26,460	26,460	26,460	26,460	26,460	24,440	23,345	21,495	19,820	18,320	16,955	15,720	14,550		
	12 000 kg – 41.4m	kg		12 000	12 000	12 000	12 000	12 000	12 000	12 000	11 540	10 590	9 750	8 990	8 310	7 690	7 130	6 600		
180 ft 55m	26,460 lbs – 144 ft	lbs		26,460	26,460	26,460	26,460	26,460	26,460	26,460	26,460	25,395	23,415	21,625	20,020	18,520				
	12 000 kg – 43.8m	kg		12 000	12 000	12 000	12 000	12 000	12 000	12 000	12 000	11 520	10 620	9 810	9 080	8 400				
164 ft 50m	26,460 lbs – 150 ft	lbs		26,460	26,460	26,460	26,460	26,460	26,460	26,460	26,460	26,460	25,065	23,150						
	12 000 kg – 45.8m	kg		12 000	12 000	12 000	12 000	12 000	12 000	12 000	12 000	12 000	11 370	10 500						
148 ft 45m	26,460 lbs – 148 ft	lbs		26,460	26,460	26,460	26,460	26,460	26,460	26,460	26,460	26,460								
	12 000 kg – 45m	kg		12 000	12 000	12 000	12 000	12 000	12 000	12 000	12 000	12 000								
131 ft 40m	26,460 lbs – 148 ft	lbs		26,460	26,460	26,460	26,460	26,460	26,460	26,460										
	12 000 kg – 45m	kg		12 000	12 000	12 000	12 000	12 000	12 000	12 000										
115 ft 35m	26,460 lbs – 148 ft	lbs		26,460	26,460	26,460	26,460	26,460												
	12 000 kg – 45m	kg		12 000	12 000	12 000	12 000	12 000												
98 ft 30m	26,460 lbs – 148 ft	lbs		26,460	26,460	26,460														
	12 000 kg – 45m	kg		12 000	12 000	12 000														

*Minimum hook reach.

1-PART OPERATION

Figure 39: Radius and capacities for a sample luffing boom tower crane (Example 1).

To read a luffing boom tower crane load chart, follow these steps:

1. **Identify the Hook Reach and Maximum Capacity**: The load chart will have columns indicating the hook reach and maximum capacity for different radii or distances from the crane's centre. The hook reach is typically provided in feet (ft) and meters (m), while the maximum capacity is given in pounds (lbs) and kilograms (kg).

2. **Locate the Specific Hook Reach**: Look for the hook reach that corresponds to the distance you intend to place the load from the centre of the crane. This will determine the specific row of data you need to reference in the load chart.

3. **Read the Maximum Capacity**: Once you've located the correct hook reach, find the corresponding maximum capacity for that distance. The capacity will indicate the maximum weight that the crane can safely lift at that particular radius.

4. **Interpret Additional Information**: Some load charts may include additional information such as special notes, minimum hook reach, or specific operating conditions. Pay attention to these details as they may impact how you interpret the load chart.

5. **Consider the Configuration**: Keep in mind that the load chart may vary depending on the configuration of the crane, including factors such as boom length, jib angle, counterweight position, and environmental conditions. Ensure that you're using the appropriate load chart for the specific configuration of the crane.

"Hook reach" and "maximum capacity - radius" represent different aspects of crane operation:

1. Hook Reach: Hook reach refers to the maximum horizontal distance from the centre of rotation of the crane to the load that the crane can reach. It indicates the furthest point the crane's hook can be positioned horizontally from the crane's centre.

2. Maximum Capacity - Radius: This represents the maximum weight (capacity) that the crane can lift at a given radius (distance) from the centre of rotation. It provides information about the crane's lifting capacity at various distances from its centre.

So, while hook reach focuses on the maximum horizontal distance the crane can reach, maximum capacity - radius specifies the maximum weight the crane can lift at different radial distances from its centre. They are related in the sense that the maximum capacity at a certain radius determines the crane's ability to lift loads at that distance from its centre.

Suppose we want to lift a load weighing 9,750 kg. We'll use the chart to determine the maximum radius at which this can be done.

1. First, locate the row corresponding to the weight of 9,750 kg. According to the chart, this weight falls in the 156 ft hook reach column.

2. Now, look across the row to find the corresponding maximum capacity at various radii. In this case, the maximum capacity varies at different radii, ranging from 26,460 lbs (12,000 kg) at a radius of 127 ft (38.8 m) to 9,750 kg at a radius of 156 ft.

3. So, the maximum radius for lifting 9,750 kg is 156 ft.

Let's use the load chart for the luffing boom tower crane with a hook reach of 40 meters to for a further illustration. Suppose we want to lift a load weighing 9,750 kg. We'll use the chart to determine the maximum radius at which this can be done.

1. First, locate the row corresponding to the weight of 9,750 kg. According to the chart, this weight falls in the 40m hook reach column.

2. Now, look across the row to find the corresponding maximum capacity at various radii. In this case, the maximum capacity varies at different radii, ranging from 26,460 lbs (12,000 kg) at a radius of 148 ft (45 m) to 9,750 kg at a radius of 40 meters.

3. So, the maximum radius for lifting 9,750 kg with a hook reach of 40 meters is 40 meters.

In a luffing tower crane, the hook reach is determined by the length and configuration of the jib or boom. The hook reach refers to the horizontal distance from the centre of the crane's rotation to the point where the load is lifted or positioned. It is essentially the maximum distance that the crane's hook can reach while maintaining stability and lifting capacity.

The hook reach of a luffing tower crane can vary depending on several factors:

1. Boom Length: The length of the boom or jib directly affects the hook reach. Longer booms allow the crane to reach further distances from its centre of rotation, while shorter booms have shorter hook reaches.

2. Jib Angle: The angle of the jib or boom also influences the hook reach. By adjusting the angle of the jib, operators can extend or reduce the hook reach as needed for specific lifting tasks.

3. Counterweight Position: The position and configuration of counterweights on the crane's structure can affect its overall stability and reach. Adjusting the counterweights may impact the crane's ability to reach certain distances safely.

4. Operating Conditions: Factors such as wind speed, load weight, and environmental conditions may affect the crane's performance and maximum hook reach. Operators must consider these conditions when determining the safe operating range of the crane.

Overall, the hook reach of a luffing tower crane is determined by a combination of these factors, and it is crucial for operators to adhere to the manufacturer's specifications and load charts to ensure safe and efficient crane operation.

In a luffing boom tower crane load chart, "1-Part Operation" typically refers to a lifting configuration where the crane utilizes a single line to hoist the load. This means that the hook is attached directly to the load, and there are no additional parts or components involved in the lifting process.

One-part operation is often used when lifting lighter loads or when precision is required in positioning the load. It allows for simpler rigging arrangements and may be preferred in situations where space is limited or where the load needs to be precisely controlled.

In the load chart, one-part operation may be indicated alongside specific load capacities and radius combinations to provide operators with the maximum allowable lifting capacity under these conditions. It helps operators determine the crane's capabilities and ensure safe lifting practices are followed during operations.

It's important for crane operators to consult the load chart and adhere to the recommended procedures for different lifting configurations, including one-part operation, to maintain safety and prevent overloading the crane.

"Two-part operation" in a luffing boom tower crane load chart refers to a lifting configuration where the load is hoisted using two parts of line. This means that the hook is attached to the load via a system that involves two lines, typically achieved through a block and tackle arrangement.

A block and tackle arrangement is a mechanical system consisting of one or more pulleys (blocks) and a length of rope or cable (tackle). It is used to multiply the force applied to lift or move a heavy object.

The basic principle behind a block and tackle is that the pulleys reduce the amount of force required to lift a load by distributing it over multiple lines of rope or cable. As a result, the load is divided among the multiple lines, allowing the user to apply less force to lift the object.

In a block and tackle system, there are typically two types of pulleys: fixed pulleys and movable pulleys. Fixed pulleys are attached to a stationary object, while movable pulleys are attached to the load being lifted. When the rope is pulled, the movable pulleys move with the load, while the fixed pulleys remain in place, creating a mechanical advantage.

The mechanical advantage provided by a block and tackle arrangement depends on the number of pulleys and the configuration of the system. By adding more pulleys or changing the arrangement, the mechanical advantage can be increased, allowing for heavier loads to be lifted with less force.

In two-part operation, the load is distributed between the two lines, allowing the crane to lift heavier loads than in one-part operation while maintaining control and stability. This configuration provides mechanical advantage, allowing the crane to lift loads beyond the capacity achievable in one-part operation.

Compared to one-part operation, two-part operation requires more complex rigging arrangements and may involve additional equipment such as blocks and sheaves. It is typically used when lifting heavier loads that exceed the capacity achievable in one-part operation or when greater lifting power is required.

Operators must consult the load chart and follow the recommended procedures for two-part operation to ensure safe lifting practices and prevent overloading the crane. Additionally, they should be trained in rigging techniques specific to two-part operation to ensure proper setup and execution of lifts.

In a load chart for a crane, "hook reach" refers to the horizontal distance from the centre of rotation of the crane (typically the centre of the slew ring) to the point where the load is attached via the crane's hook. This distance is measured perpendicular to the centreline of the crane's mast or boom.

The hook reach is an essential parameter in crane operations as it determines how far the crane can extend its hook to reach a load. It helps operators understand the maximum horizontal distance the crane can cover while maintaining its lifting capacity.

When reading a load chart, the hook reach values are provided alongside corresponding load capacities for different radii or distances from the centre of rotation. This information helps operators determine the crane's lifting capacity at various distances from its pivot point, enabling them to plan and execute lifts safely and efficiently.

Based on the load chart, let's say we wanted to determine how the crane should be configured for both point A and point B to lift a 8000 kg load from a loading point A on the ground at a radius of 15 metres to raise the load to point B which is at a radius of 32 metres. To lift an 8000 kg load from a loading point A at a radius of 15 meters to point B at a radius of 32 meters, we need to find the appropriate configuration of the crane based on the load chart provided.

1. **Point A (Radius 15 meters):** Looking at the load chart, we find that a radius of 15 meters falls within the range of capacities listed under the hook reach of 30 meters. The maximum capacity for a 30-meter hook reach is 12,000 kg, which is more than sufficient for the 8000 kg load. Therefore, we can configure the

crane with a hook reach of 30 meters for lifting the load from point A.

2. **Point B (Radius 32 meters):** For lifting the load to point B at a radius of 32 meters, we need to ensure that the crane configuration can handle this radius. From the load chart, a radius of 32 meters falls within the capacities listed under the hook reach of 40 meters. The maximum capacity for a 40-meter hook reach is also 12,000 kg, which is sufficient for the 8000 kg load. Therefore, we can configure the crane with a hook reach of 40 meters for lifting the load to point B.

In summary:
- Configure the crane with a hook reach of 30 meters for lifting the load from point A.
- Configure the crane with a hook reach of 40 meters for lifting the load to point B.

The relationship between the boom angle and the crane's capacity is crucial in determining the crane's configuration for lifting loads at different radii. The hook reach, which corresponds to the boom angle, plays a significant role in this.

In the provided scenario:

1. Point A (Radius 15 meters): The crane needs to be configured with a hook reach of 30 meters to lift the load from point A. The hook reach of 30 meters corresponds to a specific boom angle that enables the crane to reach the desired radius while maintaining its maximum capacity of 12,000 kg.

2. Point B (Radius 32 meters): To lift the load to point B at a radius of 32 meters, the crane needs to be configured with a hook reach of 40 meters. This configuration allows the crane to extend its

boom to the required angle to reach the desired radius while still ensuring that the load remains within its maximum capacity.

Therefore, the boom angle, indirectly represented by the hook reach, determines the crane's capacity to lift loads at different radii. It's essential to select the appropriate hook reach (boom angle) from the load chart to ensure safe and efficient lifting operations for each specific lifting scenario.

The load chart provides valuable information about the relationship between the radius (distance from the centre of rotation to the load) and the maximum weight that can be lifted by the crane. Here's what we can understand from the load chart:

1. Increasing Radius, Decreasing Capacity: As the radius increases, the maximum weight capacity of the crane decreases. This relationship is evident as we move from left to right across each row in the chart. For example, at a hook reach of 30m, the maximum capacity is 12,000 kg, but as the hook reach increases to 40m, the maximum capacity decreases to 11,530 kg.

2. Non-Linear Relationship: The relationship between radius and maximum capacity is not strictly linear. While there is a general trend of decreasing capacity with increasing radius, the rate of decrease varies. For instance, the decrease in capacity from 30m to 40m hook reach is more significant compared to the decrease from 40m to 45m hook reach.

3. Minimum Hook Reach: The chart also provides information about the minimum hook reach, which indicates the minimum distance from the crane's centre of rotation to the load. This is important for understanding the operational limitations of the crane.

Overall, the load chart helps crane operators and planners determine the appropriate configuration of the crane (such as boom length and counterweight) based on the specific lifting requirements, considering factors like load weight and radius.

To further illustrate these points, let's consider an alternative representation of a load chart. The load chart shown as Figure 40 provides information on the maximum load capacity of a crane at various combinations of counterweight and jib length.

Here's how to interpret the load chart:

- **Counterweight:** The weight of the counterweight installed on the crane.

- **Jib Length:** The length of the jib (or boom) of the crane, which affects its lifting capacity.

- **Maximum Load:** The maximum load capacity of the crane, given in kilograms (kg) or metric tons (t), corresponding to each combination of counterweight and jib length.

For example:

- At a counterweight of 21749 kg and a jib length of 55.0 meters, the maximum load capacity is 8639 kg.

- At a counterweight of 21749 kg and a jib length of 50.0 meters, the maximum load capacity is 9764 kg.

- At a counterweight of 18642 kg and a jib length of 28.0 meters, the maximum load capacity is 10450 kg.

To use the chart, you would select the appropriate counterweight and jib length combination based on the specific requirements of your lifting operation, ensuring that the selected combination supports the weight of the load you intend to lift.

Counterweight	Jib	Maximum Load	28.0	33.5	39.0	44.5	50.0	55.0
kg	m	14.0 t			m			
21749	55.0	20.0	8639	7000	5708	4268	3153	**2255**
21749	50.0	22.0	9764	7211	5869	4419	**3300**	
21749	44.5	22.3	9886	7346	5859	**4510**		
21749	39.0	22.4	10094	7508	**6050**			
18642	33.5	22.5	10287	**7700**				
18642	28.0	23.0	**10450**					

Figure 40: Alternative luffing boom tower crane (Example 2).

These configurations correspond to the graphical representation of the crane shown as Figure 42.

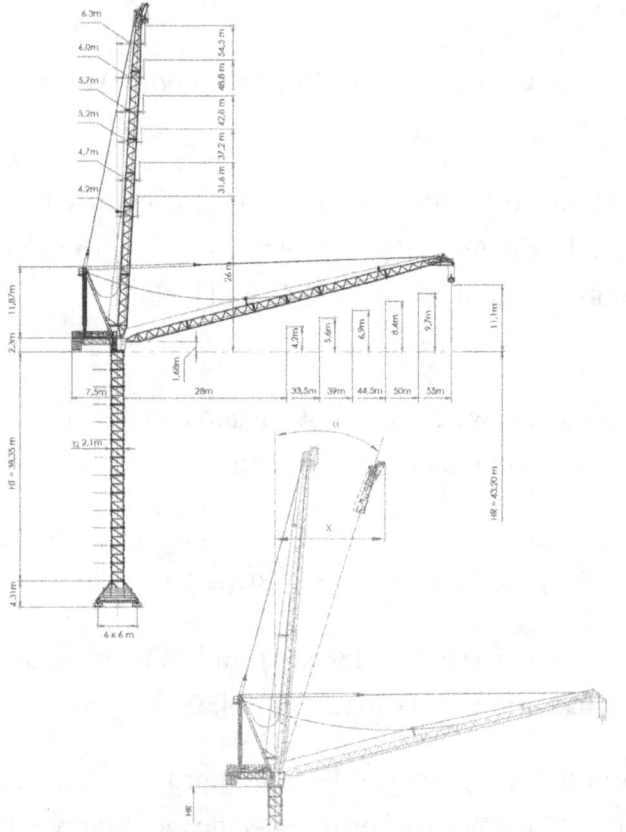

Figure 41: Example jib configurations.

Jib	28.0m	33.5m	39.0m	44.5m	50.0m	55.0m
x	22.1m	19.6m	18.5m	17.6m	17.7m	17.5m
α	46°	31°	24°	20°	18°	16°

Figure 42: Jib lengths and angles.

Figure 42, referring to Figure 41, outlines the relationship between the jib length (measured in meters), the horizontal distance from the crane's centre of rotation to the load attachment point (measured in meters), and the angle (α) of the jib.

Let's break down the components:

- Jib Length: This column lists different jib lengths in meters. The jib length refers to the horizontal distance from the crane's centre of rotation to the load attachment point.

- x: This column represents the horizontal distance from the crane's centre of rotation to the load attachment point when the jib is at a certain length. It's also measured in meters.

- α (Alpha): This column indicates the angle of the jib in degrees. The angle refers to the inclination or slope of the jib relative to the horizontal plane.

For each jib length listed, the table provides the corresponding horizontal distance (x) and the angle (α) of the jib. This information helps crane operators understand how the jib's length affects its horizontal reach and the angle at which the load is lifted relative to the ground.

As an example of using these charts, if you wanted to lift 4500 kg with a 39m jib I could determine the angle the luffing boom needs to be set at.

To ensure that the weight being lifted is within the rated capacity for a given jib length and counterweight configuration, you can refer to the chart shown as Figure 40. For a 39.0m jib length, the corresponding counterweight configuration is 21749 kg.

From Figure 40:
- At a counterweight of 21749 kg and a jib length of 39.0 meters, the maximum load capacity is 10094 kg.

Since you are lifting 4500 kg, which is well below the maximum load capacity of 10094 kg for this jib length and counterweight configuration, the weight being lifted is within the rated capacity.

Using the load charts, the straightforward way to determine the angle from the provided charts is to look at the second table (Figure 42), the angle α is given for each jib length. You want to lift the load with a 39m jib length, so you can simply look up the corresponding angle α for that jib length.

From the given table:
- For a 39.0m jib length, the corresponding angle α is 24°.

Therefore, without calculation, you can determine that the angle the boom needs to be set at to lift 4500 kg with a 39m jib is 24°.

As an aside, a more precise answer can be determined mathematically for this example.

To determine the angle the boom needs to be set at to lift 4500 kg with a 39m jib, we can use the given data from the load charts:

From Figure 42:
- Jib length (m) = 39.0m

- x = 18.5m (this represents the horizontal distance between the mast foot and the load's centre of gravity)

- α = 24° (this represents the angle between the boom and the horizontal)

Now, to find the angle at which the boom needs to be set, we can use trigonometry. The angle α represents the angle between the boom and the horizontal, so it's the angle we need to find.

Using the tangent function:

$$\tan(\alpha) = \frac{x}{\text{Jib length}}$$

Substituting the given values:

$$\tan(24°) = \frac{18.5}{39.0}$$

$$\tan(24°) = \frac{18.5}{39.0}$$

$$\tan(24°) = 0.474$$

Now, to find the angle α:

$$\alpha = \arctan(0.474)$$

Using a calculator or a trigonometric table, we find:

$$\alpha \approx 25.86°$$

Figure 43: Calculation to determine angle of boom to lift 4500kg with a 39m boom.

So, the boom needs to be set at approximately 25.86° to lift 4500 kg with a 39m jib.

Self-Erecting Tower Crane Operating Radius and Rated Capacity

Reading and interpreting a self-erecting tower crane load chart is crucial for safely operating the crane and ensuring that it doesn't exceed its capacity. This includes:

1. **Understand the Load Chart Basics:**

    - A load chart is a graphical representation provided by the crane manufacturer that shows the crane's lifting capacity at various boom lengths and radii, as shown in Figure 44.

    - It typically includes information such as boom length, radius, load capacity, and allowable configurations for lifting.

- Load charts are specific to each model of crane and should always be referenced for accurate information.

2. **Identify the Load Chart**:

- The load chart is usually located in the crane's operator manual. It might also be displayed on the crane itself for quick reference.

- Ensure that you have the correct load chart for the specific model of the self-erecting tower crane you are using.

3. **Understand the Parameters**:

- Before interpreting the load chart, familiarize yourself with the parameters it uses:

    - Boom Length: The horizontal distance from the mast to the end of the jib.

    - Radius: The horizontal distance from the crane's centre to the load.

    - Load Capacity: The maximum weight the crane can safely lift at a given boom length and radius.

4. **Select the Proper Load Chart**:

- Different load charts may be provided for various configurations of the crane, such as with or without jib extensions. Ensure you are referencing the correct chart for the current setup.

5. **Locate the Boom Length and Radius**:

CRANE OPERATIONS

- Find the boom length and radius you intend to use on the load chart.

- The boom length is typically listed on one axis, while the radius is listed on the other axis.

6. **Determine Load Capacity**:

    - Once you have located the intersection of the boom length and radius on the chart, read the corresponding load capacity.

    - The load capacity is usually provided in terms of weight (e.g., tons or pounds).

7. **Account for Additional Factors**:

    - Some load charts may provide adjustments for factors like wind speed, boom angle, or specific configurations of the crane. Make sure to consider these adjustments if they apply to your lifting operation.

8. **Ensure Safety Margins**:

    - It's essential to never exceed the load capacity indicated on the chart. Always leave a safety margin to account for unexpected variables or changes in conditions.

9. **Verify Stability**:

    - In addition to load capacity, ensure that the crane is stable for the planned lift. Pay attention to factors such as ground conditions, outrigger positioning, and the crane's levelness.

10. **Regularly Refer to the Load Chart**:

○ Throughout the lifting operation, periodically check the load chart to ensure that you remain within safe operating limits, especially if conditions change.

By following these steps and thoroughly understanding the load chart provided by the manufacturer, you can effectively read and interpret a self-erecting tower crane load chart, promoting safe and efficient lifting operations.

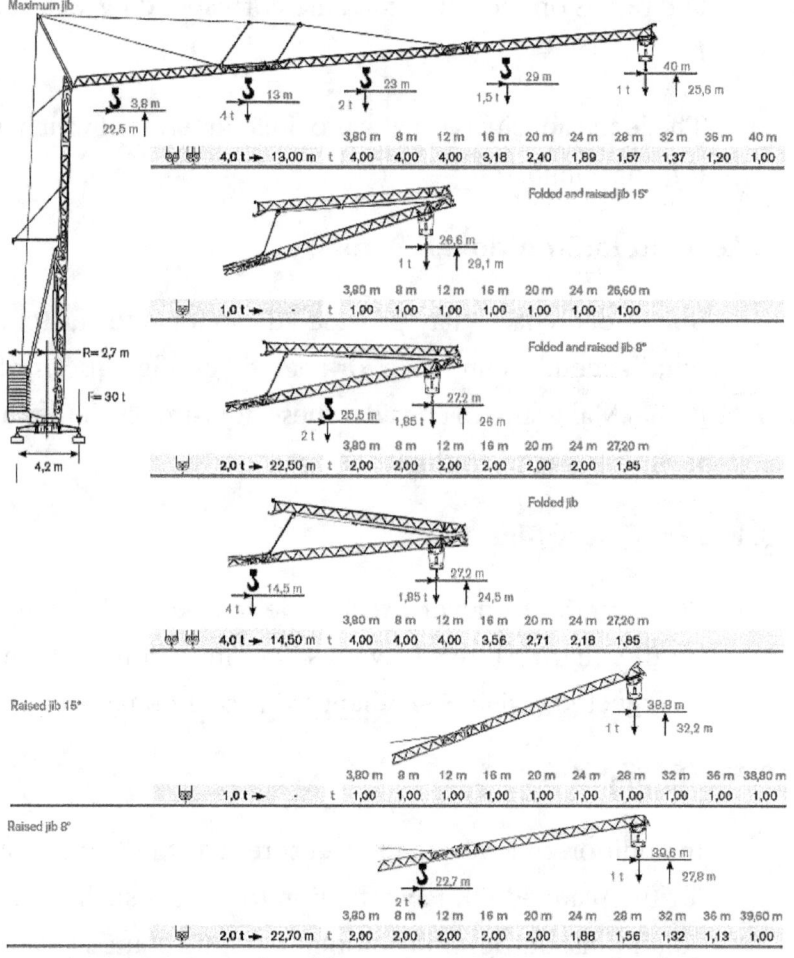

Figure 44: Sample self-erecting tower crane load chart.

Reading the load chart, shown as Figure 44, we can see for example, that the maximum weight that can be lifted with at a 24 metre radius with the jib fully extended and in 4 parts of line is 1.89 tonnes. Likewise with the jib folded and raised to 15°, at the same radius of 24, the maximum weight is reduced to 1 tonne.

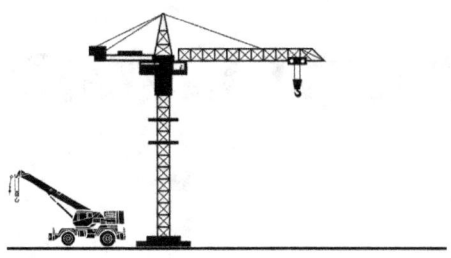

Chapter Four

Derrick and Portal Boom Cranes

Derrick Cranes

A derrick crane is a type of lifting equipment commonly used in construction, maritime, and industrial settings. It is characterized by a vertical mast or tower, which supports a boom or jib that can be raised and lowered to lift and move heavy loads. Derrick cranes have been in use for centuries and were historically employed in activities such as shipbuilding, dockside loading and unloading, and construction of large structures like bridges and buildings.

Here are some key features and components of a typical derrick crane:

1. Mast or Tower: The mast or tower of a derrick crane is a vertical structure that provides support for the entire crane assembly. It is usually constructed of steel and is designed to withstand the forces generated during lifting operations.

2. Boom or Jib: The boom or jib is an inclined or horizontal beam that extends from the top of the mast or tower. It is the primary

lifting arm of the crane and is used to support the load and provide reach.

3. Hoist System: A hoist system is mounted on the boom or jib and consists of a drum or winch mechanism with wire ropes or chains. The hoist system is responsible for raising and lowering the load.

4. Counterweights: Counterweights are often used on derrick cranes to balance the load and prevent the crane from tipping over. They are typically located on the opposite side of the mast or tower from the load.

5. Base or Foundation: Derrick cranes are usually anchored to a solid base or foundation to provide stability during lifting operations. This can include concrete footings, steel platforms, or specially designed supports depending on the specific application.

Derrick cranes come in various configurations and sizes, ranging from small portable models used for light-duty lifting to large fixed structures capable of lifting extremely heavy loads. They are valued for their simplicity, durability, and ability to handle heavy loads in confined spaces or areas with limited access.

Derrick cranes come in various types, each designed for specific applications and environments. Here are some of the most common types of derrick cranes:

1. **Stiffleg Derrick:**

    - A Stiffleg Derrick features a triangular arrangement of two inclined booms or jibs connected to a vertical mast. Guy lines are used to stabilize the crane, and it's commonly used in bridge construction, marine construction, and other applications where precise lifting with stability is required.

2. **Hammerhead Derrick**:

- A Hammerhead Derrick, also known as a Trolley Boom Derrick, is characterized by a horizontal boom that extends from the top of the mast. It has a trolley mechanism that allows the boom to move horizontally along the mast. This type of derrick crane is often used in shipyards and ports for lifting heavy loads onto ships.

3. **Gantry Derrick**:

- A Gantry Derrick, also known as a Portal Derrick, is a derrick crane mounted on a gantry structure that allows it to move along a set of rails or tracks. It typically consists of a vertical mast with a horizontal boom extending from it. Gantry Derricks are used in construction, shipbuilding, and other industrial applications where mobility and flexibility are required.

4. **Tender Derrick**:

- A Tender Derrick, also known as a Floating Derrick or Barge Derrick, is a derrick crane mounted on a floating platform or barge. It is commonly used in marine construction, offshore oil and gas operations, and port facilities for lifting heavy loads onto and off of ships and offshore structures.

5. **Guy Derrick**:

- A Guy Derrick, also known as a Guyed Derrick or Mast Derrick, is a simple type of derrick crane supported by guy wires anchored to the ground. It typically consists of a vertical mast with a single boom or jib extending from it. Guy Derricks are used in construction, mining, and other industries for lifting and moving heavy loads.

Each type of derrick crane has its own advantages and limitations, and the choice of crane depends on factors such as the specific lifting requirements, site conditions, and budget constraints. However, all derrick cranes share the common feature of using a vertical mast or tower for support and a system of booms, jibs, and rigging for lifting and moving heavy loads.

Figure 45: Two guy derricks at a granite quarry. Z22, CC BY-SA 3.0, via Wikimedia Commons.

While derrick cranes were once prevalent in many industries, they have been largely replaced by more versatile and mobile crane designs such as tower cranes, crawler cranes, and mobile cranes. However, they are still used in specific applications where their unique capabilities are advantageous, such as in shipyards, oil rigs, and certain types of construction projects.

A Stiffleg Derrick, as shown in Figure 46, is a specific type of derrick crane characterized by its distinctive support structure and rigging system. It is commonly used in construction, particularly in bridge construction, marine construction, and other applications where heavy loads need to be lifted and moved with precision and stability.

Here are the key components and features of a Stiffleg Derrick:

1. Mast or Tower: Like other derrick cranes, a Stiffleg Derrick consists of a vertical mast or tower that provides the primary support for the crane structure. The mast is typically made of steel and anchored firmly to the ground or a concrete foundation.

2. Boom or Jib: Unlike traditional derrick cranes, which have a single boom or jib extending from the mast, a Stiffleg Derrick typically has two booms or jibs arranged in a triangular configuration. These booms are inclined at an angle and are connected to the top of the mast.

3. Guy Lines: Stiffleg Derricks are stabilized using a system of guy lines, which are attached to the tops of the booms and extend outward to ground anchors or counterweights. The guy lines are tensioned to provide stability and prevent the crane from tipping over during lifting operations.

4. Hoist System: Similar to other types of cranes, a Stiffleg Derrick is equipped with a hoist system mounted on one or both of the booms. The hoist system typically consists of a winch or drum mechanism with wire ropes or chains used to raise and lower the load.

5. Counterweights or Ballast: Depending on the specific design and configuration, Stiffleg Derricks may require counterweights or ballast to balance the load and provide stability. These counterweights are often located at the base of the mast or attached to the guy lines.

Stiffleg Derricks are valued for their ability to lift heavy loads with precision and stability, particularly in situations where space is limited or access is restricted. They are commonly used in bridge construction to lift and position heavy beams and girders, as well as in marine construction for tasks such as pile driving and dock construction.

Figure 46: Stiffleg Derrick Lifting Mechanical Equipment on a rooftop in NYC, operated by BUDCO Enterprises, Inc. Username1187, CC BY-SA 4.0, via Wikimedia Commons.

A Hammerhead Derrick is a type of derrick crane commonly used in shipyards, ports, and other industrial settings for lifting and moving heavy loads, particularly onto ships or other vessels.

Key features of a Hammerhead Derrick include:
1. Mast: The vertical mast serves as the main support structure for the crane. It is usually constructed of steel and anchored firmly to the ground or a concrete foundation.

2. Boom or Jib: Unlike traditional derrick cranes with inclined booms, a Hammerhead Derrick features a horizontal boom that extends from the top of the mast. This boom can pivot around

a central point on the mast.

3. Trolley Mechanism: One of the distinguishing features of a Hammerhead Derrick is its trolley mechanism. This mechanism allows the horizontal boom to move horizontally along the length of the mast. The trolley is typically motorized for smooth and precise movement.

4. Hoist System: Similar to other types of cranes, a Hammerhead Derrick is equipped with a hoist system mounted on the horizontal boom. The hoist system typically consists of a winch or drum mechanism with wire ropes or chains used to raise and lower the load.

5. Counterweights or Ballast: Depending on the specific design and configuration, a Hammerhead Derrick may require counterweights or ballast to balance the load and provide stability. These counterweights are often located at the base of the mast or integrated into the crane structure.

Hammerhead Derricks are valued for their ability to lift heavy loads with precision and manoeuvrability, particularly in situations where space is limited or access is restricted. They are commonly used in shipyards and ports for tasks such as loading and unloading cargo onto ships, assembling ship components, and handling heavy machinery.

Figure 47: A view of a 350-ton hammerhead crane. PICRYL - Public Domain Media Search Engine.

One of the advantages of a Hammerhead Derrick is its ability to move horizontally along the length of the mast, allowing it to reach different areas within its operating radius without repositioning the entire crane. This makes it particularly useful in congested or confined spaces such as busy ports or industrial yards.

Overall, Hammerhead Derricks are versatile and efficient lifting solutions for a wide range of applications, offering high lifting capacities and precise load control in demanding industrial environments.

A guy derrick crane, also known simply as a guy derrick or a guyed derrick, is a type of crane commonly used in construction, mining, and other industries for lifting heavy loads.

The crane consists of a vertical mast or tower, which is supported by guy wires or ropes that are anchored at the base of the mast and extend outward and upward to provide stability. These guy wires are typically arranged in a triangular pattern, with multiple sets of wires providing support in different directions.

At the top of the mast, there is typically a horizontal boom or jib with a pulley system, which allows for the lifting and lowering of loads. The crane may be fixed in place or mounted on a movable base, such as a truck or a stationary platform.

Guy derrick cranes are often used in situations where space is limited or where a high degree of stability is required, such as in construction sites with tall buildings or in mining operations where the ground may be uneven. They are capable of lifting very heavy loads and are often used for tasks such as erecting steel structures, lifting heavy machinery, or handling large containers or materials.

Planning to Operate a Derrick Crane

Planning to operate a derrick crane involves several key steps to ensure safety and efficiency. These include:

1. **Task Requirements Identification:**

   - Review work orders or equivalent documents to understand the scope of work.

   - Discuss lift plan with relevant personnel, including riggers, supervisors, and site managers.

   - Conduct a thorough site inspection to assess conditions and potential hazards.

2. **Confirmation of Work Area Suitability:**

   - Assess the operating surface to ensure it can support the weight of the crane and the load being lifted.

   - Check for any obstructions or uneven terrain that could affect crane stability.

   - Follow workplace procedures to confirm the suitability of

the ground for crane operation.

3. **Establishment of Rated Capacity and Working Load Limit:**

    - Determine the Rated Capacity (RC) of the derrick crane as specified by the manufacturer.

    - Calculate the Working Load Limit (WLL) of the lifting gear based on the load and task requirements.

    - Ensure that the RC and WLL are not exceeded during operations.

4. **Assessment of Operating Paths and Hazards:**

    - Identify appropriate paths for crane operation and load movement within the work area.

    - Assess potential hazards, such as overhead obstacles, power lines, or unstable ground.

    - Implement measures to eliminate or control identified risks.

5. **Application of Hazard Identification and Risk Control Measures:**

    - Conduct a comprehensive hazard identification process, considering all potential risks associated with crane operation.

    - Implement appropriate control measures to mitigate identified hazards.

    - Communicate hazard information and control measures to associated personnel.

6. **Confirmation of Traffic Management Plan Implementa-**

tion:

- ○ Confirm the implementation of the traffic management plan to ensure the safe movement of vehicles and personnel around the work area.
- ○ Follow workplace procedures and guidelines for traffic management.

7. **Identification and Testing of Communication Procedures:**

- ○ Identify communication procedures for coordinating crane operations with associated personnel.
- ○ Test communication systems and protocols to ensure effectiveness and clarity.
- ○ Establish clear signals and protocols for communication between the crane operator and ground personnel.

8. **Confirmation of Task Requirements Compliance:**

- ○ Verify that all tasks and requirements outlined in the lift plan and workplace procedures have been met.
- ○ Ensure that the work area is prepared and all necessary precautions are in place before beginning crane operations.

9. **Obtaining and Interpreting Information for Lifting Equipment:**

- ○ Obtain relevant information on inspection, use, maintenance, and storage of lifting equipment from the manufacturer's specifications and guidelines.
- ○ Interpret this information to ensure that all lifting equipment

is used and maintained correctly and in compliance with manufacturer requirements.

Operating a derrick crane can present various hazards, which need to be identified and mitigated to ensure the safety of personnel and property. Here are some common hazards associated with derrick crane operation and ways to mitigate them:

1. **Overload Hazard:**

   - Hazard: Exceeding the crane's rated capacity can cause structural failure, leading to crane collapse and potential injury or fatality.

   - Mitigation:

     - Always know the crane's rated capacity and adhere to it strictly.

     - Conduct thorough load calculations before lifting.

     - Ensure proper rigging techniques and use appropriate lifting gear.

     - Utilize load moment indicators and overload protection devices on the crane.

2. **Collision Hazard:**

   - Hazard: Collisions with structures, equipment, or other cranes on the site can cause damage, injury, or fatalities.

   - Mitigation:

     - Maintain clear communication between crane operators and ground personnel.

- Implement and follow site-specific traffic management plans.

- Use spotters to guide crane movement and ensure clear paths.

- Mark and identify hazard zones around the crane's operating area.

3. **Electrocution Hazard:**

    - Hazard: Contact with overhead power lines can result in electrocution, leading to severe injuries or death.

    - Mitigation:

        - Conduct a thorough assessment of the work area for the presence of overhead power lines.

        - Maintain safe working distances from power lines as per regulations and guidelines.

        - Utilize proximity warning devices to alert operators when nearing power lines.

        - Implement and follow proper procedures for working near electrical hazards.

4. **Falling Object Hazard:**

    - Hazard: Objects or materials being lifted by the crane can fall, causing injuries or fatalities to personnel below.

    - Mitigation:

        - Secure all loads properly with appropriate rigging and attachments.

- Conduct regular inspections of lifting gear to ensure they are in good condition.

- Use barricades or exclusion zones to prevent unauthorized personnel from entering the danger zone.

- Implement a clear communication protocol to signal when loads are being moved.

5. **Structural Failure Hazard:**

    - Hazard: Structural failure of the crane components, such as the mast, boom, or jib, can occur due to fatigue, corrosion, or inadequate maintenance.

    - Mitigation:

        - Implement a robust inspection and maintenance program for the crane.

        - Conduct regular structural inspections by qualified personnel.

        - Monitor crane components for signs of wear, fatigue, or corrosion and replace as necessary.

        - Adhere to manufacturer's guidelines for maintenance and inspection intervals.

6. **Wind Hazard:**

    - Hazard: High winds can affect the stability and operation of the crane, leading to potential accidents or structural damage.

    - Mitigation:

- Monitor weather conditions regularly and cease crane operations during high winds or adverse weather conditions.

- Use anemometers or wind gauges to measure wind speeds on-site.

- Secure loose objects and materials that could become projectiles in high winds.

- Follow manufacturer's guidelines for operating the crane in windy conditions.

By identifying these hazards and implementing appropriate mitigation measures, the risks associated with derrick crane operation can be significantly reduced, ensuring a safer work environment for all personnel involved.

Preparing for Derrick Crane Operations

In the context of operating a derrick crane, meticulous consultation with workplace personnel is paramount, ensuring clarity and consistency in all crane and lifting operations vis-a-vis site requirements, adhering diligently to the stipulated lift plan, and workplace procedures. This collaborative approach guarantees that the execution aligns seamlessly with established protocols, fostering a safe and efficient work environment. Furthermore, thorough risk assessment is conducted, scrutinizing identified hazards to verify the implementation of requisite risk control measures as delineated in the lift plan and safe work procedures. This diligent oversight mitigates potential risks, safeguarding personnel and property.

Prior to commencement, rigorous pre-start checks are undertaken on the derrick crane, examining for any damage or defects. Prompt reporting and recording of identified issues facilitate swift corrective action in accordance with safe work procedures and manufacturer requirements. Once cleared for operation, precise positioning of the derrick crane is confirmed, meticulously adhering to manufacturer guidelines and load chart specifications. This meticulous setup extends to the arrangement of lifting gear, ensuring compliance with the lift plan and safe work procedures, as well as specific manufacturer requirements.

The following provides an example of a lift plan:

Project Name: *Construction of High-rise Building*
Location: *Construction Site XYZ*
Date: *[Insert Date]*
Prepared By: *[Insert Name of Crane Supervisor or Qualified Person]*
Approved By: *[Insert Name of Site Manager or Project Engineer]*
Purpose of Lift: *Hoisting steel beams to the 10th floor of the building under construction.*

Description of Load:
- *Type: Steel beams*
- *Weight: 5 tons each*
- *Dimensions: 10 meters long*
- *Quantity: 4 beams*

Crane Details:
- *Type: Guyed Derrick Crane*
- *Model: ABC-1000*
- *Rated Capacity: 10 tons*
- *Boom Length: 40 meters*

Lifting Equipment:

- *Rigging: Steel wire ropes with appropriate slings and hooks*
- *Shackles: Grade 80 alloy steel shackles, 2-ton capacity*
- *Spreaders: Adjustable beam spreader bars, 4-ton capacity*

Lift Procedure:

1. *Pre-Start Checks:*

   - Conduct pre-start checks on the derrick crane, ensuring all mechanical and safety systems are operational.
   - Verify fluid levels, check for leaks, inspect lights, and confirm controls.

2. *Positioning:*

   - Position the derrick crane on stable ground, ensuring outriggers are securely deployed.
   - Clear the surrounding area of personnel and obstructions.

3. *Load Preparation:*

   - Attach rigging to each steel beam using appropriate slinging techniques.
   - Ensure the load is balanced and properly secured to prevent shifting during lifting.

4. *Crane Setup:*

   - Set up the derrick crane boom to the appropriate angle and height for the lift.
   - Confirm load chart calculations for the specified boom length

and load weight.

5. *Communication:*

    ○ *Establish clear communication channels between the crane operator and ground personnel.*

    ○ *Designate signallers to communicate lift instructions using standardized hand signals.*

6. *Lifting Procedure:*

    ○ *Slowly raise the load vertically, ensuring smooth and controlled movement.*

    ○ *Monitor load stability and adjust crane controls as necessary to maintain balance.*

7. *Load Placement:*

    ○ *Position the load over the designated area on the 10th floor of the building.*

    ○ *Lower the load gently and precisely into place, guided by ground personnel.*

8. *Post-Lift Checks:*

    ○ *Conduct post-lift checks on the derrick crane to ensure it remains in proper working condition.*

    ○ *Inspect rigging and lifting equipment for any signs of damage or wear.*

Emergency Procedures:
- *In the event of an emergency, immediately stop crane operations and follow site-specific emergency procedures.*

- *Notify all personnel of the emergency and evacuate the area if necessary.*

Notes:
- *All lift operations must be conducted by trained and qualified personnel.*
- *Monitor weather conditions and cease crane operations if adverse weather poses a safety risk.*
- *Follow manufacturer guidelines and safe work procedures at all times.*

Approval Signatures:

[Signature of Crane Supervisor/Qualified Person] [Signature of Site Manager/Project Engineer]

This example provides a structured outline of the lift plan, including details of the load, crane, lift procedure, communication protocols, emergency procedures, and approval signatures. It ensures that all aspects of the lift are carefully planned and executed in accordance with safety requirements and industry standards.

Operational readiness is validated through comprehensive checks, with any discrepancies promptly reported and addressed in accordance with manufacturer requirements and safe work procedures. The crane logbook is meticulously scrutinized, verifying compliance, accuracy, and completion, with any necessary rectifications duly noted and signed off in accordance with stipulated protocols. Moreover, a thorough assessment of prevailing weather and work environment conditions is conducted, considering potential impacts on derrick crane operations as per manufacturer requirements and safe work procedures.

Integral to the lifting process is the identification or calculation of the load's weight, ensuring adherence to safety parameters and operational limitations. Additionally, the calculation and confirmation of the derated Working Load Limit (WLL) of lifting equipment resulting from selected slinging techniques are imperative, guaranteeing suitability in line with the lift plan requirements. Identifying suitable lifting points and employing appropriate slinging techniques further enhance operational safety and efficiency.

With meticulous preparation complete, lifting equipment and gear are confirmed as ready for safe use, culminating in the final confirmation of load destination stability. This crucial step ensures that the load's landing point can bear the weight securely, with preparations made to facilitate safe access and landing, thereby concluding the comprehensive operational sequence with utmost safety and efficiency.

Undertaking a pre-start check on a derrick crane is a crucial step to ensure its safe and efficient operation. The pre-start check includes:

1. **Engine/Mechanical Fluid Level Checks:**

   - Check engine oil, hydraulic fluid, coolant, and any other fluid levels as specified by the manufacturer.

   - Top up fluids if necessary to ensure they are at the correct levels for safe operation.

2. **Presence of Correct Logbook:**

   - Confirm the presence of the crane's logbook, which should contain records of previous inspections, maintenance, and repairs.

   - Ensure that the logbook is up to date and contains all relevant information for the crane's operation.

3. **Evidence of Damage:**

   - Inspect the crane for any visible signs of damage, such as dents, scratches, or cracks.

- Pay particular attention to critical components such as the boom, jib, and mast.

4. **Fluid Leaks:**

- Look for any signs of fluid leaks, such as puddles or stains on the ground beneath the crane.
- Investigate the source of any leaks and address them promptly to prevent loss of hydraulic or other fluids.

5. **Lights Work Effectively:**

- Test all lights on the crane, including headlights, brake lights, turn signals, and hazard lights.
- Ensure that all lights are functioning correctly and are visible from the appropriate angles.

6. **Locating, Identifying, and Confirming All Controls:**

- Familiarize yourself with the location and function of all controls on the crane, including joysticks, levers, switches, and buttons.
- Confirm that each control operates smoothly and responds as expected.

7. **Fire Extinguisher:**

- Check the presence and condition of the fire extinguisher mounted on the crane.
- Ensure that the fire extinguisher is fully charged and has not expired.

8. **Safety Equipment Checks:**

   - Inspect all safety equipment on the crane, including harnesses, lanyards, and fall arrest systems.

   - Ensure that safety equipment is in good condition and is properly stored and secured when not in use.

9. **Signage and Labels:**

   - Check all signage and labels on the crane to ensure they are visible, legible, and in good condition.

   - Pay attention to important safety labels, load capacity indicators, and operating instructions.

10. **Checking for Signs of Paint Separation and Stressed Welds:**

    - Inspect the crane's structure for signs of paint separation, which may indicate corrosion or rust.

    - Look for stressed welds, cracks, or other signs of structural weakness, especially in high-stress areas.

11. **Updating Records:**

    - Update inspection records and maintenance logs as required, documenting any findings or actions taken during the pre-start check.

12. **Visual Damage or Equipment Faults:**

    - Conduct a thorough visual inspection of the crane, looking for any damage or equipment faults that may affect its safe operation.

- Document any issues found and take appropriate action to address them before proceeding with crane operation.

Checking for signs of paint separation and stressed welds on a crane's structure is a critical aspect of routine maintenance and safety inspection. Firstly, inspecting the crane's structure for signs of paint separation is essential as it can indicate underlying corrosion or rust. Paint separation often occurs when moisture infiltrates the surface of the crane's metal components, causing the paint to lift or flake away. Areas where paint separation is observed should be carefully examined for signs of corrosion, which can weaken the structural integrity of the crane over time. Addressing any areas of paint separation promptly by removing the affected paint, treating the surface for corrosion, and applying a protective coating can help prevent further deterioration and maintain the crane's structural integrity.

Additionally, it's crucial to look for stressed welds, cracks, or other signs of structural weakness during the inspection. Welded joints are critical points of connection in the crane's structure, and any defects or weaknesses in these areas can compromise the crane's stability and safety. High-stress areas, such as where the boom connects to the mast or where the jib attaches to the boom, should be closely examined for signs of fatigue or failure. Stressed welds may exhibit visual indications such as discoloration, distortion, or irregularities in the weld bead. Cracks or fractures in the metal components should also be carefully inspected, as they can indicate underlying structural issues that require immediate attention. Any signs of stressed welds, cracks, or structural weakness should be thoroughly evaluated by a qualified inspector or engineer, and appropriate repairs or reinforcements should be implemented to ensure the crane's continued safe operation. Regular inspection and maintenance of the crane's structure are essential for identifying and addressing potential issues before they escalate into safety hazards.

Once the prestart checks are completed, the crane can be started. The following provides an example of a start-up procedure to start a derrick crane:

Derrick Crane Start-Up Procedure
1. Pre-Start Checks:
- *Before starting the crane, conduct a visual inspection to ensure there are no visible signs of damage or defects.*

- *Check the area around the crane for any obstructions or hazards that could interfere with its operation.*

- *Ensure that all necessary safety gear, such as hard hats and safety harnesses, is worn by personnel involved in the start-up procedure.*

2. Check Fluid Levels:
- *Verify that all fluid levels, including engine oil, hydraulic fluid, and coolant, are at the correct levels as per manufacturer specifications.*

- *Top up fluids as necessary to ensure proper lubrication and cooling during operation.*

3. Power On:
- *Turn the main power switch to the "On" position to supply power to the crane's electrical systems.*

- *If the crane is equipped with a diesel engine, start the engine by turning the ignition key and allowing the engine to warm up for a few minutes before proceeding.*

4. Test Controls:
- *Test all controls on the crane, including joysticks, levers, switches, and buttons, to ensure they respond correctly and move*

smoothly.

- Verify that all controls are functioning as expected and that there are no jams or malfunctions.

5. Check Warning Systems:
- Test all warning systems, including audible alarms and visual indicators, to ensure they are functioning correctly.
- Verify that lights, horns, and other warning devices are operational and emit a clear signal when activated.

6. Warm-Up Procedure (If Applicable):
- If the crane's engine requires a warm-up period, allow it to idle for a few minutes to reach operating temperature.
- Monitor engine gauges and indicators during the warm-up period to ensure that all readings are within normal ranges.

7. Conduct Operational Checks:
- Perform operational checks on the crane's hydraulic functions, lifting gear, and other critical components.
- Verify that all movements are smooth and controlled, with no signs of abnormal noises or vibrations.
- Check for any leaks or abnormalities in hydraulic lines, fittings, or connections.

8. Confirm Readiness:
- Once all checks have been completed and the crane is operating smoothly, confirm that it is ready for use.
- Communicate with ground personnel to ensure that the work area is clear and that all necessary precautions have been taken.

9. Log Start-Up:

- *Record the start-up procedure in the crane's logbook, including any abnormalities or issues encountered during the process.*

- *Sign and date the logbook to indicate that the crane has been properly started and is ready for operation.*

10. Final Preparations: - *Double-check that all safety measures are in place, including barricades, signage, and personal protective equipment. - Confirm that communication channels between the crane operator and ground personnel are established and functional.*

11. Crane Ready for Operation: - *With all checks completed and preparations finalized, the derrick crane is now ready for safe and efficient operation.*

This start-up procedure ensures that the derrick crane is properly prepared and in optimal condition for use, prioritizing safety and efficiency throughout the process.

Performing operational checks on a derrick crane is essential to ensure its safe and efficient operation. To conduct these checks effectively, attention to detail is crucial in ensuring that all controls, functions, and safety systems are functioning correctly.

Firstly, locating, identifying, and testing controls is paramount. This involves identifying all controls on the derrick crane, such as joysticks, levers, switches, and buttons, and testing each one individually to ensure they respond as expected. Clear labelling and accessibility are imperative to facilitate ease of use for the operator.

Next, checking hydraulic functions is essential. This entails testing all hydraulic functions of the crane, including raising and lowering the boom, extending and retracting the jib, and swinging the crane. It's imperative to verify that hydraulic movements are smooth and responsive, with no jerking or hesitation, while also checking for any leaks or abnormalities in hydraulic lines or fittings.

Testing lifting gear movements is another crucial step. This involves operating the crane's lifting gear, such as winches, hoists, and trolleys, to ensure they function smoothly and in accordance with the lift plan. It's important to verify that lifting gear movements are controlled and precise, with proper speed and alignment, and ensure that the lifting gear is capable of lifting the anticipated load as specified in the lift plan.

Additionally, checking hazard warning systems is essential for safety. This includes testing all audible and visual warning devices to ensure they are functional, checking lights, such as headlights, brake lights, turn signals, and hazard lights, to ensure they are working correctly and are visible from the appropriate angles, and verifying the operation of anti-two block alarms, if fitted, to prevent two-blocking incidents.

Following a proper start-up procedure is imperative. This involves starting the crane's engine or power source in accordance with manufacturer requirements and safe work procedures, following any specific start-up procedures outlined in the crane's operating manual, and monitoring engine gauges and indicators for any abnormal readings or warnings during start-up.

Lastly, checking for unusual noises is crucial. This entails listening for any unusual noises coming from the crane during operation, investigating the source of any unusual noises, and taking appropriate action to address them, such as lubricating moving parts or tightening loose connections. Special attention should be paid to hydraulic systems, gears, and bearings, as unusual noises may indicate mechanical problems.

Operating a Derrick Crane

In the context of operating a derrick crane, lifts are meticulously planned and executed within the Rated Capacity (RC) of the crane, adhering closely to the load charts and lift plan specifications. Before initiating any lifting operation, thorough consideration is given to the weight and dimensions of the load, ensuring it falls within the safe lifting capacity of the crane. This meticulous planning ensures the safety of personnel and equipment involved in the lift.

Once the lift plan is established, the boom/jib and hook block are positioned safely over the load with precision, following instructions from associated personnel. Every movement is executed with care and attention to detail, in strict accordance with the lift plan and safe work procedures. Clear communication channels are maintained between the crane operator and ground personnel to ensure seamless coordination throughout the lifting process.

The main hook, along with any necessary lifting gear, is connected to the load securely and used in a manner that prioritizes safety. All connections are inspected for proper engagement and integrity before lifting begins. A test lift is conducted in accordance with dogging and safe work procedures to verify the stability and balance of the load, providing reassurance that the lift can proceed safely.

Throughout the lifting operation, loads are transferred using relevant crane movements and tag lines, as required by the lift plan and safe work procedures. Constant monitoring of both the load and crane movements is essential to ensure smooth and controlled operation. Any deviations from the lift plan or safety protocols are promptly addressed to mitigate risks and maintain safety standards.

Operating a derrick crane involves several principles to lift and move loads safely and efficiently. Each movement is carefully controlled by the crane operator using a combination of mechanical controls, visual observation, and communication with ground personnel. Here's an explanation of the principles behind each movement:

1. **Hoist Up:**

    - To hoist up a load, the crane operator activates the hoist mechanism, which raises the load vertically.

    - The operator controls the speed and direction of the hoist using the crane's controls, ensuring smooth and controlled movement.

    - The hoist mechanism may be powered by an electric motor, hydraulic system, or other means, depending on the design of the crane.

2. **Luff Boom Down:**

    - Luffing refers to the vertical movement of the crane's boom or jib.

    - To luff the boom down, the operator adjusts the angle of the boom downward, bringing the load closer to the ground or desired location.

    - This movement is typically controlled by hydraulic cylinders or other mechanical means, allowing for precise positioning of the load.

3. **Luff Boom Up:**

    - Conversely, luffing the boom up involves adjusting the angle of the boom upward, lifting the load higher off the ground or raising it to a higher elevation.

    - The operator controls the speed and angle of the luffing movement to ensure the load is raised safely and accurately to the desired height.

CRANE OPERATIONS

4. **Slew Left/Right:**

   - Slew refers to the horizontal rotation of the crane's superstructure or turntable.

   - To slew left, the operator activates the slew mechanism, causing the crane to rotate in a counterclockwise direction when viewed from above.

   - Similarly, to slew right, the operator rotates the crane in a clockwise direction.

   - Slew movements allow the crane to position the load precisely over the desired location, providing flexibility in load placement.

5. **Stop:**

   - The stop command halts all crane movements and locks the crane's controls in place.

   - It is essential for the operator to stop crane movements promptly when the load reaches its intended position or in case of an emergency.

   - The stop command ensures that the crane remains stationary and stable, preventing unintended movements or accidents.

Each of these crane movements requires careful coordination and control to ensure the safe and efficient lifting and movement of loads. Proper training, experience, and adherence to safety protocols are essential for crane operators to execute these movements effectively and minimize the risk of accidents or injuries.

Derrick cranes typically slew, or rotate, by utilizing a slewing mechanism located at the base of the crane's mast or tower. This mechanism allows the entire crane superstructure, including the boom and jib, to rotate horizontally, enabling the crane to position the load precisely over the desired location. The slewing mechanism consists of several components, including:

1. Slewing Motor: Derrick cranes are equipped with an electric, hydraulic, or diesel-powered motor that drives the slewing motion. This motor provides the necessary torque to rotate the crane's superstructure.

2. Slewing Gear: The slewing motor is connected to a gear mechanism that translates the rotational motion of the motor into the horizontal movement of the crane. The gear system allows for smooth and controlled slewing operation.

3. Slewing Ring or Turntable: At the base of the crane's mast or tower, there is typically a large slewing ring or turntable upon which the crane superstructure is mounted. This turntable acts as a bearing surface, allowing the crane to rotate freely.

4. Slewing Controls: The crane operator controls the slewing motion using dedicated controls located in the crane's cab or control station. These controls may consist of joysticks, levers, or buttons that enable the operator to initiate and control the slewing movement.

When the operator activates the slewing controls, the slewing motor engages, causing the crane's superstructure to rotate horizontally. The operator can control the direction and speed of the slewing motion to position the load precisely where needed. Slewing movements are typically smooth and precise, allowing the crane operator to manoeuvre the load with accuracy and efficiency.

Overall, the slewing mechanism is an integral part of derrick crane operation, providing the crane with the versatility to reach various points within its working radius and effectively perform lifting tasks in construction, industrial, and other applications.

In a typical derrick crane, the hook is usually fixed in place at the end of the boom and does not move along the length of the boom. Instead, the hook is attached to the load, and the crane's operation involves raising, lowering, and positioning the load by adjusting the boom's angle (luffing) and rotating the crane's superstructure (slewing).

However, there are variations of derrick cranes, such as telescopic boom derrick cranes or certain specialized models, where the hook may have the capability to move along the length of the boom. These types of cranes may feature additional mechanisms such as a trolley or a telescoping section of the boom that allows the hook to be moved horizontally along the boom.

In such cases, the ability to move the hook along the boom provides increased flexibility and versatility in positioning the load precisely where needed. This feature is particularly useful in applications where precise load placement is required over a large area or where access to different parts of a work site is necessary.

However, it's essential to note that not all derrick cranes have this capability, and the design and functionality of the crane will vary depending on the specific model and manufacturer. Therefore, it's crucial for crane operators to be familiar with the features and capabilities of the particular crane they are operating.

Luffing in a derrick crane primarily involves adjusting the angle of the boom or jib to raise or lower the load vertically, controlling the height of the load relative to the crane's centreline. Luffing does not directly result in significant horizontal displacement of the load.

Horizontal movement of the load is indeed achieved through slewing, which is the rotation of the crane's superstructure horizontally. By slewing the crane left or right, the load can be positioned horizontally over the desired location within the crane's working radius. Slewing and luffing are distinct movements with different purposes and control mechanisms, as you described.

So, in summary, luffing primarily controls the vertical position of the load, while slewing facilitates horizontal movement, allowing the crane operator to position the load precisely where needed. Both movements are essential for efficient and accurate lifting operations but serve different functions in controlling the position of the load.

When operating a derrick crane, managing various load dynamics is crucial for safe and efficient operations:

1. Dynamic Loads: Dynamic loads refer to forces that change over time, often due to factors like wind, sudden movements, or changes in load distribution. To manage dynamic loads, crane operators must constantly monitor environmental conditions and adjust operations accordingly. This may involve reducing crane speed, implementing additional counterweights, or even temporarily halting operations during adverse weather conditions to ensure stability and safety.

2. Load Swing: Load swing occurs when the load being lifted starts to swing or pendulum, which can pose significant safety risks to both personnel and property. To manage load swing, operators must employ smooth and controlled movements, avoiding sudden accelerations or decelerations. Additionally, the use of tag lines or anti-swing devices can help minimize load swing by providing additional control and stability during lifting and placement operations.

3. Overloading: Overloading happens when the weight of the load exceeds the crane's rated capacity, risking structural failure or collapse. To prevent overloading, operators must always verify the weight of the load and ensure it falls within the crane's specified capacity. Utilizing load indicators and limit switches can

provide real-time feedback and alerts to prevent overloading situations. Additionally, implementing strict operational procedures and conducting regular inspections help mitigate the risk of overloading incidents.

4. Lifting and Placing Load: When lifting and placing loads, operators must execute precise manoeuvres to ensure the safe and accurate placement of the load. This involves carefully positioning the crane, accurately aligning the lifting gear with the load, and utilizing appropriate rigging techniques. Operators should communicate effectively with signalpersons and ground personnel to coordinate movements and ensure proper load placement. Additionally, maintaining a stable load path and avoiding sudden movements during lifting and placement operations enhance safety and efficiency.

5. Asymmetric Loads: Asymmetric loads refer to loads with uneven weight distribution, which can cause the load to tilt or become unstable during lifting and placement. To manage asymmetric loads, operators must carefully assess the load's centre of gravity and employ proper rigging techniques to maintain balance and stability. This may involve using additional support or adjusting the rigging configuration to distribute the load evenly. Constant vigilance and adjustments are essential when dealing with asymmetric loads to prevent accidents and ensure safe lifting and placement operations.

Managing asymmetric loads requires a detailed understanding of the load's weight distribution and centre of gravity. The centre of gravity is the point around which the load's mass is evenly distributed in all directions. When dealing with asymmetric loads, this centre of gravity may not be located at the geometric centre of the load.

To begin managing asymmetric loads, operators must assess the load's centre of gravity. This assessment involves analysing the shape, weight distribution, and composition of the load to determine where its centre of gravity lies. Once identified, operators can plan how to rig the load to maintain balance and stability during lifting and placement.

Proper rigging techniques play a crucial role in managing asymmetric loads. Rigging involves attaching lifting equipment, such as slings or hooks, to the load in a way that evenly distributes the weight and minimizes the risk of tilting or instability. This may include using multiple attachment points or adjusting the rigging configuration to ensure that the load remains level and balanced throughout the lifting process.

By carefully assessing the load's centre of gravity and employing appropriate rigging techniques, operators can effectively manage asymmetric loads, mitigating the risk of accidents and ensuring safe lifting and placement operations.

Effective communication is key during crane operation, with all required signals correctly interpreted and followed by the crane operator. This ensures that all personnel involved in the lift are aware of the intended movements and can adjust their actions accordingly to maintain safety.

As the lift nears completion, the load is lowered and landed safely in accordance with the lift plan and safe work procedures. Once the load is securely in place, lifting gear is disconnected, and the crane is positioned safely and efficiently for the next task, following the guidelines outlined in the lift plan and safe work procedures.

Finally, lifting equipment and gear are subjected to thorough inspection for defects, with any defective items promptly isolated, tagged, and reported. This proactive approach to equipment maintenance helps to prevent accidents and ensures the continued safe operation of the derrick crane.

Completing Derrick Crane Operation

Initially, the crane boom/jib, lifting gear, and associated equipment must be carefully stowed and secured in adherence to manufacturer specifications and established safe work procedures. This meticulous process not only facilitates the smooth transition from operation to storage but also mitigates the risk of damage or accidents.

Simultaneously, relevant motion locks and brakes must be diligently applied in accordance with both manufacturer requirements and prescribed safe work procedures. These crucial safety mechanisms serve to immobilize the crane, preventing any unintended movement or potential hazards that could arise during the post-operation phase.

Following the secure stowing and immobilization of the crane, the shutdown procedure must be executed meticulously. The crane is shut down and secured to thwart unauthorized access or inadvertent use, aligning precisely with safe work procedures. This step is essential in safeguarding against any unauthorized operation, minimizing the potential for accidents, and maintaining the integrity of the equipment.

Finally, comprehensive shutdown checks are conducted in strict accordance with safe work procedures and manufacturer requirements. These checks serve as a final verification process, ensuring that all safety protocols have been diligently followed and that the crane is in a safe and secure state for storage. By adhering rigorously to these steps, operators uphold the highest standards of safety and professionalism, thereby concluding the operation of the derrick crane with utmost diligence and care.

Derrick Crane Load Charts

Load charts are essential tools used in derrick cranes to determine the safe lifting capacity of the crane under various operating conditions. These charts provide valuable information regarding the crane's capabilities based on factors such as boom length, boom angle, and operating radius. Load charts typically list load capacities in terms of weight (such as short tons or metric tons) corresponding to different combinations of operating parameters.

Here's how load charts are used in derrick cranes:

1. Safety: Load charts help ensure safe crane operation by providing operators with guidelines on the maximum weight the crane can safely lift under different conditions. By consulting the load chart before lifting, operators can avoid overloading the crane, which could lead to equipment failure, accidents, or injuries.

2. Planning: Load charts aid in planning lifts by allowing operators to determine the crane's capabilities for specific lifting scenarios. Operators can assess whether the crane is suitable for lifting a particular load at a given radius and boom angle, or if adjustments need to be made to the crane setup or lifting technique.

3. Efficiency: Load charts enable operators to maximize the crane's efficiency by optimizing load capacities while maintaining safety. By selecting the appropriate boom length, angle, and radius based on the load chart, operators can achieve the desired lifting capacity while minimizing the risk of overloading.

4. Training: Load charts are valuable educational tools for crane operators, providing them with a clear understanding of the crane's capabilities and limitations. Training programs often include instruction on how to read and interpret load charts to ensure safe and effective crane operation.

Overall, load charts play a crucial role in promoting safe, efficient, and informed decision-making during derrick crane operations. They serve as a fundamental reference tool for crane operators, supervisors, and others involved in lifting operations, helping to mitigate risks and

CRANE OPERATIONS 213

ensure successful outcomes. A sample derrick crane load chart is shown as Figure 48 and Figure 49.

Operating Radius - ft (m)		Boom Angle (°)	Boom Sheave Height - ft (m)	Load Capacity Short Tons (Metric Tons) Operating Radius - ft (m)	Operating Radius - ft (m)		Boom Sheave Height - ft (m)	Boom Sheave Height - ft (m)	Load Capacity Short Tons (Metric Tons)	Boom Sheave Height - ft (m)	Load Capacity Short Tons (Metric Tons)
Outreach	Centerline				Boom Angle (°)	Boom Sheave Height - ft (m)	Load Capacity Short Tons (Metric Tons)				
100 (30.5)	240 (73.2)	80.3	577 (175.9)	4,000 (3,629)	315 (96.0)	455 (138.7)	56.4			489 (149.1)	1,442 (1,308)
105 (32.0)	245 (74.7)	79.8	576 (175.6)	3,877 (3,517)	320 (97.5)	460 (140.2)	55.8			486 (148.1)	1,421 (1,289)
110 (33.5)	250 (76.2)	79.3	575 (175.3)	3,754 (3,406)	325 (99.1)	465 (141.7)	55.1			482 (147.0)	1,399 (1,269)
115 (35.1)	255 (77.7)	78.8	574 (175.0)	3,632 (3,295)	330 (100.6)	470 (143.3)	54.5			479 (145.9)	1,377 (1,250)
120 (36.6)	260 (79.2)	78.2	573 (174.7)	3,509 (3,183)	335 (102.1)	475 (144.8)	53.9			475 (144.8)	1,356 (1,230)
125 (38.1)	265 (80.8)	77.7	572 (174.4)	3,386 (3,072)	340 (103.6)	480 (146.3)	53.2			471 (143.6)	1,334 (1,210)
130 (39.6)	270 (82.3)	77.2	571 (174.0)	3,263 (2,960)	345 (105.2)	485 (147.8)	52.6			467 (142.4)	1,313 (1,191)
135 (41.1)	275 (83.8)	76.7	570 (173.6)	3,140 (2,849)	350 (106.7)	490 (149.4)	51.9			463 (141.2)	1,291 (1,171)
140 (42.7)	280 (85.3)	76.1	568 (173.3)	3,018 (2,738)	355 (108.2)	495 (150.9)	51.3			459 (140.0)	1,270 (1,152)
145 (44.2)	285 (86.9)	75.6	567 (172.9)	2,895 (2,626)	360 (109.7)	500 (152.4)	50.6			455 (138.7)	1,250 (1,134)
150 (45.7)	290 (88.4)	75.1	566 (172.4)	2,772 (2,515)	365 (111.3)	505 (153.9)	49.9			451 (137.4)	1,229 (1,115)
155 (47.2)	295 (89.9)	74.5	564 (172.0)	2,712 (2,460)	370 (112.8)	510 (155.4)	49.3			447 (136.1)	1,209 (1,096)
160 (48.8)	300 (91.4)	74.0	563 (171.6)	2,652 (2,405)	375 (114.3)	515 (157.0)	48.6			442 (134.8)	1,188 (1,078)
165 (50.3)	305 (93.0)	73.5	561 (171.1)	2,591 (2,351)	380 (115.8)	520 (158.5)	47.9			438 (133.4)	1,167 (1,059)
170 (51.8)	310 (94.5)	72.9	560 (170.6)	2,531 (2,296)	385 (117.3)	525 (160.0)	47.2			433 (131.9)	1,147 (1,040)
175 (53.3)	315 (96.0)	72.4	558 (170.1)	2,471 (2,241)	390 (118.9)	530 (161.5)	46.5			428 (130.5)	1,126 (1,022)
180 (54.9)	320 (97.5)	71.9	556 (169.6)	2,411 (2,187)	395 (120.4)	535 (163.1)	45.8			423 (129.0)	1,106 (1,003)
185 (56.4)	325 (99.1)	71.3	555 (169.1)	2,350 (2,132)	400 (121.9)	540 (164.6)	45.0			418 (127.4)	1,085 (984)
190 (57.9)	330 (100.6)	70.8	553 (168.5)	2,290 (2,078)	405 (123.4)	545 (166.1)	44.3			413 (125.9)	1,062 (963)
195 (59.4)	335 (102.1)	70.2	551 (168.0)	2,230 (2,023)	410 (125.0)	550 (167.6)	43.5			408 (124.2)	1,038 (942)
200 (61.0)	340 (103.6)	69.7	549 (167.4)	2,170 (1,968)	415 (126.5)	555 (169.2)	42.8			402 (122.6)	1,015 (920)
205 (62.5)	345 (105.2)	69.1	547 (166.8)	2,133 (1,935)	420 (128.0)	560 (170.7)	42.0			397 (120.9)	991 (899)
210 (64.0)	350 (106.7)	68.6	545 (166.2)	2,097 (1,903)	425 (129.5)	565 (172.2)	41.2			391 (119.1)	968 (878)
215 (65.5)	355 (108.2)	68.0	543 (165.6)	2,061 (1,870)	430 (131.1)	570 (173.7)	40.5			385 (117.3)	944 (856)
220 (67.1)	360 (109.7)	67.5	541 (164.9)	2,025 (1,837)	435 (132.6)	575 (175.3)	39.6			379 (115.5)	921 (835)
225 (68.6)	365 (111.3)	66.9	539 (164.3)	1,989 (1,804)	440 (134.1)	580 (176.8)	38.8			373 (113.6)	897 (814)
230 (70.1)	370 (112.8)	66.4	537 (163.6)	1,953 (1,771)	445 (135.6)	585 (178.3)	38.0			366 (111.6)	874 (792)
235 (71.6)	375 (114.3)	65.8	535 (162.9)	1,916 (1,739)	450 (137.2)	590 (179.8)	37.1			360 (109.6)	850 (771)
240 (73.2)	380 (115.8)	65.2	532 (162.2)	1,880 (1,706)	455 (138.7)	595 (181.4)	36.3			353 (107.5)	820 (744)
245 (74.7)	385 (117.3)	64.7	530 (161.5)	1,844 (1,673)	460 (140.2)	600 (182.9)	35.4			346 (105.3)	790 (717)
250 (76.2)	390 (118.9)	64.1	527 (160.7)	1,808 (1,640)	465 (141.7)	605 (184.4)	34.5			338 (103.1)	760 (689)
255 (77.7)	395 (120.4)	63.5	525 (159.9)	1,778 (1,613)	470 (143.3)	610 (185.9)	33.5			331 (100.8)	730 (662)
260 (79.2)	400 (121.9)	62.9	522 (159.2)	1,748 (1,586)	475 (144.8)	615 (187.5)	32.6			323 (98.4)	700 (635)
265 (80.8)	405 (123.4)	62.4	520 (158.4)	1,718 (1,558)	480 (146.3)	620 (189.0)	31.6			315 (95.9)	670 (608)
270 (82.3)	410 (125.0)	61.8	517 (157.5)	1,688 (1,531)	485 (147.8)	625 (190.5)	30.6			306 (93.3)	640 (581)
275 (83.8)	415 (126.5)	61.2	514 (156.7)	1,658 (1,504)	490 (149.4)	630 (192.0)	29.6			297 (90.6)	610 (553)
280 (85.3)	420 (128.0)	60.6	511 (155.8)	1,627 (1,476)	495 (150.9)	635 (193.5)	28.5			288 (87.8)	580 (526)
285 (86.9)	425 (129.5)	60.0	508 (154.9)	1,597 (1,449)	500 (152.4)	640 (195.1)	27.4			278 (84.8)	550 (499)
290 (88.4)	430 (131.1)	59.4	505 (154.0)	1,567 (1,422)	505 (153.9)	645 (196.6)	26.2			268 (81.7)	500 (454)
295 (89.9)	435 (132.6)	58.8	502 (153.1)	1,537 (1,394)	510 (155.4)	650 (198.1)	25.0			257 (78.5)	450 (408)
300 (91.4)	440 (134.1)	58.2	499 (152.1)	1,507 (1,367)	515 (157.0)	655 (199.6)	23.7			246 (75.0)	400 (363)
305 (93.0)	445 (135.6)	57.6	496 (151.1)	1,485 (1,348)	520 (158.5)	660 (201.2)	22.4			234 (71.3)	350 (318)
310 (94.5)	450 (137.2)	57.0	493 (150.1)	1,464 (1,328)	525 (160.0)	665 (202.7)	21.0			221 (67.4)	300 (272)

Figure 48: Sample derrick crane load chart.

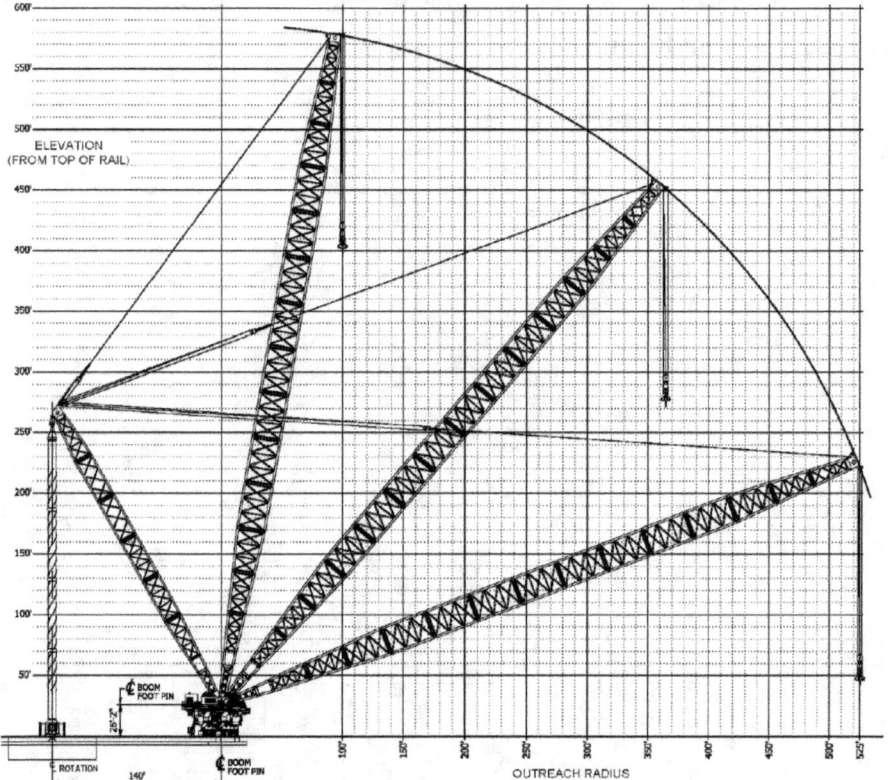

Figure 49: Sample derrick crane load chart.

To interpret the derrick crane load chart shown as Figure 48, follow these steps:

1. Identify Parameters: The chart lists various parameters including Operating Radius (measured in feet and meters), Boom Angle (measured in degrees), Boom Sheave Height (measured in feet and meters), Load Capacity in Short Tons and Metric Tons.

2. Understand Operating Radius and Boom Angle: The Operating Radius indicates the horizontal distance from the crane's centreline to the load. The Boom Angle represents the angle formed between the crane's boom and the horizontal plane.

3. Determine Load Capacity: Locate the specific Operating Ra-

dius and Boom Angle corresponding to your lifting scenario. Cross-reference these values to find the corresponding Load Capacity in both Short Tons and Metric Tons. The Load Capacity indicates the maximum weight the crane can safely lift at the given Operating Radius and Boom Angle.

4. Interpret Other Parameters: Boom Sheave Height indicates the vertical distance from the ground to the boom sheave, which may impact the crane's lifting capacity. It is essential to consider this height when calculating load capacities.

5. Use Caution: Note that load capacities may vary based on factors such as boom length, crane configuration, and environmental conditions. Always consult the crane manufacturer's guidelines and adhere to safety protocols when operating the crane.

6. Consider Jurisdictional Variations: Keep in mind that crane operations and terminology can vary across jurisdictions. Ensure compliance with local regulations and standards when interpreting and applying the load chart data.

Here are some example interpretations from the provided load chart data:

1. At 100 feet (30.5 meters) Operating Radius and 577 feet (175.9 meters) Boom Sheave Height: The crane's load capacity is 4,000 short tons (3,629 metric tons) when configured for Centerline.

2. At 120 feet (36.6 meters) Operating Radius and 573 feet (174.7 meters) Boom Sheave Height: The crane can lift up to 3,509 short tons (3,183 metric tons) when configured for Centerline.

3. At 160 feet (48.8 meters) Operating Radius and 563 feet (171.6 meters) Boom Sheave Height: The load capacity is 2,652 short tons (2,405 metric tons) when configured for Centerline.

4. At 215 feet (65.5 meters) Operating Radius and 543 feet (165.6 meters) Boom Sheave Height: The crane's load capacity is 2,061 short tons (1,870 metric tons) when configured for Centerline.

5. At 320 feet (97.5 meters) Operating Radius and 486 feet (148.1 meters) Boom Sheave Height: The crane can lift up to 1,421 short tons (1,289 metric tons) when configured for Centerline.

These interpretations demonstrate how variations in operating radius and boom sheave height impact the crane's load capacity in Centerline configuration.

Note that, "configured for centreline" in the context of a crane load chart typically refers to the crane's configuration where the boom is extended directly out from the centreline of the crane's rotation. This means that the boom is not angled or offset to the side but is aligned straight with the centreline of the crane.

When a crane is configured for centreline, it often achieves its maximum load capacity because the load is being lifted in a direct line from the crane's centre of rotation. This configuration provides optimal stability and lifting capacity for the crane.

In the load chart data provided, the load capacities specified under the "Centerline" column represent the maximum loads that the crane can lift when configured in this manner, given the specific combinations of operating radius and boom sheave height.

Note also that weights are given as short ton. A short ton, also known simply as a "ton" in the United States, is a unit of weight or mass commonly used in the US customary system. It is equal to 2,000 pounds. This unit is distinct from the long ton used in the UK and the metric ton (tonne) used in most other parts of the world.

The short ton is primarily used in the United States for measuring weights of goods, materials, and commodities, particularly in industries such as shipping, agriculture, and manufacturing. It is important to distinguish between different ton units to avoid confusion, especially in international contexts where different systems of measurement are used.

Portal Boom Cranes

A portal boom crane, also known as a gantry crane or a portal crane, is a type of crane that is typically mounted on a framework with wheels or rails, allowing it to move along a fixed path or track. The distinctive feature of a portal boom crane is its horizontal boom or girder, which is supported by upright legs or columns on either side of the crane. This design provides stability and allows the crane to lift and move heavy loads with precision.

Portal boom cranes, as shown in Figure 50, are commonly used in industrial settings, construction sites, shipping ports, and warehouses for tasks such as loading and unloading cargo from ships or trucks, moving materials within a facility, and assembling large structures. They offer versatility in handling various types of loads and are capable of reaching high elevations and extending over long distances.

Figure 50: Portal Harbour Crane Ganz Quay 16 Tallin. Pjotr Mahhonin, CC BY-SA 3.0, via Wikimedia Commons.

The mobility of portal boom cranes makes them well-suited for applications where a fixed-position crane may not be practical or feasible. Additionally, some portal boom cranes are equipped with features such as adjustable height and outreach, hydraulic systems for smooth operation, and advanced controls for precise positioning of loads.

Portal cranes, also known as gantry cranes, come in various types, each designed for specific applications and environments. Here are some common types of portal cranes:

1. **Rail-Mounted Gantry Crane (RMG)**:

    - **Description**: RMGs are typically used in intermodal yards and container terminals. They run on rails installed at ground level or elevated on gantries.

    - **Features**: RMGs are highly automated and can be remotely operated. They feature a spreader beam for lifting containers and can stack containers vertically.

- **Advantages**: Efficient for handling containers in large storage yards. They offer high stacking capabilities and precise positioning.

2. **Rubber-Tyred Gantry Crane (RTG)**:

    - **Description**: RTGs are similar to RMGs but run on rubber tyres instead of rails. They are commonly used in container terminals.

    - **Features**: RTGs are mobile and flexible, allowing them to move easily around the terminal. They typically have a higher lifting capacity than RMGs.

    - **Advantages**: Versatility in navigating terminal layouts. They can move containers between stacks and onto trucks or railcars.

3. **Ship-to-Shore Gantry Crane (STS)**:

    - **Description**: STS cranes are massive cranes installed at seaports and used for loading and unloading containers from ships.

    - **Features**: STS cranes have a high lifting capacity and are designed to reach over the width of a ship's deck. They use a spreader beam to lift containers from the ship's hold.

    - **Advantages**: Efficient handling of containers directly from ships, minimizing turnaround time for vessels in port.

4. **Straddle Carrier**:

- **Description**: While not strictly a crane, straddle carriers are often included in discussions of portal cranes. They consist of a wheeled vehicle with legs that can straddle containers, lifting them and transporting them within a terminal.

- **Features**: Straddle carriers are highly mobile and can handle containers of various sizes. They are commonly used in container terminals and storage yards.

- **Advantages**: Flexibility in handling containers directly from storage stacks or transferring them between different modes of transport.

Each type of portal crane offers specific advantages and is tailored to meet the demands of different industries and operational requirements.

The typical gantry crane features an "A" frame design, although variations with L-shaped and U-shaped legs are also accessible. Regardless of whether they incorporate a single or double girder configuration, all gantry cranes are engineered to manage substantial loads over prolonged periods. It is precisely this capability that renders them the preferred choice for heavyweight lifting tasks.

Gantry cranes can be either single or double girder (see Figure 51arrangements. The key differences between single girder and double girder portal cranes include:

1. **Structure:**

    - **Single Girder:** Utilizes a single horizontal beam (girder) for supporting the hoist and trolley.

    - **Double Girder:** Features two horizontal beams (girders) for supporting the hoist and trolley.

2. **Load Capacity:**

- **Single Girder:** Typically suitable for lighter loads compared to double girder cranes.

- **Double Girder:** Offers higher load capacities due to the added strength and stability provided by the second girder.

3. **Height of Lift:**

- **Single Girder:** Generally has a lower height of lift compared to double girder cranes.

- **Double Girder:** Allows for greater height of lift, making it suitable for lifting loads to higher elevations.

4. **Cost and Maintenance:**

- **Single Girder:** Generally more cost-effective to purchase and maintain due to its simpler design.

- **Double Girder:** Tends to be more expensive both in terms of initial investment and ongoing maintenance requirements.

5. **Headroom and Hook Height:**

- **Single Girder:** Offers reduced headroom and hook height compared to double girder cranes.

- **Double Girder:** Provides increased headroom and hook height, making it suitable for lifting taller loads.

6. **Span and Working Area:**

- **Single Girder:** Suitable for applications where the span and working area are relatively smaller.

- **Double Girder:** Ideal for applications requiring a larger span and working area, providing greater coverage.

7. **Usage and Application:**

    - **Single Girder:** Commonly used in light to moderate industrial applications such as warehouses, workshops, and assembly lines.

    - **Double Girder:** Preferred for heavy-duty industrial applications such as shipyards, steel mills, and heavy manufacturing plants.

8. **Flexibility and Versatility:**

    - **Single Girder:** Offers sufficient flexibility for various lifting tasks within its capacity range.

    - **Double Girder:** Provides enhanced versatility and flexibility, capable of handling a wider range of loads and applications.

9. **Installation and Space Requirements:**

    - **Single Girder:** Typically requires less installation space compared to double girder cranes.

    - **Double Girder:** Requires more space for installation due to the larger structure and higher lifting capabilities.

These differences can influence the selection of the appropriate portal crane based on specific project requirements, budget constraints, and operational needs.

CRANE OPERATIONS

Figure 51: 100t Double Girder Gantry Crane. Alex.huang, CC BY-SA 4.0, via Wikimedia Commons.

The Rail-Mounted Gantry Crane (RMG), as shown in Figure 52, is a specialized crane extensively utilized in intermodal yards and container terminals to streamline container handling processes. Designed specifically for this purpose, RMGs offer several notable features and advantages:

RMGs are tailor-made for operation within intermodal yards and container terminals, where the efficient movement and stacking of shipping containers are paramount. These cranes are mounted on rails, either at ground level or elevated on gantries, facilitating horizontal traversal along designated tracks for container pickup and stacking. Equipped with a spreader beam, RMGs securely lift and position containers during loading and unloading operations, maximizing efficiency and safety. RMGs are engineered to vertically stack containers, optimizing storage space utilization within container yards and terminals.

Rail-Mounted: RMGs move horizontally along designated tracks within container terminals, enhancing operational flexibility and efficiency. Gantry Structure: Some RMGs operate on elevated gantries spanning multiple lanes of container stacks, allowing for versatile manoeuvring and stacking capabilities. Automation: Highly automated, RMGs can be remotely operated from control rooms, streamlining operations and improving overall efficiency. Spreader Beam: Fitted with a spreader beam, RMGs can lift and transport containers of various sizes and weights securely. Vertical Stacking: RMGs stack containers vertically, maximizing storage space and container density within terminals. Safety Features: Advanced safety features like collision avoidance systems and load monitoring sensors ensure safe and reliable crane operation.

Efficiency: RMGs excel in handling containers in large storage yards and terminals, reducing turnaround times and increasing overall productivity. High Stacking Capability: The ability to stack containers vertically maximizes storage space utilization and enhances operational efficiency. Precise Positioning: Automated operations ensure precise container positioning, minimizing damage risks and enhancing operational safety. Remote Operation: RMGs can be operated remotely from control rooms, allowing operators to monitor and control crane operations from a safe distance. Flexibility: Versatile in handling various container sizes and types, RMGs adapt to diverse shipping and logistics requirements.

CRANE OPERATIONS

Figure 52: RMG (Rail-mounted gantry) container crane (loading/unloading device), BNSF freight yard, Sodo, Seattle, Washington. Joe Mabel, CC BY-SA 3.0 <http://creativecommons.org/licenses/by-sa/3.0/>, via Wikimedia Commons.

Rail-Mounted Gantry Cranes (RMGs) are indispensable in efficiently managing container operations within intermodal yards and container terminals. With their advanced features and automation capabilities, RMGs offer substantial advantages in terms of efficiency, stacking capability, and operational safety.

Figure 53: Operator's Cabin on a Rail Mounted Gantry Crane. Bengt Oberger, CC BY-SA 4.0, via Wikimedia Commons.

Rubber-Tyred Gantry Cranes (RTGs) represent a specialized crane type extensively utilized in container terminals, providing enhanced mobility and flexibility for container handling operations. Let's delve into a comprehensive overview covering their description, features, and advantages:

RTGs share functional similarities with Rail-Mounted Gantry Cranes (RMGs) but diverge in their mobility mechanism. Instead of traversing on rails, RTGs are affixed atop rubber tyres, affording them the freedom to manoeuvre autonomously around the terminal. These cranes predominantly populate container terminals, where the seamless movement and strategic stacking of shipping containers are imperative for logistical efficiency. Equipped with a spreader beam akin to RMGs, RTGs facilitate the lifting and precise positioning of containers during loading and unloading procedures. Their architectural design permits the vertical stacking of containers, optimizing storage space allocation within the confines of the terminal yard.

Mobility: RTGs boast superior mobility and adaptability due to their rubber tyre configuration, enabling effortless navigation across diverse terminal layouts. This manoeuvrability significantly enhances container handling efficacy and placement within the terminal premises. Lifting Capacity: RTGs typically exhibit a heightened lifting capacity relative to RMGs, rendering them well-suited for managing bulkier containers and cargo loads. Spreader Beam: Similar to RMGs, RTGs come equipped with a spreader beam mechanism, facilitating the secure lifting and transportation of containers with varying dimensions and weights. Stacking Capability: RTGs excel in vertically stacking containers, thereby optimizing storage space utilization and augmenting operational efficiency within the terminal environment.

Figure 54: Rubber tyred gantry crane. Alf van Beem, CC0, via Wikimedia Commons.

Versatility: RTGs offer unparalleled versatility in traversing terminal configurations, facilitating seamless container movement between stacks and enabling effortless transfers onto trucks or railcars. Mobility: Leveraging the rubber tyre mechanism, RTGs enjoy unhindered mobility throughout the terminal precincts, enhancing operational flexibility in container handling endeavours and curtailing turnaround times. High Lifting Capacity: Possessing a robust lifting capacity, RTGs are adept at managing heavier containers and cargo loads, thereby enhancing operational efficiency and productivity levels. Efficient Container Handling: RTGs streamline container handling operations within container terminals, ensuring a fluid operational workflow and minimizing operational bottlenecks. Optimized Storage Space: By virtue of their ability to vertically stack containers, RTGs contribute to the maximization of storage space utilization within terminal yards, ultimately optimizing container density.

Rubber-Tyred Gantry Cranes (RTGs) play a pivotal role in container terminals by delivering enhanced mobility, adaptability, and efficiency in container handling operations. With their superior lifting capacity and unparalleled versatility in negotiating terminal layouts, RTGs emerge as indispensable assets for optimizing container logistics and elevating overall operational efficiency within container terminals.

Ship-to-Shore Gantry Cranes (STS) represent colossal crane structures strategically positioned at seaports, dedicated to the pivotal task of loading and unloading containers from maritime vessels. Let's delve into a detailed exploration of their description, features, and advantages:

CRANE OPERATIONS

Figure 55: Ship-to-shore cranes at the Davao International Container Terminal in Panabo City. ROBINSON NIÑAL/PPD, Public domain, via Wikimedia Commons.

STS cranes are imposing structures erected at seaport terminals, meticulously designed to facilitate the seamless transfer of containers between ships and terminal facilities. These immense cranes serve as the linchpin of port logistics, orchestrating the efficient movement of cargo containers from the expansive holds of maritime vessels to the shoreside storage areas. Characterized by their towering stature and formidable reach, STS cranes command attention as they loom over the maritime landscape, embodying the monumental scale of global trade and shipping operations. Equipped with sophisticated lifting mechanisms and advanced control systems, STS cranes epitomize the convergence of engineering ingenuity and logistical efficiency in the maritime domain.

High Lifting Capacity: STS cranes boast a prodigious lifting capacity, enabling them to effortlessly hoist containers of varying sizes and weights from the cavernous confines of cargo ships' holds. Extensive

Reach: Designed to extend over the width of a ship's deck, STS cranes possess an expansive reach that facilitates the swift and precise extraction of containers from vessels berthed at the port. Spreader Beam Utilization: STS cranes employ a specialized spreader beam mechanism to securely grasp and lift containers, ensuring safe and efficient handling throughout the loading and unloading process. Precision Control: Equipped with state-of-the-art control systems and automation technologies, STS cranes offer precise control over container movements, optimizing operational efficiency and minimizing turnaround times.

Efficient Container Handling: STS cranes streamline the process of loading and unloading containers directly from ships, significantly reducing the turnaround time for vessels berthed at the port. Minimized Dwell Time: By expediting the transfer of cargo between maritime vessels and terminal facilities, STS cranes contribute to the reduction of dwell time for ships in port, enhancing overall port throughput and efficiency. Enhanced Productivity: The deployment of STS cranes enhances the productivity and operational performance of seaport terminals, allowing for the expeditious handling of containerized cargo and facilitating seamless cargo flows within the global supply chain.

Ship-to-Shore Gantry Cranes (STS) stand as monumental structures at seaports, playing a pivotal role in the efficient transfer of containerized cargo between maritime vessels and terminal facilities. With their remarkable lifting capacity, extensive reach, and precision control capabilities, STS cranes epitomize the epitome of efficiency and effectiveness in modern port operations, facilitating the seamless flow of goods across international borders and fostering global trade and commerce.

Straddle Carriers, although not categorized strictly as cranes, are integral components often associated with discussions involving portal cranes. Here's an in-depth exploration of their description, features, and advantages:

CRANE OPERATIONS

Figure 56: SISU Valmet 44011 Straddle carrier container mover. Alf van Beem, CC0, via Wikimedia Commons.

Straddle carriers are specialized wheeled vehicles uniquely designed for the handling and transportation of containers within terminal facilities, such as container terminals and storage yards. Distinguished by their distinctive configuration, straddle carriers feature a set of legs that can straddle containers, enabling them to securely lift and transport these containers with precision and efficiency. Unlike conventional cranes, straddle carriers operate at ground level, utilizing their manoeuvrability and lifting capabilities to facilitate the seamless movement of containers within the terminal environment. These versatile vehicles are commonly employed in port facilities, where the efficient handling and transfer of containers between storage stacks and various modes of transportation are essential for optimizing terminal operations.

High Mobility: Straddle carriers are highly mobile, equipped with robust wheeled mechanisms that enable them to traverse terminal environments with agility and ease. Their mobility allows for efficient container handling across expansive terminal facilities. Versatile Container Handling: Straddle carriers are designed to handle containers of various sizes and dimensions, offering versatility in accommodating different types of cargo units commonly encountered in maritime and intermodal operations. Ground-Level Operation: Operating at ground level, straddle carriers eliminate the need for elevated structures or tracks, providing a cost-effective solution for container handling within terminal facilities. This ground-level operation enhances operational flexibility and simplifies maintenance requirements. Precise Lifting and Positioning: Equipped with sophisticated lifting mechanisms and control systems, straddle carriers offer precise control over container movements, ensuring accurate positioning during loading, unloading, and transportation operations.

CRANE OPERATIONS

Figure 57: Straddle carrier. Matti Blume, CC BY-SA 4.0, via Wikimedia Commons.

Flexibility: Straddle carriers offer unparalleled flexibility in container handling operations, capable of lifting containers directly from storage stacks or transferring them between different modes of transportation, such as ships, trucks, and railcars. Efficient Terminal Operations: By streamlining container handling processes within terminal facilities, straddle carriers contribute to the optimization of terminal operations, reducing turnaround times and enhancing overall operational efficiency. Cost-Effective Solution: The ground-level operation of straddle carriers eliminates the need for costly infrastructure investments, such as elevated cranes or rail-mounted systems, offering a cost-effective solution for container handling in port and terminal environments. Enhanced Safety: Straddle carriers are designed with safety features to mitigate the risk of accidents and injuries during container handling operations. These safety features include collision avoidance systems, load monitoring sensors, and ergonomic operator controls.

Straddle Carriers play a vital role in modern port and terminal operations, providing a versatile and cost-effective solution for container handling and transportation. With their high mobility, versatility, and efficiency, straddle carriers contribute to the seamless flow of cargo within terminal facilities, enhancing operational productivity and facilitating global trade and commerce.

Portal Crane Operation

A portal crane, also known as a gantry crane, is a type of crane commonly used in industrial settings, such as ports, shipyards, and construction sites, for lifting and moving heavy loads over a relatively short distance. It consists of a horizontal bridge or gantry that runs along rails mounted on the ground or elevated beams, with a lifting mechanism (such as a hoist or winch) suspended from the gantry. Here's a detailed explanation of how a portal crane works:

1. **Structure**: A portal crane typically consists of the following components:

    - **Gantry**: This is the horizontal structure that spans the area where the crane operates. It is usually supported by vertical legs at either end and can move along rails or tracks laid on the ground or on elevated beams.

- **Trolley**: The trolley is a mechanism that runs along the length of the gantry. It carries the lifting mechanism and moves horizontally, allowing the crane to position the load precisely.

- **Lifting Mechanism**: This includes the hoist or winch, which is mounted on the trolley and is responsible for raising and lowering the load.

2. **Power Source**: Portal cranes are typically powered by electricity. The motors that drive the movement of the gantry and the lifting mechanism are usually electrically powered. In some cases, diesel engines may be used for outdoor applications where electricity is not readily available.

3. **Control System**: Portal cranes are controlled by operators who use a control panel or pendant attached to the crane. The control system allows the operator to move the gantry along the rails, move the trolley along the gantry, and raise or lower the load with precision.

4. **Operation**:

    - **Positioning**: To begin lifting a load, the operator positions the gantry crane so that the trolley is directly above the load.

    - **Lowering the Hook**: The operator uses the control system to lower the hook or attachment of the lifting mechanism until it reaches the load.

    - **Attaching the Load**: Once the hook is positioned above the load, it is attached securely using rigging equipment such as slings or chains.

    - **Lifting**: The operator then uses the control system to activate the lifting mechanism, which raises the load off the ground.

- **Horizontal Movement**: If needed, the operator can move the trolley along the length of the gantry to position the load over its desired destination.

- **Lowering**: Once the load is in the desired location, the operator lowers it carefully using the lifting mechanism until it reaches the ground or the designated storage area.

- **Release**: Finally, the load is released from the hook, and the crane is ready for the next operation.

5. **Safety Features**: Portal cranes are equipped with various safety features to prevent accidents and ensure the safe operation of the equipment. These may include overload protection systems, emergency stop buttons, limit switches to prevent collisions, and warning signals such as lights or alarms.

Figure 58: Portal crane components. Back image Jurgen from Netherlands, CC BY 2.0, via Wikimedia Commons

Planning for Work with a Portal Boom Crane

Operating a portal boom crane safely involves a systematic approach that includes planning, inspection, and adherence to safety protocols. Here's how to address each of the specified tasks in a safe and efficient manner:

1. Task Requirements and Lift Plan Confirmation

- **Work Orders Review:** Begin by carefully reviewing the work orders or equivalent documents to understand the specifics of the task at hand, including the type and weight of the load, destination, and any special handling instructions.

- **Lift Plan Confirmation:** Consult with associated personnel, such as riggers, site supervisors, and safety officers, to confirm the lift plan. This plan should detail the lifting process, including the path of the load, any obstructions, and coordination with other site activities.

- **Site Inspection:** Conduct a thorough site inspection to identify any potential hazards or obstacles in the crane's operating area and along the load's path. Check for overhead obstructions, ground conditions, and proximity to power lines.

2. Work Area and Ground Suitability

- **Surface Inspection:** Confirm that the operating surface is stable, level, and capable of supporting the crane's weight, especially when it is carrying loads. Look for soft ground, potholes, or other conditions that could compromise stability.

3. Crane and Lifting Gear Capacity

- **Rated Capacity (RC) Check:** Verify the portal boom crane's Rated Capacity for the specific lift configuration you'll be using. This involves checking the crane's load charts, which provide the maximum load it can safely lift at various boom angles, lengths, and radii.

- **Working Load Limit (WLL) Assessment:** Ensure that all lifting gear, such as slings, shackles, and hooks, have a Working Load Limit that is appropriate for the load's weight. The WLL should be clearly marked on the equipment and must not be exceeded.

4. Path Assessment for Crane Operation and Load Movement
   - Path Planning: Assess the entire path the crane and the load will take during the operation. Identify the safest and most efficient route, considering the load's dimensions and weight, crane mobility, and site constraints.

5. Hazard Identification and Risk Management
   - Hazard Identification: Identify potential hazards associated with the lift, including wind conditions, the potential for load swing, and personnel working nearby.

   - Risk Elimination/Control: Implement control measures to mitigate identified risks, such as using tag lines to control the load, establishing exclusion zones, and ensuring all personnel are aware of the crane's movements.

6. Traffic Management Plan
   - Plan Implementation: Confirm that a traffic management plan is in place and followed, particularly in areas where the crane's operation may intersect with vehicles or pedestrian traffic. This may include signage, barricades, and designated spotters.

7. Communication Procedures
   - Communication Identification: Determine the communication methods to be used during the operation, such as two-way radios, hand signals, or air horns. Ensure all involved personnel understand and are proficient in these communication methods.

   - Testing: Test communication devices and methods before commencing the lift to ensure clarity and reliability.

8. Task Confirmation
   - Final Check: Before starting the operation, confirm that all preparations align with the lift plan and workplace procedures.

Ensure all personnel are briefed and understand their roles.

9. Lifting Equipment and Gear Compliance
- Inspection and Compliance: Ensure that lifting equipment and gear are regularly inspected and maintained in accordance with the manufacturer's recommendations and workplace procedures. Keep records of these inspections.
- Storage: Properly store all lifting gear when not in use to prevent damage and ensure its readiness for the next operation.

By methodically addressing each of these aspects, you can ensure the safe and effective operation of a portal boom crane, protecting personnel, the load, and the crane itself from potential hazards.

Path planning for the operation of a portal boom crane is a meticulous process that ensures the safety, efficiency, and minimal disruption of site operations as the crane and its load move from the starting point to the destination. The first step involves a thorough analysis of the load, including its dimensions, weight, and nature, which significantly influences the crane setup and the chosen path. Concurrently, the crane's specifications such as its maximum reach, height, load capacity, mobility, and turning radius are reviewed to understand its operational capabilities.

A detailed site inspection is essential to identify potential obstacles like buildings, overhead lines, and uneven terrain, ensuring that the ground conditions can support the crane and the load. Creating a detailed map of the site, marking all relevant features and obstacles, aids significantly in planning the crane's path and load movement. The initial route is selected based on this map, taking into account the most direct path, potential obstacles, and the need for safety margins to account for overhead hazards and load swing.

Managing obstacles is a critical step, with plans to temporarily remove or alter obstructions and a keen focus on avoiding overhead hazards by maintaining a safe distance. Assessing and possibly stabilizing ground conditions, especially if the crane will travel with the load, are vital to prevent any risk of collapse or the crane becoming bogged down.

Coordination with other site activities is crucial to minimize disruption and ensure the safety of all personnel. Establishing exclusion zones prevents unauthorized access during the operation. Effective communication and signage are essential to warn of the crane operation, especially where the path intersects with other work areas. A dry run, if feasible, can identify any unforeseen obstacles or challenges, ensuring the crane can navigate the planned path without issues.

Finally, a final review and adjustments are made based on observations from the dry run and any new site conditions, culminating in obtaining final approval from a qualified supervisor or site safety officer. This methodical approach to path planning for both the crane and the load mitigates risks, enhances operational efficiency, and safeguards the operation and all involved personnel.

To ensure the safe operation of a portal boom crane, it's crucial to conduct a Rated Capacity (RC) Check and a Working Load Limit (WLL) Assessment. These procedures are fundamental to determining the crane's lifting capabilities and the safety of the lifting gear involved in the operation.

The Rated Capacity Check involves verifying the portal boom crane's ability to lift a specified load safely, considering the specific configuration you plan to use. This check is essential because the crane's lifting capacity can vary significantly depending on factors such as the boom length, the angle of the lift, and the radius of operation. To perform this check, you must consult the crane's load charts, which are typically provided by the manufacturer. These charts detail the maximum load the crane can safely lift under various conditions and configurations. It's important to carefully review these charts and ensure that the planned lift falls within the crane's safe operating parameters. Factors such as the weight of the load, the height to which it needs to be lifted, and the distance from the crane's centre must all be considered to ensure the operation does not exceed the crane's rated capacity.

The Working Load Limit (WLL) Assessment is equally critical and focuses on the lifting gear that will be used with the crane, such as slings, shackles, and hooks. Each piece of lifting gear has a specified WLL, which is the maximum load that it can safely support. This limit is determined by the manufacturer based on the strength of the material, the design of the equipment, and safety factors. To ensure a safe lifting operation, it's imperative to verify that the WLL of each piece of lifting gear is greater than the weight of the load being lifted. The WLL should be clearly marked on each piece of equipment. If it's not visible or legible, the equipment should not be used until it has been properly inspected and re-marked by a competent person. Exceeding the WLL can result in equipment failure, posing serious risks to both personnel and the load.

Conducting a thorough RC Check and WLL Assessment before any lifting operation is essential for ensuring the safety and success of the operation. These checks help prevent overloading the crane and the lifting gear, minimizing the risk of accidents and equipment damage. Always adhere to the manufacturer's guidelines and workplace safety standards when performing these assessments.

Preparing for Portal Boom Crane Operations

Operating a portal boom crane safely involves a comprehensive process that ensures the safety of personnel, the crane, and the load being handled. This includes:
1. Consultation with Workplace Personnel
    - Establish and maintain clear communication with all workplace

personnel involved in crane operations. This ensures that crane activities are consistent with site requirements and the lift plan. Regular meetings and briefings can be used to discuss and align on the lift plan and any changes in site conditions or requirements.

2. Risk Control Measures
   - After identifying potential hazards, ensure that risk control measures outlined in the lift plan and safe work procedures are in place and effective. Regular checks should be performed to verify the implementation and effectiveness of these measures.

3. Safe Access to Crane
   - Access the portal boom crane safely, following manufacturer guidelines and workplace safety procedures. This may include using designated access points, wearing appropriate personal protective equipment (PPE), and adhering to any specific entry protocols.

4. Pre-start Checks
   - Perform thorough pre-start checks of the crane to identify any damage or defects. This should include visual inspections and functional tests as per the manufacturer's checklist. Any issues should be immediately reported, recorded, and addressed following legislative requirements and manufacturer guidelines.

5. Crane Setup
   - Set up the crane and any lifting gear according to the lift plan, ensuring compliance with manufacturer requirements and safe work procedures. This includes verifying the crane's configuration against the lift plan and ensuring the correct setup of boom/jib and lifting gear.

6. Rigging and Lifting Gear Setup
   - Rig the boom/jib and lifting gear as required, adhering to specific manufacturer requirements and safe work procedures. Ensure that all components are correctly configured and secured for the planned lift.

7. Operational Checks
   - Conduct operational checks to ensure the crane is functioning correctly. Report and record any damage or defects found during these checks, and take appropriate action to address them before proceeding with crane operations.

8. Crane Logbook Inspection
   - Check the crane's logbook to confirm it is up to date and compliant with manufacturer requirements and safe work procedures. The logbook should be correctly completed and signed, with all required rectifications signed off.

9. Weather and Environmental Conditions Assessment
   - Assess weather and work environment conditions to determine their impact on crane operations. Adjust operations as needed to ensure safety in changing conditions, in line with manufacturer guidelines and safe work procedures.

10. Load Weight Confirmation
    - Confirm the weight of the load to ensure it is within the crane's lifting capacity and the operation complies with the lift plan.

11. Derated WLL Calculation
    - Calculate the derated Working Load Limit (WLL) of the lifting equipment, considering the slinging techniques to be used. Confirm that the derated WLL is suitable for the requirements of the lift plan.

12. Identification of Lifting Points and Slinging Techniques
    - Identify suitable lifting points and slinging techniques for the load, ensuring they are appropriate for the load's size, shape, and weight, and comply with the lift plan.

13. Lifting Equipment and Gear Readiness
    - Confirm that all lifting equipment and gear are in good condition and ready for safe use. This includes checking for wear, damage, and compliance with safety standards.

14. Load Destination Stability
    - Ensure the stability of the load destination, confirming that it can bear the load's weight and is prepared for safe access and landing of the load.

Portal crane operations, including Rail-Mounted Gantry Crane (RMGC), Rubber-Tyred Gantry Crane (RTGC), Ship-to-Shore Gantry Crane (STSG), and Straddle Carrier, pose various hazards to personnel, equipment, and the environment. Understanding these hazards is essential for implementing appropriate safety measures. Here are potential hazards associated with each type of portal crane:

1. **Rail-Mounted Gantry Crane (RMGC):**

    - **Rail Accidents**: RMGCs operate on rails, increasing the risk of accidents such as derailments, collisions, or malfunctions due to improper track alignment or defects.

    - **Electrical Hazards**: Electrically powered RMGCs pose a risk of electrical shock or fires if there are exposed wires, damaged cables, or improper grounding.

    - **Falling Objects**: Loads being lifted or moved by the RMGC may become unstable, leading to falling objects that can injure personnel or damage equipment.

- **Overhead Hazards**: Working underneath the crane's gantry poses a risk of being struck by moving parts, counterweights, or materials accidentally dropped from overhead.

2. **Rubber-Tyred Gantry Crane (RTGC)**:

    - **Collision Risks**: RTGCs manoeuvre in tight spaces, increasing the risk of collisions with other cranes, containers, or vehicles operating in the same area.

    - **Tipping Hazard**: RTGCs may tip over if they are operated on uneven ground or if loads are improperly distributed, leading to serious injuries or damage.

    - **Crushing Hazards**: Workers may be caught between moving parts of the crane, such as the spreader and the container, resulting in crushing injuries.

    - **Visibility Challenges**: Limited visibility from the operator's cab can lead to blind spots, increasing the risk of accidents involving pedestrians or other equipment in the vicinity.

3. **Ship-to-Shore Gantry Crane (STSG)**:

    - **Pinch Points**: STSGs have numerous pinch points where personnel or objects can become trapped between moving parts, such as the crane trolley and the rails or the crane boom and the ship's structure.

    - **Toppling Risks**: STSGs operate at significant heights, making them susceptible to toppling over in high winds or if load weights are miscalculated.

    - **Entanglement Hazards**: Workers may be at risk of entanglement in wires, ropes, or rigging used for lifting and securing loads during crane operation.

- **Container Movement**: Moving containers on and off ships with STSGs involves precise coordination and control to avoid accidents such as dropped containers or collisions with the ship's structure.

4. **Straddle Carrier**:

- **Overturning**: Straddle carriers can overturn if operated on uneven or unstable ground or if loads are improperly secured or positioned, posing a risk of injury or equipment damage.

- **Crush Injuries**: Workers may be at risk of crush injuries if caught between the straddle carrier and stationary objects, such as containers, racks, or other equipment.

- **Falling Objects**: Loads being lifted or moved by the straddle carrier may become unstable, leading to falling objects that can injure personnel or damage equipment.

- **Visibility Issues**: Limited visibility from the operator's cab can result in blind spots, increasing the risk of accidents involving pedestrians, vehicles, or other equipment in the vicinity.

Mitigating these hazards requires comprehensive risk assessments, proper training for personnel, adherence to safety procedures, regular equipment inspections and maintenance, and effective communication among all parties involved in portal crane operations.

After identifying potential hazard, it's crucial to implement effective risk control measures outlined in the lift plan and safe work procedures. Thoroughly reviewing the lift plan and safe work procedures developed for each specific crane operation is essential. This ensures that all potential hazards identified during the risk assessment process are addressed in the lift plan, and appropriate control measures are outlined.

Implementing control measures based on the identified hazards is paramount to mitigate risks. This may include establishing exclusion zones or restricted areas to prevent unauthorized personnel from entering hazardous areas, providing barriers, warning signs, or safety nets to prevent falls or keep personnel away from moving parts, installing safety interlocks or emergency stop systems to quickly halt crane operations in case of emergencies, conducting thorough inspections of equipment, including cranes and lifting accessories, to ensure they are in good working condition, and providing adequate training to personnel on safe work practices, crane operation procedures, and emergency response protocols.

Conducting regular checks and inspections is crucial to verify the implementation and effectiveness of the control measures. This includes performing daily pre-operational checks of the crane and its components to ensure they are functioning correctly, inspecting lifting accessories, such as slings, shackles, and hooks, for signs of wear, damage, or deformation, reviewing the condition of safety devices, such as limit switches, overload protection systems, and emergency stop buttons, to ensure they are operational, and conducting periodic audits or safety assessments to evaluate compliance with safe work procedures and identify areas for improvement.

Maintaining comprehensive documentation and records of risk assessments, lift plans, safe work procedures, inspection reports, and training records is essential. This information should be readily accessible to relevant personnel and authorities for reference and review. Continuous monitoring and evaluation of the effectiveness of risk control measures and safe work procedures are necessary for ongoing safety improvement. Soliciting feedback from crane operators, maintenance personnel, and other stakeholders helps identify areas for improvement and implement corrective actions as necessary.

Safely accessing a portal crane for operation involves a series of specific procedures aimed at ensuring the safety of personnel and the effective functioning of the crane. First, it's essential to review the site-specific safety procedures and protocols outlined in the company's safety manual or workplace guidelines. Understanding potential hazards associated with crane operation and the necessary precautions to mitigate risks is crucial.

Before accessing the crane, personnel must don appropriate personal protective equipment (PPE) as required by workplace regulations. This may include items such as hard hats, safety vests, steel-toed boots, gloves, and eye protection. Ensuring that clothing fits properly and isn't loose or baggy, which could pose a risk of entanglement in moving parts, is essential.

Approaching the portal crane cautiously is paramount. Personnel should maintain a safe distance from any moving parts or potential hazards and utilize designated walkways or pathways, if available. It's crucial to avoid walking under suspended loads or in areas where visibility may be limited.

A thorough inspection of the surrounding area should be conducted before climbing onto the crane. This includes checking for hazards, obstacles, or obstructions that may pose a risk during operation. Ensuring that the crane is on stable ground and that there are no loose materials or debris nearby is vital for safe access.

Access to the crane may be provided via platforms, stairs, or ladders attached to the structure, depending on its design. Personnel should utilize these access points, maintaining three points of contact at all times while ascending to ensure stability and prevent falls. If handholds or guardrails are provided on the crane structure, they should be utilized to maintain stability and prevent falls.

If accessing the crane at height, such as climbing a ladder or platform, fall protection equipment such as harnesses and lanyards must be properly worn and secured according to manufacturer instructions and workplace policies.

Once safely positioned on the crane, a brief inspection should be performed to ensure that all necessary controls, instruments, and safety features are in working order. Communication systems should be tested to ensure proper functioning, and emergency stop mechanisms should be easily accessible.

If operating the crane as part of a team, communication with other personnel is crucial. Confirming roles, responsibilities, and safety procedures ensures that all team members are aware of their tasks and are positioned safely before initiating crane operation.

Following these steps carefully and adhering to workplace safety guidelines ensures safe access to a portal crane for operation, minimizing the risk of accidents or injuries. Prioritizing safety and remaining vigilant throughout the entire operation is paramount.

Performing thorough pre-start checks is essential for ensuring the safety and operational efficiency of various types of gantry cranes and straddle carriers. These checks help identify any potential damage or defects that could compromise the equipment's performance or pose safety risks. Below are detailed guidelines for pre-start inspections tailored to Rail-Mounted Gantry Cranes (RMG), Rubber-Tyred Gantry Cranes (RTG), Ship-to-Shore Gantry Cranes (STS), and Straddle Carriers.

Rail-Mounted Gantry Crane (RMG)
1. Visual Inspection:

- Inspect the crane structure for any visible signs of wear, cracks, or corrosion, particularly in the legs, main girder, and support beams.

- Check the rail tracks for alignment, wear, and obstructions.
- Examine all wires, ropes, and pulleys for fraying, kinking, or other damage.

2. Functional Tests:

- Test the movement of the crane along the rails to ensure smooth operation.
- Operate the trolley and hoist to check for any unusual noises or vibrations.
- Verify the functionality of safety devices, including overload indicators, limit switches, and emergency stop mechanisms.

3. Electrical and Control Systems:

- Check all electrical connections and wiring for signs of wear or damage.
- Test control systems and operator interfaces for responsiveness and accuracy.

Rubber-Tyred Gantry Crane (RTG)

1. Visual Inspection:

- Inspect the tyres for wear, damage, and proper inflation.
- Examine the gantry structure for structural integrity, focusing on welds, joints, and any signs of deformation.
- Check lifting devices, including spreader bars, for proper attachment and condition.

2. Functional Tests:

- Test the crane's mobility by driving it a short distance, paying attention to steering, braking, and stability.
- Operate the lifting mechanism to ensure smooth and responsive movement.
- Test all safety systems, including anti-collision devices and emergency stops.

3. Power Systems:

- For diesel-powered RTGs, check engine levels (oil, coolant, fuel) and inspect for leaks.
- For electric RTGs, inspect the power cable reel, connectors, and battery condition.

Ship-to-Shore Gantry Crane (STS)

1. Visual Inspection:

- Check the boom and spreader for any signs of damage or wear, especially in high-stress areas.
- Inspect the wires and ropes for integrity, and ensure the pulleys are free of obstructions.
- Examine the crane's legs and feet for stability and any signs of settling or movement.

2. Functional Tests:

- Conduct a test lift to assess the crane's lifting performance and responsiveness.
- Test the boom's movement, including raising, lowering, and telescoping functions, if applicable.

- Ensure that all operator controls are functioning correctly and that safety systems, such as load moment indicators, are operational.

3. Electrical and Hydraulic Systems:

    - Inspect electrical panels and hydraulic systems for leaks or signs of wear.

    - Check hydraulic fluid levels and the condition of hoses and fittings.

Straddle Carrier

1. Visual Inspection:

    - Inspect the frame and lifting mechanism for structural integrity.

    - Check the wheels and tyres for condition and pressure.

    - Examine all hydraulic and mechanical lifting components for signs of wear or leaks.

2. Functional Tests:

    - Drive the straddle carrier to assess engine performance, steering, and braking.

    - Test the lifting operation, including the alignment and locking mechanisms of the spreader.

    - Verify the effectiveness of safety features, such as warning alarms and visibility aids (lights, cameras).

For all equipment types:

- Documentation: Review and update the maintenance and inspection log, noting any findings from the pre-start checks.

- Reporting: Any issues identified during the pre-start checks should be immediately reported to the relevant authority within the organization, following established reporting protocols.

- Addressing Issues: Do not operate the equipment until all identified issues have been adequately addressed and rectified in accordance with legislative requirements and manufacturer guidelines.

Calculating the derated Working Load Limit (WLL) of lifting equipment is a crucial step in ensuring the safety and efficiency of lifting operations. The WLL is the maximum load that the lifting equipment can safely handle under normal conditions. However, various factors, such as the angle of the sling, the type of hitch (way the sling is applied to the load), and environmental conditions, can affect this limit. The process of adjusting the WLL to account for these factors is known as derating. Here's how to perform a derated WLL calculation:

1. Understand the Standard WLL
    - Start by identifying the standard WLL for each piece of lifting equipment you plan to use, as specified by the manufacturer. This information is typically found on the equipment's identification tag or in the manufacturer's documentation.

2. Identify Slinging Techniques and Angles
    - Determine the slinging technique(s) you will use, such as straight lift, basket hitch, choker hitch, or any combination thereof. Each technique has a different impact on the WLL.

    - Measure or calculate the angle(s) between the sling legs and the horizontal plane, especially in configurations where multiple slings are used. The greater the angle (away from vertical), the more the WLL is reduced.

3. Consult Manufacturer's Derating Tables
   - Most manufacturers provide tables or charts that show how the WLL should be derated for different angles and slinging techniques. These tables account for the increased stress and decreased lifting capacity caused by various angles and configurations.

4. Apply Derating Factors
   - Use the information from the manufacturer's derating tables to apply the appropriate derating factor to the standard WLL based on the sling angles and techniques you're using. For example, a sling used at a 60-degree angle from the horizontal may have a derating factor of 0.87, meaning its effective WLL is 87% of its standard WLL.

5. Consider Environmental Factors
   - If applicable, consider additional derating factors that may be necessary due to environmental conditions, such as extreme temperatures, which can affect the strength and reliability of lifting gear.

6. Calculate Derated WLL
   - Multiply the standard WLL by the derating factor(s) to get the derated WLL. If multiple factors apply, multiply the standard WLL by each factor sequentially.

7. Confirm Suitability for Lift Plan
   - Once you have calculated the derated WLL, confirm that it is suitable for the requirements of the lift plan. The derated WLL must be greater than the total weight of the load, including any rigging or attachments, to ensure safe lifting.

Example Calculation

Suppose you have a sling with a standard WLL of 1000 kg, and you plan to use it in a basket hitch at a 45-degree angle. The manufacturer's table indicates a derating factor of 0.8 for a 45-degree angle in a basket hitch. The derated WLL would be calculated as follows:

Derated WLL = Standard WLL × Derating Factor

Derated WLL = 1000kg × 0.8 = 800kg

This means the sling, when used in a basket hitch at a 45-degree angle, can safely support a load of up to 800 kg. Ensure this derated capacity meets or exceeds the weight of the load specified in the lift plan.

By carefully performing derated WLL calculations and ensuring they align with the lift plan's requirements, you can maintain the safety and integrity of lifting operations.

Once checks have been made and the plant is ready to be started, the operator should follow manufacturer's starting processes and workplace policies and procedures. As a guide, the following provides an overview of the starting sequence for each type of crane and straddle carrier:

Rail-Mounted Gantry Crane (RMGC):

1. Conduct a pre-operational inspection of the crane, including checking for any signs of damage, leaks, or malfunctions.

2. Ensure that the crane is positioned correctly on the rails and that the track alignment is proper.

3. Activate the power source and control systems of the crane.

4. Test the movement of the crane along the rails to ensure smooth operation.

5. Verify that all safety features, such as emergency stop buttons and limit switches, are functional.

6. Communicate with other personnel to confirm readiness for operation.

7. Begin crane operation according to the lift plan, taking into account load weight, position, and destination.

Rubber-Tyred Gantry Crane (RTGC):

1. Perform a visual inspection of the crane, checking for any visible damage or abnormalities.

2. Ensure that the RTGC is parked on stable ground and that the wheels are properly aligned.

3. Start the engine or power source of the RTGC.

4. Activate the control systems and test the movement of the crane, including driving, steering, and lifting functions.

5. Check that all safety devices, such as alarms and lights, are operational.

6. Coordinate with other personnel to confirm clearance and safety measures.

7. Commence crane operation in accordance with the lift plan, ensuring proper load handling and movement.

Ship-to-Shore Gantry Crane (STSG):

1. Conduct a pre-operational inspection of the crane, focusing on structural integrity, lifting mechanisms, and safety features.

2. Ensure that the STSG is properly positioned alongside the vessel, with sufficient clearance and stability.

3. Power up the crane's systems, including the main motors and control panels.

4. Test the movement of the crane along the rails or tracks, ensuring smooth and precise operation.

5. Verify the functionality of safety devices, such as load sensors and collision avoidance systems.

6. Coordinate with ship personnel to confirm readiness for cargo handling operations.

7. Initiate crane operation as per the lift plan, maintaining close communication with ship crew and ground personnel.

Straddle Carrier:
1. Perform a visual inspection of the straddle carrier, checking for any visible damage or leaks.

2. Ensure that the straddle carrier is parked on stable ground and that the wheels are properly aligned.

3. Start the engine or power source of the straddle carrier.

4. Activate the control systems and test the movement of the carrier, including driving, steering, and lifting functions.

5. Check that all safety features, such as alarms and emergency stop buttons, are operational.

6. Coordinate with other personnel to confirm clearance and safety measures around the carrier.

7. Begin carrier operation according to the lift plan, ensuring proper load handling and movement.

Each starting sequence should be tailored to the specific requirements and operational procedures of the crane or straddle carrier, ensuring safety and efficiency throughout the lifting and handling process.

Conducting operational checks on a portal crane is essential to ensure that it is functioning correctly and safe for operation. Here's how to perform these checks and address any issues found:

1. **Pre-Operational Inspection:**

    - Before starting any crane operations, conduct a pre-operational inspection of the crane. This inspection should be thorough and cover all critical components of the crane, including the structure, lifting mechanisms, electrical systems, and safety features.

    - Begin by visually inspecting the crane's structure for signs of damage, corrosion, or wear. Check for any loose or missing bolts, welds, or components.

    - Inspect the lifting mechanisms, including the hoist, trolley, and spreader, for proper functioning. Look for any signs of wear or damage to ropes, chains, hooks, or attachments.

    - Check the electrical systems of the crane, including control panels, switches, and cables, to ensure they are in good condition and properly connected.

    - Verify the functionality of safety features such as limit switches, overload protection systems, emergency stop buttons, and audible alarms. Test each safety device to ensure it activates as intended.

2. **Functional Testing:**

    - After completing the visual inspection, conduct functional testing of the crane's movements and operations.

    - Test the crane's movements, including hoisting, lowering, trolley travel, and gantry travel. Ensure that each movement is smooth, controlled, and without unusual noises or vibrations.

- Test the load-lifting capacity of the crane by lifting a test load to the maximum capacity specified by the manufacturer. Observe the crane's performance and verify that it can lift and lower the load safely and without strain.

- Test the emergency stop system by activating the emergency stop button and verifying that all crane movements come to an immediate halt.

3. **Reporting and Recording Defects**:

    - If any damage or defects are found during the operational checks, immediately report them to the appropriate personnel, such as a supervisor or maintenance technician.

    - Use a standardized reporting form or checklist to document the details of the damage or defect, including its location, nature, and severity.

    - Record the date and time of the inspection, as well as the name of the person conducting the inspection.

    - Take photographs of the damage or defect if possible, as visual documentation can help communicate the issue more effectively.

4. **Taking Appropriate Action**:

    - Once defects are reported and recorded, take appropriate action to address them before proceeding with crane operations.

    - Depending on the nature and severity of the defect, this

may involve temporarily suspending crane operations until repairs can be made, or implementing alternative safety measures to mitigate the risk.

- Notify relevant personnel, such as maintenance technicians or safety officers, to schedule repairs and ensure that the crane is returned to a safe and operational condition as soon as possible.

Portal Crane Load Charts

Reading a portal crane's load chart is crucial for safe and efficient crane operation. The load chart provides vital information on the crane's lifting capacity under various conditions and configurations. Here's a step-by-step guide on how to interpret these charts:

1. Identify the Chart
    - Ensure you're looking at the correct load chart for the specific model and configuration of the portal crane you're operating. Cranes can have multiple load charts based on different configurations, such as with different boom lengths, jib attachments, or counterweights.

2. Understand the Units
    - Load charts typically use specific units of measurement, such as tons or kilograms for weight and feet or meters for length. Ensure you understand the units used in the chart to avoid any confusion.

3. Analyse the Configuration
    - The load chart may start with a diagram or description of the crane's configuration, including boom length, jib length (if ap-

plicable), counterweights, and other relevant setup details. Ensure your crane's setup matches the configuration described in the load chart.

4. Lifting Capacity
   - The main part of the load chart lists the crane's lifting capacities. This is usually presented in a table or grid format, showing how the maximum safe lifting capacity varies with the boom length, boom angle, and radius (the horizontal distance from the crane's centre to the load).

5. Boom Length and Angle
   - Locate the column or section of the chart that corresponds to the desired or current boom length. Alongside or within this section, there should be information about the boom angle or height, which also affects lifting capacity.

6. Radius
   - The radius is crucial in determining the lifting capacity. Find the row or column that corresponds to the radius at which you plan to lift the load. The intersection of the boom length and radius will give you the maximum lifting capacity for those specific conditions.

7. Deductions for Attachments
   - If the crane uses any attachments, like a fly jib or special hooks, the load chart might include deductions for these. These deductions must be subtracted from the gross capacity to get the net capacity available for lifting the load.

8. Wind Speed and Other Environmental Factors
   - Some load charts include adjustments for wind speed and other environmental conditions. Be aware of these factors, as they can

significantly reduce the safe lifting capacity.

9. Safety Margins
   - Keep in mind that the values on the load chart are maximum capacities. It's good practice to operate well within these limits to account for unforeseen factors and to maintain a safety margin.

10. Notes and Warnings
    - Pay close attention to any notes, warnings, or symbols on the load chart. These may provide critical information on operational limits, safety precautions, or specific conditions under which the listed capacities are valid.

Example of Reading a Load Chart:

Suppose you need to lift a load with a weight of 10 tons using a portal crane. The load is located 20 meters away from the crane's centre (radius), and you plan to use a boom length of 30 meters.

1. Look for the section of the load chart that corresponds to a 30-meter boom length.

2. Find the row that corresponds to a 20-meter radius.

3. The intersection of these two will give you the maximum lifting capacity for that boom length and radius. Ensure this capacity is equal to or greater than the weight of your load (10 tons in this example).

A portal crane load chart is a critical tool used in the operation of portal cranes, providing the operator with essential information on the crane's lifting capacity at various boom lengths and angles. Below is a simplified example of what a sample portal crane load chart might look like. Please note that actual load charts are more complex and specific to each crane model, considering factors like wind speed, outrigger positioning, and operational conditions. A simplified load chart follows.

Sample Portal Crane Load Chart

Crane Model: PC-1000

Maximum Load Capacity: 50 Tons
  Boom Lengths: 20m - 50m

Boom Length (m)	Load at Min. Radius (Tons)	Max. Radius for Full Load (m)	Load at Max. Radius (Tons)
20	50	10	48
25	48	12	46
30	46	15	44
35	44	18	40
40	40	20	35
45	35	22	30
50	30	25	25

Figure 59: Basic Sample Load Chart.

Operational Notes:

- *The load chart values assume the crane is operating on firm, level ground and in wind speeds less than 20 km/h.*

- *Loads must be reduced by 5% for each 10 km/h increase in wind speed above 20 km/h.*

- *The crane's counterweight must be set according to the manufacturer's specifications for the specific boom length and load.*

- *Always refer to the crane's operational manual and load chart specific to the crane model before operation.*

This sample load chart provides a basic framework. For actual lifting operations, it's crucial to use the precise load chart provided by the crane's manufacturer, as it contains detailed information tailored to the specific crane model, including safety margins and operational conditions. Figure 60 shows a more detailed load chart.

Boom Length (m) → Working Radius ↓	15.2	18.3	21.3	24.4	27.4	30.5	33.5	36.6	39.6	42.7	45.7	48.8	51.8	54.9	57.9	61.0	64.0	67.1	70.1	73.2	76.2
4.5	4.4 m/150.																				
5.0	131.1	5.1 m/128.4	5.6 m/117.2																		
6.0	110.4	110.1	109.8	6.1 m/107.8	6.7 m/95.1																
7.0	95.1	94.8	93.3	91.1	89.3	7.2 m/84.2	7.7 m/75.3														
8.0	79.5	79.9	79.1	77.4	75.9	74.8	72.4	8.2 m/67.8	8.8 m/61.7												
9.0	67.7	68.8	68.5	67.2	66.0	64.9	62.5	61.5	60.0	9.3 m/56.3	9.8 m/51.8										
10.0	58.4	59.0	59.0	58.8	58.3	57.4	56.5	55.0	53.6	52.2	50.9	10.4 m/47.8	10.9 m/44.2	11.4 m/40.1	11.9 m/38.4						
12.0	44.3	45.7	45.8	45.4	45.2	45.2	45.1	44.9	44.1	43.0	42.0	41.0	40.0	39.1	38.2	12.5 m/35.8	13.0 m/33.4	13.5 m/26.7			
14.0	33.5	37.1	37.0	36.8	36.6	36.5	36.5	36.3	36.2	36.1	35.6	34.7	33.9	33.2	32.5	31.7	30.9	26.7	14.1 m/26.7	14.6 m/24.4	15.1 m/20.4
16.0	14.8 m/29.3	30.0	31.0	30.8	30.6	30.5	30.4	30.2	30.1	30.0	29.9	29.6	29.3	28.7	28.1	27.4	26.7	26.3	25.7	22.7	19.4
18.0		17.5 m/24.8	25.6	26.4	26.2	26.1	26.0	25.8	25.7	25.6	25.4	25.3	25.2	25.1	24.6	24.0	23.4	23.0	22.5	20.8	17.5
20.0			21.7	23.0	22.8	22.7	22.6	22.4	22.3	22.2	22.0	21.9	21.7	21.6	21.5	21.2	20.7	20.4	19.9	18.6	15.8
22.0			20.1 m/21.3	19.9	20.1	20.0	19.9	19.7	19.6	19.5	19.3	19.2	19.0	18.9	18.8	18.6	18.4	18.1	17.7	17.1	14.3
24.0				22.8 m/18.5	18.0	17.9	17.7	17.5	17.4	17.3	17.1	17.0	16.8	16.7	16.6	16.4	16.2	16.2	15.8	15.4	13.0
26.0					25.4 m/16.0	16.1	16.0	15.7	15.6	15.5	15.3	15.2	15.0	14.9	14.7	14.6	14.4	14.4	14.2	13.8	11.8
28.0						14.2	14.5	14.2	14.1	13.9	13.8	13.6	13.5	13.4	13.2	13.1	12.9	12.8	12.7	12.4	10.7
30.0						28.1 m/14.1	13.2	12.9	12.8	12.7	12.5	12.3	12.2	12.1	11.9	11.7	11.6	11.5	11.4	11.2	9.7
32.0							30.7 m/12.5	11.8	11.7	11.5	11.4	11.2	11.1	10.9	10.8	10.6	10.4	10.4	10.2	10.0	8.8
34.0								33.3 m/10.9	10.8	10.6	10.4	10.3	10.1	10.0	9.8	9.6	9.4	9.4	9.2	9.1	8.0
36.0									9.7	9.8	9.6	9.4	9.2	9.1	8.9	8.8	8.6	8.5	8.4	8.2	7.2
38.0										8.9	8.8	8.7	8.5	8.4	8.2	8.0	7.8	7.8	7.6	7.4	6.5
40.0										38.6 m/8.6	8.1	8.0	7.8	7.7	7.5	7.3	7.1	7.1	6.9	6.7	5.8
42.0											41.2 m/7.5	7.4	7.2	7.1	6.9	6.7	6.5	6.5	6.3	6.1	5.2
44.0												43.9 m/6.9	6.7	6.5	6.4	6.2	6.0	5.9	5.7	5.5	4.6
46.0													5.9	6.0	5.9	5.7	5.4	5.3	5.2	4.9	4.0
48.0													46.5 m/5.7	5.3	5.4	5.2	4.9	4.9	4.7	4.4	3.5
50.0														49.2 m/4.8	4.7	4.7	4.5	4.4	4.2	4.0	2.9
52.0															51.8 m/4.1	4.2	4.1	4.0	3.8	3.6	2.4
54.0																3.6	3.6	3.5	3.4	3.2	
56.0																54.4 m/3.4	3.0	3.1	3.0	2.8	
58.0																	57.1m/2.8	2.6	2.5	2.4	
60.0																		59.7 m/2.2	2.1		
Reeves	12	10	9	8	8	7	6	6	5	5	4	4	3	3	3	3	3	2	2	2	2

Figure 60: Sample Portal Crane Load Chart.

The load chart shown as Figure 60 provides detailed information on the crane's lifting capacity across various working radii and boom lengths. Here are some observations we can derives from the load chart:

1. Lifting Capacity at Various Radii: The crane's lifting capacity is contingent on the working radius. At a smaller radius, the crane can lift heavier loads.

2. Increased Capacities with Closer Radii: As the working radius decreases, the lifting capacity increases, which is evident in the significant jump in capacity at closer radii. For example, at

a 5.0-meter working radius, the crane can lift 131.1 tons at a 15.2-meter boom length.

3. Variable Capacities at Different Boom Lengths: The crane's capacity varies not just with the working radius but also with changes in boom length. For a 6.0-meter working radius, the capacity is 110.4 tons at a 15.2-meter boom length, which slightly decreases as the boom length extends, showing a capacity of 109.6 tons at a 21.3-meter boom length.

4. Specific Capacities and Minimum Boom Lengths: Some entries indicate a minimum boom length necessary to achieve a certain lifting capacity at a specific working radius. For instance, at a 7.0-meter working radius, the crane can lift 84.2 tons, but this capacity is only achievable with a minimum boom length of 7.2 meters.

5. Trend of Decreasing Capacity with Increased Radius and Length: As the working radius and boom length increase, the crane's lifting capacity generally decreases. This is highlighted at larger working radii and boom lengths, where the crane's capacity diminishes significantly.

6. Operational Limits at Extremes: The chart also outlines the operational limits of the crane at extreme working radii and boom lengths. For example, at a 60.0-meter working radius, the crane can lift a maximum of 2.2 tons, which indicates the maximum operational reach of the crane.

7. Reeve Configurations: The chart mentions reeve configurations, which affect the mechanical advantage and lifting capacity. The configuration changes based on the working radius and boom length, influencing the crane's operational capabilities.

The position of the trolley on the boom directly affects the reeving system, particularly in terms of the amount of reeving that remains on the drum and the mechanical advantage achieved. Here's how it works:

1. Closer Trolley Position: When the trolley (and thus the load) is closer to the pivot point or base of the boom, it allows for more reeving between the load and the hoisting machinery. This is because the load is closer, requiring less rope to reach from the drum to the trolley. This position enables a higher mechanical advantage due to more reeves, which effectively increases the lifting capacity of the crane.

2. Further Trolley Position: As the trolley moves further out along the boom, towards the tip, the length of rope required to reach the trolley from the drum increases. This can reduce the amount of reeving on the drum because more of the rope is used to span the distance between the drum and the trolley. With fewer reeves, the mechanical advantage is reduced, which typically results in a lower lifting capacity.

3. Mechanical Advantage and Rope Tension: The mechanical advantage provided by multiple reeves allows the crane to lift heavier loads by distributing the tension across multiple lines of rope. However, as the trolley moves further out, the increased distance requires more rope length, reducing the number of lines between the drum and the trolley, thus affecting the overall lifting capacity.

4. Impact on Crane Operations: The changing reeve configuration based on trolley position affects not just the lifting capacity, but also the crane's stability and the load's control. Operators must be aware of how the trolley position impacts the crane's capabilities and adjust their lifting plans accordingly.

5. Design Considerations: Crane designs often take into account the variability in reeving configurations due to trolley position. Safety mechanisms, load limiters, and operational guidelines are typically established to ensure that the crane is used within its safe operational envelope regardless of the trolley position.

The trolley position on the boom indeed plays a crucial role in determining the reeving configuration and, consequently, the lifting capacity, stability, and operational efficiency of the crane. This relationship underscores the importance of careful planning and operation within the specified limits to ensure safety and effectiveness in crane operations.

Operating a Portal Crane

Operating a Rail-Mounted Gantry Crane (RMG) safely involves adhering to a set of procedures and protocols to ensure efficient and secure lifting operations. First and foremost, lifts must be executed within the Rated Capacity (RC) of the crane, following the guidelines outlined in the load chart/s and lift plan. This ensures that the crane is not overloaded, maintaining safety for both personnel and equipment.

Portal cranes typically have a comprehensive set of crane controls designed to facilitate precise and efficient operation. These controls are usually located in the crane cab or control room and are operated by a trained crane operator. Here's an overview of the common crane controls:

1. Joysticks or Control Levers: Joysticks or control levers are used to manoeuvre the crane in various directions. They allow the operator to control the crane's movements such as forward, backward, left, and right. Some joysticks may also control vertical movements like hoisting and lowering the load.

2. Master Switches: Master switches are used to power on/off the crane's electrical systems. They are essential for starting up or shutting down the crane safely.

3. Hoist Controls: These controls are used to operate the hoisting mechanism, allowing the operator to lift and lower loads. Hoist controls typically include buttons or levers for raising and lowering the hook or lifting gear.

4. Trolley Controls: Trolley controls are used to move the trolley along the length of the crane bridge. They enable the operator to position the load precisely along the crane's span.

5. Bridge Controls: Bridge controls allow the operator to move the entire crane along the rails. They control the lateral movement of the crane, allowing it to traverse the length of the rail tracks.

6. Emergency Stop Button: An emergency stop button is a crucial safety feature present in all crane controls. It allows the operator to immediately halt all crane movements in case of an emergency or hazardous situation.

7. Safety Interlocks: Safety interlocks are integrated into the crane controls to prevent unsafe operations. These interlocks may include features such as overload protection, collision avoidance systems, and limit switches to ensure safe crane operation.

8. Display Panels: Display panels provide the operator with essential information about the crane's status, including load weight, crane position, operating conditions, and any potential alarms or warnings.

9. Radio Remote Controls: Some portal cranes may also be equipped with radio remote controls, allowing operators to

control the crane from a distance. This can enhance safety and productivity in certain operational scenarios.

Overall, the crane controls in a portal crane are designed to provide operators with intuitive and responsive control over the crane's movements, ensuring safe and efficient operation in a variety of lifting tasks. Regular training and adherence to safety protocols are essential for operators to effectively utilize these controls and minimize the risk of accidents.

Positioning the boom/jib and hook block over the load is a critical step, and it must be done cautiously. This positioning is typically guided by associated personnel and follows the directives outlined in the lift plan and safe work procedures. This ensures that the load is correctly aligned for lifting and minimizes the risk of accidents or damage to the cargo.

Once positioned, the hook and lifting gear, if required, are connected to the load following strict safety protocols. This includes adhering to manufacturer requirements, lift plan specifications, and safe work procedures. Ensuring proper connection of lifting gear is essential for maintaining the integrity of the lift and preventing any mishaps during the operation.

Before proceeding with the actual lift, a test lift is often conducted in accordance with dogging and safe work procedures. This test helps verify the stability of the load and ensures that all equipment is functioning correctly before committing to the full lift.

During the transfer of loads, relevant crane movements and tag lines are utilized as necessary, following the instructions outlined in the lift plan and safe work procedures. Continuous monitoring of both load and crane movement is essential to identify and address any potential hazards promptly.

Clear communication is vital throughout the operation, with all required signals being correctly interpreted and followed. This communication ensures coordination between crane operators and ground personnel, minimizing the risk of accidents and ensuring smooth workflow.

After completing the lift, the load is safely lowered and landed according to the lift plan and safe work procedures. Once the load is secured, lifting gear is disconnected, and the crane is positioned safely for the next task, following the lift plan and safe work procedures to maintain efficiency and safety.

Finally, a thorough inspection of lifting equipment and gear is conducted to identify any defects. Any defective items are isolated, tagged, and reported for immediate attention, ensuring that only safe and reliable equipment is used for future operations.

Loading and unloading cargo from ships using a portal boom crane involves additional precautions due to the dynamic environment of a maritime setting. Here are some key precautions to consider:

1. Weather Conditions: Monitor weather forecasts and sea conditions before and during loading/unloading operations. High winds, rough seas, or adverse weather can affect the stability of the ship and crane operations. Operations may need to be suspended or altered based on weather conditions to ensure safety.

2. Ship Stability: Assess the stability of the ship before loading or unloading operations commence. Ensure that the ship is properly ballasted and moored to prevent excessive movement during cargo handling. Unstable ships pose risks to both personnel and cargo.

3. Communication: Establish clear communication protocols between the ship's crew, crane operators, and ground personnel. Effective communication is critical for coordinating movements and ensuring the safety of all involved. Utilize radios, hand signals, or other communication methods as necessary.

4. Load Distribution: Ensure proper distribution of cargo on the ship's deck to maintain stability and prevent overloading. Follow guidelines provided by the ship's captain or loading supervisor to distribute weight evenly and avoid exceeding weight limits.

5. Securing Cargo: Properly secure cargo on the ship's deck and within containers to prevent shifting during transit. Use lashings, twist locks, or other securing mechanisms as appropriate to ensure cargo remains stable during loading, unloading, and transportation.

6. Maritime Regulations: Familiarize yourself with relevant maritime regulations and guidelines governing cargo handling operations. Compliance with regulations ensures safety and prevents potential legal issues. This includes regulations related to cargo stowage, handling equipment, and personnel safety.

7. Emergency Preparedness: Have emergency response procedures in place in case of accidents or incidents during loading/unloading operations. This includes procedures for medical emergencies, fire, spills, or equipment malfunctions. Conduct regular drills to ensure all personnel are familiar with emergency protocols.

8. Personal Protective Equipment (PPE): Ensure that all personnel involved in loading/unloading operations wear appropriate PPE, including helmets, safety vests, gloves, and steel-toed boots. PPE helps protect against potential hazards such as falling objects, slips, trips, and falls.

9. Training and Certification: Ensure that crane operators, riggers, and other personnel involved in cargo handling operations are properly trained and certified. Training should cover safe

operating procedures, equipment use, hazard recognition, and emergency response.

Figure 61: Portal crane loading the ship Maersk Sembawang in the JadeWeserPort in Wilhelmshaven. Rhetos, CC0, via Wikimedia Commons.

Completing Portal Crane Operations

Shutting down and completing the operation of a portal boom crane safely is as crucial as operating it. This includes:

Firstly, ensure that the crane boom/jib, lifting gear, and associated equipment are stowed and secured as required. This involves following manufacturer requirements and safe work procedures to properly secure all components of the crane. This ensures that loose equipment does not pose a hazard during shutdown or when the crane is not in use.

Next, apply relevant motion locks and brakes as required by manufacturer specifications and safe work procedures. These locks and brakes prevent unintended movement of the crane components, enhancing safety during shutdown and storage.

After securing the crane components, proceed to shut down the crane and secure it to prevent unauthorized access or use. This may involve turning off power sources, locking control panels, and physically securing access points to the crane. Following safe work procedures ensures that the crane is safely immobilized and inaccessible to unauthorized personnel.

Perform shutdown crane checks in accordance with safe work procedures and manufacturer requirements. These checks typically involve inspecting various components of the crane to ensure they are in a safe and secure state for shutdown and storage. Checking for any abnormalities or issues ensures that the crane is properly maintained and ready for the next use.

By following these steps and adhering to safe work procedures and manufacturer requirements, you can ensure that the portal boom crane is safely shut down and ready for storage. This not only prevents accidents and damage to the equipment but also promotes a safe working environment for all personnel involved.

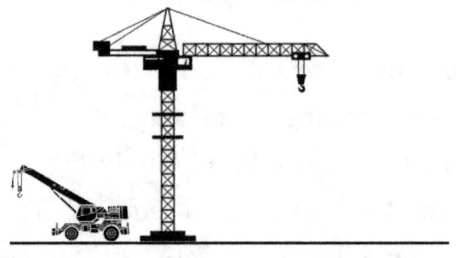

Chapter Five
Bridge Cranes

A bridge crane, as defined, is a type of crane that comprises a bridge beam or beams mounted to end carriages at each end. These end carriages enable the bridge crane to travel along elevated runways. The bridge crane typically features one or more hoisting mechanisms arranged to traverse across the bridge beam(s). In essence, a bridge crane moves horizontally along a fixed path, utilizing the bridge beam(s) as its primary structural element.

Figure 62: An overhead crane at the factory of Rajaville, a manufacturer of concrete products, in Alppila, Oulu, Finland. Methem (Mikko J. Putkonen), Public domain, via Wikimedia Commons.

A bridge crane is a specific type of crane that is designed with a bridge beam or beams as its primary structural element. This bridge beam is mounted to end carriages at each end, which allows the crane to travel along elevated runways. These runways provide a fixed path for the bridge crane to move horizontally.

The key components of a bridge crane include the bridge beam(s) and the end carriages. The bridge beam serves as the horizontal framework of the crane, while the end carriages support and guide the movement of the crane along the runways. By utilizing these end carriages, the bridge crane can traverse along the length of the elevated runways with precision and stability.

In addition to the bridge beam and end carriages, a bridge crane typically features one or more hoisting mechanisms. These mechanisms are arranged to traverse across the bridge beam(s), allowing the crane to lift and lower loads vertically. The hoisting mechanisms may include hooks, chains, or other lifting attachments, depending on the specific requirements of the crane's application.

Overall, a bridge crane operates by moving horizontally along a fixed path using the bridge beam(s) and end carriages, while also providing vertical lifting capabilities through its hoisting mechanisms. This design makes bridge cranes well-suited for tasks that require precise and controlled movement of heavy loads within a defined area, such as manufacturing facilities, warehouses, and shipping yards.

There are several different types of bridge cranes, each designed for specific applications and industries. Some common types include:

Single Girder Bridge Crane: This type of crane, as shown in Figure 63, has one bridge beam supported by end trucks on each side. Single girder bridge cranes are typically used for light to moderate lifting tasks in facilities such as warehouses, workshops, and assembly lines.

CRANE OPERATIONS

Figure 63: Single girder over head crane. Overhead crane, CC BY-SA 4.0, via Wikimedia Commons.

Double Girder Bridge Crane: Double girder bridge cranes feature two bridge beams supported by end trucks on each side. These cranes offer higher lifting capacities and greater spans compared to single girder cranes, making them suitable for heavy-duty applications such as steel mills, foundries, and shipyards.

Figure 64: 25t Double Girder Overhead Crane. Alex.hu ang, CC BY-SA 4.0, via Wikimedia Commons.

Top Running Bridge Crane: In a top running bridge crane, the bridge travels on top of rails mounted on the runway beams. This configuration allows for greater lifting heights and capacities, as well as smoother travel compared to an under-running crane.

Under Running Bridge Crane: Under running bridge cranes have the bridge supported by wheels that run on rails attached to the bottom flange of the runway beams. These cranes are often used in buildings with low ceiling heights or where overhead clearance is limited.

Figure 65: 15t Under-running Overhead Crane. Alex.huang, CC BY-SA 4.0, via Wikimedia Commons.

Single girder top running cranes typically offer load capacities ranging from 0.25 to 20 tons, with spans typically under 65 feet (Mazzella Companies, 2024). They are well-suited for light-duty applications, characterized by low deadweight and ample overhead space. Single girder configurations are known for their high speed and comparatively lower production costs, making them an economical choice for various lifting tasks.

On the other hand, double girder top running cranes are capable of handling heavier loads, typically ranging from 20 to 400 tons, with spans extending beyond 65 feet. These cranes excel in heavy-duty applications, offering superior performance in environments where robust lifting capabilities are required. Double girder configurations provide exceptional hook height, making them ideal for situations demanding extremely high lifting positions. Moreover, they offer the most overhead space and can achieve greater lift heights compared to single girder cranes. Despite higher production costs, double girder top running cranes deliver unparalleled lifting power and speed, making them a preferred choice for demanding industrial settings (Mazzella Companies, 2024).

Freestanding Bridge Crane: Freestanding bridge cranes are designed to be self-supporting and do not require support from the building's structure. They are often used in outdoor applications such as loading docks, storage yards, and construction sites.

Box Girder Bridge Crane: Box girder bridge cranes feature a box-shaped bridge beam that offers increased strength and stiffness compared to traditional I-beam designs. These cranes are commonly used in heavy-duty applications where high precision and stability are required.

Wall-Mounted Bridge Crane: Wall-mounted bridge cranes are attached directly to the walls of a building, eliminating the need for overhead support structures. They are ideal for facilities with limited floor space or where overhead clearance is restricted.

Figure 66: Wall Travelling JIB Crane. Alex.huang, CC BY-SA 4.0, via Wikimedia Commons.

Workstation Bridge Crane: Workstation bridge cranes are designed for light-duty lifting and positioning tasks within a specific work area. They are often installed above individual workstations or assembly lines to improve efficiency and ergonomics.

These are just a few examples of the various types of bridge cranes available, each with its own unique features and advantages. The choice of crane depends on factors such as lifting capacity, span, height, and the specific requirements of the application.

A bridge crane consists of several key components, identified in Figure 67, that work together to facilitate the lifting and movement of loads within a defined area. Here are the main components of a bridge crane:

1. Bridge Girder/Beam: The bridge girder or beam is the primary horizontal structure of the crane, spanning the width of the lifting area. It supports the hoisting mechanism and travels along the length of the crane runway on end trucks or wheel assemblies.

2. End Trucks: End trucks are wheeled assemblies located at each end of the bridge girder. They support and guide the movement of the bridge girder along the crane runway or tracks. End trucks typically include wheels or rollers that run along rails or tracks mounted on the runway beams.

3. Runway Beams: Runway beams are horizontal beams installed parallel to each other along the length of the crane runway. They provide a stable track for the bridge girder to travel on and support the weight of the crane and its load.

4. Hoist Trolley: The hoist trolley is a mechanism that moves horizontally along the length of the bridge girder. It supports the hoisting mechanism and allows the load to be lifted, lowered, and moved horizontally across the lifting area. The hoist trolley may be powered by electric motors or manually operated.

5. Hoisting Mechanism: The hoisting mechanism is responsible for lifting and lowering the load. It typically consists of a drum or winch mounted on the bridge girder, along with lifting cables or chains connected to a hook or lifting attachment. The hoisting mechanism may be powered by electric motors, pneumatic systems, or hydraulic systems.

6. Load Block/Hook: The load block or hook is the attachment point for the load being lifted. It is suspended from the hoisting mechanism and is used to securely hold the load during lifting and movement. Load blocks or hooks may be equipped with safety latches or other devices to prevent accidental disengagement of the load.

7. Electrical Controls: Electrical controls include switches, buttons, and control panels used to operate the crane and its vari-

ous functions. They may be located in a control cabin or pendant station and allow the operator to control the movement of the crane, hoist, and trolley.

8. Safety Features: Bridge cranes are equipped with various safety features to prevent accidents and ensure safe operation. These may include overload protection devices, limit switches to prevent over-travel, emergency stop buttons, and warning lights or alarms.

These components work together to provide efficient and safe lifting and movement of loads within a facility or work area. Regular maintenance and inspection of these components are essential to ensure the continued safe operation of the bridge crane.

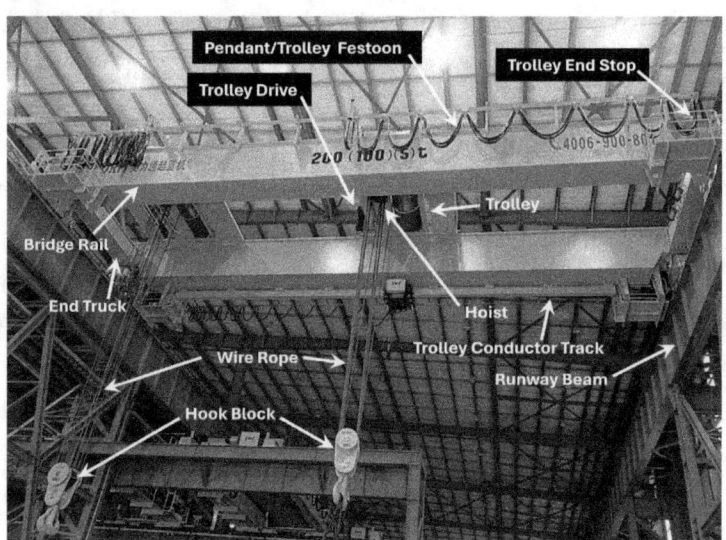

Figure 67: Bridge crane components. Background - Ale x.huang, CC BY-SA 4.0, via Wikimedia Commons.

Bridge Crane Control

Bridge cranes are controlled using a combination of manual and automated control systems, depending on the specific requirements of the application and the sophistication of the crane. Here are some common methods used to control bridge cranes:

1. Pendant Control: Pendant controls are handheld devices connected to the crane by a flexible cable. They typically feature buttons or switches that allow the operator to control the movement of the crane, hoist, and trolley. Pendant controls provide the operator with direct, intuitive control over the crane's movements and are often used for precise positioning of loads.

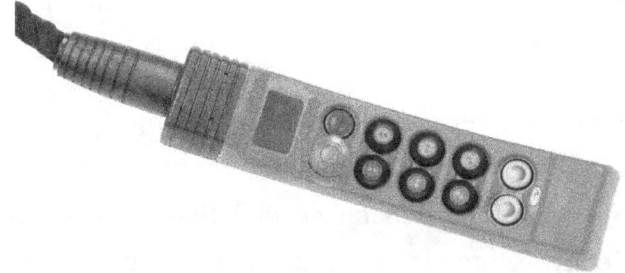

Figure 68: Pendant control. Source: Canva.

1. Radio Remote Control: Some bridge cranes are equipped with radio remote control systems that allow the operator to control the crane from a distance. Radio remote controls provide flexibility and freedom of movement for the operator, particularly in applications where direct line-of-sight control is not feasible or safe.

2. Cab Control: Bridge cranes may be equipped with a control cabin or operator's cab located on the bridge girder. The operator sits inside the cabin and uses a control panel or joystick to operate the crane. Cab controls provide a comfortable and ergonomic working environment for the operator, particularly for long-duration operations.

3. Automated Control Systems: In modern bridge cranes, automated control systems may be used to optimize crane operation and improve efficiency. These systems may include programmable logic controllers (PLCs) or computerized control systems that monitor and control various aspects of crane operation, such as load positioning, speed control, and collision avoidance.

4. Safety Interlocks and Limit Switches: Bridge cranes are equipped with safety interlocks and limit switches that prevent unsafe operation and protect against overloading or over-travel. These devices automatically stop the crane or trigger alarms if certain conditions are exceeded, ensuring safe operation at all times.

5. Variable Frequency Drives (VFDs): Some bridge cranes are equipped with variable frequency drives that allow for precise control of motor speed and acceleration. VFDs improve energy efficiency, reduce wear and tear on equipment, and provide smoother and more controlled crane movements.

Overall, bridge cranes can be controlled using a variety of methods, ranging from manual pendant controls to advanced automated systems. The choice of control method depends on factors such as the complexity of the crane operation, the skill level of the operator, and the specific requirements of the application.

A bridge crane is equipped with several powered operations that enable it to efficiently lift, move, and position loads within a defined area. These powered operations are controlled by electric motors or hydraulic systems and include:

1. Hoisting: Hoisting is the vertical movement of the load, accomplished by raising or lowering the load block or hook attached to the hoist mechanism. The hoisting operation is powered by an electric motor or hydraulic system located on the bridge girder.

The motor drives a drum or winch, which spools or unspools the lifting cable or chain to raise or lower the load.

2. Trolley Travel: Trolley travel refers to the horizontal movement of the hoist trolley along the length of the bridge girder. The trolley is powered by an electric motor or hydraulic system and is typically mounted on rails or tracks attached to the bridge girder. The motor drives the trolley wheels or drives mechanism, allowing the trolley to move smoothly along the length of the bridge girder.

3. Bridge Travel: Bridge travel involves the horizontal movement of the entire bridge crane along the length of the crane runway or tracks. The bridge travel operation is powered by electric motors or hydraulic systems located on the end trucks or wheel assemblies at each end of the bridge girder. The motors drive the wheels or drives mechanism, propelling the bridge crane along the runway beams.

4. Cross Travel: Cross travel, also known as lateral travel or crab travel, refers to the horizontal movement of the load across the width of the lifting area. This operation is achieved by moving the entire hoist trolley assembly laterally along the bridge girder. Cross travel is powered by electric motors or hydraulic systems located on the hoist trolley, which drive the lateral movement of the trolley assembly.

5. Auxiliary Functions: In addition to the main powered operations, bridge cranes may also feature auxiliary functions powered by electric motors or hydraulic systems. These functions may include rotating the load, tilting or manipulating the load orientation, or operating additional attachments or accessories such as magnets or grabs.

These powered operations allow bridge cranes to perform a wide range of lifting and handling tasks with precision and efficiency. The integration of electric or hydraulic power systems enables smooth and controlled movement of loads, enhancing productivity and safety in industrial environments.

Figure 69: Various powered operations in action. Alex.huang, CC BY-SA 4.0, via Wikimedia Commons.

Planning for Bridge Crane Operations

Operating a bridge crane involves a systematic approach to ensure the safe and efficient handling of loads. To begin, task requirements are identified by reviewing work orders or similar documentation. Following this, the lift plan is confirmed with associated personnel, and a comprehensive site inspection is conducted to assess conditions and hazards present in the work area. Thorough planning and preparation are essential, and adherence to workplace procedures is paramount throughout this phase.

Once task requirements are established, the working area undergoes a detailed inspection to identify potential obstacles, obstructions, or hazards that could impact crane operations. Paths for operating the bridge or gantry crane and moving or placing loads are determined based on this assessment, ensuring compliance with workplace procedures. Additionally, the quality and suitability of the operating surface are evaluated to confirm its ability to support the crane's operational requirements.

Furthermore, the Rated Capacity (RC) of the crane and the Working Load Limit (WLL) of the lifting gear are determined based on load and task requirements. Manufacturer specifications and workplace procedures are referenced to establish safe lifting capacities and limits. Hazard identification and risk control measures are then applied to mitigate potential risks associated with the lifting operation, with relevant personnel advised accordingly.

Establishing the Rated Capacity (RC) of a bridge or gantry crane and the Working Load Limit (WLL) of the lifting gear is crucial to ensure safe lifting operations. Here's a detailed guide on how to accomplish this:

1. Understand Terminology: Before proceeding, it's essential to understand the terminology. The Rated Capacity (RC) refers to the maximum load that a crane is designed to lift safely under normal operating conditions. The Working Load Limit (WLL) pertains to the maximum load that the lifting gear, such as hooks, slings, or chains, can safely handle.

2. Review Load Requirements: Begin by reviewing the load re-

quirements for the lifting task. This includes determining the weight of the load to be lifted, as well as any additional factors that may affect lifting operations, such as load dimensions, centre of gravity, and lifting points.

3. Consult Manufacturer Specifications: Refer to the manufacturer's specifications for the bridge or gantry crane. These specifications provide detailed information about the crane's design, capabilities, and limitations. Look for the crane's Rated Capacity (RC), which is typically specified in terms of maximum load capacity and span.

4. Consider Crane Configuration: Take into account the configuration of the crane, including whether it is a single-girder or double-girder crane, as well as its operating environment. Different crane configurations may have varying Rated Capacities and limitations.

5. Review Workplace Procedures: Consult workplace procedures and guidelines related to lifting operations. These procedures may include specific instructions or limitations regarding crane usage, load handling, and safety protocols.

6. Calculate Load Characteristics: Calculate the characteristics of the load being lifted, including its weight, dimensions, centre of gravity, and any dynamic factors that may affect lifting operations, such as acceleration, deceleration, or wind loads.

7. Apply Safety Factors: Apply appropriate safety factors to account for uncertainties and variations in load conditions. Safety factors are typically specified by industry standards or workplace procedures and may include factors for load dynamics, environmental conditions, and equipment reliability.

8. Verify Compliance: Ensure that the Rated Capacity (RC) of the crane and the Working Load Limit (WLL) of the lifting gear meet or exceed the calculated load requirements. Verify that the crane and lifting gear are in compliance with manufacturer specifications and workplace procedures.

9. Document Findings: Document the established Rated Capacity (RC) of the crane and the Working Load Limit (WLL) of the lifting gear, along with any relevant calculations, specifications, or workplace procedures. This documentation serves as a reference for future lifting operations and ensures compliance with safety standards and regulations.

10. Communicate Information: Communicate the established Rated Capacity (RC) and Working Load Limit (WLL) to all relevant personnel involved in the lifting operation. Ensure that everyone understands the limitations and safety requirements associated with the lifting task.

By following these steps and carefully considering all relevant factors, you can effectively establish the Rated Capacity (RC) of a bridge or gantry crane and the Working Load Limit (WLL) of the lifting gear, ensuring safe and efficient lifting operations.

Operating a bridge crane, also known as an overhead crane, involves various tasks that can expose operators and nearby personnel to specific hazards. It's crucial to identify and mitigate these risks to ensure safety during crane operations. Here are some of the specific hazards related to operating a bridge crane:

1. Electrical Hazards
   - Overhead cranes often operate in close proximity to electrical power sources, which can pose electrocution risks, especially if the crane or its load comes into contact with overhead power lines or electrified components.

2. Mechanical Failures
   - Mechanical issues such as brake failure, wire rope degradation, or structural failure of the crane components (e.g., the bridge, hoist, or trolley) can lead to catastrophic drops or uncontrolled movements of the load.

3. Load Dropping
   - Dropping the load, whether due to operator error, mechanical failure, or improper rigging, can cause severe injury, fatalities, or significant damage to property and equipment.

4. Collision Hazards
   - The crane's movement along the bridge and trolley's path can lead to collisions with other cranes on the same rails, nearby structures, or personnel if the area is not adequately cleared or if the crane's travel path is not correctly planned.

5. Overloading
   - Lifting a load that exceeds the crane's rated capacity can lead to structural overloading and potential failure of the crane, posing significant risks to all personnel involved and nearby equipment.

6. Falling Objects
   - Parts of the load, rigging hardware, or even components of the crane itself can become dislodged and fall, posing a risk to anyone beneath or near the crane's operation area.

7. Poor Visibility
   - Operators may have limited visibility when moving large loads or when the control station is not adequately positioned, leading to potential collisions or improper load placement.

8. Human Error
   - Mistakes made by crane operators or rigging personnel, such

as incorrect rigging, exceeding the crane's operational limits, or misjudgement of distances and clearances, can result in accidents.

9. Environmental Conditions
   - Operating a crane in adverse weather conditions, such as high winds, lightning, or extreme temperatures, can affect crane stability, load control, and operator judgment.

10. Unauthorized Access
    - Personnel who are not involved in the crane operation entering the crane's operating area can be at risk, especially if they are unaware of ongoing lifting activities.

To mitigate these hazards, it's essential to implement comprehensive safety measures, including but not limited to:
- Regular maintenance and inspection of crane components.
- Strict adherence to the crane's operational limits and load capacities.
- Proper training and certification for crane operators and rigging personnel.
- Use of spotters or signal persons to assist with lifts when visibility is poor or when navigating tight spaces.
- Implementing and enforcing exclusion zones around the crane's operating area to prevent unauthorized access.
- Utilizing warning signs, signals, and barriers to alert personnel to the crane's movements and active lifting areas.
- Monitoring environmental conditions and adjusting crane operations accordingly to ensure safety.

By recognizing these hazards and implementing effective safety protocols, the risk of accidents and injuries during bridge crane operations can be significantly reduced.

Confirmation of the implementation of the traffic management plan is essential to ensure the safe movement of personnel and equipment within the work area. Adhering to workplace procedures, appropriate communication procedures are identified and tested with associated personnel to facilitate clear and effective communication during crane operations.

Prior to proceeding with crane operations, the alignment of all tasks with workplace requirements, including safety, efficiency, and procedural compliance, is verified. Finally, information required for equipment inspection and maintenance is obtained to ensure compliance with manufacturer requirements. Interpretation of this information ensures that all equipment is properly maintained and operated safely in accordance with workplace procedures.

Preparing for Bridge Crane Operations

Operating a bridge crane requires thorough consultation with workplace personnel to ensure clarity and consistency in all crane and lifting operations, aligning with site requirements, lift plans, and workplace procedures. Risk control measures for identified hazards are meticulously checked to ensure implementation according to the lift plan and safe work procedures.

Accessing the bridge or gantry crane safely is paramount, adhering strictly to manufacturer specifications and safe work procedures. Pre-start checks are diligently carried out, and any observed damage or defects are promptly reported, recorded, and addressed in line with safe work procedures and manufacturer specifications.

Completing a pre-start check on a bridge crane is a crucial step to ensure that the crane is in proper working condition and safe to operate. Here's a detailed guide on how to conduct a prestart check:

1. Review Documentation: Begin by reviewing the crane's documentation, including the manufacturer's manual and any relevant maintenance records. Ensure that all necessary inspections, servicing, and repairs have been completed as required.

2. Visual Inspection: Conduct a thorough visual inspection of the crane, starting from the ground and working your way up. Look for any signs of damage, wear, or corrosion on structural components, such as the bridge girders, end trucks, and runway beams.

3. Electrical Components: Check all electrical components of the crane, including cables, wiring, connectors, and junction boxes. Look for any signs of fraying, exposed wires, loose connections, or damage to insulation.

4. Hoisting Mechanism: Inspect the hoisting mechanism, including the hoist drum, wire ropes or chains, and hook assembly. Ensure that the wire ropes or chains are properly seated on the drum and that there are no signs of wear, corrosion, or distortion.

5. Trolley Mechanism: Check the trolley mechanism for smooth operation along the bridge girder. Ensure that the trolley wheels are in good condition and properly aligned with the runway beams. Check for any signs of binding, excessive wear, or damage to the trolley wheels or rails.

6. Bridge Travel: Test the bridge travel mechanism by moving the crane along the length of the runway beams. Ensure that the movement is smooth and controlled, with no excessive noise, vibration, or irregularities. Check for any signs of misalignment

or damage to the end trucks or runway beams.

7. Control Systems: Test all control systems and functions of the crane, including pendant controls, radio remote controls, and cabin controls. Ensure that all buttons, switches, and joysticks are functioning correctly and that the crane responds appropriately to commands.

8. Safety Features: Verify the operation of all safety features and devices, including limit switches, emergency stop buttons, overload protection systems, and travel limiters. Ensure that these safety features are functioning correctly and provide adequate protection for personnel and equipment.

9. Documentation Check: Review the crane's logbook and maintenance records to ensure that all required inspections, servicing, and repairs have been documented. Verify that any outstanding issues or maintenance tasks have been addressed before operating the crane.

10. Final Assessment: After completing the prestart check, make a final assessment of the crane's condition and readiness for operation. If any issues or concerns are identified during the inspection, take appropriate action to address them before using the crane.

Subsequently, setting up and rigging the bridge or gantry crane correctly with lifting gear follows the lift plan and relevant manufacturer specifications, including load charts and safe work procedures. Operational checks are conducted to verify functionality, with any identified damage or defects reported, recorded, and managed in accordance with manufacturer requirements and safe work procedures.

All controls are located, identified, and tested as per relevant manufacturer specifications and safe work procedures, ensuring their proper functionality. Inspection of the crane logbook is performed to verify correctness for the crane and type, with necessary rectifications signed off in line with manufacturer requirements and safe work procedures.

Assessment of weather and work environment conditions is essential to determine any potential impact on bridge or gantry crane operations, following manufacturer requirements and safe work procedures.

Identification, calculation, or estimation of the weight of the load is crucial, along with calculating the derated Working Load Limit (WLL) of lifting equipment resulting from selected slinging techniques. Suitable lifting points and slinging techniques are identified, and lifting equipment and gear are prepared for safe use.

Finally, confirmation of the load destination for stability is ensured, verifying its ability to bear the load and preparing it for safe access and landing. By meticulously following these steps and adhering to manufacturer specifications and safe work procedures, bridge crane operations can be conducted safely and efficiently.

Operating a Bridge Crane

Operating a bridge crane involves a systematic approach to ensure safe and efficient lifting operations. To begin, it's essential to determine lifts within the Rated Capacity (RC) of the crane by reviewing the load chart/s and lift plan. This ensures that all lifts remain within the crane's safe lifting capacity, preventing overloading and potential accidents.

Once the lifts are determined, the next step is to safely position the hook block over the load in accordance with safe work procedures. If controlling the crane from the cabin, directions from associated personnel should be followed to accurately position the hook block over the load. Ensuring precise positioning is crucial for the safety and stability of the lift.

After positioning the hook block, the lifting equipment and gear are connected to the load securely, following the guidelines outlined in the lift plan and safe work procedures. Double-checking the connections for proper security is essential before proceeding with the lift to avoid any risks of load instability or detachment during lifting.

Before proceeding with the actual lift, it's important to conduct a test lift in accordance with safe work procedures. This ensures that both the crane and lifting equipment are functioning correctly, and that the load can be lifted smoothly and without any issues. Verification of the test lift's success is crucial before proceeding with the actual operation.

Conducting a test lift using a bridge crane is a critical step to ensure the crane's proper functioning and the safety of lifting operations. This includes:

1. Preparation: Before conducting the test lift, ensure that all necessary preparations have been made. This includes verifying that the crane is properly set up, rigged, and operational, as well as confirming that the load and lifting equipment are ready for use.

2. Safety Checks: Perform pre-start checks on the bridge crane to ensure that it is in good working condition. This may involve inspecting the crane's structural integrity, electrical components, hoisting mechanisms, brakes, and other safety features. Any damage or defects should be reported, recorded, and addressed before proceeding with the test lift.

3. Load Selection: Select a suitable test load that is within the crane's rated capacity and representative of typical lifting tasks. Ensure that the weight of the test load is accurately known or calculated to prevent overloading the crane.

4. Lifting Plan: Develop a lifting plan that outlines the specific procedures and safety measures to be followed during the test lift. This plan should include details such as the intended lifting location, lifting technique, load handling procedures, and communication protocols.

5. Communication: Establish clear communication channels with all personnel involved in the test lift, including crane operators, signalpersons, and ground crew. Ensure that everyone understands their roles and responsibilities and that communication signals are agreed upon and clearly understood.

6. Execution: Begin the test lift by slowly and smoothly lifting the load off the ground. Pay close attention to the crane's operation and monitor for any signs of instability, unusual noises, or other issues. Use caution and ensure that the load remains balanced and under control throughout the lifting process.

7. Observation: Observe the behaviour of the crane and the load during the test lift. Monitor factors such as load sway, crane movement, and any changes in operating conditions. Be prepared to stop the lift immediately if any safety concerns arise.

8. Lowering: Once the test lift has been completed successfully, carefully lower the load back to the ground using controlled and precise movements. Ensure that the load is landed safely and securely before releasing the lifting equipment.

9. Evaluation: After the test lift is complete, evaluate the crane's performance and the effectiveness of the lifting procedures. Identify any issues or areas for improvement and make necessary adjustments to the lifting plan or crane operation as needed.

10. Documentation: Record the details of the test lift, including the

load weight, lifting procedures, observations, and any findings or recommendations. Maintain thorough documentation for future reference and compliance with regulatory requirements.

By following these steps and conducting a test lift with careful attention to safety and precision, you can ensure that the bridge crane is operating correctly and that lifting operations can be performed safely and efficiently.

Figure 70: Conduct a test lift prior to moving the load. Overhead Crane for Coil Lifting. Sclaferriere, CC BY-SA 4.0, via Wikimedia Commons.

Once the test lift is successful, the loads are transferred using relevant bridge or gantry crane movements and tag lines as required by the lift plan and safe work procedures. Constant monitoring of both the load and crane movement is essential throughout the lifting operation to ensure compliance with the lift plan and safe work procedures, with adjustments made as needed.

Clear and effective communication with associated personnel is maintained by interpreting and following all required communication signals while operating the crane. Prompt responses to signals or instructions help maintain safe crane operations and prevent potential accidents or disruptions.

After the load is safely lowered in accordance with the lift plan and safe work procedures, the lifting gear is disconnected from the load and positioned safely and efficiently for the next task as outlined in the lift plan and safe work procedures.

Finally, a thorough inspection of all lifting equipment and gear is conducted for defects, wear, or damage following the lift. Any defective items are isolated, tagged appropriately, and reported to the relevant personnel for further action. By following these steps and adhering to lift plans and safe work procedures, the operation of a bridge or gantry crane can be effectively conducted while ensuring the safety of personnel and equipment during lifting operations.

Completing Bridge Crane Operations

Operating a bridge crane safely involves several important steps to ensure that the crane is properly parked, secured, and shut down after use. Here's how you would execute these tasks:

1. Parking the Crane: Park the bridge or gantry crane in accordance with manufacturer specifications and safe work procedures. This may involve positioning the crane at a designated parking area or location where it will not obstruct other operations or traffic flow.

2. Stowing Lifting Gear: Stow and secure the lifting gear and associated equipment in accordance with safe work procedures. This includes retracting the hook block, securing any loose cables or chains, and storing any auxiliary equipment in designated storage areas on the crane.

3. Applying Motion Locks and Brakes: Apply relevant motion locks and brakes as required by manufacturer specifications and safe work procedures. These locks and brakes prevent unintended movement of the crane while parked, reducing the risk of accidents or damage.

4. Shutting Down the Crane: Shut down the bridge or gantry crane in accordance with safe work procedures. This typically involves turning off the power supply, shutting down control systems, and securing any movable components or operating mechanisms.

5. Securing the Crane: Ensure that the crane is secured to prevent unauthorized access or use. This may involve locking control panels or access doors, removing key components, or implementing other security measures as specified in safe work procedures.

6. Post-Operational Checks: Conduct post-operational checks on the bridge or gantry crane in accordance with safe work procedures and manufacturer specifications. This includes inspecting the crane for any signs of damage, wear, or malfunction that may have occurred during operation.

By following these steps and adhering to safe work procedures and manufacturer specifications, you can safely park, secure, and shut down a bridge or gantry crane after use, minimizing the risk of accidents and ensuring the continued safe operation of the equipment.

CRANE OPERATIONS

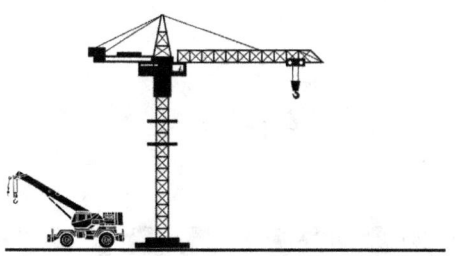

Chapter Six

Personnel and Materials Hoist

A materials or personnel hoist is used to hoist personnel, goods and/or materials. It comprises a car, structure, machinery or other equipment associated with the hoist, and may be either a cantilever hoist, tower hoist or a multiple winch operation (WorkSafe Queensland, 2024).

A personnel and materials hoist, as shown in Figure 71, often simply referred to as a hoist, is a type of lifting equipment designed to transport both people and materials vertically between different levels of a building or structure. Unlike a traditional materials-only hoist, which is primarily used for moving goods or equipment, a personnel and materials hoist is specifically engineered to accommodate both materials and personnel simultaneously.

These hoists are commonly used in construction, maintenance, and renovation projects where workers and materials need to be transported to various heights efficiently and safely. They provide a convenient and reliable means of accessing different levels of a building or structure, especially in high-rise construction projects where conventional methods like stairs or elevators may be impractical or unavailable.

Figure 71: STROS Personnel and Material Construction Hoists on Orbion business center. Niklitov, CC BY-SA 4.0, via Wikimedia Commons.

Personnel and materials hoists typically feature a sturdy platform or cage that can accommodate both workers and materials. The platform is equipped with safety features such as guardrails, gates, and interlocking doors to ensure the safety of personnel during transportation. Additionally, these hoists often include load-sensing devices, emergency stop buttons, and overload protection systems to prevent accidents and ensure safe operation.

The lifting mechanism of a personnel and materials hoist may be powered by electric motors, hydraulic systems, or other means, depending on the specific design and requirements of the application.

Some hoists are also equipped with variable-speed controls and remote operation capabilities to enhance efficiency and flexibility in operation.

The fundamental operation of a personnel and material hoist comprises two primary elements: the lift car (or cage), responsible for conveying passengers or materials vertically, and the drive system, which propels the lift car along its designated track(s).

The drive system encompasses either electric motors or hydraulic cylinders that are connected to winches, which in turn manipulate cables attached to pulleys positioned at each end of the track(s). As these cables are tensioned by the winch systems, they facilitate the movement of the lift car either upward or downward accordingly.

Depending on the nature of the project being undertaken, additional safety features may also be incorporated. These may include emergency stop buttons strategically located within close proximity from both inside and outside of each cabin or cage. This enables workers to promptly halt the hoist's operation in the event of an emergency or malfunction, thereby swiftly regaining control of the system.

Personnel and materials hoists come in various types, each designed to meet specific requirements and applications in construction and industrial settings. Some common types of personnel and materials hoists include:

1. Single-Cage Hoists: These hoists feature a single cage or platform for transporting both personnel and materials. They are suitable for smaller construction projects or sites with limited space.

2. Twin-Cage Hoists: Twin-cage hoists consist of two separate cages or platforms that operate independently. They allow for simultaneous transportation of personnel and materials, increasing efficiency and productivity on larger construction sites.

3. Rack and Pinion Hoists: Rack and pinion hoists utilize a rack and

pinion system for vertical movement. They are known for their smooth and stable operation, making them suitable for high-rise construction projects.

4. Wire Rope Hoists: Wire rope hoists use wire ropes and a drum or winch system for lifting and lowering. They are versatile and can handle heavy loads, making them suitable for various construction and industrial applications.

5. Hydraulic Hoists: Hydraulic hoists utilize hydraulic power to lift and lower the hoist car. They offer precise control and are ideal for applications where smooth and precise movement is required.

6. Electric Chain Hoists: Electric chain hoists use an electric motor and chain mechanism for lifting and lowering. They are compact, lightweight, and easy to operate, making them suitable for smaller-scale construction projects.

7. Customized Hoists: Some personnel and materials hoists are custom-designed to meet specific project requirements. These hoists may incorporate unique features or modifications tailored to the project's needs.

Overall, the choice of personnel and materials hoist depends on factors such as project size, lifting capacity, vertical transportation requirements, and site conditions. By selecting the appropriate type of hoist, construction and industrial companies can ensure safe and efficient transportation of personnel and materials on their worksites.

Setting up a personnel and materials hoist involves several essential steps to ensure its proper installation and safe operation. First, selecting a suitable location is crucial, considering factors such as ground stability, accessibility, and proximity to the work area. Once a location is chosen, the foundation must be prepared to provide stable support for the hoist. This may entail pouring concrete footings or installing steel support beams, depending on the hoist's specific requirements.

Next, the various components of the hoist, including the lift car (or cage), drive system, track(s), and safety features, need to be assembled. It's important to follow the manufacturer's instructions and specifications meticulously during this process to ensure proper assembly and installation of each component. Once assembled, the track(s) along which the lift car will travel must be securely anchored to the foundation and aligned correctly to facilitate smooth movement.

Figure 72: Material Handler general arrangement. Background W. Bulach, CC BY-SA 4.0, via Wikimedia Commons.

The drive system, whether powered by electric motors or hydraulic cylinders, must be mounted according to manufacturer guidelines and connected to the track(s). Ensuring proper positioning and securing of the drive system is essential for the hoist's functionality and safety. Subsequently, attaching the lift car (or cage) to the track(s) and connecting it to the drive system is crucial. All connections must be securely fastened and tightened to prevent any movement or instability during operation.

After assembly, the hoist should undergo thorough testing to ensure all components are functioning correctly. This includes testing the lift car's movement along the track(s) as well as the effectiveness of safety features such as emergency stop buttons and overload protection systems. Safety checks should be performed to ensure compliance with relevant safety regulations and standards, addressing any signs of damage or defects before putting the hoist into service.

Operators must receive comprehensive training on the hoist's safe operation, including loading and unloading procedures, emergency protocols, and routine maintenance tasks. It's essential to ensure that operators are familiar with all safety features and procedures before using the hoist. Finally, documenting the installation process, including assembly instructions, safety checks, and operator training, is crucial for future reference and maintenance purposes.

Planning for Personnel and Materials Hoist Operations

Operating a personnel and materials hoist involves several important steps to ensure safety and efficiency. Here's how you would carry out the tasks you've described:

1. Review Task Instructions and Obtain Relevant Information: Be-

gin by reviewing task instructions and consulting with relevant personnel to clarify any uncertainties. Obtain workplace-specific information and ensure you understand the scope of work.

2. Interpret Safe Work Method Statements (SWMSs): Obtain and interpret safe work method statements (SWMSs) to understand the specific procedures and safety requirements for the task at hand. Ensure compliance with workplace-specific and safe work requirements outlined in the SWMSs.

3. Interpret Equipment Information: Obtain and interpret information regarding the inspection, use, maintenance, and storage of the hoist equipment. Ensure compliance with manufacturer requirements to maintain the equipment's safety and functionality.

4. Identify Hazards and Determine Risk Controls: Identify workplace and task-specific hazards associated with hoist operation. Determine required risk controls and safety measures, as well as the necessary safety equipment to mitigate identified hazards.

5. Calculate Load Weight and Ensure Compliance: Calculate the weight of the load to be lifted using the hoist. Check that the load weight is within the working load limit (WLL) of the hoist and distribute it evenly according to manufacturer requirements to ensure safe lifting operations.

6. Establish Communication Methods: Establish communication methods with relevant personnel involved in the hoisting operation. Ensure clear and effective communication channels are in place to coordinate tasks and address any issues that may arise during operation.

7. Review Emergency Procedures: Review emergency procedures

in consultation with relevant personnel. Familiarize yourself with emergency protocols, including evacuation procedures, emergency stop mechanisms, and communication protocols, to ensure a prompt and coordinated response to any emergencies.

Personnel and materials hoist operations present a range of hazards and risks that demand careful management to safeguard the well-being of personnel and the integrity of transported materials. Among these hazards, falls from height represent a significant risk, particularly during loading and unloading activities. To address this, personnel should utilize suitable fall protection equipment such as harnesses and lanyards, coupled with the installation of guardrails around hoist openings. Additionally, comprehensive training in loading and unloading procedures is crucial to mitigate the risk of slips, trips, and falls.

Mechanical failure of hoist components, including cables, pulleys, and brakes, poses another potential hazard. Regular maintenance and inspection of hoist equipment are essential to detect and rectify issues before they escalate. Implementing a preventive maintenance program and adhering to manufacturer recommendations can further minimize the risk of mechanical failure, enhancing overall safety.

Overloading the hoist beyond its rated capacity can lead to structural damage, equipment failure, and accidents. Preventing overloading requires accurate calculation of load weight prior to hoisting and adherence to the hoist's rated capacity. Establishing a robust load management system, incorporating indicators and sensors, aids in monitoring and preventing overloading incidents.

Personnel working near hoist machinery are susceptible to entanglement and crush injuries from moving parts such as cables and pulleys. Mitigation strategies include posting clear warning signs and establishing safety zones to restrict access to hazardous areas. Comprehensive training on safe work practices and maintaining a safe distance from moving components further minimizes the risk of entanglement and crush hazards.

Electrical hazards pose a threat to personnel working on or near electrical hoist equipment, risking electric shock and electrocution. Effective mitigation involves ensuring proper grounding of hoist equipment, along with training personnel in electrical safety procedures and the use of insulated tools and personal protective equipment (PPE). Regular inspections and testing of electrical systems are imperative to identify and address potential hazards promptly.

A comprehensive approach encompassing hazard identification, risk assessment, and mitigation is vital for ensuring the safe operation of personnel and materials hoists. This involves implementing engineering and administrative controls, as well as personal protective measures, to minimize the likelihood and severity of accidents and injuries. Regular training, inspection, and maintenance activities are integral components of a robust hoist safety program, promoting a safer work environment overall.

Selecting and Preparing for Personnel and Materials Hoist Operations

Operating a personnel and materials hoist involves several critical steps to ensure safety and efficiency. Here's how you would carry out the tasks you've described:

1. Put Risk Controls and Safety Measures in Place: In consultation with relevant personnel, identify potential hazards associated with hoist operation and implement appropriate risk controls and safety measures. This may include installing guardrails, safety harnesses, and signage, as well as establishing safe work procedures and protocols.

2. Access Hoist Safely: Ensure safe access to the hoist by using designated access points and following established safety protocols, such as using ladders, stairs, or platforms. Take precautions to prevent slips, trips, and falls during access.

3. Visually Check Hoist for Damage and Defects: Conduct a visual inspection of the hoist to identify any signs of damage, wear, or defects. Inspect components such as cables, pulleys, hooks, and structural elements for integrity and ensure they are free from any abnormalities.

4. Carry Out Pre-Start Checks: Before starting the hoist, perform pre-start checks to ensure all components are functioning correctly. Check the hoist logbook for any maintenance or operational issues, and verify the condition of controls, switches, and safety devices.

5. Perform Operational Checks: Conduct operational checks to verify the hoist's functionality during operation. Test safety devices such as limit switches, overload protection systems, and emergency stop buttons to ensure they activate correctly. Check the availability and condition of fire extinguishers and other emergency equipment.

6. Ensure Hoist is Operating Correctly: Monitor the hoist during operation to ensure it is functioning correctly and smoothly. Verify that the hoist moves without hesitation or abnormal noises and that there are no obstructions or impediments to its operation.

7. Check Communication Equipment and Alarm Systems: Inspect communication equipment, including two-way radios or intercom systems, to ensure they are operational and reliable. Test

lighting and alarm systems to confirm they are functional and visible in case of emergency.

8. Conduct Test Run and Identify Abnormalities: Perform a test run of the hoist to simulate typical operating conditions. Listen for abnormal noises or vibrations and observe any irregularities in the hoist's performance. If any abnormalities are detected, shut down the hoist, tag it out of service, and report the issues to relevant personnel.

9. Isolate, Report, Tag Out, and Record Defective Equipment: If defective equipment is identified during inspection or operation, isolate it from use, report the issue to appropriate personnel, tag it out of service, and record the details of the defect in maintenance logs or records.

Accessing the hoist safely is paramount to ensuring the overall safety of personnel involved in its operation. To begin, it's crucial to identify and utilize designated access points designated for entering and exiting the hoist area. These access points are typically established in accordance with safety regulations and are equipped with features that facilitate safe entry and exit.

Once the designated access points are identified, it's important to adhere to established safety protocols while accessing the hoist. This may involve using ladders, stairs, or platforms provided specifically for this purpose. These structures are designed to provide stable footing and support for personnel as they ascend or descend to the hoist area.

During the process of accessing the hoist, it's essential to take precautions to prevent slips, trips, and falls. This can be achieved by maintaining three points of contact with the ladder, stair railing, or platform at all times, ensuring proper footwear with adequate traction is worn, and avoiding rushing or making sudden movements that could lead to accidents.

Furthermore, it's important to keep the access area clear of any obstacles or debris that could pose tripping hazards. Regular inspections should be conducted to identify and address any potential hazards promptly. Additionally, adequate lighting should be provided in the access area to ensure visibility, especially in low-light conditions.

By following these safety protocols and precautions, personnel can access the hoist safely, minimizing the risk of accidents or injuries associated with entering or exiting the hoist area. This proactive approach to safety helps create a secure working environment for all personnel involved in hoist operations.

Conducting a visual inspection of the hoist is a critical step in ensuring its safe and effective operation. To begin, personnel should carefully examine the various components of the hoist, including cables, pulleys, hooks, and structural elements, to identify any signs of damage, wear, or defects. This inspection should be thorough and systematic, covering all areas of the hoist that are accessible for visual examination.

During the inspection, attention should be paid to potential areas of vulnerability, such as areas where wear and tear are more likely to occur due to frequent use or exposure to environmental conditions. Personnel should look for indications of fraying or kinking in cables, cracks or deformations in pulleys, distortion or bending in hooks, and any signs of corrosion or structural damage in the hoist's framework.

It's essential to ensure that all components are free from any abnormalities that could compromise the hoist's integrity or safety during operation. Any identified damage or defects should be documented and addressed promptly to prevent further deterioration and mitigate the risk of accidents or equipment failure.

In addition to visual inspection, personnel should also be trained to recognize potential indicators of hidden defects or underlying issues that may not be immediately apparent. This may include abnormalities in the hoist's operation, such as unusual noises, vibrations, or irregularities in movement, which could signal underlying mechanical problems requiring further investigation.

Before initiating hoist operations, it is imperative to conduct thorough pre-start checks to verify the functionality and safety of all components involved. To begin, personnel should consult the hoist logbook, which serves as a repository for maintenance records and operational history. This logbook provides valuable insights into any previous issues or maintenance tasks performed on the hoist, allowing personnel to identify any recurring problems or areas of concern that may require attention.

During the pre-start checks, particular attention should be given to the condition of controls, switches, and safety devices that govern the operation of the hoist. Personnel should visually inspect these components to ensure they are free from damage, wear, or signs of malfunction. Additionally, functional tests should be conducted to verify that controls and switches operate as intended and that safety devices such as limit switches and emergency stop buttons are responsive and effective.

In addition to assessing the condition of individual components, personnel should also inspect the overall condition of the hoist, including its structural integrity and cleanliness. Any signs of damage, corrosion, or deterioration should be noted and addressed promptly to prevent further degradation and ensure the hoist's continued safe operation.

Furthermore, personnel should verify that all necessary safety precautions are in place before commencing hoist operations. This may include confirming the availability and functionality of safety features such as guardrails, safety harnesses, and emergency stop mechanisms.

By diligently performing pre-start checks and addressing any identified issues, personnel can help ensure the safe and efficient operation of the hoist, minimizing the risk of accidents or equipment failure during use. Regular maintenance and inspection practices contribute to the overall reliability and longevity of the hoist, enhancing workplace safety and productivity.

Performing operational checks is a critical step in ensuring the safe and efficient operation of the hoist. During this stage, personnel conduct thorough assessments to verify the functionality of various components while the hoist is in operation. This includes testing safety devices such as limit switches, overload protection systems, and emergency stop buttons to confirm their proper activation and responsiveness. By ensuring these safety mechanisms are functioning correctly, personnel can effectively mitigate potential risks and enhance overall safety.

Additionally, personnel should inspect the availability and condition of essential emergency equipment, such as fire extinguishers, located near the hoist. These emergency resources play a vital role in addressing unforeseen hazards or incidents that may occur during hoist operations. By ensuring that fire extinguishers and other emergency equipment are readily accessible and in good working condition, personnel can respond promptly to emergencies and minimize their impact on safety and operations.

Conducting operational checks allows personnel to identify any issues or abnormalities that may compromise the safe operation of the hoist. Any anomalies observed during the checks should be promptly addressed and rectified to prevent potential accidents or disruptions. By adhering to a systematic approach to operational checks, personnel can maintain the integrity and reliability of the hoist, contributing to a safer working environment for all personnel involved in hoist operations.

Ensuring that the hoist operates correctly is paramount to the safety and efficiency of its operation. Throughout the hoisting process, personnel must maintain vigilant monitoring to confirm that the hoist functions smoothly and without interruption. This involves observing the movement of the hoist and verifying that it operates without hesitation or abnormal noises, which could indicate potential issues or malfunctions. By continuously monitoring the hoist's performance, personnel can promptly identify any irregularities and take appropriate action to address them before they escalate into more significant problems.

In addition to observing the hoist's movement, personnel should also assess the surrounding environment to ensure there are no obstructions or impediments that could interfere with its operation. This includes checking for any debris, equipment, or other objects that may obstruct the hoist's path or pose a safety hazard. Clearing the work area of any potential obstacles helps to maintain smooth and uninterrupted hoist operation, minimizing the risk of accidents or damage to materials being transported.

Regular monitoring of the hoist's operation is essential throughout the duration of the lifting process. Personnel should remain attentive and vigilant, ready to respond quickly to any signs of abnormality or deviation from normal operation. By maintaining a proactive approach to monitoring, personnel can ensure the safe and efficient operation of the hoist, promoting a productive and secure work environment for all involved.

Checking communication equipment and alarm systems is crucial to maintaining a safe and efficient hoist operation environment. Personnel must conduct thorough inspections to verify the functionality and reliability of communication equipment, such as two-way radios or intercom systems. These communication tools facilitate effective communication between personnel operating the hoist and those on the ground, enabling seamless coordination and response to potential hazards or emergencies. By ensuring that communication equipment is operational, personnel can promptly convey critical information and instructions, enhancing overall safety and efficiency.

In addition to inspecting communication equipment, personnel should also test lighting and alarm systems to confirm their functionality and visibility in case of emergency situations. Adequate lighting is essential for maintaining visibility in low-light conditions, ensuring that personnel can safely navigate and operate the hoist even during nighttime or low-visibility scenarios. Similarly, functional alarm systems provide timely alerts in the event of emergencies, allowing personnel to initiate appropriate response actions promptly. Regular testing of lighting and alarm systems helps ensure their effectiveness and reliability when needed most, minimizing the risk of accidents or injuries during hoist operations.

During the inspection process, personnel should pay close attention to any signs of damage, wear, or malfunction in communication equipment and alarm systems. Any issues identified should be promptly addressed and rectified to maintain the integrity and effectiveness of these critical safety features. By conducting thorough checks and testing of communication equipment and alarm systems, personnel can enhance situational awareness, communication, and emergency preparedness, contributing to a safer and more efficient hoist operation environment overall.

Conducting a test run of the hoist is a critical step in ensuring its proper function and identifying any potential issues or abnormalities. During this process, personnel simulate typical operating conditions to assess the hoist's performance and reliability. As the hoist operates, personnel should listen attentively for any abnormal noises or vibrations that may indicate mechanical problems or malfunctions. Additionally, they should closely observe the hoist's movement and behaviour to detect any irregularities in its performance.

If any abnormalities are detected during the test run, personnel must take immediate action to address them and prevent further risks or hazards. This involves promptly shutting down the hoist to halt its operation, tagging it out of service to indicate its status, and reporting the issues to relevant personnel responsible for maintenance and repairs. By following these procedures, personnel can ensure that any identified abnormalities are addressed promptly and effectively, minimizing the risk of accidents or disruptions during hoist operations.

Regular testing and inspection of the hoist are essential components of proactive maintenance and safety protocols. By conducting test runs and promptly addressing any abnormalities, personnel can maintain the integrity and reliability of the hoist, promoting a safer and more efficient work environment for all involved. Additionally, documenting and reporting identified issues help facilitate timely repairs and preventive maintenance efforts, ensuring the continued safe operation of the hoist over time.

When defective equipment is identified during inspection or operation of the hoist, it is essential to take immediate action to mitigate risks and prevent further use of the faulty equipment. The first step is to isolate the defective equipment from use, ensuring that it is no longer accessible or operational. This helps prevent any unintended or unauthorized use of the equipment, reducing the risk of accidents or injuries.

Next, personnel must report the issue to appropriate personnel responsible for maintenance and repairs. This involves notifying supervisors, maintenance technicians, or other designated individuals who are trained to address equipment defects and malfunctions. Providing detailed information about the nature of the defect and its location helps ensure that the issue can be addressed promptly and effectively.

In addition to reporting the issue, personnel should tag out the defective equipment to clearly indicate its status and prevent its use until repairs are completed. Tagging out involves attaching a visible tag or label to the equipment, typically indicating that it is out of service or undergoing maintenance. This helps communicate the status of the equipment to other personnel and reinforces the importance of avoiding its use until it has been repaired and deemed safe for operation.

Finally, it is important to record details of the defect in maintenance logs or records for documentation and tracking purposes. This includes noting the nature of the defect, the date and time it was identified, any actions taken to isolate or address the issue, and the outcome of any repairs or maintenance activities. Maintaining accurate records helps track the status of equipment defects, monitor repair progress, and identify any recurring issues that may require further investigation or intervention.

By following these steps to isolate, report, tag out, and record defective equipment, personnel can effectively manage equipment defects and malfunctions, reduce safety risks, and ensure the continued safe operation of the hoist and associated equipment.

Conducting Hoist Operations

Operating a personnel and materials hoist involves several critical procedures aimed at ensuring safe and efficient operations while effectively managing communication and responding to emergency situations.

Firstly, maintaining communication is paramount throughout hoist operations. Clear and constant communication with relevant personnel, including operators and workers on the ground, is essential. Utilizing two-way radios, intercom systems, or other designated communication devices helps convey instructions, updates, and alerts as required. In emergency scenarios, it's vital to keep communication lines open and ensure all personnel are promptly informed of the situation and any necessary actions to be taken.

Operating a loaded hoist requires strict adherence to manufacturer requirements and guidelines. Ensuring the hoist is properly configured and rated for the load being lifted is crucial for safe operations. Following all safety precautions is imperative, and operators should aim to operate the hoist smoothly and steadily, avoiding sudden movements or excessive speeds that could compromise safety. Continuous monitoring of the hoist's performance during lifting and lowering operations allows for prompt adjustments to maintain stability and control.

Identifying and interpreting the Working Load Limit (WLL) of personnel and materials hoists involves several critical steps to ensure safe and efficient operations:

Firstly, reference the manufacturer's documentation, which typically comprises the hoist's specifications, operating manual, and load charts. These documents provide crucial information regarding the hoist's WLL, including its maximum capacity and any specific guidelines for its safe operation.

Understanding load ratings is essential. Familiarize yourself with load ratings and their significance in hoist operations. The WLL signifies the maximum load that the hoist can safely lift under normal operating conditions, considering factors such as structural integrity, mechanical components, and safety margins.

Consulting load charts provided by the hoist manufacturer is key. These charts outline the hoist's WLL for various configurations, such as different lift heights, boom lengths, or operating conditions. This allows operators to select the appropriate settings for their specific lifting tasks.

Environmental factors must also be considered. Take into account variables like temperature, wind conditions, and altitude, as they can impact the hoist's performance. Adjustments to the WLL may be necessary to ensure safe operation under varying conditions.

Calculate the weight of the load accurately using suitable measurement tools, such as scales or load cells. Ensure that the calculated load weight does not exceed the hoist's WLL as specified in the manufacturer documentation and load charts.

Verify compliance with all relevant safety regulations and guidelines. Double-check all calculations and confirm that the selected hoist configuration and operating parameters are suitable for the intended lifting task.

Communicate load information effectively to all personnel involved in the lifting operation, including operators, riggers, and supervisors. Clear communication ensures that everyone understands the WLL limitations and operates the hoist safely within its capacity.

Continuously monitor the load during hoist operation to ensure it remains within the WLL and that there are no signs of overload or instability. Promptly stop the lift if any issues or concerns arise and take corrective action as needed to maintain safety.

Familiarizing oneself with standard communication signals used during hoist operations is essential. These signals, which may include hand signals, audible alarms, or visual indicators, convey specific instructions or warnings. Accurately interpreting and responding to these signals ensures that all personnel involved in the hoisting process are aware of and understand the communicated messages. Effective communication signals facilitate coordinated movements and actions, reducing the risk of accidents or mishaps.

In the event of an emergency necessitating the lowering of the hoist, adhering to manufacturer requirements and procedures for emergency lowering is crucial. Activating the emergency lowering mechanism or controls as directed ensures a controlled and safe descent. Communicating the emergency situation to all relevant personnel and coordinating actions is essential to safeguard everyone involved. Following the emergency, conducting a thorough inspection of the hoist helps assess any potential damage or issues that may have occurred during the emergency lowering process.

Completing Hoist Operations

In operating a personnel and materials hoist, ensuring the safe shutdown of the equipment is crucial. Here's a detailed guide on how to carry out the shutdown procedures effectively:

1. Shut Down Hoist: Begin by shutting down the hoist strictly in accordance with the manufacturer's guidelines. Refer to the specific procedures outlined in the manufacturer's manual or operating instructions to ensure a safe and controlled shutdown process. Follow any recommended sequences or steps to power off the hoist systematically.

2. Carry Out Shut-Down Checks: After the hoist has been shut down, conduct comprehensive shut-down checks to confirm that all systems are deactivated and properly secured. This involves inspecting various components such as control panels, emergency stop buttons, power sources, and any other relevant parts to ensure they are in the appropriate state for shutdown. Verify that all moving parts have come to a complete stop.

3. Isolate and Secure Power: Take steps to isolate and secure the power source to prevent unauthorized access or accidental activation of the hoist. This may include actions such as turning off circuit breakers, disconnecting power cables, or implementing lockout/tagout procedures to ensure that the hoist cannot be restarted inadvertently. Use appropriate locking mechanisms or barriers to prevent access to power controls.

4. Report, Tag Out, Isolate, and Record Damages and Defects: If any damages or defects are discovered during the shutdown process, promptly report them to the relevant personnel or maintenance department. Tag out the affected components to indicate that they are not to be used until necessary repairs have been completed. Isolate any damaged or defective equipment to prevent further safety risks or accidents. Ensure that details

of any identified damages or defects are recorded accurately in maintenance logs or records for future reference and follow-up actions.

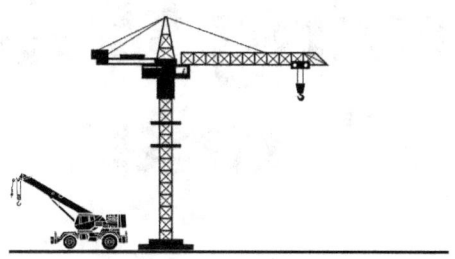

Chapter Seven
Slewing Mobile Cranes

The primary distinction between a static crane and a mobile crane lies in their mobility and respective applications. A static crane is immobile and installed at a fixed location, typically mounted on a stationary structure such as a building, tower, or fixed gantry. It lacks mobility and cannot be easily relocated without significant disassembly and reassembly efforts. Conversely, a mobile crane, such as the example shown as Figure 73, is specifically engineered for mobility, equipped with its own propulsion system or capable of being towed. Mounted on a wheeled chassis or truck, it possesses the ability to transport between different job sites, facilitating lifting operations as required.

Figure 73: Slewing mobile crane. ozz13x, CC BY 2.0, via Wikimedia Commons.

Static cranes find common usage in construction projects necessitating prolonged periods of heavy lifting, such as the erection of steel structures, assembly of large machinery, or loading and unloading tasks at ports. While they offer stable and precise lifting capabilities, they are confined to a fixed location. In contrast, mobile cranes exhibit versatility and are employed across various industries and applications, including construction, road and bridge construction, utility maintenance, and disaster recovery efforts. Their adaptability and accessibility to diverse job sites make them well-suited for tasks requiring frequent relocation or lifting operations in remote areas.

Although both static and mobile cranes excel in lifting heavy loads, their fundamental discrepancy lies in mobility. While static cranes are anchored to specific locations, providing stability and precision, mobile cranes offer flexibility and adaptability by manoeuvring between different job sites as required.

Mobile cranes are recognized for their high mobility, operational flexibility, and the ability to work on sites that may not be pre-equipped

(Lagerev et al., 2021). This mobility is a key advantage over static cranes, allowing them to be efficiently utilized in various construction projects (Azami et al., 2022).

The setup process of static cranes involves on-site assembly, which can be time-consuming and may require additional resources. On the other hand, mobile cranes can be quickly set up at different locations without the need for extensive manual input or additional data collection time prior to the lift (Fang et al., 2016). This ease of setup contributes to the overall efficiency and productivity of mobile cranes in construction projects.

Mobile cranes come in different configurations and sizes, ranging from small, compact models suitable for light lifting in urban areas to large, heavy-duty models capable of lifting massive loads on construction sites or industrial projects. They are widely used in construction, infrastructure development, maintenance, and other industries where lifting heavy objects or materials is necessary. Mobile cranes offer versatility, mobility, and flexibility, making them essential equipment for many lifting operations.

Mobile cranes come in various types, each designed for specific lifting tasks and operating conditions. Some of the most common types of mobile cranes include:

All-Terrain Crane: These cranes are designed to operate on both rough terrain and public roads, offering excellent mobility and versatility. All-terrain cranes feature multi-axle steering and often have telescopic booms for extended reach.

CRANE OPERATIONS

Figure 74: Terex AC 500-2 All-Terrain crane. Lutz Blohm from Schifferstadt, Germany, CC BY-SA 2.0, via Wikimedia Commons.

Rough Terrain Crane: Rough terrain cranes are specifically built to operate on rugged and uneven surfaces, such as construction sites. They feature robust tires, independent suspension systems, and often have lattice booms for heavy-duty lifting.

Figure 75: Grove RT600E Rough Terrain Crane. AlfvanBeem, CC0, via Wikimedia Commons.

Truck-Mounted Crane: These cranes are mounted on a truck chassis, providing mobility and convenience for various lifting tasks. Truck-mounted cranes are commonly used in urban areas and can quickly travel between job sites without the need for additional transportation. In some countries, these are referred to as a vehicle loading crane. Truck mounter cranes are discussed in the next chapter.

Figure 76: Truck mounter crane. Reise Reise, CC BY-SA 4.0, via Wikimedia Commons.

Crawler Crane: Crawler cranes are equipped with tracks instead of wheels, allowing them to move smoothly on soft or uneven terrain. These cranes are known for their stability and lifting capacity, making them suitable for heavy lifting operations on construction sites and industrial projects.

Figure 77: Telescopic crawler crane. Telescopic crawler crane by Graeme Yuill, CC BY-SA 2.0, via Wikimedia Commons.

Pick and Carry Crane: Pick and carry cranes, also known as carry deck cranes and mobile articulated crane, are compact mobile cranes designed for lifting and transporting loads within confined spaces. They feature a telescopic boom and can lift loads while moving, making them ideal for indoor construction or warehouse operations. These cranes are non-slewing and are outlined in Chapter 9.

Figure 78: Mobile articulated crane.

Each type of mobile crane has its unique features, advantages, and limitations, making it essential to select the right crane for the specific lifting task and operating conditions.

Slewing Mobile Cranes

A slewing mobile crane is a type of crane that is mounted on a mobile chassis and equipped with a rotating boom. This crane is designed for versatility and mobility, allowing it to be easily transported to various job sites and perform a wide range of lifting tasks.

The key feature of a slewing mobile crane is its ability to rotate or slew the entire upper structure, including the boom and load, in a full circle. This rotation capability enables the crane operator to position the load precisely and reach different areas within the crane's operating radius without having to reposition the entire crane.

Slewing mobile cranes come in various sizes and configurations, ranging from compact models mounted on truck chassis to larger models with telescopic or lattice booms mounted on crawler tracks. They are commonly used in construction, infrastructure development, industrial maintenance, and other applications requiring heavy lifting and precise load placement.

The operational principles of a slewing mobile crane encompass several fundamental components and procedures crucial for its safe and efficient functioning:

- Mobility: Slewing mobile cranes are affixed to a mobile chassis, facilitating easy transportation between different job sites. Equipped with either wheels or tracks, depending on the model, they possess the capability to traverse various terrains and access remote or challenging areas.

- Slewing Mechanism: A pivotal aspect of slewing mobile cranes is the slewing mechanism, which enables the crane's upper structure—including the boom and load—to rotate or slew in a complete circle. This controlled rotation, typically driven by hydraulic or electric motors, is indispensable for precisely positioning loads and reaching diverse areas within the crane's operational radius.

- Boom Configuration: Slewing mobile cranes exhibit varying boom configurations, comprising telescopic booms, lattice booms, or a blend of both. Hydraulically extended or retracted, the boom facilitates reaching different heights and distances, enhancing versatility in lifting operations.

- Load Capacity: Slewing mobile cranes are assigned specific load capacities, defining the maximum weight they can safely lift. Adherence to these load capacity limits is imperative for preventing overloading, which could result in accidents or structural damage.

- Stabilization: Maintaining stability during lifting activities is ensured through outriggers or stabilizer legs extending from the crane's chassis. Deployed prior to lifting commencement, these stabilizing mechanisms are adjusted as necessary to uphold balance and avert tipping.

- Operator Controls: Operators manoeuvre slewing mobile cranes from a control cabin positioned atop the crane's upper structure or via remote control systems. Utilizing joysticks, levers, and other controls, they manage crane movements, boom extension or retraction, and slewing motions.

- Safety Systems: Slewing mobile cranes are equipped with an array of safety features and systems aimed at safeguarding both personnel and equipment during lifting operations. These encompass overload protection devices, emergency stop buttons, load moment indicators, and collision avoidance systems, among others.

The major components of a slewing mobile crane include:
1. Chassis: The chassis forms the base of the crane and supports all other components. It typically includes the wheels or tracks that enable the crane's mobility.

2. Upper Structure: Mounted on the chassis, the upper structure houses the engine, operator's cab, slewing mechanism, and other essential components. It rotates on the chassis to facilitate positioning of the crane and its load.

3. Boom: The boom is an extendable arm that supports the load

and enables the crane to reach varying heights and distances. Slewing mobile cranes may feature different types of booms, such as telescopic or lattice booms, depending on the model and application.

4. Counterweights: Counterweights are used to balance the crane and offset the weight of the load being lifted. They are typically located near the rear of the upper structure and can be added or removed as needed to maintain stability.

5. Outriggers or Stabilizers: Outriggers or stabilizers are deployed from the chassis to provide additional support and stability during lifting operations. They are essential for preventing tipping and ensuring safe crane operation, especially when lifting heavy loads or operating on uneven terrain.

6. Slewing Mechanism: The slewing mechanism allows the crane's upper structure to rotate or slew in a full circle. It is typically driven by hydraulic or electric motors and controlled by the operator to position the crane and its load accurately.

7. Operator's Cab: The operator's cab is where the crane operator controls the crane's movements and operations. It is equipped with controls, instruments, and displays that provide the operator with essential information and enable them to safely operate the crane.

8. Hydraulic System: Slewing mobile cranes rely on hydraulic systems to power various functions, including boom extension and retraction, lifting, and slewing. The hydraulic system consists of hydraulic pumps, cylinders, valves, and hoses that work together to generate and control hydraulic power.

9. Electrical System: The electrical system provides power to the

crane's electrical components, including lights, indicators, safety devices, and control systems. It includes wiring, switches, relays, and other electrical components necessary for the crane's operation.

10. Load Handling Equipment: Load handling equipment, such as hooks, slings, and lifting attachments, are used to secure and manipulate loads during lifting operations. These components are essential for safely lifting and moving materials using the crane.

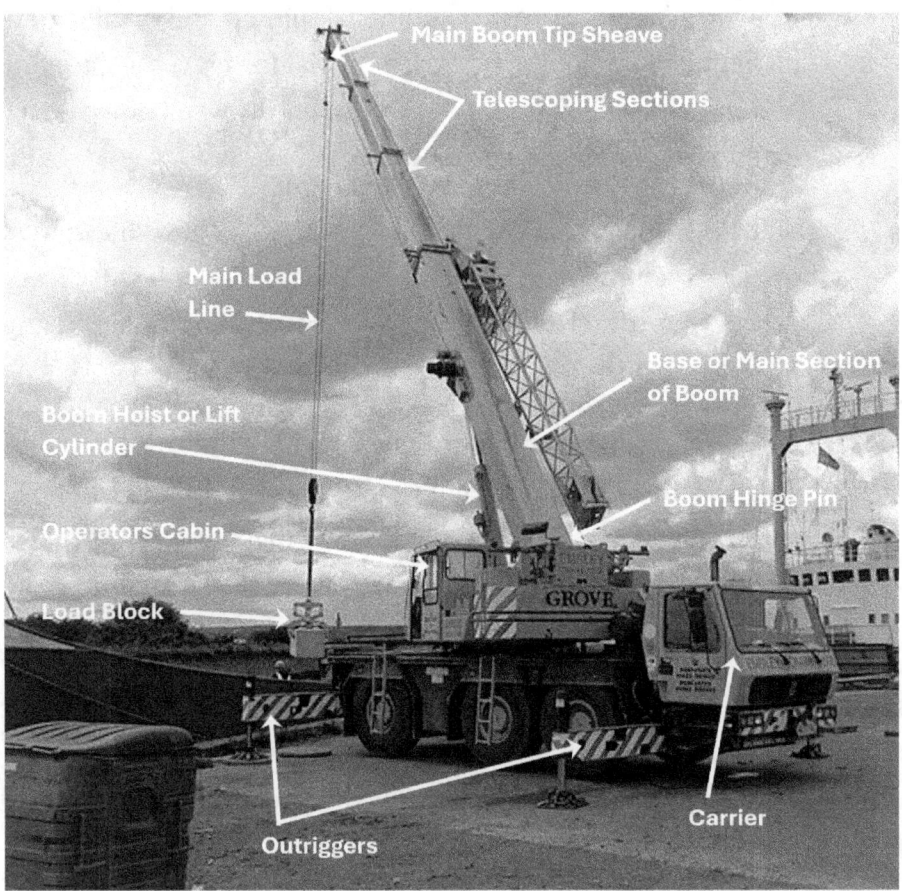

Figure 79: Slewing mobile crane components. Background David Wright, CC BY 2.0 , via Wikimedia Commons.

A slewing upper structure entails the installation of a boom, hoisting/derricking crane equipment, or similar apparatus within a welded structure known as a "slewing frame." This frame is affixed atop the base carrier via a slewing bearing, enabling the entire structure to rotate left and right.

In rough terrain crane configurations, the slewing base within the slewing frame houses a boom, derricking mechanism (such as a derricking cylinder), hoisting mechanism, and an operational cab for crane and driving activities. A counterweight or comparable weighted structure is typically positioned at the rear of the hoisting mechanism to maintain equilibrium.

Rough-terrain cranes, also known as off-road cranes, are affixed to a four-wheeled undercarriage, designed with wider wheels and base to enhance the crane's stability, while taller wheels increase ground clearance over rugged terrain.

Equipped with a telescoping boom and outriggers, rough-terrain cranes ensure stability and support during lifting operations. They boast a lighter weight compared to all-terrain cranes, attributable to two main factors: rough-terrain cranes feature a single, compact cab from which both operations and driving are conducted, and they are powered by a single engine responsible for both the boom and the undercarriage functionalities.

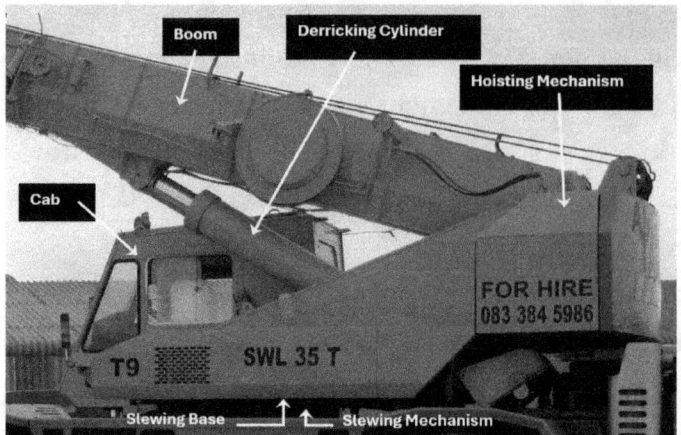

Figure 80: Rough Terrain Crane Slewing Upper Structure. Background Tadano 35T crane on rough terrain chassis, Bob Adams from Amanzimtoti, South Africa, CC BY-SA 2.0, via Wikimedia Commons.

The slewing mechanism facilitates the rotational movement of the slewing upper structure to the left and right while being affixed to the base carrier. In numerous designs, the slewing bearing is situated atop the base carrier frame, with the slewing upper structure mounted on the upper surface of the slewing bearing. This configuration allows for unrestricted 360° rotation.

Crane stability is critical to prevent serious incidents involving cranes. Several factors influence crane stability, including:

- Operating the crane close to or at its maximum rated capacity.

- Ground conditions and how the crane's outrigger pads, tires, or tracks are supported.

- The slope of the ground, including side slope and the slope in the direction of crane travel, especially relevant for non-slewing mobile cranes.

- Wind conditions, which vary based on the size and shape of the suspended load and crane boom.

Counterweights play a crucial role in maintaining crane stability. If the counterweight is insufficient for the load and boom setup, the crane may tilt towards the direction of the suspended load. Conversely, if the counterweight is too heavy for the boom configuration, the crane could overturn backward. This risk increases when the crane travels uphill with the boom extended or when the outrigger pads beneath the counterweight lack proper support on soft ground. Additionally, failure to extend or lower the outriggers into position can contribute to instability.

On smaller mobile cranes, counterweights are typically fixed and not easily removable. However, some designs allow for counterweights to be removed for transportation or when handling lighter loads. It's crucial to attach the appropriate type and quantity of counterweights for each specific lift, following the manufacturer's instructions meticulously.

When counterweights are removable, they should be clearly marked with the crane manufacturer's name or logo and their respective weight. Furthermore, if the crane is equipped with a rated capacity limiter, accurate data regarding the counterweight and boom configuration must be inputted into the system, aligning with the information provided on the relevant load chart.

Crane instrumentation, including indicators, encompasses safety instruments and electronic load monitoring equipment installed on mobile cranes, which include:

- Rated Capacity Limiters: Mobile cranes manufactured since 2002, with a rated capacity exceeding 3 tonnes, should be equipped with rated capacity limiters. These limiters aim to prevent exceeding the crane's rated capacity, maintaining it within a tolerance of 100 to 110 percent to avoid lifting and radius increases. Operating mobile cranes within their rated design capacity is crucial for safety.

- Working Radius Indicators: A working radius indicator typically measures the radius of the suspended load from the centre of the slew ring. It should be present on all mobile cranes originally designed with this feature. The indicator, displayed in meters, should be accurate to within +10 percent and -3 percent of the actual radius.

- Load Indicators: Mobile cranes with a maximum rated capacity exceeding 3 tonnes should have load indicators installed. These indicators measure and display the mass of the load being lifted, assisting the crane operator in adhering to the load chart and the crane's rated capacity. The load indicator should be capable of continuously displaying the mass of the suspended load.

- Load Charts: Load charts, also known as rated capacity charts, outline the safe lifting capabilities of the crane. These charts should be accessible in the crane cabin for the operator to verify that the crane is not being overloaded. Some mobile cranes may feature multiple load charts for different boom and counterweight configurations, each containing various conditions that must be followed to ensure safe lifting.

- Stability Function of Load Charts: When the load being lifted causes the crane to become unstable and potentially overturn, it's referred to as tipping. The maximum load that the crane can lift before tipping occurs is determined by applying a stability factor, recorded on the crane load charts. This stability factor accounts for dynamic factors such as crane motion, load swaying, and wind effects. Typically, the stability factor is 75.0 percent when operating on rubber or outriggers and 66.6 percent when in mobiling mode. However, overturning can still occur with smaller loads in windy conditions, on sloping ground, or if the crane is not operated smoothly.

Planning Slewing Mobile Crane Operation

When operating a slewing mobile crane, a series of steps are followed to ensure safe and effective operations:

- Identification of Task Requirements: Initially, task requirements are identified by reviewing work orders or similar documents. The lift plan is then confirmed with relevant personnel, and a thorough site inspection is conducted in accordance with workplace protocols.

- Confirmation of Work Area Operating Surface: The quality of the ground surface in the work area is carefully verified to ascertain its suitability for the mobile crane's operational use. This process aligns with workplace procedures to ensure safety and stability during crane operations.

- Establishment of Rated Capacity and Working Load Limit: The Rated Capacity (RC) of the mobile crane and the Working Load Limit (WLL) of the lifting gear are established for the specific load and task requirements. This is done in strict adherence to both manufacturer specifications and workplace procedures.

- Assessment of Operating Paths: An assessment is made to determine appropriate paths for operating the mobile crane and manoeuvring loads within the work area. This assessment follows established workplace procedures to optimize efficiency and safety.

- Application of Hazard Identification and Risk Control Measures: Relevant hazards are identified, and appropriate risk elimination or control measures are implemented. Associated personnel are informed of these measures, ensuring compliance with workplace protocols and enhancing safety.

- Confirmation of Traffic Management Plan: The implementation of the traffic management plan is confirmed, and adherence to it is ensured. This step is crucial for maintaining safe operations in areas with vehicular or pedestrian traffic, in accordance with workplace procedures.

- Identification and Testing of Communication Procedures: Communication procedures are identified and tested with associated personnel to facilitate effective communication during crane operations. This ensures clear and efficient communication channels, as outlined by workplace protocols.

- Confirmation of Task Requirements: All tasks are confirmed to ensure alignment with the requirements specified in the lift plan and adherence to workplace procedures. This step verifies that operations proceed as planned and in accordance with safety guidelines.

- Obtaining and Interpreting Information for Lifting Equipment and Gear: Information necessary for compliance with manufacturer requirements regarding the inspection, use, maintenance, and storage of lifting equipment and gear is obtained and interpreted. This ensures proper equipment handling and maintenance practices, promoting safety and equipment longevity.

Ensuring the suitability of the work area operating surface involves a systematic assessment of ground quality to ascertain its capability to sustain the safe and efficient operation of the mobile crane. Initiate the process by conducting a comprehensive site inspection encompassing the entirety of the work area slated for the deployment of the mobile crane. This inspection should encompass not only the immediate vicinity but also the surrounding terrain. Evaluate the ground conditions meticulously, considering factors such as soil composition, texture, and stability. Determine whether the ground is sufficiently firm and level to bear the weight of the crane and the loads it will be lifting.

Identify any potential obstacles or hazards on the ground that could obstruct crane operations or pose safety threats. These may encompass debris, uneven terrain, overhead obstacles, or subsurface utilities. Evaluate the accessibility of the work area for the mobile crane, ensuring unimpeded pathways for manoeuvring. Verify that there are no obstructions hindering the crane's movement.

Adhere to workplace procedures and guidelines governing the assessment of ground suitability. Follow prescribed protocols for conducting site inspections and recording observations. Seek input from site supervisors, engineers, or safety personnel if necessary, to validate ground conditions and ensure all pertinent factors are considered. Document the findings of the ground assessment comprehensively, including any noted observations or concerns regarding ground quality or suitability. This documentation serves as a vital record for compliance purposes and aids in the formulation of lift plans.

Ground conditions play a pivotal role in ensuring the stability of cranes during operations, with various factors influencing the suitability of the ground for crane deployment. Ground-related considerations include:

- Factors Affecting Ground Support: Ground conditions can vary significantly, impacted by factors such as surface water, soil composition (e.g., mud, clay, sand, or rock), backfilled ground, hidden underground cavities, continued crane operation in one location, and the presence of pressurized underground services. The location of underground services, like shallow fire hydrant mains, must also be considered to prevent accidents.

- Ground Inspection and Assessment: Decisions regarding ground suitability rely on visual inspection, but in cases where it's challenging to assess, documented information on ground bearing pressure from a geotechnical engineer can provide valuable insights. Rock formations, while typically stable, may not extend far below the surface, necessitating careful examination of nearby excavations or trenches to gauge ground integrity.

- Crane Operation Impact: Continuous crane operation in one location can compact the ground underneath the outriggers, potentially compromising stability. Sloping ground poses additional risks, affecting the crane's working radius and stability, leading to overturning hazards. Manufacturers typically recommend operating cranes on firm, level ground to minimize risks associated with sloping or uneven terrain.

- Side Slope Considerations: Side slopes, even as minimal as 2 or 3 degrees, can significantly impact crane stability, particularly when combined with factors like high boom luff angles, telescoped booms, high load centre of gravity, or articulated crane articulation. Soft ground, pneumatic tires, and suspension movement further exacerbate the risk of overturning on side slopes.

- Crane Proximity to Excavations: Setting up cranes near excavations or trenches introduces risks of collapse, especially in softer ground conditions or areas with groundwater presence. The distance between crane outrigger support dunnage and excavation edges should be carefully determined based on ground stability, with stricter guidelines for loose or backfilled ground.

Figure 81: Outcome of operating a mobile crane on soft ground. Pl77, CC BY-SA 3.0, via Wikimedia Commons.

Outriggers and stabilizers are integral components of crane systems, featuring various configurations depending on the crane type. They serve to mitigate the risk of rollover incidents by expanding the vehicle's support base beyond its natural footprint. While outriggers elevate the vehicle's wheels off the ground, stabilizers, primarily found on vehicle loading cranes, stabilize the vehicle without lifting its wheels.

The deployment of outriggers on mobile cranes significantly enhances stability during lifting operations, regardless of ground conditions. It's essential to place timbers or other load-distributing materials under the outriggers, except in cases where engineering dictates direct outrigger pad application. Proper outrigger setup should align with the manufacturer's instructions for the specific crane type, and markings should indicate partial or full extension positions for operator guidance.

Crane operators must adhere to manufacturer-approved practices and employ suitable overload interlocks when using partially extended outriggers for lifting operations. The correct outrigger configuration, as outlined in the relevant load chart, should be followed for such lifts to ensure safety and stability.

The maximum pressure exerted by a crane on the ground depends on several factors, including crane mass, configuration (e.g., boom length and centre of gravity), and load mass. Ground bearing capacity must exceed the maximum pressure applied by the crane to ensure adequate support. Before conducting a lift, operators must verify ground bearing capacity and consider using control measures like outrigger pads.

Manufacturers typically furnish information on maximum loads and outrigger pressure for various boom configurations in the crane operation manual stored in the operator's cabin. Additionally, a range of materials, including timber, plastic, metal pads, and bog mats, can be utilized to distribute the crane and load mass to the ground effectively.

Timbers with rectangular cross-sections are commonly used as outrigger pads, but plastic or metal pads are also available for certain crane models. In situations with low ground bearing capacity or when ground protection is necessary, plastic or timber bog mats may be employed. For crawler cranes, which exert less point load due to their larger track contact area, bog mats or other supportive materials may be necessary for heavy lifts or poor ground conditions.

Figure 82: Outriggers extended with metal pads. PvOberstein, CC0, via Wikimedia Commons.

It's crucial to adhere to manufacturer-specified material dimensions and configurations for outrigger pads, timbers, steel plates, and bog mats. If such information is not provided by the manufacturer, a competent person should determine the appropriate material size and layout based on load requirements and ground conditions.

Figure 83: Outriggers extended and padded with timbers. High Contrast, CC BY 3.0 DE, via Wikimedia Commons.

Calculating the pressure exerted by outriggers involves considering the ground bearing capacity, which varies depending on the ground type. In cases where the ground comprises a mix of soil types, the lowest bearing capacity among them should determine the maximum permissible ground pressure when the crane is set up on outriggers. Many crane manufacturers offer data on the maximum ground pressure applicable when the crane operates at its maximum capacity within the load chart's stability range.

For instance, hard rock can typically withstand a maximum permissible ground pressure (PMAX) of 200 tonnes per square meter, while shale rock and sandstone have a PMAX of 80 tonnes per square meter.

Compacted gravel, asphalt, and compacted sand have PMAX values of 40, 20, and 20 tonnes per square meter, respectively. Stiff clay (when dry) and soft clay (when dry) can tolerate up to 20 and 10 tonnes per square meter, respectively. Loose sand and wet clay have even lower tolerances, with PMAX values of 10 tonnes per square meter and less than 10 tonnes per square meter, respectively.

Ground bearing pressure, also known as soil bearing pressure or simply bearing pressure, refers to the pressure exerted by a structure or load on the ground surface. It is the force per unit area that the weight of a structure or load applies to the supporting ground underneath.

In the context of cranes or heavy equipment, ground bearing pressure is particularly important as it determines whether the ground can adequately support the weight of the crane or equipment without causing soil failure or instability. Ground bearing pressure is typically measured in units such as tonnes per square meter (t/m^2) or pounds per square inch (psi).

Understanding ground bearing pressure is essential for ensuring the stability and safety of operations involving heavy machinery, as exceeding the ground's bearing capacity can lead to ground failure, sinking, or even tipping of the equipment. Therefore, calculations and assessments of ground bearing pressure are crucial for selecting appropriate equipment, determining proper ground preparation, and ensuring safe operation on various types of terrain.

The maximum force exerted by any outrigger on the ground occurs at the tipping point, precisely when the crane is on the verge of overturning, and the crane boom directly aligns with an outrigger foot. This critical scenario underscores the importance of accurately calculating and adhering to the permissible ground pressures to ensure crane stability and prevent accidents.

Crane pads or mats, which can be made of various materials such as timber, steel, HDPE, among others, serve to evenly distribute the load of the crane onto the ground surface. The adequacy of the crane pad is assessed based on two main criteria:

1. The size of the mat should be sufficient to spread the load over the ground, ensuring that the stress level remains below the ground bearing capacity. This helps prevent excessive pressure on the ground, minimizing the risk of soil compaction or damage.

2. The strength and structural integrity of the mat are essential factors in determining its suitability. The mat must be robust enough to withstand the load exerted by the crane without deforming or failing. This ensures the stability and safety of the crane operation by providing reliable support to the equipment on various ground surfaces.

There are a number of calculations that can be done to determine correct pad size.

Outrigger Point Load

An outrigger point load refers to the amount of force exerted on each outrigger point of a crane. It is a critical factor in crane operations as it directly affects the stability and safety of the crane during lifting operations.

The outrigger point load is calculated by dividing the total weight supported by the crane's outriggers by the area over which this weight is distributed. Here's the basic formula for calculating the outrigger point load:

Outrigger Point Load = Total Weight Supported / Area of Load Distribution

Assuming you know the ground bearing pressure, to calculate the total weight supported, you need to add up the weights of various components, including:

- The weight of the crane itself

- The weight of any counterweights attached to the crane

- The weight of the load being lifted

- The weight of any additional attachments such as hook blocks, tackle, or fly jibs

Once you have determined the total weight supported, you then divide this by the area over which the weight is distributed. This area is typically determined by dividing the total weight by the ground bearing pressure (GBP), which is the maximum allowable pressure that the ground can support without risk of failure. The resulting outrigger point load provides crucial information for ensuring that the crane is set up safely and that the ground can adequately support the load during lifting operations.

This calculation is used to determine the outrigger point loading of a crane based on a ground bearing pressure of 25 tonnes for this example. Here's how the calculation works:

1. **Determine the Total Weight Supported:** Add the weight of the crane, counterweight, load being lifted, hook block/tackle, and fly jib.

    - Crane weight: 72 tonnes

    - Counterweight: 60 tonnes

    - Load weight: 11.4 tonnes

    - Hook block/tackle: 0.7 tonnes

    - Fly jib: 0.5 tonnes Total weight = 72 + 60 + 11.4 + 0.7 + 0.5 = 144.6 tonnes

2. **Calculate the Area of Load Distribution:** Divide the total weight by the ground bearing pressure (25 tonnes) to find the

CRANE OPERATIONS 349

area in square meters (m²) over which the load is distributed.

- Area = Total weight / Ground Bearing Pressure
- Area = 144.6 tonnes / 25
- Area ≈ 5.784 m²

3. **Determine the Pad Size:** Take the square root of the calculated area to find the dimensions of a square pad that would distribute the load evenly. Round up to the nearest suitable pad size.

   - √5.784 ≈ 2.4056 meters
   - Pad size: 2.4 meters (rounded up from 2.4056)

4. **Calculate the Outrigger Point Load:** Divide the total weight by the area of the chosen pad size to find the outrigger point load.

   - Outrigger Point Load = Total weight / Pad area
   - Outrigger Point Load ≈ 144.6 tonnes / 5.29 m²
   - Outrigger Point Load ≈ 27.34 tonnes

Therefore, the outrigger point load is approximately 21 tonnes.

Assuming the crane was being set up on asphalt, let's repeat the calculation with a ground bearing pressure of 20 tonnes per square metre:

1. **Determine the Total Weight Supported:**

   - Crane weight: 72 tonnes
   - Counterweight: 60 tonnes

- Load weight: 11.4 tonnes
- Hook block/tackle: 0.7 tonnes
- Fly jib: 0.5 tonnes
- Total weight = 72 + 60 + 11.4 + 0.7 + 0.5 = 144.6 tonnes

2. **Calculate the Area of Load Distribution:**

    - Area = Total weight / Ground Bearing Pressure
    - Area = 144.6 tonnes / 20 tonnes
    - Area ≈ 7.23 square meters (m²)

3. **Determine the Pad Size:**

    - Take the square root of the calculated area to find the dimensions of a square pad that would distribute the load evenly.
    - √7.23 ≈ 2.6896 meters
    - Pad size: 2.7 meters (rounded up from 2.6896)

4. **Calculate the Outrigger Point Load:**

    - Divide the total weight by the area of the chosen pad size to find the outrigger point load.
    - Outrigger Point Load = Total weight / Pad area
    - Outrigger Point Load ≈ 144.6 tonnes / 7.29 m²
    - Outrigger Point Load ≈ 19.83 tonnes

Therefore, based on a ground bearing pressure of 20 tonnes per square meter, the outrigger point load is approximately 19.83 tonnes.

And now assuming the same lift was being performed on loose sand, having a ground bearing pressure of 10 tonnes per square metre:

1. **Determine the Total Weight Supported:**

    - Crane weight: 72 tonnes
    - Counterweight: 60 tonnes
    - Load weight: 11.4 tonnes
    - Hook block/tackle: 0.7 tonnes
    - Fly jib: 0.5 tonnes
    - Total weight = 72 + 60 + 11.4 + 0.7 + 0.5 = 144.6 tonnes

2. **Calculate the Area of Load Distribution:**

    - Area = Total weight / Ground Bearing Pressure
    - Area = 144.6 tonnes / 10 tonnes
    - Area ≈ 14.46 square meters (m^2)

3. **Determine the Pad Size:**

    - Take the square root of the calculated area to find the dimensions of a square pad that would distribute the load evenly.
    - $\sqrt{14.46}$ ≈ 3.8 meters
    - Pad size: 3.8 meters

4. **Calculate the Outrigger Point Load:**

    - Divide the total weight by the area of the chosen pad size to find the outrigger point load.
    - Outrigger Point Load = Total weight / Pad area

- Outrigger Point Load ≈ 144.6 tonnes / 14.46 m²

- Outrigger Point Load ≈ 10 tonnes

Therefore, based on a ground bearing pressure of 10 tonnes per square meter, the outrigger point load is approximately 10 tonnes.

It is clear from these calculations that a larger pad is required to support the crane as the maximum permissible ground pressure decreases.

This calculation is crucial for ensuring the safe operation of a crane by determining the load exerted on the outrigger points. Here's why it's important:

1. Determining Total Weight Supported: By adding up the weights of the crane, counterweight, load, and additional attachments, we get the total weight that needs to be supported by the outrigger points. This step ensures that the crane does not exceed its capacity, which could lead to instability and potential accidents.

2. Calculating Area of Load Distribution: Dividing the total weight by the ground bearing pressure helps us understand how much area the load is distributed over. This is crucial for determining the pressure exerted on the ground and ensuring it does not exceed the ground's capacity to support the crane.

3. Determining Pad Size: Taking the square root of the calculated area helps find the dimensions of a square pad that would evenly distribute the load. Choosing the appropriate pad size ensures that the load is spread out over a sufficient area, minimizing the risk of the crane sinking into the ground or causing damage to the surface.

4. Calculating Outrigger Point Load: Dividing the total weight by the area of the chosen pad size gives us the outrigger point load. This value indicates the amount of force exerted on each

outrigger point, helping crane operators determine if the ground is suitable for supporting the crane safely. If the outrigger point load exceeds the ground's capacity, it could lead to instability and pose a risk to both personnel and equipment.

This calculation provides essential information for crane operators to ensure that the crane is set up safely and securely on the ground, minimizing the risk of accidents and ensuring smooth and efficient crane operations.

Crane Pad Suitability Calculation

This following outlines how to calculate the pressure imposed by a crane on the ground and how to determine if the crane pad size is suitable for the lift.

Firstly, the pressure exerted by the crane on the ground is calculated using the formula (The Crane Industry Council of Australia, 2017):

Pressure=Force ÷ Area

The force exerted by the crane is typically known and is determined by the load being lifted. For example, if a lift study indicates that a crane imposes a maximum load of 48 tonnes on the outrigger, then the force can be calculated by multiplying the load by the acceleration due to gravity (9.8 m/s^2) to convert tonnes to kilonewtons (kN). Thus, the force would be:

Force=48 tonnes×9.8 m/s^2=470.4 kN

The area over which the force is distributed is determined by the size of the crane pad. For instance, if the available crane pad size is 1.7 meters by 1.7 meters, then the area would be:

Area of the crane pad=1.7 m×1.7 m=2.89 m^2

Substituting the calculated force and area into the pressure formula, we can find the pressure exerted by the crane on the ground:

Pressure=470.4 kN ÷ 2.89 m^2

Once the pressure is calculated, it is compared with the maximum permissible ground pressure. If the pressure exerted by the crane is less than or equal to the maximum permissible ground pressure, then the crane pad size is considered adequate for the lift. For example, if the maximum permissible ground pressure is 200 kPa, and the calculated pressure is lower than this value, then the crane pad size is suitable for the lift.

To repeat the calculation with the provided weights in the prior example, we'll follow the same process:

Given:
- Crane weight: 72 tonnes
- Counterweight: 60 tonnes
- Load weight: 11.4 tonnes
- Hook block/tackle weight: 0.7 tonnes
- Fly jib weight: 0.5 tonnes
- Crane pad size: 1.7 meters by 1.7 meters

1. Calculate the total weight supported by the crane:

Total weight=72 tonnes+60 tonnes+11.4 tonnes+0.7 tonnes+0.5 tonnes

Total weight=144.6 tonnes s

1. Calculate the force exerted by the total weight:

Force=144.6 tonnes×9.8 m/s^2

Force=1418.28 kN

1. Calculate the area of the crane pad:

Area of the crane pad=1.7 m×1.7 m

Area of the crane pad=2.89 m^2

1. Calculate the pressure exerted by the total weight on the ground:

Pressure=1418.28 kN ÷ 2.89 m2

Pressure≈490.73 kN/m²

Again, converting the pressure to kilopascals (kPa):

1 kN/m2=0.1 kPa

490.73 kN/m²×0.1=49.073 kPa

1. Compare the calculated pressure with the maximum permissible ground pressure. If the calculated pressure is lower than or equal to the maximum permissible ground pressure, then the crane pad size is suitable for the lift. If not, the mat size needs to be reconsidered.

It is crucial to ensure that when outriggers apply pressure to the ground, they do not sink into the soil or cause adjacent excavations to collapse, as this could result in the crane tipping over. The pressure exerted by outriggers creates stresses on the ground beneath them, commonly referred to as the "zone of influence" (The Crane Industry Council of Australia, 2017). Typically, this zone operates at a 45-degree angle or extends one meter from the top, depending on whichever measurement is greater, as shown in Figure 84. However, the angle may vary depending on factors such as ground composition and outrigger support design. In situations where ground conditions are uncertain or further clarification is needed, it may be necessary to seek input from an engineer.

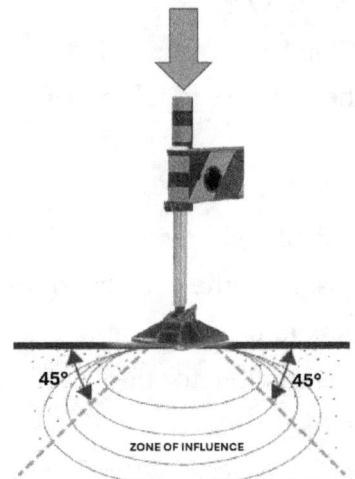

Figure 84: Zone of influence.

When positioning a crane near a trench, it is essential to adhere to specific guidelines. The crane should be set up in a manner where the nearest outrigger to the trench is positioned at a distance equal to or greater than the depth of the trench (The Crane Industry Council of Australia, 2017). This guideline operates under the assumption that the zone of influence operates at a 45-degree angle. Trench and batter collapse potential are shown in Figure 85 and Figure 86.

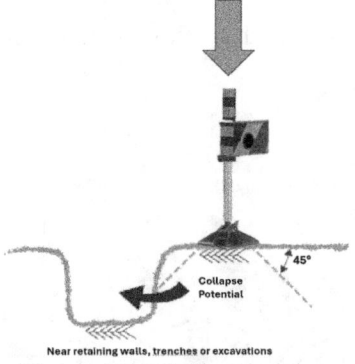

Figure 85: Collapse potential near trenches and excavations.

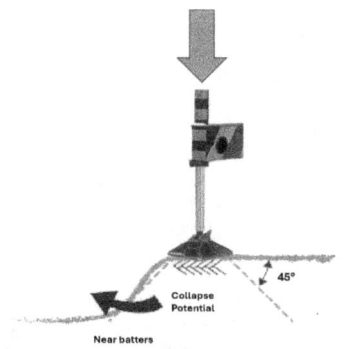

Figure 86: Collapse potential near batters.

Various load scenarios can subject the ground to varying loads and forces. When operating a crane, factors such as boom length, slew angle, and slew arc can fluctuate, leading to changes in the forces acting on the outriggers. While it's commonly assumed that maximum loads and forces occur during operation at full capacity, this isn't always true. For instance, outrigger loads could peak without any load on the hook at minimum radius due to the backward moment from the counterweight. Additionally, in certain load situations, the entire crane load may predominantly affect a single outrigger or crawler track when the boom or counterweight is slewed over that outrigger or over the side of that track. These scenarios are shown in Figure 87 through to Figure 90.

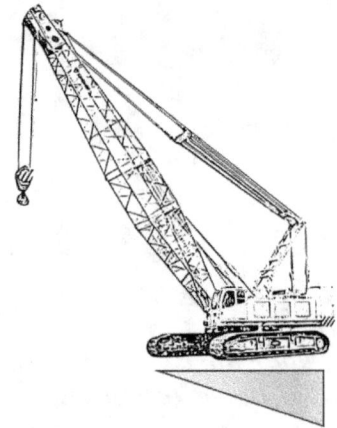

Figure 87: With no load on the hook the pressure is at highest under the rear end of the tracks due to the counterweight.

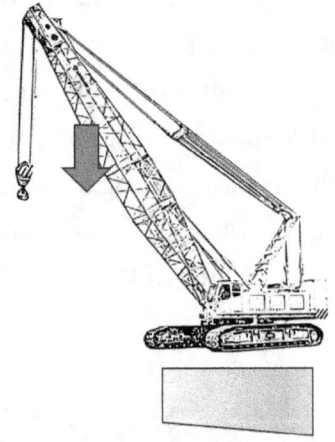

Figure 88: With no load on the hook and the jib luffing down, the pressure changes from triangular to trapezoidal distribution.

CRANE OPERATIONS

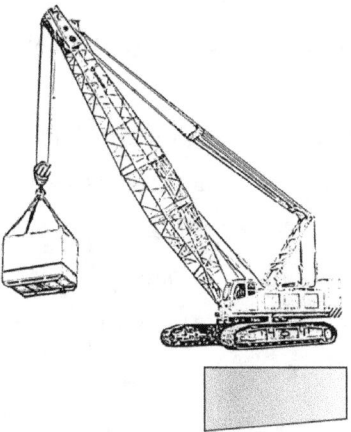

Figure 89: With load on the hook, the pressure changes from triangular to trapezoidal distribution.

Figure 90: With load on the hook and the jib luffing down the pressure changes from trapezoidal to triangular distribution, with the highest under the front end of the tracks.

Operating a slewing mobile crane involves several steps, including the establishment of the rated capacity and working load limit. This includes:

1. Understand Manufacturer Specifications: Begin by thoroughly understanding the manufacturer's specifications for the slewing mobile crane. These specifications outline the crane's capabilities, including its rated capacity, operational limitations, and safety guidelines. Pay close attention to any load charts provided by the manufacturer.

2. Assess Task Requirements: Identify the specific load and task requirements that the crane will be used for. This includes understanding the weight of the load to be lifted, the distance it needs to be moved, and any other relevant factors that may impact the crane's operation.

3. Determine Rated Capacity: The rated capacity (RC) of the crane refers to the maximum load weight that the crane is designed to lift safely under ideal conditions. Refer to the load charts provided by the manufacturer to determine the rated capacity for the specific configuration of the crane, including boom length, angle, and other variables.

4. Identify Working Load Limit: The working load limit (WLL) refers to the maximum load weight that the lifting gear, such as slings, shackles, or hooks, can safely handle during the lifting operation. Consult the manufacturer's specifications for the lifting gear being used to determine its working load limit.

5. Adhere to Workplace Procedures: Ensure that all procedures and protocols outlined by the workplace are followed rigorously. This includes complying with any safety regulations, conducting pre-operation inspections, and obtaining necessary

permits or approvals before beginning the lift.

6. Verify Compatibility: Confirm that the rated capacity of the crane aligns with the working load limit of the lifting gear being used. The combined weight of the load and the lifting gear must not exceed the rated capacity of the crane.

7. Document Information: Keep detailed records of the established rated capacity, working load limit, and any other relevant information pertaining to the lift. This documentation serves as a reference for all personnel involved in the operation and may be required for regulatory compliance purposes.

Operating a slewing mobile crane presents numerous hazards that both operators and individuals working in its vicinity must be cognizant of. Among the prominent risks are overloading, where exceeding the crane's rated capacity can result in structural failure, tipping, or collapse, leading to severe injuries, fatalities, and property damage. Improper setup or operation may induce instability, particularly evident when lifting heavy loads or operating on uneven terrain, potentially causing the crane to tip over and cause accidents. Accidental contact with overhead power lines poses a significant danger, risking electrocution, fires, and fatalities if any part of the crane, including the boom or load, makes contact.

Moreover, there's a risk of falling objects, as materials being hoisted or maneuvered by the crane can fall, endangering workers, bystanders, and nearby structures. Operators and workers nearby are susceptible to being crushed or pinched by moving crane parts, necessitating clear communication and situational awareness. Additionally, working at height on the crane's platform or climbing onto it presents fall hazards, emphasizing the importance of proper fall protection measures. Mechanical failures, such as malfunctioning brakes or hydraulics, can lead to accidents, underscoring the need for regular maintenance and inspections.

Environmental conditions like high winds or adverse weather can affect crane stability and safe operation, requiring operators to be vigilant and take appropriate precautions. Inadequate training and supervision of operators and workers elevate the risk of accidents, emphasizing the need for comprehensive training and adherence to safety protocols. Lastly, communication errors among crane operators, signal persons, and other workers can lead to accidents and injuries, highlighting the importance of clear and effective communication protocols. By identifying and addressing these hazards, implementing safety measures, and providing proper training and supervision, the risks associated with operating a slewing mobile crane can be effectively managed.

Wind conditions can significantly impact the operation and stability of a mobile crane, necessitating careful consideration of various factors to ensure safe operations in windy environments. Wind-related concerns are addressed by:

- Manufacturer's Instructions: Refer to the crane manufacturer's instructions and load charts to determine the maximum wind speed at which the crane can safely operate. These guidelines provide essential information regarding the crane's wind load capacity.

- Adjustment for Surface Area: While the manufacturer may specify a maximum wind speed, it's crucial to consider factors such as the surface area of the load and boom. In cases where large surface areas are involved, a lower maximum wind speed may need to be applied to maintain stability.

- Impact on Rated Capacity: Wind speed becomes particularly critical when the crane is lifting close to its rated capacity. Lower safety margins under such circumstances make the crane more susceptible to wind-induced instability.

- Microbursts and Thunderstorm Activity: Be mindful of nearby thunderstorm activity, which can lead to sudden and severe wind conditions known as microbursts. These unpredictable changes in wind load can jeopardize the stability of both the crane and the load being lifted.

- Non-Standard Lifts: For non-standard lifts involving suspended loads or large surface areas in windy conditions, seek advice from a competent person. This individual can provide written guidance on safe lifting conditions, potentially recommending a lower maximum wind speed than indicated by the manufacturer.

- Wind Gauge Operation: Ensure that wind gauges, also known as anemometers, are functional and accurately measuring wind speed. Position wind gauges at the boom tip, where the highest wind loading occurs, adhering to manufacturer instructions for proper mounting.

Mobile cranes are designed with a standard drag factor of 1.2 and a wind area/weight of 1.2 m^2/tonne as per standards EN 13000 – 2010 / ISO 4306-2:2012 (Ritchies Offsore Services, 2024). This indicates that specific loads may generate side forces on the crane that exceed its intended capacity to withstand such forces.

The drag factor and wind area/weight ratio are parameters used in crane design to assess the effects of wind on the crane structure when lifting loads. A drag factor of 1.2 implies that when exposed to wind, the crane experiences forces that are 1.2 times greater than the actual wind speed due to the crane's shape and other factors. Similarly, the wind area/weight ratio of 1.2 m^2/tonne indicates that for every tonne of weight being lifted, the crane presents a wind-exposed area of 1.2

square meters, which affects the magnitude of wind forces acting on the crane.

In practical terms, this means that certain loads being lifted by the crane may generate higher lateral forces caused by wind than what the crane is designed to safely handle. As a result, careful consideration of wind conditions and load characteristics is necessary during crane operations to ensure safety and prevent structural failures or accidents due to excessive side loads.

The term "Sail Area of Load" refers to the effective surface area presented by the load being lifted by a crane when it is exposed to wind. Just like the sail of a boat catches wind to propel it forward, certain types of loads lifted by cranes can catch wind, creating additional forces on the crane structure.

The sail area of the load is an important consideration, especially when working in windy conditions, as it can significantly increase the lateral forces exerted on the crane. This increased force can impact the stability of the crane and may require adjustments in crane operation or additional safety measures to ensure safe lifting practices.

Crane operators and supervisors typically take into account factors such as the size, shape, and orientation of the load, as well as wind speed and direction, to assess the potential sail area of the load and its implications for crane stability and safety during lifting operations.

The sail area of a load can be calculated by determining the effective surface area presented by the load to the wind. For a rectangular load, the sail area can be calculated using the formula:

Sail Area = Length × Width × $\sin(\theta)$

Where:
- Length is the length of the load facing the wind.

- Width is the width of the load perpendicular to the wind direction.

- θ (theta) is the angle between the wind direction and the plane of the load.

If the wind is perpendicular to one side of the load, then the angle θ would be 90 degrees. However, if the wind direction is at an angle to the load, then trigonometric functions can be used to calculate the effective surface area.

For example, let's consider a rectangular load with dimensions:
- Length = 4 meters

- Width = 2 meters

If the wind is blowing perpendicular to the length of the load (θ = 90 degrees), then the sail area would be: Sail Area=4×2×sin(90°)

Sail Area=8m^2

This means that when the wind blows directly against the 4-meter side of the load, the effective sail area presented to the wind is 8 square meters. However, if the wind direction changes, and the angle θ is different, the sail area would be recalculated accordingly using the appropriate trigonometric function.

A wind resistance coefficient, also known as drag coefficient or aerodynamic coefficient, is a dimensionless quantity that characterizes the drag or resistance experienced by an object moving through a fluid, such as air. It quantifies how effectively an object can overcome air resistance as it moves through the air.

In the context of slewing mobile crane operations, the wind resistance coefficient is crucial because it determines how much force the wind exerts on the crane when it's in operation. Slewing mobile cranes are tall and have large surface areas, making them susceptible to wind forces. The wind resistance coefficient helps crane operators understand the impact of wind on crane stability and operation.

By considering the wind resistance coefficient, crane operators can:

1. Assess Wind Loads: Understanding the wind resistance coef-

ficient allows operators to calculate the wind loads acting on the crane. This information helps ensure that the crane can safely withstand wind forces without tipping over or becoming unstable.

2. Determine Operating Limits: By knowing the wind resistance coefficient and the crane's structural capacity, operators can establish safe operating limits, including maximum wind speeds for crane operation.

3. Enhance Safety: Proper consideration of wind forces helps prevent accidents and ensures the safety of personnel working near or with the crane. It allows operators to take appropriate precautions, such as reducing crane loads or ceasing operations during high wind conditions.

4. Optimize Crane Performance: Factoring in wind resistance coefficient enables operators to optimize crane performance by adjusting crane configurations, positioning, and operational practices to mitigate the effects of wind on crane stability and efficiency.

The wind resistance coefficient for an object is determined through experimentation, numerical simulations, or reference tables. Here's how it's typically determined:

1. **Experimental Testing:** Engineers conduct wind tunnel tests where models of the object are subjected to airflow at various speeds. Instruments measure the drag force acting on the model, and the wind resistance coefficient is calculated using the formula:

$$C_d = \frac{F_d}{\frac{1}{2}\rho A V^2}$$

Where:
- F_d is the drag force experienced by the object,
- ρ is the air density,
- A is the reference area of the object (such as frontal area),
- V is the wind speed.

Figure 91: Wind resistance coefficient calculation.

1. **Numerical Simulations:** Computational Fluid Dynamics (CFD) simulations are used to model airflow around the object and calculate the drag force. By inputting the object's geometry and properties into specialized software, engineers can simulate airflow and calculate the wind resistance coefficient.

2. **Reference Tables:** For common shapes and objects, wind resistance coefficients may be available in reference tables or literature based on past experimental data or theoretical calculations. These values provide a convenient reference for engineers and designers when assessing wind effects on standard objects.

Once the wind resistance coefficient is determined, it serves as a crucial parameter for analysing wind loads on structures, vehicles, or equipment like slewing mobile cranes, aiding in design, safety assessments, and operational considerations.

Reference tables containing wind resistance coefficients for various shapes and objects can be found in engineering handbooks, building codes, standards publications, and academic textbooks. Here are some common sources where you can find such reference tables:

1. Engineering Handbooks: Many engineering handbooks, such as the "Handbook of Steel Construction" or the "CRC Handbook of Mechanical Engineering," include tables of wind resistance

coefficients for different shapes and structures.

2. Building Codes and Standards: National and international building codes and standards, such as those published by the American Society of Civil Engineers (ASCE), the International Building Code (IBC), or Eurocode, often provide guidelines and reference values for wind loads and coefficients.

3. Academic Textbooks: Textbooks on fluid mechanics, aerodynamics, structural engineering, and civil engineering may include sections on wind effects and provide reference coefficients for common shapes.

4. Online Databases: Some engineering organizations and institutions provide online databases or resources where wind resistance coefficients for various objects can be accessed or calculated.

5. Research Papers and Journals: Scientific research papers and academic journals in the fields of fluid dynamics, aerospace engineering, and civil engineering may contain experimental data and coefficients for specific shapes and objects.

When using reference tables, it's essential to ensure that the data is relevant to your specific application and complies with applicable standards and regulations. Additionally, consider consulting with experienced engineers or professionals in the field for guidance on interpreting and applying the data effectively.

Using the formula below, we can calculate the maximum allowable wind speed (V^{Max}) that a crane can withstand for a given load.

Maximum wind speed (v^{Max}) calculation for a given load:

$v^{Max} = V^{Chart} \times \sqrt{((1.2 \times M) \div (A^P \times C^W))}$

where:

V^{Chart} = Maximum wind speed of the crane

1.2 = Manufacture Test Standards (EN 13000 – 2010 / ISO 4306-2:2012)

M = Maximum Gross Weight

A^P = Sail Area of Load

C^W = Resistance Coefficient (1.4) (Example)

As an example of the calculation:

1.2 x 15.5 = 18.6

(Manufacture Test Standards) X (Load Weight)

20 x 1.4 = 28 (wind load Area)

18.6 ÷ 28 = 0.6643

√0.6643 = 0.81504

0.81504 x 12.8 = 10.43

The maximum windspeed that this load can safely be lifted in is 10.43 m/s.

Here's a breakdown of each component and how they contribute to the calculation:

- **vMax**: This represents the maximum wind speed that the crane can handle without exceeding its safety limits. It is the value we are trying to determine with the calculation.

- **VChart**: This is the maximum wind speed of the crane, typically specified by the manufacturer. It serves as a reference point for calculating the maximum wind speed for a given load.

- **1.2**: This value is a constant derived from manufacturing test standards such as EN 13000 – 2010 or ISO 4306-2:2012. It is used in the calculation as a standardized factor.

- **M**: This represents the maximum gross weight of the load being lifted by the crane. It is a crucial parameter as heavier loads may increase the wind force exerted on the crane.

- **Ap**: Sail Area of Load. This is the effective area exposed to the wind created by the load being lifted. It is essential to accurately determine this area, especially for irregularly shaped loads.

- **CW**: This is the resistance coefficient, representing the wind resistance of the crane and the load. It is typically provided by the manufacturer or based on industry standards. In the example provided, a value of 1.4 is used.

The calculation combines these parameters to determine the maximum allowable wind speed. First, it calculates the wind load area ($A^P \times C^W$) and divides it by the product of the maximum wind speed of the crane and a constant (1.2 x M). Then, it takes the square root of this result to obtain the maximum wind speed (v^{Max}).

In the example provided:
- The maximum wind speed of the crane (V^{Chart}) is 20.

- The maximum gross weight of the load (M) is 15.5.

- The resistance coefficient (CW) is 1.4.

- The wind load area (Ap x CW) is 28.

- The calculation yields a v^{Max} of approximately 10.43, indicating that the crane can safely operate in wind speeds up to this value for the given load.

The calculation for the maximum wind speed (v^{Max}) tells a slewing mobile crane operator the maximum allowable wind speed that the crane can safely operate in while lifting a given load. This information is crucial for ensuring the safety of crane operations, as operating in high winds can significantly increase the risk of accidents, structural damage, and injury.

By determining the v^{Max} using the provided formula, the operator can assess whether the current wind conditions are within the safe operating range of the crane for the specific load being lifted. If the actual wind speed exceeds the calculated v^{Max}, it indicates that the conditions may pose a safety risk, and the operator should take appropriate measures to mitigate these risks.

Operating a slewing mobile crane in windy conditions beyond its capacity can lead to instability, loss of control, or structural failure, endangering the operator, nearby workers, and property. Therefore, understanding and adhering to the v^{Max} calculation is essential for maintaining safe crane operations, preventing accidents, and protecting personnel and equipment on the job site.

Traffic management plans for slewing mobile crane operations are essential to ensure the safety of workers, pedestrians, and motorists in the vicinity of the crane. These plans typically involve several key elements to effectively manage traffic flow and minimize the risk of accidents. Here's an overview of the components of a traffic management plan for slewing mobile crane operations:

1. Traffic Control Personnel: Trained personnel should be designated to manage traffic around the crane operation area. This includes flagpersons positioned strategically to direct traffic, control access to the work zone, and communicate with crane operators and other workers.

2. Traffic Signs and Signals: Clear signage and signals should be installed to alert drivers and pedestrians of the crane operation zone, restricted areas, and detours. Signs indicating speed limits, lane closures, and pedestrian crossings help maintain order and safety.

3. Work Zone Identification: The work zone should be clearly demarcated using barricades, cones, or barriers to define the

boundaries of the crane operation area. Visible markings on the ground can also indicate restricted zones and safe pathways for pedestrians.

4. Traffic Routing: Traffic routing plans should be developed to divert vehicles away from the crane's swing radius and lifting path. Temporary road closures, detours, or lane shifts may be implemented to ensure adequate clearance for crane movements.

5. Pedestrian Safety Measures: Safe pathways for pedestrians should be established, clearly marked, and separated from vehicular traffic. Pedestrian crossings, walkways, and barriers protect pedestrians from entering hazardous areas and maintain a safe distance from the crane.

6. Communication Protocols: Effective communication channels should be established between traffic control personnel, crane operators, and construction crews. Two-way radios or hand signals facilitate real-time communication and coordination to manage traffic and crane movements efficiently.

7. Emergency Procedures: Emergency response protocols should be in place to address unforeseen incidents, such as accidents, breakdowns, or medical emergencies. Clear evacuation routes and procedures ensure the swift and safe evacuation of workers and bystanders if necessary.

8. Regular Monitoring and Review: Ongoing monitoring and evaluation of the traffic management plan are essential to identify potential hazards, address issues promptly, and implement corrective measures. Regular reviews ensure that the plan remains effective and responsive to changing conditions.

Road travel preparations for a mobile crane should strictly adhere to the instructions provided by the crane manufacturer to mitigate the risk of harm to the crane operator, pedestrians, and other drivers sharing the road. Several control measures are essential for safe road travel, including:

- Verifying and adjusting tyre pressure to the recommended levels.

- Securing both hydraulic and manual outriggers using locking devices and positioning them appropriately for travel to prevent lateral movement.

- Ensuring loose components are properly stored in designated storage areas to prevent them from becoming hazards during transit.

- Disengaging drives to hydraulic pumps, booms, and outriggers, and switching controls to the off position to prevent unintended activation during travel.

- Restraining the boom and hook securely to prevent any accidental movement during transit.

Preparing for Slewing Mobile Crane Operation

Preparing to operate a slewing mobile crane involves several steps to ensure safety and efficiency. Firstly, consultation with workplace personnel is essential to understand site requirements and ensure clarity and consistency with the lift plan. Regular communication is vital to address any potential discrepancies or changes in the plan.

Next, it's crucial to verify the implementation of risk control measures for identified hazards in accordance with the lift plan and safe work procedures. This involves inspecting the work area and ensuring that all necessary precautions are in place.

When accessing the mobile crane, following manufacturer requirements and safe work procedures is paramount. This includes using designated access points and adhering to safety protocols such as wearing appropriate personal protective equipment (PPE).

Conducting thorough pre-start checks of the mobile crane is essential, noting any damage or defects. Any issues should be reported promptly, and appropriate action should be taken as per manufacturer requirements and safe work procedures.

Ensuring that the crane is set up correctly according to the lift plan and relevant manufacturer requirements is crucial. This involves stabilizing the crane and configuring any lifting gear as specified in the plan.

If required by the lift plan, setting up counterweights following manufacturer requirements and safe work procedures ensures stability during lifting operations. Similarly, if applicable, setting up the fly jib or luffing fly according to specific manufacturer requirements and safe work procedures outlined in the lift plan is necessary.

Performing operational checks to verify the crane's functionality is essential. Any issues should be reported, and necessary action should be taken in line with manufacturer requirements and safe work procedures.

Checking the crane logbook to ensure compliance, accuracy, and completion is another important step. It's crucial to confirm that any required rectifications have been addressed and signed off as per manufacturer requirements and safe work procedures.

Assessing weather conditions and other environmental factors that may impact crane operations is necessary. Plans and procedures should be adjusted accordingly to maintain safety and efficiency.

Verifying the weight of the load to ensure it aligns with the lift plan and crane capacity is essential. Similarly, determining the derated

Working Load Limit (WLL) of lifting equipment based on selected slinging techniques and confirming that the calculated WLL is suitable for the lift plan requirements is crucial.

Identifying suitable lifting points and determining appropriate slinging techniques based on load characteristics and safety considerations are important for safe lifting operations.

Finally, ensuring that all lifting equipment and gear are in proper working condition and ready for safe use is vital. Performing final checks to verify readiness before commencing lifting operations is essential for safe and effective crane operation. By following these steps meticulously and adhering to established procedures and safety protocols, one can operate a slewing mobile crane safely and effectively.

The initial and critical step in selecting the appropriate crane revolves around understanding the specific demands of the job. It is paramount to assess the nature of the load slated for lifting to ensure compatibility with the crane's capabilities. It's essential to strike a balance, ensuring that the chosen crane possesses the requisite capacity to handle the load efficiently without being overburdened. Moreover, deliberation on the required lifting height is imperative to determine the suitable boom length. While vertical lifting may necessitate a longer boom, tasks within a confined radius may not warrant an extensive load capacity.

Consideration should also extend to the characteristics of the load material. Varying payloads, such as liquid-filled tanks versus concrete blocks, mandate different equipment and accessories for safe and effective handling.

The prevailing ground and weather conditions at the jobsite significantly influence the crane's operational capacity, primarily due to their impact on the machine's stability. Wind, particularly at elevated lift heights, poses a notable challenge as it can induce sway in the crane's boom. Moreover, uneven or rugged terrain may necessitate the use of all-terrain cranes to ensure safe operation.

Assessing the required level of mobility is equally crucial. Smaller cranes, with reduced lifting capacity, often offer enhanced precision and manoeuvrability, facilitating navigation around obstacles present at the site.

Once a comprehensive understanding of the jobsite and its requirements is obtained, meticulous scrutiny of crane spec sheets and load charts is essential. This examination ensures that the selected crane aligns with the job demands and is capable of accessing the designated worksite.

It is prudent to opt for a crane with a capacity exceeding the maximum load requirement to establish a safety margin, mitigating risks and ensuring operational resilience.

Using load charts is a fundamental aspect of preparing to use a mobile slewing crane. Most load charts include a lift range diagram that illustrates the load radius, representing the horizontal distance from the centreline of the crane's rotation to the load. A shorter load radius corresponds to a higher load capacity of the crane. To determine the load radius, identify the length of the boom being used and the angle at which it will be positioned on the diagram. Then, locate the corresponding number at the bottom of the chart to find the radius.

After obtaining the load radius, locate it on the load chart and scan across to determine the lifting capacity. Load charts typically display both the gross capacity and net capacity of the crane, providing information on the machine's rated capacity and its maximum capacity. Additionally, the chart contains details regarding other factors that influence the crane's lifting capacity. For instance, it may specify if the capacity is calculated over the rear or front of the machine, at a 360-degree rotation, and whether the machine is stabilized by tires or outriggers. These factors impact the crane's net capacity, which is the actual load it can lift. Typically, the lifting capacity at the rear or front of a crane is higher due to structural considerations and weight distribution. Ensuring that the boom remains in the specified position during operation is crucial to avoid overloading.

Environmental factors such as ground conditions (e.g., slope) and wind speed are also taken into account on the load chart as they affect the crane's stability, consequently influencing its load capacity.

A standard crane load chart consists of several key components: lifting capacity, boom length, boom angle, capacity deductions, and operation notes. The lifting capacity indicates the total weight the crane can safely lift based on the load radius, while the boom length refers to the crane's arm length. The boom angle represents the angle between the boom and the ground, and capacity deductions specify the weight deductions for accessories in use. Operation notes cover considerations such as slope and wind speed. Moreover, crane load charts typically feature a bold line that divides them into two sections, indicating the crane's major limitations: structural strength and stability. Capacities below the bold line are restricted by the crane's stability, while those above it are constrained by the machine's strength.

Operators must also note that every crane model is accompanied by its own distinct load chart, which may vary depending on the crane's configurations. Manufacturers typically furnish these load charts in the operator manual, commonly located within the crane's cab.

A crane's load chart serves as a tool for the operator to determine the lifting capabilities of the crane, ensuring it operates within its safe lifting capacity. This chart accounts for variables such as lift distance, angle, and the crane's configuration, including its base and setup. Critical factors on the load chart include boom length, boom angle, and load radius.

Understanding a crane load chart involves considering various factors related to lift capacity, lift range, boom angle, and more. The following are key aspects to comprehend when reading a crane load chart:

    1. Lift Capacity: This measurement indicates the maximum load a

crane can lift, considering factors like load dimension, lift height, and angle.

2. Lift Range: The load chart diagram provides information on the required boom length for a given lift distance and height.

3. Boom Angle: The angle between the longitudinal and centreline of the boom and the horizontal centreline is crucial. Crane stability is a significant consideration, especially when lifting loads close to or exceeding the crane's angle limit.

4. Movement: Cranes often need to move or rotate during a lift. Considering the distance and speed of rotation is essential for assessing the feasibility of a lift and avoiding imbalance or tipping over.

5. Deductions: To determine the crane's net lifting capacity, deductions must be made for the weight of the crane and its accessories, including rigging, lines, ball and jib, block, windspeed, and windsail. Various factors such as load block weight, headache ball weight, jib weight, and others are subtracted from the gross capacity.

The bold line on a crane load chart divides it into two sections, indicating the crane's structural strength and stability limitations. Capacities listed on one side of the line are restricted by the crane's structural strength, while those on the other side are limited by its stability.

According to OSHA regulations, crane operators must be proficient in interpreting load charts, and the load chart must be present on the crane and consulted before each lift (Fullman, 2023). Guesswork or mathematical interpolation between chart values is not permitted, ensuring safe crane operations.

Knowing how to interpret a crane load chart enables you to determine the crane's load capacity relative to the boom angle and length. Nowadays, many lifts are planned using computer simulations, and load indicators in the crane cabs alert operators when lifts are approaching or exceeding the crane's capacity (Mollo, 2021). Nevertheless, possessing the skill to read crane load charts remains crucial for crane operations.

While crane load charts may vary in appearance from one manufacturer to another, they should all encompass fundamental information. Understanding how to interpret a Crane Load Chart is paramount for crane operators, ensuring both safety and efficiency in operations. It serves as a crucial resource for determining a crane's lifting capabilities. Given the multitude of crane manufacturers, it's essential to have a thorough grasp of the specific crane's load chart. Whether operating a boom truck like Terex, National, Manitex, Pioneer, or Altec, or a rough terrain crane such as Grove, Link-Belt, Manitowoc, Kato, or Tadano, acknowledging the variations among load charts is vital. Overlooking these differences could result in crane overturning or structural failure.

Let's make use of the following example, shown as Figure 92.

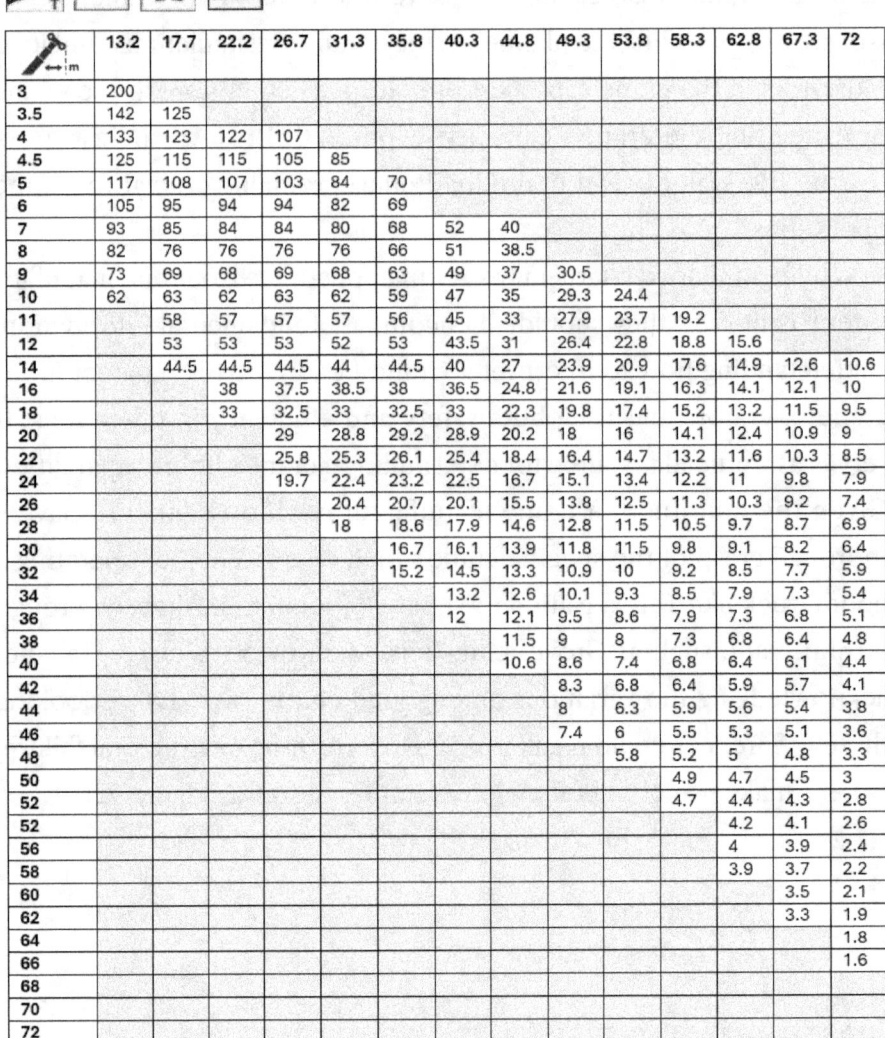

m	13.2	17.7	22.2	26.7	31.3	35.8	40.3	44.8	49.3	53.8	58.3	62.8	67.3	72
3	200													
3.5	142	125												
4	133	123	122	107										
4.5	125	115	115	105	85									
5	117	108	107	103	84	70								
6	105	95	94	94	82	69								
7	93	85	84	84	80	68	52	40						
8	82	76	76	76	76	66	51	38.5						
9	73	69	68	69	68	63	49	37	30.5					
10	62	63	62	63	62	59	47	35	29.3	24.4				
11		58	57	57	57	56	45	33	27.9	23.7	19.2			
12		53	53	53	52	53	43.5	31	26.4	22.8	18.8	15.6		
14		44.5	44.5	44.5	44	44.5	40	27	23.9	20.9	17.6	14.9	12.6	10.6
16			38	37.5	38.5	38	36.5	24.8	21.6	19.1	16.3	14.1	12.1	10
18			33	32.5	33	32.5	33	22.3	19.8	17.4	15.2	13.2	11.5	9.5
20				29	28.8	29.2	28.9	20.2	18	16	14.1	12.4	10.9	9
22				25.8	25.3	26.1	25.4	18.4	16.4	14.7	13.2	11.6	10.3	8.5
24				19.7	22.4	23.2	22.5	16.7	15.1	13.4	12.2	11	9.8	7.9
26					20.4	20.7	20.1	15.5	13.8	12.5	11.3	10.3	9.2	7.4
28					18	18.6	17.9	14.6	12.8	11.5	10.5	9.7	8.7	6.9
30						16.7	16.1	13.9	11.8	11.5	9.8	9.1	8.2	6.4
32						15.2	14.5	13.3	10.9	10	9.2	8.5	7.7	5.9
34							13.2	12.6	10.1	9.3	8.5	7.9	7.3	5.4
36							12	12.1	9.5	8.6	7.9	7.3	6.8	5.1
38								11.5	9	8	7.3	6.8	6.4	4.8
40								10.6	8.6	7.4	6.8	6.4	6.1	4.4
42									8.3	6.8	6.4	5.9	5.7	4.1
44									8	6.3	5.9	5.6	5.4	3.8
46									7.4	6	5.5	5.3	5.1	3.6
48										5.8	5.2	5	4.8	3.3
50											4.9	4.7	4.5	3
52											4.7	4.4	4.3	2.8
52												4.2	4.1	2.6
56												4	3.9	2.4
58												3.9	3.7	2.2
60													3.5	2.1
62													3.3	1.9
64														1.8
66														1.6
68														
70														
72														

Figure 92: Sample slewing mobile crane load chart for a 200t crane.

- The gross capacity, indicated as 200T, represents the tonnage a crane can lift, while its actual load capacity is referred to as the net capacity.
- The top line of the chart denotes the available boom lengths specific to the crane type.

- The numbers in the far-left column represent the operating radius in meters, indicating the crane's turning ability and operational range.
- The chart displays weight capacities for lifts from left to right, considering the correct boom length and operating radius.

In summary, one must determine the required boom length for the job and correlate it with the achievable operating angle on-site. Identifying the corresponding load rating provides the crane's lifting capacity.

Using the chart as an example: If the load to be lifted is 20T, and the operational space is limited to 26m, what boom length is needed from the 200T crane to execute the job accurately? Answer: 40.3m.

Gross Capacity Versus Net Capacity The capacities listed in a crane load chart, termed as Gross Capacities or Rated Capacities, do not represent the actual loads that can be lifted. The actual load a crane can lift is the Net Capacity, which must never exceed the crane's maximum load.

The Gross Capacity includes the weight of all components mounted or stowed on the crane's boom, including Capacity Deductions. Capacity Deductions include the weight of the main load block, headache ball or overhaul ball, effective weight of the jib, hanging cables, rigging, and the load itself:

1. Main Load Block: The main load block is a heavy-duty pulley block used in lifting operations. It is typically attached to the end of the crane's hoist line and is responsible for directly lifting the load. The main load block contains sheaves (pulleys) through which the hoist line runs, allowing for efficient lifting by distributing the load's weight across multiple lines.

2. Headache Ball or Overhaul Ball: The headache ball, also known as an overhaul ball, is a weighted attachment that hangs from the crane's hook. Its purpose is to provide counterbalance to the hoist line, maintaining tension and preventing slack in the line during lifting operations. The weight of the headache ball

helps stabilize the load and ensures smooth lifting and lowering motions.

3. Effective Weight of the Jib: The jib is an extendable arm or boom attached to the main boom of the crane, providing additional reach and flexibility in lifting operations. The effective weight of the jib refers to the mass of the jib structure itself, including any extensions or attachments. This weight is factored into the crane's load calculations and must be considered when determining the crane's lifting capacity.

4. Hanging Cables: Hanging cables refer to any additional cables or lines suspended from the crane's boom or jib. These cables may be used for various purposes, such as supporting auxiliary equipment or guiding the load during lifting operations. The weight of hanging cables is considered a capacity deduction and must be accounted for when determining the crane's net lifting capacity.

5. Rigging: Rigging encompasses all the equipment and hardware used to secure and lift a load, including slings, chains, shackles, and hooks. Rigging is essential for ensuring the safe and efficient lifting of loads by distributing the load's weight evenly and securely. The weight of rigging materials is deducted from the crane's gross capacity to determine its net lifting capacity.

6. The Load Itself: The load refers to the object or material being lifted by the crane. This could be construction materials, equipment, machinery, or any other heavy object. The weight of the load is a critical factor in determining the crane's lifting capacity and must be carefully assessed to ensure that it does not exceed the crane's capabilities. The weight of the load is also considered a capacity deduction when calculating the crane's

net lifting capacity.

Manufacturer variations exist, so it's crucial to understand the specific capacity deductions determined by the manufacturer.

As a further example, lets assume that we want to determine the maximum weight that can be lifted with the boom extended to 40.3 meters, we need to find the corresponding column in the load chart for the 40.3m boom length. Looking down the column we can see that the maximum weight is 52t with an operating radius of 7m. We can also see that as the radius increases the maximum that can be lifted decreases.

Assuming we wanted to shift a 10t load from an operating radius of 16m to a position at 24m, we can use the load chart to determine applicable boom lengths. Looking at the operating radius for 16m, we can see that with a boom length at 26.7m we can lift 37.5t down to 14.1t with a boom length of 68.2m. For the working radius of 24m, at a 26.7m boom length, 19.7t can be lifted down to 11t at 62.8m boom length. As such, given that 10t is less than the maximum weights, the boom may be set from 26.7m to 62.8m to safely lift the 10t load (assuming the load is inclusive of weight deductions such as lifting deductions such as the main load block.

Range diagrams aid crane operators in determining the optimal configuration and positioning of the crane. These diagrams provide valuable insights into the required boom length for lifting operations. Additionally, they prove useful when setting up the crane near structures. When calculations involving deductions for the wire rope are necessary, the working range diagram serves as a valuable resource. This diagram typically includes sections delineating load radius (vertical lines), boom tip height (horizontal lines), boom jib length (arched sections), boom angles (angled lines), and caution areas (prohibited zones). An example is shown as Figure 93.

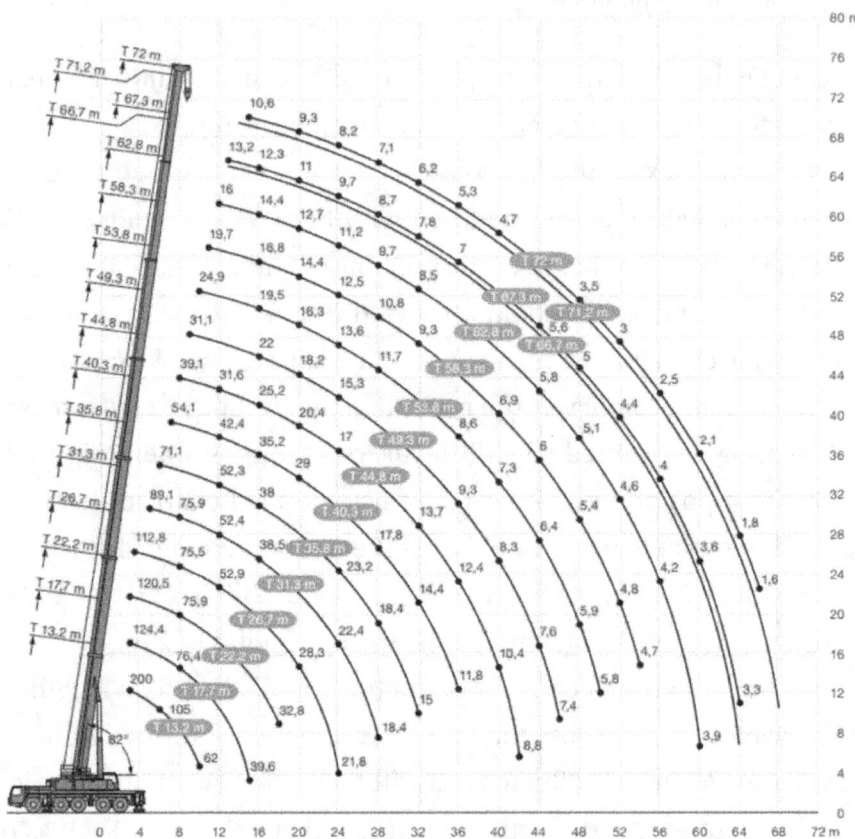

Figure 93: Sample range diagram.

In the provided example represented as Figure 93, the vertical axis on the left side of the chart indicates the boom length (in meters) at different extensions. Arched lines originating from these measurements depict the boom's positions at various lift angles. The horizontal axis at the bottom illustrates the operating radius. With knowledge of the boom length (including any jib length, if present) and its angle, this chart facilitates straightforward calculation of the load radius. Simply trace the arched line corresponding to a specific boom length until it intersects with the radial line corresponding to the desired lift angle.

Operating a Slewing Mobile Crane

Operating a slewing mobile crane involves a series of steps to ensure the safe and efficient lifting and movement of loads. Here's a detailed description of how each step is executed:

1. **Determining Lifts within Radius Control (RC):**

   - Referencing the load chart/s and lift plan, the crane operator assesses the maximum safe lifting capacity within the crane's radius control.

   - Lifts are planned within this radius to ensure that the load remains within the crane's safe operating limits.

2. **Positioning Boom/Jib and Hook Block:**

   - Following directions from associated personnel and the lift plan, the operator positions the boom/jib and hook block over the load.

   - This positioning is executed meticulously to ensure proper alignment with the load and adherence to safe work procedures.

3. **Connecting Hooks and Lifting Gear:**

   - The main and/or auxiliary hook, along with any necessary lifting gear, are securely connected to the load.

   - All connections are made in accordance with the lift plan, safe work procedures, and manufacturer requirements to ensure load stability and safety during lifting.

4. **Carrying Out Test Lift:**

- Prior to full-scale lifting operations, a test lift is conducted as per dogging and safe work procedures.
- This test lift verifies the stability of the load and ensures that all equipment functions properly before proceeding with actual lifting tasks.

5. **Transferring Loads and Monitoring Movement:**

    - Loads are transferred using relevant crane movements, such as hoisting, slewing, and booming, as specified in the lift plan.
    - Tag lines may be used as necessary to control load swing and ensure precise positioning.
    - Throughout the lifting process, the operator continuously monitors load and crane movement to detect any anomalies and ensure safe operation.

6. **Interpreting Communication Signals:**

    - The operator accurately interprets and follows all required communication signals while operating the crane.
    - Clear communication between the operator and signallers ensures coordinated and safe lifting operations in accordance with the lift plan.

7. **Lowering and Landing the Load:**

    - Once the lifting operation is complete, the load is safely lowered and landed at the designated location following the lift plan and safe work procedures.
    - Careful control of crane movements is crucial to prevent sudden drops or swings during the lowering process.

8. **Disconnecting Lifting Gear and Repositioning Crane:**

   - Lifting gear is disconnected from the load, and the crane is positioned safely and efficiently for the next task as outlined in the lift plan.

   - Proper repositioning ensures readiness for subsequent lifting operations and maintains workflow efficiency.

9. **Inspecting and Reporting Defective Equipment:**

   - After completing lifting tasks, all lifting equipment and gear are inspected for defects.

   - Any defective items are isolated, labelled, and reported as per organizational protocols to ensure prompt repair or replacement and maintain workplace safety standards.

The crane controls of a slewing mobile crane are engineered to give operators precise control over the crane's movements and functions, ensuring efficient and safe operation.

Hoist Controls: These controls manage the lifting and lowering of loads, offering various mechanisms such as levers, joysticks, or buttons, as shown in Figure 94. Operators utilize these controls to adjust the speed and direction of the hoisting motion, facilitating the raising and lowering of both the main and auxiliary hooks, along with any attached lifting gear.

Figure 94: Liebherr LTM-1750-9.1-crane cabin. Unkonw, CC BY-SA 4.0, via Wikimedia Commons.

Boom Controls: Responsible for regulating the extension and retraction of the crane's boom, these controls empower operators to customize the length and angle of the boom. This flexibility allows for reaching the desired height and distance necessary for lifting operations, with control mechanisms often comprising levers or joysticks tailored for telescoping or luffing the boom.

Slew Controls: Govern the rotation of the crane's upper structure or superstructure, enabling operators to precisely position the load horizontally. Slew controls typically feature levers or pedals that dictate the rotation speed and direction of the crane, ensuring accurate alignment of the load.

Figure 95: Liebherr LTM 1750-9.1. Background © Raimond Spekking / CC BY-SA 3.0 (via Wikimedia Commons).

Drive Controls: Manage the crane's movement on the ground, facilitating forward, reverse, and turning manoeuvres. Depending on the crane's configuration, drive controls may incorporate steering wheels, pedals, or joysticks to navigate the crane into position safely and efficiently.

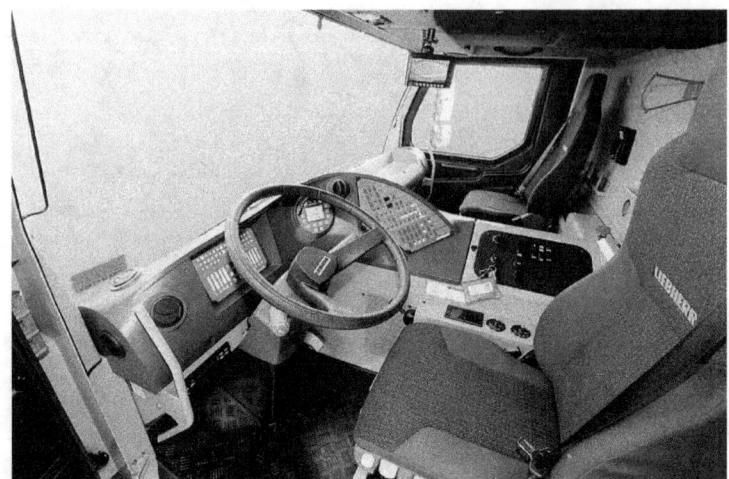

Figure 96: Liebherr LTM-1750-9.1 driving-cabin. Unkonw, CC BY-SA 4.0 <https://creativecommons.org/licenses/by-sa/4.0>, via Wikimedia Commons.

Emergency Stop Button: Serving as a crucial safety feature, the emergency stop button promptly halts all crane movements in emergency or unsafe conditions. Positioned within easy reach of the operator, it provides a quick means to shut down crane operations if necessary.

Load Monitoring System: Many modern slewing mobile cranes come equipped with load monitoring systems, offering real-time feedback on the load's weight and position. These systems often include digital displays or indicators that aid operators in ensuring the crane operates within its safe working limits.

Auxiliary Controls: Additional controls may be present depending on the crane's configuration, facilitating functions such as outrigger deployment, counterweight adjustment, or attachment operation. These controls allow operators to fine-tune the crane's setup and performance for specific lifting tasks.

The crane controls of a slewing mobile crane are thoughtfully designed to be intuitive and ergonomic, enabling operators to navigate the crane safely and efficiently while maintaining precise control over lifting operations. Proper training and familiarization with these controls are imperative for ensuring safe and effective crane operation.

Determining lifts within the radius control (RC) involves a meticulous process guided by the load chart and lift plan. Initially, the crane operator carefully references these documents to ascertain the maximum safe lifting capacity achievable within the crane's radius control. By consulting the load chart, which delineates the crane's lifting capabilities at various radii and boom configurations, the operator gains crucial insights into the permissible load weights and operating conditions.

With the load chart as a reference point, the operator then collaborates closely with the lift planning team to delineate a comprehensive lift plan. This plan meticulously outlines the sequence of lifts, positioning of the crane, and other pertinent details essential for safe and efficient lifting operations. Importantly, lifts are strategically planned within the determined radius control to ensure that the load remains well within the crane's safe operating limits throughout the operation.

By adhering to the radius control parameters established through the load chart and lift plan, the crane operator safeguards against overloading the crane and mitigates the risk of accidents or equipment damage. This systematic approach ensures that lifts are executed with precision and adherence to safety protocols, thereby fostering a secure working environment for all personnel involved in the lifting operation.

Positioning the boom/jib and hook block of a slewing mobile crane is a critical aspect of preparing for lifting operations. To execute this task accurately, the crane operator relies on directions provided by associated personnel and the comprehensive lift plan. These directives serve as invaluable guides, outlining the precise positioning requirements essential for safe and efficient load handling.

With instructions from the lift planning team and other relevant personnel, the crane operator manoeuvres the crane's boom or jib to align it directly over the load. This process demands a keen eye for detail and a thorough understanding of the lift plan's specifications. By adhering to these instructions, the operator ensures that the boom or jib is positioned optimally to facilitate smooth and controlled lifting operations.

Simultaneously, the hook block, which serves as the primary attachment point for lifting the load, is carefully positioned over the load by the crane operator. This manoeuvre requires precision to achieve proper alignment and ensure the load's secure attachment to the crane. Throughout this process, the operator remains vigilant, monitoring the positioning of the boom/jib and hook block to verify compliance with safe work procedures and lift plan requirements.

Before engaging in full-scale lifting operations, slewing mobile crane operators undertake a crucial preparatory step known as the test lift. This preliminary procedure is conducted in strict accordance with dogging procedures and established safe work protocols. The primary objective of the test lift is to validate the stability of the load and assess the functionality of all crane equipment components.

Conducting a test lift serves as a proactive measure to mitigate potential risks associated with lifting operations. By subjecting the crane and its associated equipment to a controlled test scenario, operators can identify and address any issues or abnormalities before commencing actual lifting tasks. This proactive approach not only enhances safety but also contributes to the overall efficiency and effectiveness of the lifting operation.

During the test lift, operators carefully observe and evaluate various factors, including the crane's stability, the responsiveness of control mechanisms, and the behaviour of the load under simulated lifting conditions. Any deviations from expected outcomes are promptly addressed and rectified to ensure optimal performance during subsequent lifting activities.

Furthermore, adherence to dogging procedures and safe work protocols is paramount throughout the test lift process. Operators meticulously follow established guidelines to maintain a safe working environment and minimize the risk of accidents or equipment damage. By adhering to these protocols, operators uphold safety standards and promote a culture of diligence and responsibility in crane operations.

Ultimately, the test lift serves as a critical checkpoint in the pre-operational phase, providing assurance that the crane and its associated equipment are primed for safe and efficient lifting activities. By conducting this preparatory step diligently and methodically, operators demonstrate a commitment to safety and professionalism in their crane operations, thereby safeguarding both personnel and property on the worksite.

During lifting operations with a slewing mobile crane, transferring loads is a critical phase that demands meticulous attention to detail and adherence to prescribed procedures. To execute this task effectively, operators rely on a combination of relevant crane movements, including hoisting, slewing, and booming, as outlined in the lift plan. By following these predetermined sequences of actions, operators ensure that loads are transferred smoothly and securely, minimizing the risk of accidents or damage.

In some cases, additional precautions may be necessary to control load movement and enhance precision during transfer operations. One common strategy involves the use of tag lines, which are ropes or lines attached to the load to provide manual control and minimize swinging. By applying tension to the tag lines, operators can counteract the natural momentum of the load, helping to stabilize it and facilitate more accurate positioning.

Throughout the lifting process, operators maintain vigilant oversight of both load and crane movement to detect any deviations from expected behaviour. This continuous monitoring allows operators to promptly identify and address potential issues, such as load instability or equipment malfunction, before they escalate into safety hazards. By remaining attentive and responsive, operators uphold safety standards and mitigate risks associated with lifting operations.

Effective communication and coordination among team members are essential during load transfer activities. Operators must communicate closely with riggers, signallers, and other personnel involved in the lifting operation to ensure seamless coordination of tasks and adherence to the lift plan. Clear and concise communication helps to minimize confusion and enhance safety by ensuring that everyone is aware of their roles and responsibilities.

In the operation of a slewing mobile crane, clear communication between the crane operator and signallers is paramount to ensuring the safety and efficiency of lifting operations. The operator must possess the ability to accurately interpret and promptly respond to all communication signals provided by the signallers. These signals serve as instructions guiding the crane operator's actions and manoeuvres during the lifting process, facilitating precise positioning and load management.

By attentively observing and understanding the communication signals, the crane operator maintains synchronization with the lifting team and ensures that all movements are coordinated in accordance with the lift plan. This coordination is crucial for preventing accidents, minimizing risks, and optimizing productivity on the worksite. Effective communication allows the lifting operation to proceed smoothly and efficiently, with each member of the team contributing to the overall success of the task at hand.

The crane operator relies on a combination of visual and auditory cues to interpret the signals provided by the signallers. Clear and consistent hand gestures, flags, or verbal commands convey essential instructions related to hoisting, slewing, booming, and other crane movements.

By accurately interpreting these signals, the operator can adjust the crane's operations in real-time, ensuring precise load placement and safe working conditions.

Additionally, the operator's ability to maintain open channels of communication with the signallers fosters a collaborative environment where information flows freely between team members. This communication facilitates the exchange of critical updates, such as changes in lifting conditions or unforeseen obstacles, allowing the team to adapt their approach accordingly and mitigate potential risks.

Overall, the effective interpretation of communication signals by the crane operator is essential for maintaining safety, productivity, and operational efficiency during lifting operations. Through clear communication and seamless coordination with signallers, the operator plays a central role in ensuring the success of the lifting task while prioritizing the safety of personnel and equipment on the worksite.

After successfully completing the lifting operation, the next critical step for the slewing mobile crane operator is to lower and land the load safely at the designated location. This phase of the operation requires careful precision and adherence to the lift plan and established safe work procedures to ensure the integrity of the load and the safety of personnel and equipment on the worksite.

With the lifting operation concluded, the operator begins the process of lowering the load in a controlled manner, employing the crane's hoist controls to gradually decrease the load's elevation. Careful coordination between the operator and any assisting personnel is essential during this phase to maintain clear communication and ensure that the load descends smoothly and precisely.

Throughout the lowering process, the operator exercises precise control over the crane's movements, adjusting the hoist speed and carefully monitoring the load's descent to prevent sudden drops or swings. By maintaining a steady and controlled pace, the operator minimizes the risk of damage to the load and surrounding structures, as well as the potential for injury to personnel.

As the load approaches the ground or the designated landing area, the operator continues to guide its descent with precision, making any necessary adjustments to ensure accurate placement. Clear communication with ground personnel ensures that the load is landed safely and securely, precisely aligning with the intended location as outlined in the lift plan.

Once the load has been safely lowered and landed, the operator confirms its stability and secures it in place as necessary to prevent any unintended movement. With the load securely positioned, the crane operator completes the final steps of the operation, such as retracting the boom or jib and disconnecting any lifting gear, in preparation for the next task.

Overall, the process of lowering and landing the load requires meticulous attention to detail, precise control of crane movements, and effective communication between the operator and ground personnel. By following established protocols and safe work procedures, the crane operator ensures the safe and efficient completion of the lifting operation while minimizing the risk of accidents or incidents.

Concluding Slewing Mobile Crane Operations

In slewing mobile crane operations, proper stowing and securing of equipment are essential for maintaining safety, preventing damage, and preserving the crane's integrity. Here's a comprehensive guide on how to carry out these tasks:

Stowing and Securing Crane Boom/Jib and Lifting Gear: Following the manufacturer's guidelines and safe work procedures, retract the crane's boom or jib to its designated storage position. Ensure that all lifting gear, such as hooks, slings, and shackles, is securely stowed to prevent movement during transportation or storage. Utilize appropriate securing devices like straps or chains to firmly hold the boom/jib and lifting gear in place. Conduct a thorough visual inspection to verify that all components are correctly stowed and securely fastened.

Removing and Securing Crane Fly Jib and Counterweight: If applicable, detach the crane's fly jib and counterweight from the main structure according to manufacturer specifications and safe work procedures. Lower the fly jib and counterweight carefully using the crane's hoist controls to the ground or assigned storage area. Secure the fly jib and counterweight in their storage positions using suitable locking mechanisms or securing devices. Ensure all connections and attachments are properly secured to prevent unintended movement or detachment during transportation or storage.

Applying Motion Locks and Brakes: Engage the relevant motion locks and brakes as per the manufacturer's instructions and safe work procedures to prevent unintentional movement of the crane's components. Verify that all motion locks and brakes are correctly engaged and functioning before proceeding with further shutdown procedures.

Stowing and Securing Outriggers: Retract the outriggers or stabilizers according to manufacturer requirements and safe work procedures. Secure the outriggers in their stowed positions using locking pins, bolts, or other specified securing devices. Perform a visual inspection to confirm that all outriggers are securely stowed, with no loose or protruding components.

Shutting Down and Securing the Crane: Safely shut down the crane's engine or power source following safe work procedures. Secure the crane's controls and access points to prevent unauthorized access or use, such as locking the crane cab door or control panel. Apply any additional security measures recommended by the manufacturer or site-specific safety protocols to prevent tampering or misuse of the crane.

Stowing Plates or Packing: If applicable, stow any plates or packing materials used during the lifting operation in designated storage areas. Ensure that plates or packing materials are properly secured to prevent shifting or falling during transportation or storage.

Performing Shutdown Crane Checks: Conduct a final inspection of the crane to ensure that all components are properly stowed, secured, and compliant with manufacturer requirements and safe work procedures. Address any identified discrepancies or issues before concluding the shutdown process. Document any maintenance or repair needs and report them to the relevant personnel for follow-up action.

Figure 97: Liebherr LTM-1750-9.1 secured and ready for transport. Unknown source, CC BY-SA 4.0 <https://creativecommons.org/licenses/by-sa/4.0>, via Wikimedia Commons.

CRANE OPERATIONS

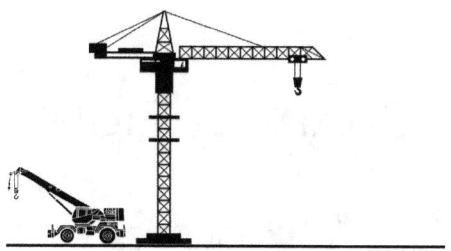

Chapter Eight

Truck Mounted/Vehicle Loading Crane

A vehicle loading crane, also known as truck mounted crane, often abbreviated as VLC, is a type of crane specifically designed and mounted onto a vehicle for the purpose of loading and unloading cargo. These cranes are commonly used in industries such as transportation, logistics, construction, and shipping to handle various types of materials and goods.

Vehicle loading cranes come in different configurations and sizes to suit different applications and requirements. They are typically mounted on trucks, trailers, or other types of vehicles, providing mobility and flexibility in transporting goods to and from various locations.

Figure 98: Truck mounted crane being used for lamp post replacement. Hullian111, CC BY-SA 4.0 , via Wikimedia Commons.

These cranes are equipped with lifting mechanisms such as hydraulic arms, winches, and booms, allowing them to lift, move, and position heavy loads with precision and efficiency. They may also feature telescopic booms or jibs to extend their reach and versatility in handling cargo.

The primary function of a vehicle loading crane is to facilitate the loading and unloading of goods onto or from vehicles, such as trucks, trailers, flatbeds, or shipping containers. They are commonly used in warehouses, ports, construction sites, and other industrial settings where the efficient movement of materials is essential.

A truck-mounted crane, as the name suggests, is a crane that is mounted onto a truck chassis or vehicle. It integrates the capabilities of both a crane and a truck, offering mobility, versatility, and lifting capacity in a single unit. These cranes are commonly used in various industries and applications where the ability to lift and transport heavy loads is required.

Truck-mounted cranes typically consist of a crane assembly mounted on a specially designed truck bed or platform. The crane assembly includes a telescopic or articulated boom, which extends and retracts to reach different heights and distances. Depending on the model, the boom may also have additional sections or attachments to enhance its flexibility and lifting capabilities.

The crane's controls, operator cab, and other necessary components are often integrated into the truck chassis, providing ease of operation and efficient manoeuvrability. The truck's engine powers the crane's hydraulic system, which operates the boom, hoist, and other crane functions.

Truck-mounted cranes come in various sizes and configurations to suit different lifting requirements and vehicle capacities. They are commonly used for tasks such as loading and unloading cargo, construction material handling, utility work, tree trimming, and recovery operations.

The main advantages of truck-mounted cranes include:

1. Mobility: They can travel on roads and highways like standard trucks, allowing them to reach multiple job sites without the need for additional transportation.

2. Versatility: They can perform a wide range of lifting and material handling tasks, thanks to their adjustable booms and manoeuvrable design.

3. Efficiency: They offer quick setup and operation, enabling faster loading and unloading of goods and reducing downtime on job sites.

4. Cost-effectiveness: They eliminate the need for separate transportation of a crane and a truck, saving on logistics and labour costs.

A vehicle loading crane serves the purpose of loading and unloading materials on construction sites from vehicles, while also facilitating lifting operations in various scenarios:

- Transferring loads from the vehicle to elevated areas within a workplace, such as lifting frames directly from the vehicle to a building floor.

- Transporting loads to and from locations other than the vehicle, allowing for versatile material handling.

- Placing loads directly into position, such as installing a sign securely while it is being connected.

To enhance safety and mitigate the risk of accidents, several risk control measures are implemented around cranes, particularly to prevent incidents like being crushed between the crane boom and the operator's control panel. These measures include:

- Utilizing remote controls to operate the crane from a safe distance.

- Rearranging the controls on the vehicle to minimize the risk of accidental contact.

- Incorporating slew limiters to restrict the crane's movement and prevent contact between the boom and the operator.

- Installing physical barriers to create a protective buffer zone around the crane.

- Implementing operator controls that can only be activated from a position where the boom or load cannot endanger the operator.

- Implementing an emergency system to ensure that the crane's boom cannot inadvertently lower due to its own weight or the weight of a load.

Furthermore, an emergency stop device is mandated for every control station on the crane. These emergency stops should be easily accessible, simple to operate, and capable of immediately halting all crane movements. Additionally, they should require manual reset after activation to ensure proper safety protocols are followed.

Truck-mounted cranes come in various types, each designed for specific lifting tasks and operational requirements. Here are some common types of truck-mounted cranes:

Hydraulic Boom Truck Crane: This type of crane features a hydraulic telescoping boom mounted on a truck chassis. It offers excellent mobility and flexibility, making it suitable for a wide range of lifting applications, from construction to utility work.

Knuckle Boom Crane (Articulating Crane): Knuckle boom cranes have a hinged boom that resembles the knuckle of a finger, allowing for greater flexibility and manoeuvrability. They are commonly used in urban areas and tight spaces where traditional cranes may have difficulty accessing.

Figure 99: Knuckle Boom loader crane. TM, CC BY-SA 2.0 DE, via Wikimedia Commons.

Telescopic Boom Truck Crane: Telescopic boom cranes have a straight, extendable boom that can be extended or retracted using hydraulic cylinders. They offer greater reach and lifting capacity compared to knuckle boom cranes, making them ideal for heavy-duty lifting tasks such as construction and infrastructure projects.

Figure 100: Telescopic boom truck mounted crane. Video13, CC BY-SA 4.0, via Wikimedia Commons.

Lattice Boom Truck Crane: Lattice boom cranes feature a lattice structure boom that can be raised and lowered using hydraulic cylinders. They are commonly used in heavy construction and industrial applications where high lifting capacities and long reach are required.

These are just a few examples of the different types of truck-mounted cranes available. Each type has its own unique features and advantages, allowing contractors and operators to choose the right crane for their specific lifting needs and job requirements.

CRANE OPERATIONS

Figure 101: Combination of knuckle and telescopic boom truck mounted crane. An Atlas 190.2 foldable truck mounted crane outside Santander by Roger A Smith, CC BY-SA 2.0, via Wikimedia Commons.

Planning and Preparing Truck Mounted Crane Operations

Operating a truck-mounted crane necessitates planning and strict adherence to safety protocols to guarantee the well-being of both personnel and equipment involved.

Identifying Task Requirements and Confirming Lift Plan: To commence operations, carefully review work orders or equivalent documentation to ascertain the specific task requirements. Subsequently, collaborate with associated personnel, including the crane operator, riggers, and site supervisors, to confirm the lift plan. Additionally, conduct a thorough site inspection to assess prevailing conditions and identify any potential hazards or obstacles that may impede crane operations.

Confirming Work Area Operating Surface: Evaluate the quality of the ground surface within the work area to ensure its suitability for accommodating the weight and operation of the truck-mounted crane. Identify and address any hazards such as soft or uneven ground, overhead obstructions, or buried utilities that could potentially compromise crane stability or safe operation.

Establishing Rated Capacity and Working Load Limit: Determine the Rated Capacity (RC) of the truck-mounted crane as specified by the manufacturer. Establish the Working Load Limit (WLL) tailored to the specific load/s and work/task requirements, taking into account the crane's RC and the lifting gear's specifications.

Each crane possesses a specific lifting capacity, typically measured in kNm or tm, known as the load moment. This capacity is determined by multiplying the payload at the hook by the crane's outreach in meters at various positions. Essentially, the lifting capacity represents the maximum load the crane can safely lift within its operational range. It's essential to understand that as the operating radius of the crane increases, the lifting capacity decreases due to the weight of the boom system itself.

Both the load plate and the load diagram on the crane indicate the maximum loads permissible within the crane's operational reach. It's crucial to heed the warnings associated with overloading, as it could lead to severe consequences such as damage to the crane, personal injury, or even fatalities. Never attempt to increase a suspended load, as doing so may trigger a load-holding valve to open or cause the vehicle to overturn. Additionally, always ensure that the crane's overload protection (OLP) system is activated during operation.

Furthermore, when using lifting accessories, it's imperative to account for their additional weight, which reduces the maximum load capacity of the crane accordingly. Therefore, with the inclusion of lifting accessories, the maximum weight that the crane can lift becomes lower.

The load plate, indicating the maximum weight permissible at a specific reach with the 1st boom in the optimal position, is often located adjacent to the main control valve. You can reference the Technical Data the crane's operational manual to access these values for your crane.

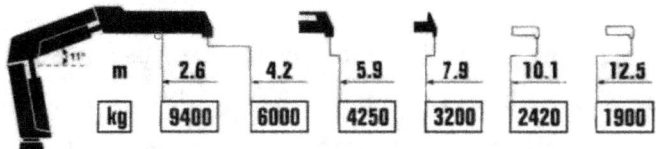

Figure 102: Sample Load plate.

Assessing Appropriate Paths and Operating Procedures: Assess and determine suitable paths for manoeuvring the truck-mounted crane and positioning loads within the work area. Consider various factors including overhead clearance, ground conditions, and proximity to adjacent structures or equipment to ensure safe and efficient crane operations.

Applying Hazard Identification and Risk Control Measures: Identify potential hazards associated with crane operations and implement effective risk elimination or control measures. Disseminate pertinent safety information to relevant personnel and advise on appropriate safety precautions to mitigate risks. Some safety considerations include:

- Avoid standing in front of the hydraulically operated stabilizer legs while operating them.

- Never rely on the stabilizer legs as a parking brake to prevent the vehicle from sliding.

- Extend the stabilizer extension fully on both sides of the vehicle whenever possible before lowering the stabilizer legs for support.

- Refrain from operating the stabilizer legs while the crane is loaded to avoid potential hazards.

- Apply low force when placing the stabilizer legs on the ground.

- Avoid lifting the vehicle using the stabilizer legs to prevent damage.

- Ensure that both add-on lifting accessories and separate lifting accessories are in good condition. Add-on lifting accessories such as hoists or jibs are sometimes installed on the crane, while separate lifting accessories like slings or chains are connected to the standard load hook.

- Avoid standing in front of the boom system when operating the crane outside of the parking position.

Confirming Traffic Management Plan Implementation: Verify the effective implementation of the traffic management plan to uphold the safety of personnel and vehicles operating in the vicinity of the crane. Adhere to prescribed procedures for managing traffic flow and maintaining safe distances from the crane during operations.

Identifying Communication Procedures: Identify and establish clear communication protocols for coordinating crane operations with associated personnel. Conduct tests to ensure the functionality and clarity of communication systems during lifting operations to facilitate seamless coordination.

Confirming Task Requirements and Compliance: Thoroughly verify that all tasks adhere to the requirements of the relevant work area and comply with established workplace procedures. Maintain strict adherence to safety protocols and operational standards throughout the lifting operation to ensure optimal safety and efficiency.

Obtaining Information for Lifting Equipment Inspection and Maintenance: Acquire essential information pertaining to the inspection, use, maintenance, and storage of lifting equipment and gear to ensure compliance with manufacturer requirements. Interpret and apply manufacturer guidelines and recommendations for the safe and proper utilization of lifting equipment and gear.

Operating a truck-mounted crane demands a systematic approach to ensure safety, efficiency, and compliance with workplace procedures. Below are detailed steps on how to operate a truck-mounted crane:

1. Consultation with Workplace Personnel:

    - Establish and maintain communication with workplace personnel to ensure clear understanding and consistency in crane and lifting operations.

    - Ensure that all operations align with site requirements, lift plans, and workplace procedures.

2. Checking Risk Control Measures:

    - Verify the implementation of risk control measures for identified hazards in accordance with the lift plan and safe work procedures.

    - Ensure that measures are in place to mitigate risks associated with crane and lifting operations.

3. Accessing Crane Controls:

    - Safely access the vehicle loading crane controls in accordance with manufacturer requirements and safe work procedures.

    - Familiarize yourself with the operation of the controls and their functions before proceeding.

4. Pre-Start Checks:

    - Perform pre-start checks on the vehicle loading crane to identify any damage or defects.

    - Report and record any issues and take appropriate action as per safe work procedures and manufacturer requirements.

5. Setting Up the Crane:

    - Set up the vehicle loading crane correctly with any required lifting gear according to the lift plan and relevant manufacturer requirements.

    - Consult the load chart/s and follow safe work procedures to ensure proper setup.

6. Setting Up Boom/Jib and Lifting Gear:

    - Configure the boom/jib and lifting gear as required, adhering to specific manufacturer requirements and safe work procedures.

    - Ensure proper alignment and attachment of lifting gear to the crane.

7. Stabilizing the Crane:

    - Stabilize the vehicle loading crane appropriately in accordance with the lift plan, relevant manufacturer requirements, and safe work procedures.

    - Use outriggers or stabilizers to enhance stability as needed.

8. Operational Checks:

    - Conduct operational checks to ensure all crane functions are working correctly.

- Report any damage or defects, record findings, and take necessary action in line with manufacturer requirements and safe work procedures.

9. Inspecting Crane Logbook:

- Inspect the vehicle loading crane logbook to ensure it is correct for the crane type and has been completed and signed.
- Verify that any required rectifications have been signed off as per manufacturer requirements and safe work procedures.

10. Assessing Weather and Work Environment:

- Assess weather and work environment conditions to determine any potential impact on crane operations.
- Take necessary precautions and adjustments in accordance with manufacturer requirements and safe work procedures.

11. Identifying Load Weight and Slinging Techniques:

- Identify, calculate, or estimate the weight of the load to be lifted.
- Calculate the derated Working Load Limit (WLL) of lifting equipment based on selected slinging techniques.

12. Preparing Lifting Equipment and Gear:

- Prepare lifting equipment and gear for safe use, ensuring they are in good condition and properly rigged.
- Identify suitable lifting points and select appropriate slinging techniques based on the load and lift plan.

13. Confirming Load Destination and Stability:

- Confirm the load destination, ensuring it is stable and capable of bearing the load weight.

- Prepare the destination area for safe access and landing of the load.

Operating a Truck Mounted Crane

Operating a truck-mounted crane requires meticulous attention to detail to ensure the safety and efficiency of lifting operations.

Determining Lifts within the RC: Consult the load chart/s and lift plan to identify lifts within the Rated Capacity (RC) of the vehicle loading crane. It's crucial to ensure that planned lifts fall within the crane's safe operating limits as specified by the load chart/s and lift plan.

Positioning Boom/Jib and Hook Block: Safely position the boom/jib and hook block over the load, following directions from associated personnel if applicable. Adhere strictly to the lift plan and safe work procedures to ensure proper alignment and positioning of the crane components over the load.

Connecting Lifting Equipment and Gear: Connect lifting equipment and gear to the load according to the lift plan, safe work procedures, and manufacturer requirements. Verify that all connections are secure and properly rigged to support the load safely during lifting operations.

Conducting Test Lift: Perform a test lift in accordance with safe work procedures to validate the stability of the load and functionality of the crane. This step ensures that all equipment and systems are operating correctly before proceeding with actual lifting tasks.

Transferring Loads: Transfer loads using relevant crane movements and tag lines, if necessary, as specified in the lift plan and safe work procedures. Exercise caution and precision to ensure smooth and controlled movement of the load throughout the lifting process.

Here are some effective lifting practices to optimize the performance of the crane:

- Maintain Clear Visibility: Always ensure that you have a clear view of the work area. Poor visibility can lead to accidents or damage.

- Working at Close Proximity: When lifting, aim to keep the load within close range while ensuring that the extension boom is partially retracted. This configuration allows the crane to maximize its lifting capacity. Position the vehicle as close to the load as possible for added efficiency.

- Working Below Ground Level: When working below ground level, adjust the first boom angle to approximately 10 to 30 degrees above the horizontal plane to facilitate loading and unloading operations.

- Handling Heavy Loads: For heavy loads, utilize the second boom, if available, positioned optimally relative to the first boom. Refer to the load plate on your crane for guidance on proper positioning.

- Smooth Crane Movements: Operate the crane with synchronized movements of various functions to ensure smooth operation. This approach not only enhances efficiency but also helps prevent rapid overheating of the hydraulic system.

Figure 103 provides an example of a Hiab control panel. Its functions include:

The stop button halts all crane movements immediately when pressed.

- The ON/OFF button toggles the safety system On or Off.

- Button is used to operate stabilizer extensions and legs. For remote-controlled stabilizer systems: The confirm view button ensures the driver has a full view while extending the stabilizer extensions outward. In this configuration, there is a user panel, SPACE 4000, on both sides of the crane. This button also functions as an OLP release button, allowing for:

  - Disconnection of the automatic dump function.
  - OLP release.

- Button if present, activates the horn.

- Button is used to toggle between remote or manual control modes.

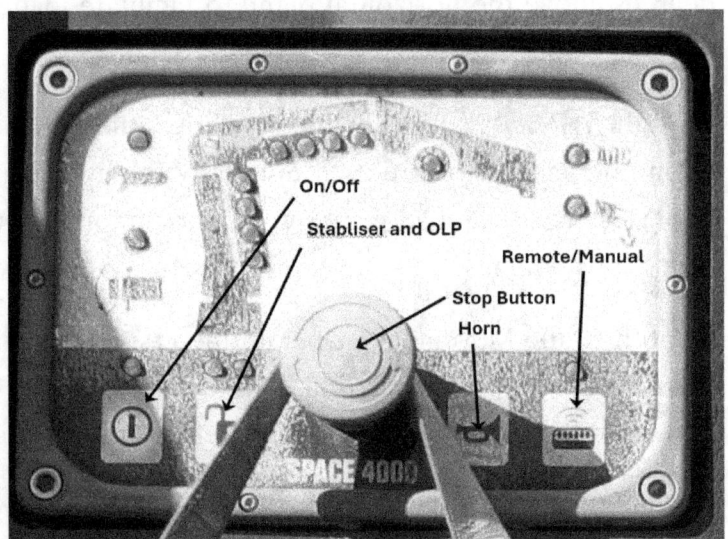

Figure 103: Hiab control panel (SPACE 4000). Leo Miregalitheo, CC BY-SA 4.0, via Wikimedia Commons.

Monitoring Load and Crane Movement: Constantly monitor load and crane movement to detect any anomalies or deviations from the lift plan. Operate the crane safely and in line with the lift plan and safe work procedures to maintain control over the lifting operation. The crane may be operated by remote, such as shown in Figure 104.

Figure 104: HIAB 195 remote control. Kenneth Allen / HIAB 195 remote control / CC BY-SA 2.0 (via Wikimedia Commons).

Interpreting Communication Signals: Accurately interpret and follow all required communication signals while operating the crane. Maintain clear and effective communication with associated personnel to coordinate lifting operations safely and efficiently.

Lowering and Landing the Load: Lower the load safely following the lift plan and safe work procedures, exercising careful control over crane movements. Ensure that the load is landed securely and stably at the designated location as specified in the lift plan.

Disconnecting Lifting Gear: Disconnect lifting gear from the load once the lifting operation is complete. Safely position the crane for the next task as per the lift plan and safe work procedures.

Inspecting Lifting Equipment and Gear: Inspect lifting equipment and gear for defects and damage post-lifting operation. Isolate, tag, and report any defective items as per safe work procedures to ensure timely repair or replacement.

Completing Truck Mounted Operations

Completing truck-mounted crane operations involves several crucial steps to ensure the safety of personnel and equipment. Here's a detailed guide on how to carry out each task effectively:

1. **Stowing and Securing Crane Boom/Jib, Lifting Gear, and Associated Equipment:**

    - Follow manufacturer requirements and safe work procedures to stow and secure the crane boom/jib, lifting gear, and associated equipment.

    - Use appropriate securing methods such as straps, chains, or locking mechanisms to prevent movement during transportation or storage.

2. **Applying Relevant Motion Locks and Brakes:**

    - Engage motion locks and brakes as required by the manufacturer and safe work procedures to prevent unintended movement of crane components.

    - Verify that all motion locks and brakes are properly applied and functioning correctly before proceeding with further shutdown procedures.

3. **Stowing and Securing Stabilisers:**

    - Retract and secure the stabilisers in accordance with manufacturer requirements and safe work procedures.

- Ensure that all locking pins, bolts, or securing devices are properly engaged to prevent accidental deployment during transportation or storage.

4. **Shutting Down and Securing the Crane**:

- Safely shut down the crane's engine or power source following safe work procedures.

- Secure the crane's controls and access points to prevent unauthorized access or use, such as locking the crane cab door or control panel.

5. **Stowing Plates or Packing**:

- If applicable, stow any plates or packing materials used during the lifting operation following safe work procedures.

- Secure plates or packing materials to prevent shifting or falling during transportation or storage.

6. **Performing Shutdown Crane Checks**:

- Conduct a thorough inspection of the crane to ensure compliance with safe work procedures and manufacturer requirements.

- Check for any damage, defects, or abnormalities and report them as per established protocols.

Figure 105: Crane boom/jib, lifting gear, and associated equipment stowed and secured. Reise Reise, CC BY-SA 4.0, via Wikimedia Commons.

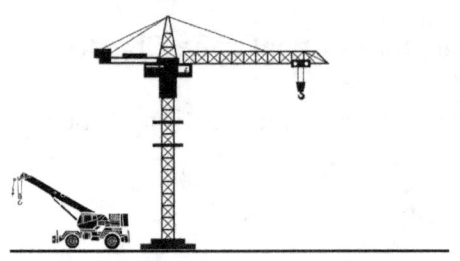

Chapter Nine

Non-Slewing Mobile Cranes

A non-slewing mobile crane, also known as a pick and carry crane or a mobile crane without slew, is a type of crane designed for lifting and carrying heavy loads horizontally without the need for a rotating upper structure. Unlike slewing cranes, which have a rotating turret or turntable, non-slewing cranes do not swivel or slew, hence the name.

Figure 106: Mobile articulated crane (Franna AT20). Ingolfson, Public domain, via Wikimedia Commons.

Non-slewing mobile cranes are commonly used in construction, industrial, and infrastructure projects where lifting and moving heavy loads over short distances is required. They are particularly useful in confined spaces or urban areas where manoeuvrability is limited, as they can navigate tight spaces and access work areas with ease.

A mobile articulated crane, as shown in Figure 106, a subtype of non-slewing cranes, is specifically engineered for road travel and the lifting and often transporting of loads to designated destinations. In contrast to slewing mobile cranes, articulated cranes typically lack stabilizer legs or outriggers, instead featuring a fixed articulation joint within their structure. This unique design attribute enables the crane to navigate and position loads without the need for additional stabilization mechanisms.

While the skill requirements for crane operators remain largely consistent across various crane types, articulated cranes possess distinct operational characteristics that set them apart from other mobile crane variants, such as slewing mobile cranes.

During road operations, the stability of articulated cranes relies solely on the condition and capacity of their tyres. Specifically, the crane's rated capacities when traveling on tyres are contingent upon factors such as tire capacity, tyre condition, tyre air pressure, and ground conditions. It is imperative that all tyres undergo thorough inspection and are inflated to the recommended pressure before embarking on road operations. Prior to commencing any operations, crane operators must diligently review and comprehend the manufacturer's instructions pertaining to site conditions, road operations, and lifting conditions.

Mobile articulated cranes are recognized by various names, including "pick and carry" cranes and designations based on their manufacturer or model, such as Franna, Terex, TIDD, Hummer, and MAC.

Usually, these cranes can operate in both two-wheel (front-wheel) and four-wheel drive modes. They are equipped with a front axle differential lock for navigating rough terrain. Additionally, the crane is outfitted with a transfer case featuring high and low range gearing.

Steering of the crane is accomplished by articulating around the centre pivot. This movement is facilitated by hydraulic cylinders, which are powered by a pump connected to the main hydraulic pump of the engine. Furthermore, a secondary emergency hydraulic pump, powered by electricity, is installed as a backup in the event of main pump failure.

Certain articulated mobile cranes come equipped with a counterweight that can be situated at the front of the crane. This counterweight can be positioned at the front of the crane or carried separately to adhere to axle weight regulations, such as those applicable during road travel. It is acceptable to lift loads without any counterweight or with front or rear counterweights, following the guidelines outlined in the rated capacity manual.

The articulated mobile crane incorporates articulated steering around a central pivot, with hydraulic cylinders supplying the necessary force. In the event of hydraulic pump failure, a backup emergency pump is available.

The suspension on articulated mobile cranes is harsh. This means every bump and undulation in the road is felt by the driver. An air suspended seat is also fitted to manufactured articulated mobile cranes, which means that the driver bounces up and down a reasonable amount relative to the vehicle as result of road roughness. The harsh suspension comes about because when the crane is being used as a crane, it needs to lift up a heavy load at the front. The entire load must be supported by its front suspension. Mobile articulated cranes are specifically intended to drive around work sites with the load suspended at its front. This stands in strong contrast to other mobile cranes, which generally are not designed to travel while suspending a load. Other mobile cranes use extendable outriggers to deal with the large lifted loads and use dedicated road suspension when travelling along roads.

Mobile articulated cranes possess unique characteristics that set them apart from conventional vehicles such as trucks, buses, cars, and even other cranes. These distinctive traits pose challenges when attempting to regain control after a loss of control at high speeds.

Unlike vehicles with Ackerman steering, which steer by turning the front wheels while the body remains stationary, articulated mobile cranes utilize frame steering. This method involves bending the crane in the middle, effectively turning the front wheels in relation to the rear wheels. Consequently, the driver experiences rapid rotation with the front half of the cabin in the direction of steering, creating a unique sensation for crane operators.

Articulated mobile cranes rely on hydraulic cylinders to push the two halves of the vehicle's body apart for steering. This hydraulic system, coupled with limited feedback in the steering wheel, results in "twitchy" steering behaviour. Rapid rotation of the steering wheel prompts sharp changes in steering response, potentially leading to over-steering if not carefully managed.

Unlike the castor effect observed in conventional vehicles, where front wheels naturally straighten up after completing a turn, articulated mobile steering cranes lack this self-centring mechanism. When the steering wheel is released, the front wheels do not automatically return to a straight line. As a result, crane operators must remain vigilant and actively manage steering to maintain control and stability at all times.

The distinctive attributes mentioned above may contribute to lateral instability when operating these cranes at high speeds. In specific scenarios, an articulated crane may exhibit slight lateral movement, initially by a few inches, which can escalate to more pronounced swerving from side to side, commonly referred to as "fishtailing." This phenomenon is sometimes colloquially termed "speed wobbles."

Lateral instability or "speed wobbles" pose significant risks, potentially leading to loss of control and serious accidents. Factors such as the driver's reactions, speed, acceleration instead of gradual braking, and excessive steering input can exacerbate the loss of control.

In the event of lateral instability, it is crucial to respond appropriately. The driver should promptly release the accelerator pedal. It is advised not to:

- Apply harsh braking

- Accelerate further

- Overcorrect steering

- Grip the steering wheel with both hands simultaneously

as these actions can exacerbate the fishtailing effect, worsening the situation.

Drivers operating articulated mobile cranes on construction sites are entrusted with the responsibility of driving safely and adhering to both road regulations and worksite rules. They must exercise caution and operate in accordance with Traffic Management Plans (TMPs) and Vehicle Movement Plans (VMPs) where applicable.

Alertness is paramount for drivers of mobile articulated cranes navigating construction sites, who must remain attentive to various factors including:

- Adherence to temporary speed zones and directives to ensure safe driving practices.

- Observation of worksite entry and exit points, allowing for ample distance for deceleration and acceleration into and out of traffic streams.

- Exercise of judgment when changing lanes or making turns within the worksite to prevent accidents or disruptions.

- Consideration of moving traffic and queued vehicles entering or exiting the worksite, navigating safely through traffic flows.

- Following directions provided by traffic controllers to ensure smooth traffic flow and coordination.

- Adaptation to changes in surface materials and conditions, such as transitioning between solid road surfaces and loose stones or dirt, which may pose hazards like slippery or uneven terrain.

- Awareness of vehicular traffic, pedestrians, and workers present within the worksite premises to avoid collisions or accidents.

- Respect for pedestrian and vehicle exclusion zones designated within the worksite to maintain safety standards.

- Utilization of preferred communication methods, such as two-way radios, to facilitate effective communication among team members.

- Compliance with worksite induction requirements to ensure familiarity with site-specific protocols and procedures.

- Adherence to guidelines regarding the use of pilot or escort vehicles and directional routes to navigate safely through the worksite.

- Consideration of crane height, width, length clearances, and weight restrictions to prevent collisions with structures or obstacles within the worksite.

- Maintenance of visibility despite obstacles like dust, smoke, darkness, or blind spots to ensure safe navigation.

- Awareness of dangerous goods and flammable storage areas within the worksite to prevent accidents or hazards.

- Utilization of warning devices like flashing lights, reversing alarms, and lights to alert others of crane movement.

- Strict adherence to wearing seat belts at all times to ensure personal safety while operating the crane.

- Prevention of unauthorized use of the crane equipment to maintain operational integrity and safety standards.

- Attention to night work conditions and sufficient lighting to ensure visibility and safety during nocturnal operations.

- Wearing appropriate Personal Protective Equipment (PPE), including high-visibility clothing, to enhance visibility and personal safety.

- Compliance with decontamination requirements for contaminated sites to prevent contamination spread.

- Awareness that site conditions may change over time, requiring adaptability and caution when revisiting the same location.

Planning Non-slewing Crane Operations

Operating a non-slewing crane entails a systematic approach to ensure safety and efficiency in lifting operations. Firstly, task requirements are identified from work orders or similar documents. This involves understanding the nature of the lift and any specific instructions provided. Subsequently, a lift plan is formulated in consultation with relevant personnel, including riggers and site supervisors. This plan outlines the steps to be taken during the lifting operation and ensures alignment with workplace procedures.

Before commencing operations, a thorough site inspection is conducted following workplace procedures. This inspection assesses the work area operating surface to determine ground suitability for crane operation. It involves evaluating factors such as ground stability and any potential hazards that may affect crane stability or operation.

Establishing the Rated Capacity (RC) of the non-slewing mobile crane and the Working Load Limit (WLL) of the lifting gear is crucial for safe lifting. This is done in accordance with manufacturer requirements and workplace procedures. The RC and WLL are determined based on the specific load and task requirements, ensuring compliance with safety standards.

Assessing appropriate paths for operating the mobile crane and moving and placing loads in the work area is essential to prevent accidents and ensure smooth operations. This involves considering factors such as overhead obstacles, ground conditions, and proximity to other structures or equipment, in line with workplace procedures.

Identifying hazards and implementing risk control measures are paramount to mitigate potential risks associated with crane operations. Relevant hazard identification techniques are applied, and appropriate risk elimination or control measures are advised to associated personnel, ensuring adherence to workplace safety protocols.

Confirming and following the traffic management plan is crucial to ensure the safety of personnel and vehicles in the vicinity of crane operations. Compliance with traffic management procedures outlined in the workplace protocols helps minimize the risk of accidents or disruptions.

Establishing effective communication procedures is vital for coordination and safety during lifting operations. Identifying and testing communication protocols with associated personnel ensures clear and timely communication, enhancing overall operational efficiency and safety.

Ensuring all tasks are confirmed in accordance with the lift plan and workplace procedures is essential to maintain consistency and adherence to safety standards. Regular confirmation of task requirements helps prevent deviations that may compromise safety or efficiency.

Obtaining and interpreting information required for lifting equipment and gear inspection, use, maintenance, and storage is necessary to ensure compliance with manufacturer requirements. This includes understanding guidelines for equipment inspection, maintenance procedures, and storage protocols to maintain equipment integrity and safety.

Preparing for Non-slewing Crane Operations

Operating a non-slewing crane requires meticulous attention to detail and adherence to safety protocols throughout the lifting operation. Initially, consultation with workplace personnel is established and maintained to ensure that the lift plan is clear and aligns with site requirements and workplace procedures. This involves continuous communication with relevant stakeholders to address any concerns or modifications necessary for the safe execution of the lift.

Following the establishment of the lift plan, thorough risk control measures for identified hazards are checked for implementation. This step ensures that all potential risks associated with the lifting operation are adequately addressed and mitigated in accordance with the lift plan and safe work procedures.

Accessing the non-slewing mobile crane safely is paramount to prevent accidents or injuries. Operators must adhere to manufacturer requirements and safe work procedures when accessing the crane, ensuring proper entry and exit protocols are followed to maintain personal safety and equipment integrity.

Prior to initiating crane operations, pre-start checks are diligently carried out to assess the condition of the crane and lifting equipment. Any damage or defects observed during these checks are promptly reported, recorded, and addressed in accordance with manufacturer requirements and safe work procedures to maintain equipment reliability and safety standards.

Correct setup of the mobile crane is essential for safe lifting operations. This includes ensuring that the crane is configured correctly with any lifting gear according to the lift plan, relevant manufacturer requirements, load charts, and safe work procedures. Additionally, if a fly jib is fitted, it must be set up in accordance with specific manufacturer requirements and safe work procedures to enhance operational safety.

Operational checks are conducted to verify the functionality of the crane and identify any operational issues or defects. Any observed damage or defects are reported, recorded, and addressed in accordance with manufacturer requirements and safe work procedures to maintain operational integrity.

Regular inspection of the crane logbook is essential to confirm current compliance with the crane type and ensure that all required documentation is completed, signed, and up to date. Any necessary rectifications are promptly addressed and signed off in accordance with manufacturer requirements and safe work procedures.

Assessment of weather and work environment conditions is crucial to determine any potential impacts on mobile crane operations. Operators must adhere to manufacturer requirements and safe work procedures when assessing weather conditions, ensuring that operations are conducted safely in various environmental conditions.

Identifying the weight of the load and calculating the derated Working Load Limit (WLL) of lifting equipment resulting from selected slinging techniques are essential steps to ensure safe lifting operations. Suitable lifting points and slinging techniques are identified in accordance with safe work procedures, and lifting equipment and gear are prepared accordingly for safe use during the lifting operation.

Finally, load destination is confirmed for stability, ensuring that the load-bearing capacity is adequate and that the area is prepared for safe access and landing of the load. This comprehensive approach to crane operations ensures the safety of personnel and equipment throughout the lifting process.

As an example of setting up for operations, with the Terex Fanna mobile articulated crane the crane operator must establish reduced Rated Capacities for the specific job, taking into consideration various adverse operating conditions. These conditions encompass factors such as the condition of the supporting surface, pendulum action of the load, abrupt stops or jerking of the load, and other elements that may affect stability, including two-machine lifts, proximity to electrical wires, adverse weather conditions such as wind, and hazardous surroundings. Additionally, the experience level of personnel involved in the operation must be considered.

Rated Capacity is typically determined based on Freely Suspended Loads with the machine positioned on a firm, level surface with a maximum slope of 1% (0.6°) and uniform ground conditions. However, lifting or traveling with a load on soft or uneven ground can pose hazards and reduce the Rated Capacity of the crane. It is crucial to refrain from attempting to drag the load along the ground in any direction to maintain safety standards.

Wind forces acting on the boom, particularly from winds up to 10 m/s (36 km/h), are factored into the Rated Capacity. Any additional Side Loading resulting from wind forces on the load will further diminish the Rated Capacity and must be taken into account during operations. Rated Capacities above a designated red line are primarily based on the machine's hydraulic or structural competence rather than its stability, whereas capacities below the red line primarily consider machine stability.

The Rated Capacities provided include the mass of various attachments such as hooks, blocks, slings, and auxiliary lifting devices. To determine the equivalent net load, their mass must be subtracted from the listed Rated Capacity.

Loaded Boom Angles specified at certain boom lengths offer only an approximate estimation of the Load Radius. It's advisable to adjust the Boom Angle before loading to a greater degree to accommodate for boom deflection, which increases the Load Radius as the load is lifted.

These mobile cranes are primarily intended for use on stable, flat, and level ground, as specified by AS 1418.5. Any deviation from this standard necessitates a reduction in the Rated Capacity of the crane.

According to AS 2550.5, mobile cranes should avoid negotiating slopes while traveling with Freely Suspended Loads. When operating on side slopes of up to 5° (8.75% gradient), certain precautions must be observed, considering that surface depressions and potholes can create effects similar to side slopes.

To ensure safe operation on side slopes, several measures should be taken. Firstly, it's essential to verify that the tyres are inflated correctly in accordance with the rated capacity manual. Additionally, the ground condition must be assessed to ensure it is firm enough to support the axle loads. The Rated Capacity of the crane should be reduced by the specified percentage value for operating on side slopes up to 5°, as illustrated in figure 1. It's important to note that the crane's load indicator does not automatically derate the Rated Capacity.

The crane's side slope inclinometer can serve as a reference guide, but its accuracy is highest when the crane's Articulation is straight ahead without a load suspended. Articulated chassis cranes will exhibit some degree of side tilt when articulated with a load, which should not be mistaken for the ground's side slope. To minimize risks, it's advisable to use the minimum boom length and Loaded Boom Angle practical to keep the boom tip as close to the ground as possible and the load as low as possible.

Furthermore, utilizing the minimum practical Articulation angle is recommended, considering that the crane will side tilt, causing the hook to move toward the direction of Articulation while steering. Placing the load on the uphill side of the crane whenever possible, especially when articulated, is advised to mitigate the increase in the working Load Radius if the load is suspended in the downhill position.

Lastly, it's crucial to prevent load swing to maintain stability. Taglining loads to prevent pendulum motion and applying travel and crane motions gently can help minimize this effect.

To recap, during lifting operations, slewing mobile cranes typically raise and lower the load between fixed positions, while pick and carry cranes often transport loads while moving across sites. When using the crane to lift and transport a load, it's imperative for the crane operator to adhere to the manufacturer's instructions. They must consider adverse operating conditions, such as the nature of the supporting surface, the pendulum action of the load, abrupt movements or stops of the crane leading to load swing, and other factors impacting stability. Additionally, crane operators must remain mindful of changing ground conditions that may arise during travel with a load, such as uneven road surfaces or potholes, as these factors can diminish the crane's rated capacity. Such conditions effectively create a scenario akin to operating on a side slope, necessitating a reduction in the crane's rated capacity to maintain stability .

Lifting a load on a side slope introduces a lateral force as the load swings downhill, influencing the tipping line of the crane. Crane operators should refer to the deration load chart provided by the crane manufacturer to ascertain the deration percentage necessary for calculating the appropriate rated capacity for their lifting task.

Figure 107 is an example of how to use the crane capacity deration chart. The deration load charts are provided by the crane manufacturers to guide the operator on how to calculate the rated capacity reduction when a side slope is encountered (Terex, 2005).

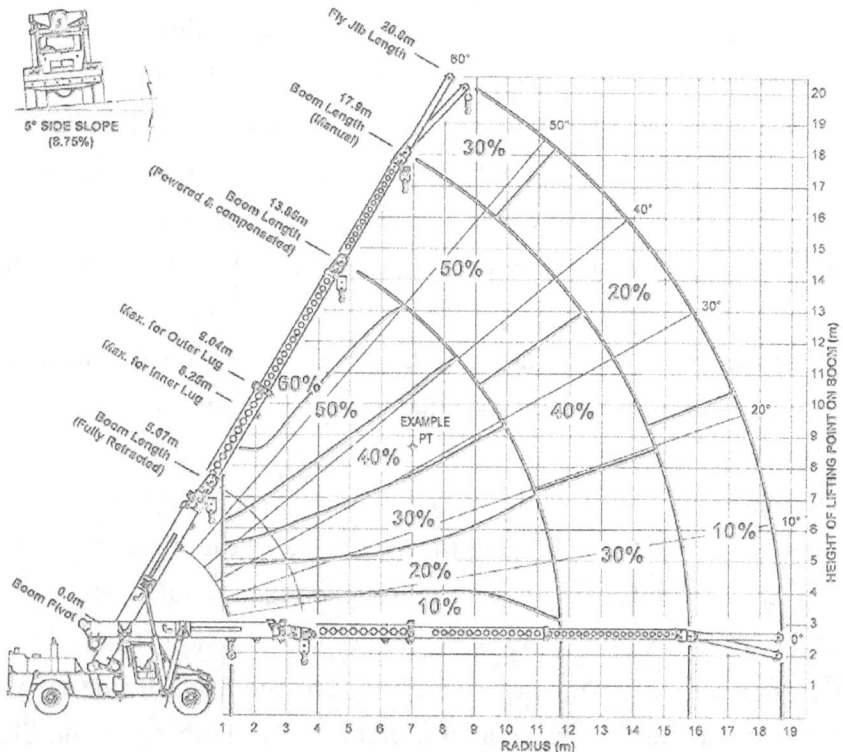

Figure 107: Percentage Deration Chart for AT-20 at 5° Side Slope. Adapted from Terex (2005).

As an example, a crane with a deration load chart in Figure 107 has a rated capacity (on level ground) of 4000kg (operating at 7m working radius with a boom angle of 34°). When it's operating on a side slope up to 5°, according to the chart, the crane capacity should reduce 40 per cent to (Arnott, 2020):

4000kg − (4000kg x40%) = 2400 kg

Crane stability can vary during crane articulation, as the positioning of the crane's weight shifts closer to the axis of rotation, resulting in a reduction of the moment exerted by the crane's weight. When operating on a side slope, if the load offset extends beyond the wheel, the crane's tipping line shifts to the side wheel line, significantly reducing the distance between the crane's weight and the tipping line.

Similarly, when operating on a side slope in an articulated configuration, the crane's tipping line also shifts to the side wheel line, resulting in a notable reduction in the distance between the crane's weight and the tipping line, while increasing the distance between the load and the tipping line. Unlike slewing mobile cranes, which can execute lifting operations with a slewing angle of 360°, articulated cranes are restricted to operating within the crane's articulation range, typically up to 40°. Above 10° articulation, most articulated cranes experience a reduction in rated capacity.

During crane articulation, the crane's centre of gravity moves closer to the axis of rotation, leading to a decrease in the moment exerted by the crane counterweight. Therefore, a reduced rated capacity chart must be utilized when operating within the articulation range of 10° to 40° (Arnott, 2020). Given that the crane often articulates during carrying operations while traversing a site, meticulous planning of the lift is essential to ensuring that the crane's capacity remains intact throughout the lifting operation.

Operating a Mobile Articulated Crane

Firstly, lifts must be determined within the Rated Capacity (RC) of the crane, adhering closely to the load chart/s and lift plan provided. These documents outline the permissible lifting capacities and ensure that the crane operates within safe limits.

Next, the boom/jib and hook block must be positioned securely over the load, following instructions from associated personnel and in alignment with the lift plan and established safe work procedures. This step is critical for ensuring the stability and safety of the lifting operation.

When mobilizing a load, it's imperative to verify the rated load capacity of the crane to prevent overloading. If necessary, the crane should be de-rated following the manufacturer's instructions or those provided by a qualified person.

During mobilization, the dogger must maintain visibility to the crane operator and avoid walking in the crane's path or between the crane and the load.

When traveling and manoeuvring with a load, the crane operator should adhere to several guidelines:

- Plan the travel pathway in advance.

- Inspect ground conditions and the intended pathway for any obstacles or hazards, such as wet ground, potholes, or uneven terrain, and address them before moving the load.

- Operate the crane according to the manufacturer's instructions.

- • Maintain a speed appropriate for the dogger, ground conditions, and the load, typically a comfortable walking pace.

- Consider the impact of wind loading, especially for loads with a large surface area.

- Keep the load at minimum boom length and as close to the ground as feasible.

- Carry the load uphill of the crane whenever possible, such as driving in reverse down a slope, to keep the load near the crane.

- Engage axle locks, if equipped, following the manufacturer's instructions.

- Execute turns with a wide radius to minimize the crane's articulation, as articulation diminishes the crane's rated capacity.

Once the load is properly positioned, lifting equipment and gear, if required, should be connected to the load in accordance with the lift plan, safe work procedures, and manufacturer requirements. This ensures that the load is securely rigged and supported during lifting.

Before proceeding with the lift, a test lift should be conducted in accordance with safe work procedures. This allows operators to verify the stability of the load and ensure that all crane systems are functioning correctly.

During the transfer of loads, relevant crane movements and tag lines should be utilized as specified in the lift plan and safe work procedures. This ensures controlled and precise movement of the load throughout the lifting process.

Constant monitoring of load and crane movement is essential to detect any deviations from the lift plan or safety procedures. Operators must vigilantly oversee crane operations to maintain control and mitigate risks.

Communication signals must be accurately interpreted and followed at all times while operating the crane, in strict accordance with the lift plan and safe work procedures. Clear communication is vital for coordinating lifting operations safely and efficiently.

Once the load has been lifted and transferred, it must be lowered and landed safely according to the lift plan and safe work procedures. Careful control of crane movements is essential to prevent accidents during this phase of the operation.

After the load has been safely lowered, lifting gear should be disconnected from the load, and the crane should be positioned safely and efficiently for the next task, following the lift plan and safe work procedures.

Finally, all lifting equipment and gear must be inspected for defects, and any defective items should be isolated, tagged, and reported as per established procedures. Regular inspection and maintenance are crucial for ensuring the ongoing safety and reliability of the crane.

For operations of the Terex Franna AT-20 for example:

- Thoroughly read and comprehend all cautionary alerts and instructional remarks provided.

- Avoid tipping the machine to ascertain permissible lifting capacities.

- Loads can be lifted from various points on the crane, including the main boom head on the winch, the rhino hook, the fixed lug, or either of the two sliding lugs on the boom. Additionally, a fly jib may extend the maximum boom length, and a manbasket can be affixed to the head of the boom. Always refer to the appropriate Rated Capacity chart for the lifting point in use, and ensure the Load Moment Indicator (LMI) is adjusted to the correct duty.

- Simultaneous lifting from multiple lifting points is not intended or sanctioned.

- The handling of personnel from the boom, except in a Terex Lifting Australia supplied manbasket correctly installed on the head of the boom or other approved arrangement, is neither intended nor approved.

- When the boom length or Load Radius falls between listed values, the smallest load indicated at the next larger Load Radius or boom length should be used, or the interpolated value displayed on the LMI may be employed.

- Side loading of the machine and load swing out may result in structural failure or machine tip-over. Side loads can be caused by lifting when not level, sudden acceleration or deceleration while articulating with a load, dragging or pushing a load, and wind forces on the load and boom structure.

- The Rated Capacity of the manual extension is determined by the Loaded Boom Angle. Although the boom may be retracted and extended manually, the Rated Capacity remains unchanged from the fully extended position for the given Loaded Boom Angle.

- It is permissible to attempt to telescope any load within the limits of the Rated Capacity Manual. However, the maximum load that may be telescoped is restricted by hydraulic pressure, Loaded Boom Angle, and lubrication of powered boom sections.

- The winch rope is fully compensated for boom extension, except when manually setting the extension. Refer to the operator's manual for the manual setting procedure. Once set, compensation is fully functional. Always ensure a minimum of 2 wraps of rope remain on the winch drum, and note the areas on the range diagram where the fall block cannot reach the ground on 4 or 3 parts of rope.

- The Rated Capacity depends on tyre rating, condition, and inflation pressure. Ensure all tyres are in good condition and inflated to the recommended pressure before attempting a lift.

- Pick and carry operation is permissible through the full Articulation range; however, Rated Capacity is reduced above 10° Articulation. Refer to the reduced capacities chart if entering this Articulation zone during operation.

- The maximum speed for pick and carry operation is 0.4m/s (1.44km/h), with the transfer case set to low range. Operating this crane beyond the Rated Capacity and disregarding instructions poses hazards.

Figure 108 shows a sample load chart for a mobile articulated crane.

CRANE OPERATIONS

Pick & Carry 0.4 m/s (1.44 km/h); On rubber 66.6%   5.67–13.85 m

RADIUS m	5.67 kg	6.00 kg	6.50 kg	7.00 kg	7.50 kg	8.00 kg	8.50 kg	9.00 kg	9.50 kg	10.00 kg	10.50 kg	11.00 kg	11.50 kg	12.00 kg	12.50 kg	13.00 kg	13.50 kg	13.85 kg
1.6	16800 / 12600 / 48°	16250 / 12600 / 51°	16450 / 12600 / 54°	14900 / 12800 / 57°														
2.0	16800 / 12600 / 42°	16300 / 12600 / 46°	16500 / 12600 / 50°	15700 / 12600 / 53°	15100 / 12600 / 56°	14700 / 12600 / 58°	14350 / 12600 / 60°											
2.5	13900 / 12150 / 34°	13900 / 12150 / 39°	13900 / 12100 / 44°	13850 / 12100 / 48°	13850 / 12100 / 51°	13850 / 12100 / 54°	13850 / 12050 / 56°	13200 / 12050 / 58°	13000 / 12050 / 60°									
3.0	11450 / 9950 / 25°	11450 / 9950 / 31°	11450 / 9950 / 37°	11400 / 9950 / 42°	11400 / 9950 / 46°	11400 / 9900 / 49°	11400 / 9900 / 52°	11400 / 9900 / 55°	11400 / 9900 / 57°	11150 / 9900 / 59°	10250 / 9900 / 60°							
3.5	9650 / 8400 / 8°	9650 / 8400 / 20°	9650 / 8400 / 29°	9650 / 8400 / 36°	9650 / 8400 / 41°	9650 / 8400 / 45°	9650 / 8400 / 48°	9650 / 8400 / 51°	9650 / 8400 / 53°	9650 / 8350 / 55°	9500 / 8350 / 57°	8150 / 8150 / 59°	7500 / 7500 / 60°					
4.0	9450 / 8200 / (3.57)	8550 / 7450 / (3.90)	8350 / 7250 / 19°	8350 / 7250 / 28°	8350 / 7250 / 35°	8350 / 7250 / 39°	8350 / 7250 / 43°	8350 / 7250 / 47°	8300 / 7200 / 49°	8300 / 7200 / 52°	8300 / 7200 / 54°	7800 / 7200 / 56°	7000 / 7000 / 57°	6700 / 6700 / 59°	6450 / 6450 / 60°			
4.5			7500 / 6500 / (4.40)	7300 / 6350 / 19°	7300 / 6350 / 27°	7300 / 6350 / 34°	7300 / 6350 / 38°	7300 / 6350 / 42°	7300 / 6300 / 45°	7300 / 6300 / 48°	7300 / 6300 / 50°	7150 / 6300 / 52°	6550 / 6300 / 54°	6250 / 6050 / 56°	6050 / 6050 / 58°	5800 / 5800 / 59°	5650 / 5650 / 60°	
5.0				6650 / 5750 / (4.90)	6500 / 5600 / 18°	6500 / 5600 / 27°	6500 / 5600 / 33°	6500 / 5600 / 37°	6500 / 5600 / 41°	6500 / 5600 / 44°	6500 / 5600 / 47°	6500 / 5600 / 49°	6150 / 5600 / 51°	5900 / 5600 / 53°	5650 / 5600 / 55°	5450 / 5450 / 56°	5300 / 5300 / 58°	5150 / 5150 / 59°
6.0						5950 / 5100 / (5.40)	5350 / 4600 / (5.90)	5250 / 4550 / 17°	5250 / 4550 / 25°	5250 / 4550 / 31°	5250 / 4500 / 35°	5250 / 4500 / 39°	5250 / 4500 / 42°	5250 / 4500 / 45°	5250 / 4500 / 47°	5050 / 4500 / 49°	4850 / 4500 / 51°	4700 / 4500 / 53°	4600 / 4500 / 54°
7.0									4850 / 4200 / (6.40)	4450 / 3800 / (6.90)	4400 / 3750 / 16°	4400 / 3750 / 24°	4400 / 3750 / 29°	4400 / 3750 / 34°	4400 / 3750 / 37°	4350 / 3750 / 40°	4350 / 3750 / 43°	4350 / 3750 / 45°	4200 / 3750 / 47°	3950 / 3750 / 48°
8.0												4100 / 3500 / (7.40)	3750 / 3200 / (7.90)	3750 / 3150 / 15°	3700 / 3150 / 23°	3700 / 3150 / 28°	3700 / 3150 / 32°	3700 / 3150 / 36°	3700 / 3150 / 38°	3700 / 3150 / 41°	3600 / 3150 / 43°
9.0														3500 / 2950 / (8.40)	3250 / 2750 / (8.90)	3200 / 2700 / 15°	3200 / 2700 / 22°	3200 / 2700 / 27°	3200 / 2700 / 31°	3200 / 2700 / 34°	3200 / 2700 / 36°
10.0																3000 / 2550 / (9.40)	2800 / 2400 / (9.90)	2800 / 2350 / 14°	2800 / 2350 / 21°	2800 / 2350 / 26°	2900 / 2350 / 29°
11.0																		2650 / 2200 / (10.40)	2500 / 2100 / (10.90)	2450 / 2050 / 13°	2450 / 2050 / 18°
11.75																				2350 / 1950 / (11.40)	2250 / 1850 / (11.75)

Legend: RC (kg) < than 10° articulation | RC (kg) > than 10° articulation | Boom angle | ( ) Radius at 0° boom angle

Figure 108: Sample load cjart for mobile articulated crane.

As an example of using the load chart, let's say we had a crane set up as follows:

- Main boom length: 10.5 metres

- Working radius: 3.5 metres

- Articulation is less than 10%

- Two fall hook block fitted with a weight of 60kg.

What is the maximum load that can be raised on the hook?
Adjustments: Two fall hook block 60 kg
Workings: 10.5 metre boom at 3.5 metre radius: rated capacity (articulation less than 10%) = 9500 kg (see Figure 109)

Radius m	5.67 kg	6.00 kg	6.50 kg	7.00 kg	7.50 kg	8.00 kg	8.50 kg	9.00 kg	9.50 kg	10.00 kg	10.50 kg	11.00 kg	11.50 kg	12.00 kg	12.50 kg	13.00 kg	13.50 kg	13.85 kg
1.6	16800 / 12600 / 48°	16250 / 12600 / 51°	15450 / 12600 / 54°	14900 / 12600 / 57°														
2.0	16800 / 12600 / 42°	16800 / 12600 / 46°	16500 / 12600 / 50°	15700 / 12600 / 53°	16100 / 12600 / 56°	14700 / 12600 / 58°	14350 / 12600 / 60°											
2.5	13900 / 12150 / 34°	13900 / 12150 / 39°	13800 / 12100 / 44°	13850 / 12100 / 48°	13850 / 12100 / 51°	13850 / 12100 / 54°	13850 / 12100 / 56°	13200 / 12050 / 58°	13000 / 12050 / 60°									
3.0	11450 / 9050 / 25°	11450 / 8950 / 31°	11450 / 8950 / 37°	11400 / 8950 / 42°	11400 / 8950 / 46°	11400 / 8900 / 49°	11400 / 8900 / 52°	11400 / 8900 / 55°	11400 / 8900 / 57°	11150 / 9900 / 59°	10250 / 9000 / 60°							
3.5	9650 / 8400 / 8°	8650 / 8400 / 20°	9650 / 8400 / 29°	9650 / 8400 / 36°	9650 / 8400 / 41°	9650 / 8400 / 45°	9650 / 8400 / 48°	9650 / 8400 / 51°	9650 / 8400 / 53°	9650 / 8400 / 55°	**9500 / 8350 / 57°**	8150 / 8350 / 59°	7500 / 8150 / 60°	7500 / —				
4.0	9450 / 8200 / (3.57)	8550 / 7450 / (3.90)	8350 / 7250 / 19°	8350 / 7250 / 28°	8350 / 7250 / 35°	8350 / 7250 / 39°	8350 / 7250 / 43°	8350 / 7250 / 47°	8350 / 7200 / 49°	8300 / 7200 / 52°	8300 / 7200 / 54°	7900 / 7200 / 56°	7000 / 7000 / 57°	6700 / 6700 / 59°	6450 / 6450 / 60°			
4.5				7500 / 6500 / (4.40)	7300 / 6350 / 19°	7300 / 6350 / 27°	7300 / 6350 / 34°	7300 / 6350 / 38°	7300 / 6300 / 42°	7300 / 6300 / 45°	7300 / 6300 / 48°	7300 / 6300 / 50°	7150 / 6300 / 52°	6550 / 6300 / 54°	6250 / 6250 / 56°	6050 / 6050 / 58°	5800 / 5800 / 59°	5650 / 5650 / 60°
5.0				8650 / 5750 / (4.90)	6500 / 5600 / 18°	6500 / 5600 / 27°	6500 / 5600 / 33°	6500 / 5600 / 37°	6500 / 5600 / 41°	6500 / 5600 / 44°	6500 / 5600 / 47°	6500 / 5600 / 49°	6150 / 5600 / 51°	5900 / 5600 / 53°	5650 / 5600 / 55°	5450 / 5450 / 56°	5300 / 5300 / 58°	5150 / 5150 / 59°
6.0						5950 / 5100 / (5.40)	5250 / 4600 / (5.90)	5250 / 4550 / 17°	5250 / 4550 / 25°	5250 / 4550 / 31°	5250 / 4500 / 35°	5250 / 4500 / 39°	5250 / 4500 / 42°	5250 / 4500 / 45°	5250 / 4500 / 47°	5050 / 4500 / 49°	4850 / 4500 / 51°	4700 / 4500 / 53° / 4600 / 4500 / 54°
7.0								4850 / 4200 / (6.40)	4450 / 3800 / (6.90)	4400 / 3750 / 19°	4400 / 3750 / 24°	4400 / 3750 / 29°	4400 / 3750 / 34°	4400 / 3750 / 37°	4350 / 3750 / 40°	4350 / 3750 / 43°	4200 / 3750 / 45° / 47°	3950 / 3750 / 48°
8.0										4100 / 3500 / (7.40)	3750 / 3200 / (7.90)	3750 / 3150 / 15°	3700 / 3150 / 23°	3700 / 3150 / 28°	3700 / 3150 / 32°	3700 / 3150 / 36°	3700 / 3150 / 38°	3600 / 3150 / 41° / 43°
9.0											3500 / 2950 / (8.40)	3250 / 2750 / (8.90)	3200 / 2700 / 15°	3200 / 2700 / 22°	3200 / 2700 / 27°	3200 / 2700 / 31°	3200 / 2700 / 34°	3200 / 2700 / 36°
10.0													3000 / 2850 / (9.40)	2800 / 2400 / (9.90)	2800 / 2350 / 14°	2600 / 2350 / 21°	2800 / 2350 / 26°	2800 / 2350 / 29°
11.0															2650 / 2200 / (10.40)	2500 / 2100 / (10.90)	2490 / 2050 / 13°	2450 / 2050 / 18°
11.75																	2350 / 1950 / (11.40)	2250 / 1850 / (11.75)

Figure 109: Workings for boom length at 10.5m and working radius of 3.5m.

Two fall hook block 60 kg

Total deductions 60 kg

Maximum load:

9500 kg − 60 kg = 9440 kg

Therefore, the maximum load that can be lifted in this configuration is 9440 kg

Completing Non-slewing Crane Operations

Before concluding crane operations, it is imperative for the non-slewing crane operator to ensure that the crane boom/jib, lifting gear, and associated equipment are meticulously stowed and secured in compliance with both manufacturer stipulations and safe work procedures. This includes properly securing all components to prevent any unintended movement or dislodgment during transport or storage.

Additionally, it is crucial to engage relevant motion locks and brakes as required by the manufacturer and in accordance with safe work procedures. These measures are essential to immobilize the crane effectively and prevent any potential motion or instability that could pose safety risks during transit or while stationary.

Following the completion of crane operations, the crane must be appropriately shut down and secured to prevent unauthorized access or use. This involves following established safe work procedures to power down the crane and implement any necessary physical security measures to deter unauthorized individuals from accessing or operating the equipment.

Finally, post-operational crane checks must be diligently conducted to fulfill legislative responsibilities, adhere to safe work procedures, and satisfy manufacturer requirements. These checks involve a comprehensive inspection of the crane and its components to identify any signs of damage, defects, or abnormalities that may have arisen during operation. Any issues discovered must be addressed promptly to ensure the crane's continued safe and effective performance.

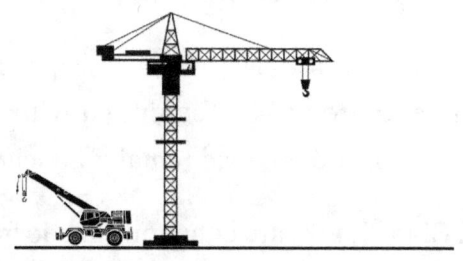

Chapter Ten
Crane Hooks and Lifting Gear

Crane hooks and lifting gear are essential components of crane operations, playing a crucial role in safely lifting, moving, and positioning heavy loads. These include:

Crane Hooks:

1. Function: Crane hooks are devices attached to the end of the crane's lifting mechanism (such as the hoist or wire rope) to engage with and lift loads securely.

2. Design: Hooks typically have a curved shape to prevent slippage of the load and are usually equipped with a latch or safety mechanism to ensure the load remains attached during lifting.

3. Materials: Crane hooks are commonly made from high-strength alloy steel to withstand heavy loads and resist wear and fatigue.

4. Types:

    - Single Hooks: Basic hook design with a single lifting point.

    - Double Hooks: Consist of two hooks connected by a shackle, providing increased stability and load-bearing capacity.

- Swivel Hooks: Allow for rotation of the load, enabling easier positioning during lifting.

- Specialty Hooks: Designed for specific applications, such as grab hooks for lifting objects with handles or coil hooks for handling cylindrical loads.

5. Load Capacity: Hooks are rated for specific load capacities, and it's essential to ensure that the load being lifted does not exceed the hook's rated capacity to prevent overloading and potential failure.

6. Inspection and Maintenance: Regular inspection and maintenance of crane hooks are critical to identify signs of wear, deformation, or damage that could compromise their integrity. Hooks should be inspected visually and, if necessary, subjected to non-destructive testing methods like magnetic particle or dye penetrant inspection.

Figure 110: Crane hook. Alexander P Kapp / CC BY-SA 2.0, via Wikimedia Commons.

Lifting Gear:

1. Definition: Lifting gear refers to the equipment used in conjunction with crane hooks to secure and lift loads safely. It includes various components such as slings, shackles, lifting beams, and spreader bars.

2. Types:

    ◦ Slings: Flexible straps or cables used to wrap around or attach to the load for lifting. Common types include wire rope slings, chain slings, and synthetic webbing slings.

    ◦ Shackles: U-shaped metal connectors with a pin or bolt for attaching slings or other lifting accessories to the crane hook or load.

- Lifting Beams: Structural beams designed to distribute the load weight evenly and provide multiple lifting points for attaching slings or hooks.

- Spreader Bars: Horizontal bars with multiple attachment points used to stabilize and evenly distribute the load when lifting wide or irregularly shaped objects.

3. Material: Lifting gear components are typically made from high-strength alloy steel, aluminium, or synthetic materials, depending on the specific application and load requirements.

4. Load Ratings: Like crane hooks, lifting gear is rated for specific load capacities, and it's crucial to select the appropriate gear based on the weight, size, and shape of the load being lifted.

5. Inspection and Maintenance: Regular inspection, maintenance, and certification of lifting gear are essential to ensure their safety and performance. Inspections should encompass visual checks for signs of wear, deformation, or damage, as well as load testing and certification by qualified personnel.

Crane hooks and lifting gear are integral components of crane operations, providing the necessary means to lift and move heavy loads safely and efficiently. Proper selection, inspection, and maintenance of these components are essential to ensure the safety of crane operations and personnel involved.

Crane Hooks

Crane hooks come in various types, each tailored to specific lifting tasks and scenarios. Here are some commonly utilized crane hook variants frequently encountered in heavy-lifting projects, also shown as Figure 111:

1. Ramshorn Hook: Recognizable by its double-horned configuration, the ramshorn hook offers enhanced load capacity and stability. Typically found in robust applications like shipbuilding and steel fabrication, it excels in heavy-duty lifting tasks. An example is shown as Figure 112

2. Single Hook: Featuring a solitary lifting point, the single hook is versatile and ideal for lighter applications with limited headroom. Widely employed across diverse industries such as construction, manufacturing, and maintenance, it offers flexibility and reliability.

3. Double Hook: Equipped with two lifting points, the double hook ensures superior load distribution and stability. Often used in conjunction with another double hook for hoisting long or oversized items like beams or girders, it enhances lifting efficiency.

4. Eye Hook: Characterized by a single-point design and an eye-shaped opening for attachment to lifting machinery, the eye hook is typically utilized in light-duty lifting tasks, providing simplicity and ease of use.

5. Clevis Hook: Similar to single hooks but featuring a clevis pin instead of a latch, the clevis hook is favoured in industrial and manufacturing settings for its ability to handle high-capacity loads efficiently.

6. Sorting Hook: Tailored for hanging, organizing, and storing items systematically, sorting hooks find common application in

warehouses and production facilities, facilitating efficient and safe sorting operations.

7. **Swivel Hook:** Offering 360-degree rotation, swivel hooks provide enhanced flexibility and manoeuvrability during lifting operations. Often paired with other hooks to bolster stability and prevent unintended slippage, they are valued for their versatility.

8. **Choker Hook:** Designed for secure gripping and lifting of objects, choker hooks are compatible with various lifting scenarios, from small-scale projects to large-scale industrial endeavours. They are typically used alongside other hooks for added support.

9. **J Hook:** Specifically engineered for lifting flat or round objects, J hooks feature a distinctive "J"-shaped design that facilitates easy insertion beneath the load. Widely utilized in construction and maintenance tasks, they offer reliable lifting solutions for various applications.

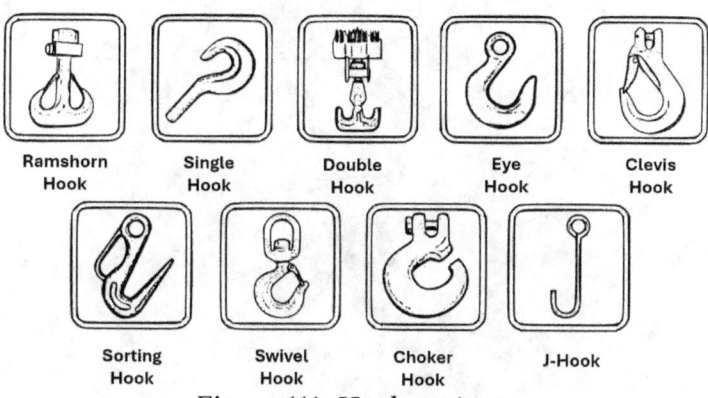

Figure 111: Hook variants.

Understanding the dimensions and load capacities of crane hooks and associated rigging equipment is essential for selecting the appropriate gear to meet your specific lifting needs.

For instance, a 5-ton crane hook is engineered to safely hoist and transport loads weighing up to 5 tons. The dimensions of such a hook can vary based on the manufacturer and design specifications. Prior to engaging in any lifting task, it is imperative to confirm both the dimensions and load capacity of the hook to ensure its suitability for the intended operation (Maxim Crane Works, 2023).

The selection of the right hook size for your project hinges on various factors, including the weight and complexity of the load, the working environment, the type of crane utilized, and any unique project requirements that may apply. Taking these considerations into account will aid in identifying the optimal hook size to achieve safe and efficient lifting operations.

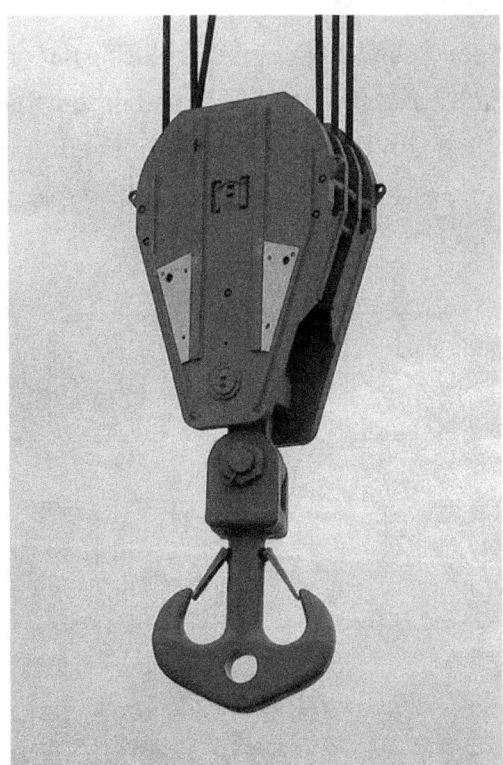

Figure 112: Ramshorn hook fitted to a 700t crane. Henryvb, CC BY-SA 3.0, via Wikimedia Commons.

Numerous terms are pertinent to the realm of lifting, each carrying significance in ensuring the safe selection of lifting equipment. These include (Certex, 2024):

WLL: stands for Working Load Limit, a prevalent abbreviation in lifting parlance. It denotes the maximum load specified by the manufacturer that a non-fixed lifting attachment is engineered to lift under stipulated conditions.

SWL: is an abbreviation for Safe Working Load, formerly extensively used. However, owing to legal implications surrounding the term "safe," SWL has largely been supplanted by WLL. Presently, SWL typically aligns with WLL for all lifting equipment beneath the crane hook. The term "Capacity" is used for cranes, hoists, and winches, where the load-bearing capability is typically influenced by the weight of the lifting apparatus assembled under the crane hook. The term "safe workload" may still be utilized to denote a reduced load contingent upon specific environmental circumstances. A competent individual must conduct a risk assessment before each lift to ascertain potential impacts on load capacity.

Minimum Breaking Strength (MBL/MBF): signifies the load or force that must be reached before there is a risk of the lifting equipment breaking or experiencing a change that could cause the load to disengage. It is measured in kilogram/ton for load and kilonewtons (kN) for force.

Safety Factor (SF): represents the ratio between WLL and MBL, delineating how much stronger the equipment is compared to its intended lifting capacity. The safety factor, specified in the standard for each lifting range, typically ranges between 4:1 and 7:1. The maximum load can be computed as WLL = MBL/SF.

Proof Load: denotes the load to which the manufacturer subjects the product during a proof load test. The minimum testing requirement is outlined in the prevailing standard.

It is imperative to note that when amalgamating multiple lifting components in lifting equipment, the component with the lowest maximum load dictates the WLL of the entire lifting apparatus.

For lifting tools, WLL specifications pertain to straight lifting in a singular part. In scenarios involving multiple parts or alternative lifting configurations, the maximum load is calculated based on the specified factor.

The Working Load Limit (WLL) of a hook is determined by the manufacturer based on various factors, including the design, materials used, construction methods, and intended application. These include:

1. Design and Engineering: The manufacturer designs the hook to meet certain specifications and standards, taking into account factors such as the intended load capacity, environmental conditions, and safety requirements.

2. Material Selection: High-quality materials with suitable strength and durability characteristics are chosen for constructing the hook. The material selection is crucial to ensure that the hook can withstand the intended loads without deformation or failure.

3. Testing and Certification: The hook undergoes rigorous testing procedures to verify its load-bearing capacity and performance under various conditions. These tests may include static and dynamic load testing, fatigue testing, and other evaluations to ensure compliance with industry standards and regulations.

4. Calculations and Analysis: Engineering calculations and analysis are performed to determine the maximum load that the hook can safely lift under different operating conditions. Factors such

as the material properties, geometry of the hook, stress distribution, and safety margins are considered in these calculations.

5. Certification and Rating: Once the hook has passed all testing and analysis requirements, it is certified by the manufacturer and assigned a specific Working Load Limit (WLL). This rating indicates the maximum load that the hook is designed to lift safely under normal operating conditions.

6. Documentation and Marking: The WLL of the hook is clearly marked on the hook itself or provided in accompanying documentation. This allows users to easily identify the maximum load capacity of the hook and ensure that it is used within its rated limits.

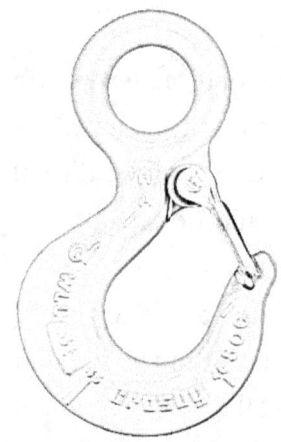

Figure 113: Exaple of a hook WLL stamped on the hook.

Hook Blocks

Crane hook blocks play a vital role in lifting operations, facilitating the even distribution of loads and enhancing overall safety and efficiency within crane systems. They are available in various types, tailored to the specific requirements of individual lifting projects. The most common hook block varieties include single-sheave, double-sheave, and multi-sheave configurations (Maxim Crane Works, 2023), shown as Figure 114.

- Single-sheave blocks are typically employed for lighter loads and feature a single pulley to support the lifting line.

- Double-sheave blocks incorporate two pulleys, enabling higher load capacities and more uniform force distribution.

- Multi-sheave blocks are equipped with three or more pulleys, offering increased load capacities and enhanced stability during lifting manoeuvres.

When using a crane, the load capacity of the block is matched to the crane's maximum load and hook capacity.

The number of sheaves, or pulleys, directly impacts the lifting capacity and stability, with additional sheaves providing superior load distribution.

The selection of the wire rope size for the lifting operation is also crucial, as it must align with the sheave diameter of the hook block (Maxim Crane Works, 2023).

Hooks and hook blocks utilized in demanding settings, such as marine or corrosive environments, may necessitate specialized materials and coatings to ensure longevity and mitigate premature wear.

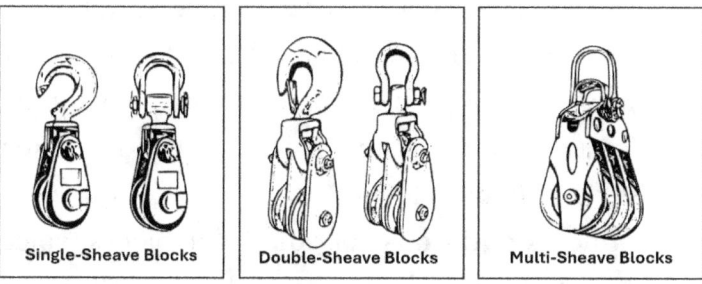

Figure 114: Common crane hook block types.

Ensuring the safety and optimal performance of crane hooks requires regular inspection and maintenance procedures. It is imperative to adhere to the manufacturer's guidelines and industry standards regarding inspection schedules and maintenance protocols. The correct usage and handling of crane hooks are pivotal in preserving their integrity and extending their lifespan.

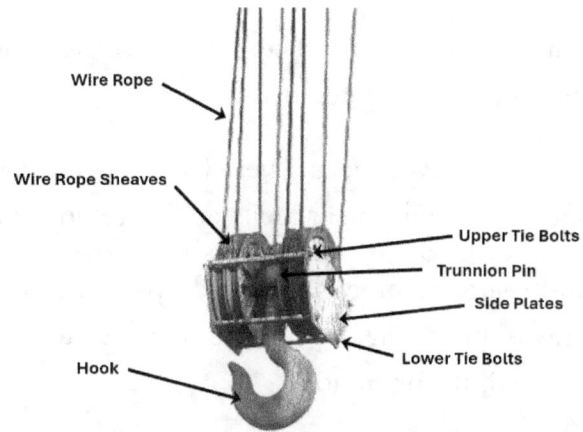

Figure 115: Hook block components.

Replacing damaged or worn hooks is a crucial aspect of crane hook safety and maintenance. If any signs of wear or damage, such as cracks, deformations, corrosion, or excessive wear in the latch or throat opening, are observed, the hook should be deemed unfit for use and replaced promptly.

Hook blocks are essential components in lifting operations, designed to facilitate the safe and efficient lifting of heavy loads. They are commonly used in conjunction with cranes, hoists, and other lifting equipment to provide a means of attaching and hoisting loads securely. Here's a detailed overview of hook blocks:

1. **Components and Construction:** Hook blocks typically consist of several key components, including a sheave or pulley wheel, a hook, a frame or housing, and various fittings for attachment to lifting equipment. The sheave is mounted on bearings within the frame, allowing it to rotate freely and accommodate the lifting line or wire rope.

2. **Types of Hook Blocks:** Hook blocks come in various types and configurations to suit different lifting applications and load capacities. Common types include:

    - Single-sheave blocks: These have a single pulley wheel and are suitable for lighter loads.

    - Double-sheave blocks: These feature two pulley wheels and offer increased load capacity and better load distribution.

    - Multi-sheave blocks: These have three or more pulley wheels, providing even greater load capacities and stability during lifting operations.

3. **Load Capacity:** The load capacity of a hook block is determined by factors such as the number of sheaves, the diameter of the sheaves, and the construction of the block. Manufacturers specify the maximum load that a hook block can safely lift, and this information is typically marked on the block or provided in accompanying documentation.

4. **Usage and Applications:** Hook blocks are used in a wide range

of industries and lifting scenarios, including construction, manufacturing, shipping, and material handling. They are commonly employed for lifting heavy equipment, machinery, materials, and structural components.

5. **Safety Features:** To ensure safe lifting operations, hook blocks are equipped with safety features such as latch mechanisms to prevent accidental release of the load, as well as overload protection devices to alert operators if the load exceeds the block's rated capacity.

6. **Maintenance and Inspection:** Regular inspection and maintenance of hook blocks are essential to ensure their safe and reliable operation. This includes checking for signs of wear, corrosion, and damage, as well as verifying proper lubrication and functionality of safety features.

7. **Training and Certification:** Operators should be properly trained in the safe use of hook blocks and lifting equipment, including understanding load capacities, rigging procedures, and safety protocols. Additionally, hook blocks should be inspected and certified by qualified personnel to ensure compliance with industry standards and regulations.

Figure 116 shows a schematic diagram of a single-sheave hook block. Overall, hook blocks are critical components in lifting operations, providing a versatile and reliable means of hoisting heavy loads safely and efficiently. Proper selection, use, and maintenance of hook blocks are essential for ensuring the safety of personnel and equipment during lifting operations.

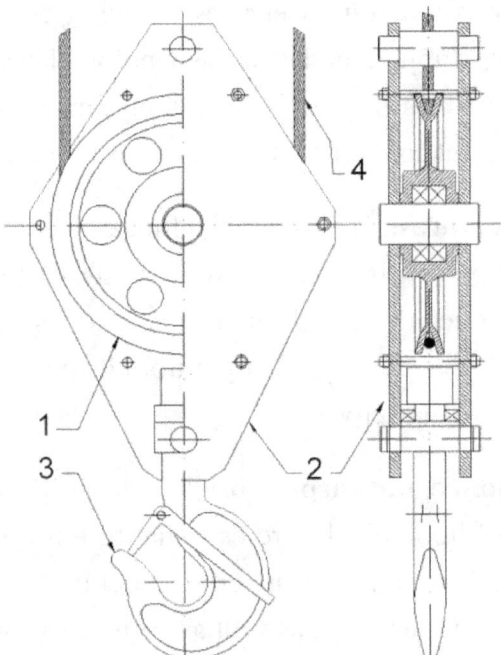

Figure 116: Schematic of a single-sheave hook block. Ssawka, CC BY-SA 3.0, via Wikimedia Commons.

A block comprises a shell (or side plates), a centre pin, and an end fitting, which can vary and include hooks, shackles, and clevices, enabling the attachment of the block to the cargo or a fixed anchorage. Additionally, blocks feature a becket or mouse ear where the end of the rope line is secured. The sheaves of the block transmit the load from the wire rope to the centre pin and then to the shell straps or side plates.

There are three primary types of blocks:

1. Crane Block: Used for long lifts under continuous service conditions, crane blocks feature multiple large diameter sheaves with long service life. Cheek plate weights are added to the block side frames to increase overhaul weight. Typically, crane blocks are equipped with a swivel hook, allowing the cargo to rotate without interfering with the multiple parts of reeving.

2. Snatch Block: Snatch blocks are utilized for intermittent service, jerking or snatching their load over short distances. These blocks are characterized by a side-opening plate that facilitates threading the wire rope through the block.

3. Wire Rope (Construction or Fixed) Blocks: Fixed blocks, also known as construction blocks, are commonly employed as upper blocks in multi-part reeving arrangements in derricks or material hoists. They feature large diameter multiple sheaves similar to crane blocks but lack the additional cheek plate weights required for overhaul.

Slings

The materials used for lifting slings typically include cable, chain, rope, or webbing, and they are employed alongside cranes or other lifting apparatuses.

There are three primary types of lifting slings available: chain slings, wire rope slings, and polyester slings. Continue reading to learn about the distinctions between these types and determine which lifting sling is suitable for your lifting equipment.

Chain slings come in various material grades, sizes, and configurations, and selecting the appropriate one is crucial for the success of your lifting tasks. Renowned for their strength and durability, chain slings are particularly favoured in heavy-duty sectors such as construction, mining, and manufacturing. Typically crafted from alloy steel, these slings can endure harsh conditions common in construction environments and are capable of securing extremely hot loads without sustaining damage.

Among the array of lifting options, lifting chains are widely preferred due to their unparalleled durability. They exhibit resilience in challenging environments and can withstand rigorous usage without faltering. Additionally, chain slings offer versatility, available in configurations ranging from single-leg to quad leg. Notably, they are adjustable and repairable, allowing for damaged chain links to be replaced, thereby enabling the sling to be recertified and redeployed.

However, chain slings do have drawbacks. Their hardness and weight make them prone to causing damage, especially when handling delicate or vulnerable items. The chains can inadvertently scratch finished surfaces, crush non-reinforced objects, or dent surfaces upon impact. Furthermore, chain slings are subject to stringent regulations, primarily governed by OSHA and ASME standards, particularly ASME B30.9, which undergoes periodic review and updating.

In terms of cost, lifting chains can be more expensive, especially for overhead lifting where grade 80 chains or higher are mandated. Although this requirement may entail higher expenses, investing in quality lifting chain slings could prove to be economical in the long run, especially when compared to the ongoing replacement costs associated with less expensive alternatives like wire rope slings.

Synthetic slings, also referred to as polyester slings, are renowned for their versatility, making them an excellent choice for various lifting applications. Their flexibility allows them to conform to irregularly shaped loads, making them particularly suitable for securing fragile or delicate items. Typically constructed from nylon or polyester fibres, synthetic slings are often favoured by doggers/riggers due to their adaptability. However, it's essential to note that synthetic slings may experience accelerated wear in rugged weather conditions compared to other sling types.

Flat webbed slings, alternatively termed synthetic slings, are gaining popularity with advancing technology. These flat lifting slings are crafted from either polyester or nylon, each material serving specific purposes. One significant distinction between nylon and polyester slings lies in their chemical resistance properties. Nylon exhibits alkaline resistance and remains unaffected by oil exposure, while polyester is resistant to bleaching agents and acidic chemicals. The choice between the two depends on the anticipated chemical exposure during lifting operations.

Stretch is another consideration when selecting between polyester and nylon slings. Polyester slings have a stretch rating of up to 3%, whereas nylon slings can stretch between 6% to 10%. This stretch factor must be accounted for, especially when nearing the lifting height limit or operating in low headroom conditions. Both polyester and nylon web slings are commonly available with eyes on each end, facilitating versatile setup options for vertical, basket, and choker lifts.

Although webbed slings have a lower lifting capacity compared to wire rope slings, their ability to conform to the shape of the load and non-abrasive material make them ideal for protecting delicate loads from damage. However, one potential issue with webbed slings is the risk of fraying if the sling's edge comes into contact with abrasive surfaces or corners. In such cases, the sling must be promptly removed from service to ensure safety. Manufacturers have addressed this concern by offering edge guards, which are additional protective materials sewn over the sling's edges. These edge-wrap slings provide added protection without compromising the sling's lifting capabilities.

Round lifting slings, another variety of synthetic sling, offer a comprehensive solution for those seeking enhanced protection beyond just the edges. Like web slings, they are crafted from durable polyester or nylon materials and feature an additional protective jacket enveloping the entire sling for added durability and resilience.

Renowned for their lightweight design and impressive lifting capabilities, round slings are often comparable to web slings in various aspects. Typically available in a continuous (infinite) loop configuration, round slings may also come in eye-to-eye variants. The full-wrap jacket renders them particularly suitable for lifting tasks involving items that require safeguarding against scratches or damage.

To facilitate ease of selection and ensure safety compliance, the jackets of round slings are frequently color-coded according to their lifting ratings. This simplifies the process of choosing the appropriate sling for the job and enables swift identification if an incorrect sling is being utilized.

However, it's essential to note that both web slings and round slings are not recommended for use with loads containing sharp edges. Despite the robustness of their fibers, they have inherent limitations and may not withstand the rigors associated with sharp-edged loads as effectively as metal alternatives.

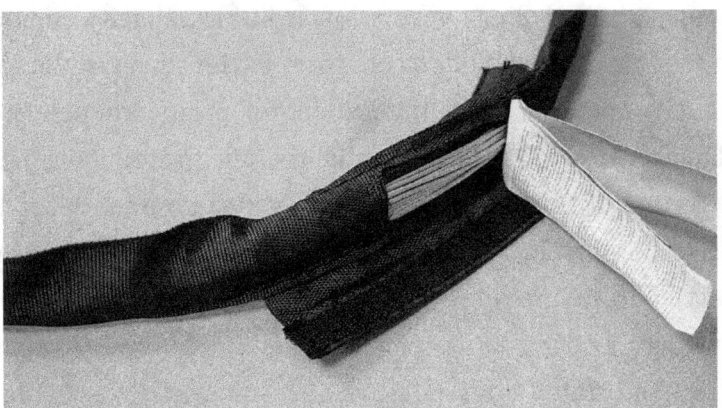

Figure 117: Close-up of round sling steel multifilament. Lhennen, CC BY-SA 4.0, via Wikimedia Commons.

Wire rope slings, offering greater durability than synthetic counterparts and a more economical option compared to chain slings, present a compelling choice for many within the construction sector. Crafted by weaving individual wires or strands around a core, these slings boast exceptional strength and resistance to abrasion or cutting, rendering them suitable for various lifting and hoisting operations. Available in diverse configurations and dimensions such as round braids, flat braids, tri-flex, and cable-laid slings, wire rope slings offer versatility to cater to different lifting needs.

One of the primary reasons wire rope slings are favoured by riggers is their wide range of materials, lays, diameters, and configurations, ensuring easy access to the ideal sling for any given task. However, it's crucial to note that wire rope slings may be prone to kinks and twists, underscoring the importance of thorough inspection prior to use.

The construction of wire rope slings involves winding wires into strands and strands into rope, with the thickness of the rope determined by the number of wires and strands, consequently influencing both flexibility and lifting capacity. Typically composed of steel in accordance with ASTM guidelines, wire rope slings feature eyes on both ends, often fashioned into flemish eyes, where strands are split and rewound into a loop, secured in place by swedging a metal cap.

While wire rope slings offer the advantage of being lighter and more cost-effective than chain slings, they possess a lower lifting limit. This makes them suitable for workers handling loads that do not require the robustness of chain slings, providing ease of use in various lifting scenarios. The inherent stiffness of wire rope facilitates easy rigging for lifting tasks, enabling straightforward manoeuvring even in spaces with low clearance, a task that would prove challenging with chain slings.

Furthermore, wire rope slings come with options for different-sized eyes, rope lengths, and various hardware configurations at each end, akin to chain slings, including multi-leg options. However, users should be aware of potential pitfalls, such as susceptibility to damage when lifting certain loads that may not pose issues for other types of slings. Instances of kinking, pinching, or wire breakage due to wear or extreme tension mandate the immediate removal of the sling from service. Additionally, similar to chain slings, wire rope slings have the potential to cause damage to fragile or delicate items and may scratch unprotected surfaces.

Crane Wire Rope

Wire rope is a crucial component in crane operations, serving as the primary means of lifting heavy loads. It is made up of individual steel wires twisted or braided together to form a flexible yet strong rope.

At the heart of crane operations, steel wire ropes serve as lifelines, tasked with bearing the weight of lifted loads and facilitating their movement. Comprising multiple strands of steel wires twisted in a helical arrangement, these ropes exhibit crucial attributes such as strength, flexibility, and durability, pivotal for crane functionality. Despite their robustness, steel wire ropes are subject to deterioration over time, driven by various factors that pose risks of failure and safety hazards.

Multiple factors render steel wire ropes on cranes vulnerable to failure. Cycles of loading and unloading induce fatigue, leading to the formation of cracks that may culminate in rope failure. Exposure to moisture, chemicals, or harsh environmental conditions initiates corrosion, compromising the structural integrity of the rope. Moreover, contact with surfaces or loads causes abrasion, gradually eroding the outer layers and diminishing the rope's strength.

A critical concern revolves around surpassing the safe working load (SWL) of the wire rope, as it can precipitate immediate or accelerated failure. The bending and flexing of the rope around sheaves and drums during crane operation contribute to localized wear and fatigue. Mishandling of the wire rope, resulting in kinks, twists, or birdcages, undermines its structural integrity and poses risks. Furthermore, internal defects such as broken wires, albeit challenging to detect visibly, can gradually erode the rope's strength and reliability over time.

Wire rope characteristics include:

1. **Construction**:

    - Wire rope is typically constructed from high-strength steel wires twisted or braided together in various configurations.

    - The wires are wound around a central core, which can be fibre core (FC) or steel core (IWRC - Independent Wire Rope Core).

    - Fibre core provides flexibility and cushioning, while steel core offers greater strength and durability.

2. **Types**:

    - There are different types of wire rope based on the number of strands and the arrangement of wires within those strands. Common types include:

        - 6x19: Comprising 6 strands with 19 wires per strand, providing flexibility and resistance to abrasion.

        - 6x37: With 6 strands containing 37 wires per strand, offering higher breaking strength and flexibility.

        - 7x19: Made up of 7 strands with 19 wires per strand, suitable for applications requiring flexibility and durability.

        - Other configurations like 6x36, 8x19, and 8x36 are also available, each offering specific characteristics suited to different lifting tasks.

3. **Features**:

    - High Strength: Wire rope is designed to withstand heavy loads and harsh operating conditions.

- Flexibility: Despite its strength, wire rope remains flexible, allowing it to bend and conform to the shape of the load.

- Abrasion Resistance: The outer wires protect the inner wires, providing resistance to abrasion and wear.

- Corrosion Resistance: Galvanized or stainless steel wire rope options are available for enhanced corrosion resistance, crucial in outdoor or marine environments.

- Fatigue Resistance: Properly maintained wire rope can withstand repeated bending and flexing without failure.

4. **Components**:

    - Core: Provides stability and support to the wire rope, helping maintain its shape and structural integrity.

    - Strands: Individual groups of wires twisted together to form the rope.

    - Wires: The basic building blocks of the wire rope, typically made of high-strength steel.

    - Lubrication: Proper lubrication helps reduce friction, prevents corrosion, and extends the lifespan of the wire rope.

5. **Maintenance**:

    - Regular inspection and maintenance are essential to ensure the safety and reliability of wire rope.

    - Inspections should include checking for signs of wear, corrosion, broken wires, and distortion.

    - Proper lubrication should be applied to reduce friction and protect against corrosion.

- Wire rope should be replaced if it shows significant signs of wear or damage to maintain safe lifting operations.

Wire rope is crafted through the intertwining of numerous strands. Each individual strand is meticulously formed by weaving together numerous cold-worked seamless wires composed of high-grade carbon steel.

- Core: An overarching term encompassing fibre cores, strand cores, and rope cores, serving as the central element of a rope or strand.

- Strand: Constituting a fundamental building block of a wire rope, a strand comprises multiple wires intricately twisted together.

- Wire: The elemental steel wires composing a strand, categorized into naked wires and plated wires.

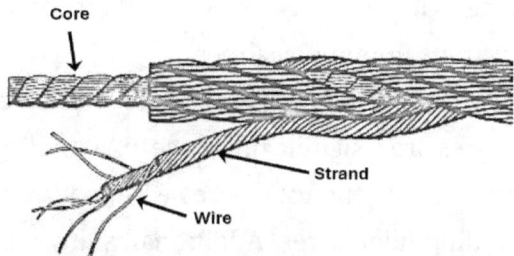

Figure 118: Wire Rope Structure.

The central fibre or rope core within the wire rope serves several vital functions: it preserves the rope's shape, imparts flexibility, and absorbs shocks and vibrations to safeguard the strands from potential breakage. This core mechanism is crucial for ensuring the rope's integrity.

In the realm of mobile cranes, wire ropes composed of six intertwined strands are frequently employed. The composition of a wire rope is typically denoted by a structural code, expressed as (the number of strands) x (the number of wires within each strand), such as 6 x 37. Generally, among wire ropes of comparable diameter, those containing a higher count of thinner wires tend to exhibit superior flexibility.

The wire rope diameter is determined by measuring the diameter of a circle that encloses its cross-section. This measurement involves using slide callipers to measure the wire rope's diameter in three directions at a specific cross-section, followed by averaging the obtained results. The tolerance level against the nominal diameter, as determined during production (according to JIS standards), should fall within 0% to +7%. It's worth noting that for wire ropes with diameters below 10 mm, this tolerance extends from 0% to +10%.

Wire rope inspection involves assessing various key points to ensure the integrity and safety of the wire rope. These inspection points include checking for the presence of broken wires, identifying any reduction in diameter and signs of wear, examining for kinks and deformations, observing evidence of corrosion, and inspecting terminations and other connections for abnormalities.

In terms of criteria for discarding wire ropes, certain conditions must be met. Broken wires are a significant concern, with disposal necessary if more than 10 percent of the total wires within a lay of the wire rope are broken, excluding filler wires. Additionally, any wires exhibiting a reduction in diameter exceeding seven percent of the nominal diameter should be discarded. Wires showing deformations, such as kinks, should not be repaired and reused. Furthermore, severe deformations and corrosion in wires warrant immediate disposal.

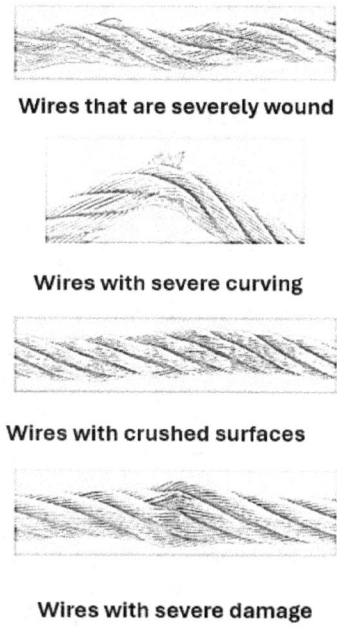

Figure 119: Wire rope deformation.

These criteria for wire rope disposal adhere to legal regulations governing safety standards. It is recommended to replace wire ropes with broken wires or significant diameter reduction promptly to mitigate safety risks. Moreover, wire ropes should be replaced if they manifest a combination of two or more issues, such as deformations, signs of wear, or broken wires. Even if individual damages do not meet the removal criteria, the cumulative effect of these factors necessitates replacement to ensure safe crane operation.

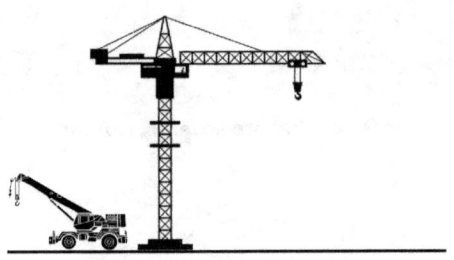

Chapter Eleven

Load Calculations

A crane operator needs to be proficient in various calculations to ensure safe and efficient crane operation. Some of the key calculations include:

1. Load Weight Calculation: Crane operators must accurately calculate the weight of the load being lifted. This involves considering the weight of the load itself along with any additional factors such as attachments, rigging equipment, and environmental conditions.

2. Load Radius Calculation: Determining the load radius involves measuring the distance from the centre of the crane's rotation to the centre of gravity of the load. This calculation is crucial for determining the load moment and ensuring that the crane's capacity is not exceeded.

3. Crane Capacity Calculation: Crane operators need to calculate the crane's capacity based on factors such as the crane's configuration, boom length, angle, and load radius. This ensures that the crane is not overloaded and operates within its safe working limits.

4. Boom Angle Calculation: The angle of the crane's boom affects

its lifting capacity. Crane operators must calculate the boom angle accurately to ensure safe lifting operations.

5. Wind Load Calculation: Wind can exert significant force on a crane and the load being lifted, affecting stability and safety. Crane operators need to calculate wind loads and consider them when planning and executing lifts, especially in outdoor settings.

6. Ground Bearing Pressure Calculation: When operating on soft or uneven ground, crane operators must calculate the ground bearing pressure to ensure that the crane's outriggers or tracks distribute weight evenly and prevent sinking or instability.

7. Rigging Tension Calculation: Calculating the tension in rigging lines is essential for ensuring that the load is lifted safely and securely. Crane operators need to consider factors such as the weight of the load, the angle of the rigging lines, and the type of rigging equipment being used.

8. Center of Gravity Calculation: Determining the centre of gravity of the load is crucial for maintaining stability during lifting operations. Crane operators must calculate the centre of gravity accurately to ensure that the load is balanced and does not tip or swing unexpectedly.

These calculations require a solid understanding of physics, mathematics, and crane operation principles. Crane operators must undergo thorough training and certification to perform these calculations accurately and safely. Additionally, they should continually update their skills and knowledge to stay abreast of advancements in crane technology and safety standards. Many of these calculations were covered within previous chapters and some others will be addressed here.

Load Weight Calculations

Before initiating a lift, one of the primary tasks is to ascertain the total weight of the load. This crucial step should be undertaken during the initial planning phases of the lift, as the weight of the load dictates various aspects of the overhead lift, encompassing:

- Selection of equipment or the type of crane required for the lift
- Determination of the appropriate lifting slings, rigging hardware, and below-the-hook devices necessary for the operation
- Assessment of the suitable sling hitch and sling angle for the lift

The total weight of the load must encompass the entirety of lifting gear engaged in the operation, including the hook and all components below it, such as the hook block, ropes, lifting beams, shackles, hoist rings, and other hardware, along with the lifting slings.

Several methodologies can be employed to ascertain the weight of the load and various methods exist to determine the weight of a load without resorting to complex calculations.

1. Inspection of Load Markings: Check the load for any markings indicating its weight, which may have been provided by the manufacturer or calculated beforehand. Visual cues on the load can aid in selecting appropriate lifting and rigging equipment.

2. Load Familiarity: If the load is a familiar one that is regularly handled in your facility, such as a steel coil or a bundle of pipes or lumber, its weight may already be known. Often, overhead cranes are designed with specific capacities for routine lifting tasks, taking into account the known weight of the load.

3. Engineering Prints or Design Plans: Consult product prints or engineered drawings related to the load, as they may specify the

final assembled weight.

4. Review Shipping Documentation: Examine the bill of lading or shipping documents associated with the load, as they typically include weight information from the shipment.

5. Utilize Industrial Scales: For smaller or lighter loads, industrial floor scales commonly available in production areas or shipping and receiving departments can be used to measure weight accurately.

6. Manufacturer's Specifications or Catalogue Data: If the load is a product or machinery component, weight information may be provided through various sources such as paperwork from the manufacturer, details on their website, or product specifications in catalogues or brochures.

If load weight information isn't available, you'll need to perform calculations to ascertain the weight of the load for lifting. Below, we outline basic calculations for estimating the weight of different-sized loads comprising various materials.

Step 1: Calculate the Load Volume

- Rectangle/Square: Volume = Length x Width x Height

- Hollow Cylinder: Volume = 3.14 x Length x Wall Thickness x (Diameter − Wall Thickness)

- Complex Shapes: For irregular shapes, envision enclosing the object in a rectangle or break it down into smaller rectangles for volume calculation.

Step 2: Identify the Material Being Lifted

Refer to the table shown as Figure 120 for approximate weight values of common materials (or other suitable chart).

CRANE OPERATIONS

Material	Pounds / Cubic Foot	Material	Pounds / Cubic Foot
Aluminium	165	Iron Casting	450
Asbestos	153	Lead	708
Asphalt	81	Lumber (Fir)	32
Brass	524	Lumber (Oak)	62
Brick	120	Lumber (RR Ties)	50
Bronze	534	Oil, Motor	58
Coal	56	Paper	58
Concrete	150	Portland Cement	94
Crushed Rock	95	River Sand	120
Diesel	52	Rubber	94
Dry Earth (loose)	75	Steel	480
Gasoline	45	Water	63
Glass	162	Zinc	437

Figure 120: Approximate weight values of common materials.

Step 3: Determine the Load Weight

Multiply the pounds per cubic foot of the material by the calculated volume to obtain the load weight.

Example #1: Block of Aluminium

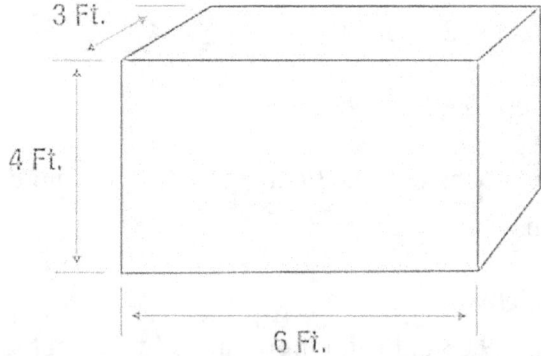

Figure 121: Example load, block of aluminium.

- Volume = 6 ft x 3 ft x 4 ft = 72 cubic ft

- Aluminium weighs 165 lbs/cubic ft

- Block weight = 72 cubic ft x 165 lbs/cubic ft = 11,880 lbs / 5.94 tons

In metric weights:

- Volume = 6 ft x 3 ft x 4 ft = 72 cubic ft (approximately 2.04 cubic meters)

- Aluminium weighs 165 lbs/cubic ft (approximately 2,648 kg/cubic meter)

- Block weight = 72 cubic ft x 165 lbs/cubic ft = 11,880 lbs (approximately 5,386 kg) / 5.94 tons (approximately 5.42 metric tons)

Example #2: Steel Pipe

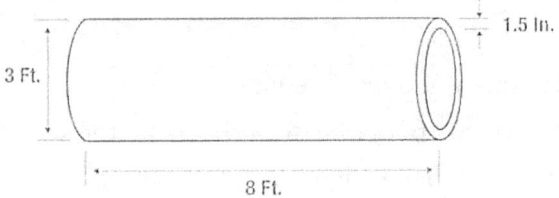

Figure 122: Example load, steel pipe.

- Volume = 9.03 cubic ft

- Steel weighs 480 lbs/cubic ft

- Steel tube weight = 9.03 cubic ft x 480 lbs/cubic ft = 4,334 lbs / 2.17 tons

In metric weights:
- Volume = 9.03 cubic ft (approximately 0.26 cubic meters)

- Steel weighs 480 lbs/cubic ft (approximately 7,706 kg/cubic meter)

- Steel tube weight = 9.03 cubic ft x 480 lbs/cubic ft = 4,334 lbs (approximately 1,965 kg) / 2.17 tons (approximately 1.98 metric tons)

Example #3: Complex Shapes (Concrete)

CRANE OPERATIONS

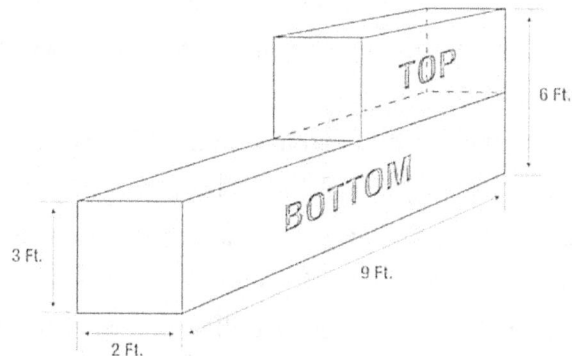

Figure 123: Example load, complex concrete shape.

- Total Volume = 78 cubic ft

- Concrete weighs 150 lbs/cubic ft

- Complex concrete shape = 78 cubic ft x 150 lbs/cubic ft = 11,700 lbs / 5.85 tons

In metric weights:
- Total Volume = 78 cubic ft (approximately 2.21 cubic meters)

- Concrete weighs 150 lbs/cubic ft (approximately 2,401 kg/cubic meter)

- Complex concrete shape = 78 cubic ft x 150 lbs/cubic ft = 11,700 lbs (approximately 5,307 kg) / 5.85 tons (approximately 5.32 metric tons)

By following these calculations, you can accurately estimate the weight of loads before conducting overhead lifting operations.

Areas and Volumes

Area refers to the amount of space enclosed within a two-dimensional object, while volume pertains to the space contained within a three-dimensional object.

Area is typically measured in square units (^{2}) because it involves two dimensions, such as length multiplied by width. On the other hand, volume is measured in cubic units (^{3}) since it encompasses three dimensions, like length multiplied by width multiplied by depth. Cubic units can include cubic centimetres (cm³), cubic meters (m³), and cubic feet. Volume can also denote liquid capacity.

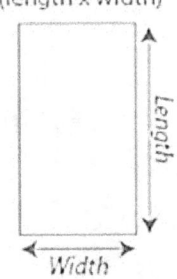

Figure 124: Rectangular Area.

In the metric system, liquid capacity is quantified in litres, which correlates directly with cubic measurements, as 1 millilitre (ml) is equivalent to 1 cubic centimetre (cm³). Specifically, 1 litre equals 1,000 ml or 1,000 cm³. In the imperial or English system, liquid capacity is expressed in fluid ounces, pints, quarts, and gallons, which do not directly convert into cubic feet. Therefore, it is advisable to use either liquid or solid volume units consistently.

For solids based on rectangular shapes, the volume is calculated using the formula length multiplied by width multiplied by height. This formula remains consistent regardless of the terminology used for the dimensions, such as using 'depth' instead of 'height'. The key is to multiply all three dimensions together. For instance, a box measuring 15 cm in width, 25 cm in length, and 5 cm in height would have a volume of 1875 cm³.

Calculated as:

$15 \times 25 \times 5 = 1875 cm^3$

Volume

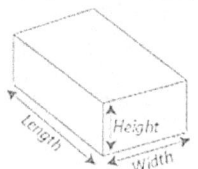

Figure 125: Rectangular volume.

Similarly, for prisms and cylinders, the volume formula is the area of the end shape multiplied by the height or depth of the shape. The area of the end shape could be a circle for cylinders or any polygon for prisms. For instance, to find the volume of a straight length of circular pipe with an internal diameter of 2 cm and a length of 1.7 m, you calculate the area of the circle (πr^2) and then multiply it by the length, ensuring consistent units.

The volume of cones and pyramids follows the same principle but involves multiplying the area of the base or end shape by the height and then taking one-third of that result due to their pointed structure.

Finally, the volume of a sphere is calculated using the formula 4/3 multiplied by π multiplied by the radius cubed (r^3). The radius can be determined by measuring the circumference of the widest point of the sphere and dividing it by 2π.

To determine the weight of an unidentified load, you need to multiply the load's volume by the material's unit weight.

For instance: Consider a rectangular stack of hardwood measuring 3 meters in length, 1 meter in height, and 0.5 meters in width.

Volume of the rectangular solid: = length x width x height 3 m x 1 m x 0.5 m = 1.5 cubic meters

The unit weight of hardwood is 1120 kg per cubic meter. 1.5 x 1120 = 1680

Hence, the total weight of the load is 1680 kg.

Centre of Gravity

Gravity affects all objects uniformly. When objects are divided into multiple parts, gravity exerts force on each individual part. The resultant force of these gravitational forces can be simplified by considering all the individual forces concentrated at a single point. This point, where the resultant force acts, is termed the "centre of gravity." The centre of gravity of an object remains constant regardless of changes in the object's position or orientation. It's important to note that the centre of gravity may not always reside within the physical boundaries of the object itself.

When a crane lifts a load, the load has the freedom to tilt and shift. In simple lifts without specialized equipment, the load typically tilts until its centre of gravity (CoG) aligns directly under the crane hook.

For instance, if the load, such as a box as shown in Figure 126, is heavier on one side, it will have an offset centre of gravity, even if the lifting point is centrally located on the box. As the box is hoisted, it will tilt until its centre of gravity aligns beneath the crane hook. Understanding the centre of gravity of a load, either through prior knowledge or calculation, allows for the prediction of the precise angle of tilt during the lift. This prediction is crucial for lift planning and assessing the stability of the lift. Additionally, it plays a vital role in the design of lifting aids like counterweighted lifting beams.

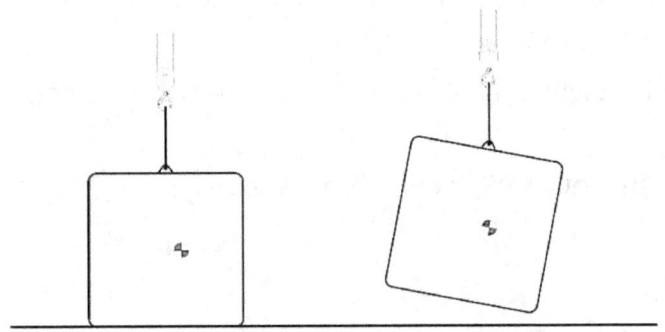

Figure 126: Load with a centre of gravity offset to one side.

When a crane lifts a load, the load is capable of tilting and shifting. In simpler lifting scenarios without specialized equipment, the load typically tilts until its centre of gravity (CoG) aligns directly under the crane hook. For instance, if a box being lifted has an uneven distribution of weight, resulting in an offset CoG, yet the lifting point is centrally located on the box, upon elevation, the box will tilt until its CoG aligns beneath the crane hook.

Understanding the CoG of a load is crucial for predicting the precise tilt angle before lifting. This information is vital for lift planning and assessing lift stability. Additionally, it plays a significant role in the design of lifting aids like counterweighted lifting beams.

In general, loads rigged to lift from above, with lift points positioned higher than the CoG, tend to be stable. This stability arises from the CoG being below the lift points. When external forces such as wind or crane acceleration act on the load, the CoG naturally seeks to return the load to equilibrium, akin to hanging a broom by its handle. This setup ensures stability, as illustrated in Figure 1 below.

Conversely, caution is warranted when lift points are situated below the CoG, as this configuration poses a risk of load instability.

Let's consider a straightforward method for determining the Center of Gravity (CoG), which can be applied to any object requiring its CoG to be identified (Hatton, 2024). Consider Figure 127, depicting a two-dimensional object, such as a steel plate with a random shape, where the CoG needs to be pinpointed. This process, as outlined by Hatton (2024) involves a series of steps rather than a single one.

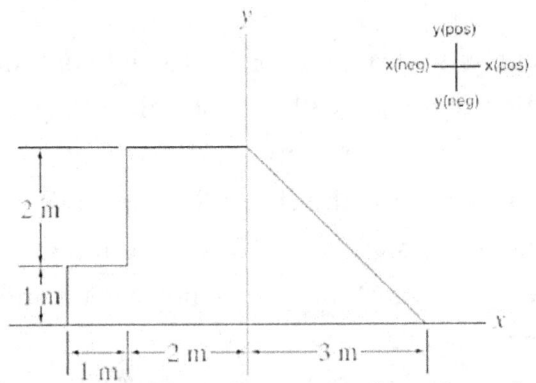

Figure 127: Shape for centre of gravity calculation.

Step 1: First, select the positions for the x-axis and the y-axis. These axes can be chosen arbitrarily, as the outcome of the calculation remains consistent regardless of their placement. For this illustration, let's position the x-axis at the base of the object and the y-axis vertically from the midpoint between the triangular and rectangular shapes.

Step 2: Next, designate which side of the x-axis is positive and which is negative. This distinction is necessary since a 1-meter distance from the y-axis could fall on either side. Without indicating the positive or negative designation, the calculation outcome would be incorrect by definition.

Step 3: Now, divide the object into smaller "sub-objects" to facilitate the determination of the CoG. Refer to Figure 128 for a visual representation. There is no strict rule for selecting these smaller objects; any configuration will suffice as long as the entire object is covered without omission. In this instance, we've chosen:

1. A triangle (formed by halving a 3 x 3 m square)

2. A square (3 x 3 m), which includes a "void"

3. A rectangle (1 x 2 m), representing the void within the aforementioned square at 2.

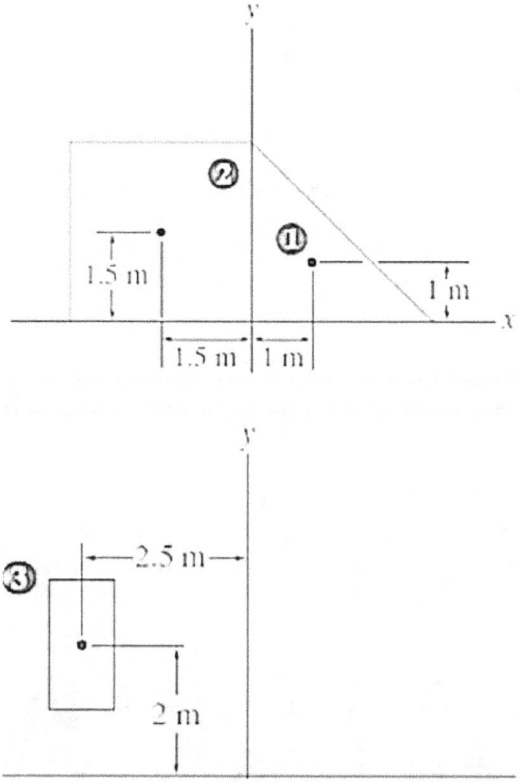

Figure 128: Object sub-sections.

Step 4: Determine the CoG of each sub-object and express it in coordinates. Figure 129 demonstrates this process. For squares and rectangles, the CoG location can be identified by drawing assist lines (depicted in red) from one corner to the opposite corner. Triangular CoG locations can be found by drawing assist lines from one corner to the center of the opposite side. The CoG is situated at the intersection of these lines. The resulting CoG locations are:

CoG 1. (+1.0, +1.0)
CoG 2. (-1.5, +1.5)
CoG 3. (-2.5, +2.0)

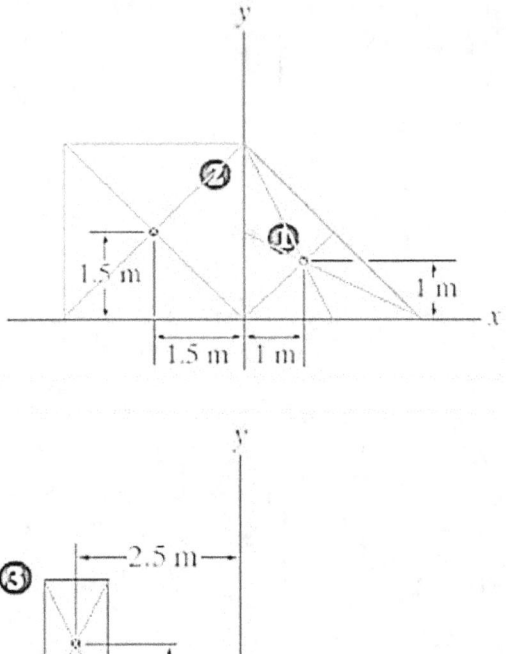

Figure 129: CoG of each sub-object.

Step 5: Arrange all the numbers to prepare for the CoG calculation.

Step 6: The formula for calculating the CoG is:

CoG = (ΣD * W) / ΣW

This formula suggests that the CoG location can be determined by summing (Σ) the product of the distance and the weight (area) and dividing it by the sum of all the weights (areas). Since this is a two-dimensional object, this calculation must be performed in both the x-direction and the y-direction. For a three-dimensional object, the calculation extends to the z-direction as well. In numerical terms:

CoGx = (-0.35) / 11.5

CoGy = (1.13) / 11.5

The CoG is located at coordinates (-0.35, 1.13), as shown in Figure 130.

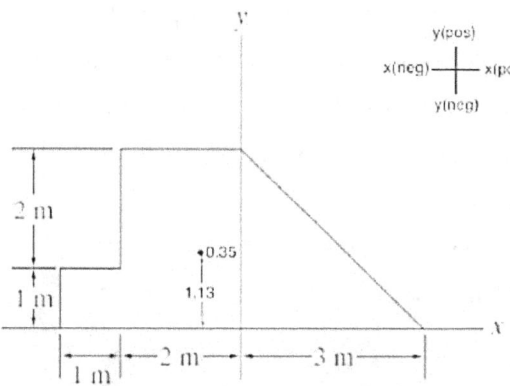

Figure 130: CoG location coordinates.

Sheave Blocks and Force

When hoisting a load using a wire rope, the greater the weight of the load, the greater the force needed. Sheave blocks are employed either to diminish the force needed for lifting the load or to alter the direction of the force.

The fixed sheave remains immobile in its designated position and serves to alter the direction of force. By utilizing it, a simple downward pull on the rope translates into an upward lift of the load. While the force's direction changes, its magnitude remains constant. To raise a load by 1 metre, the rope must be drawn downward by 1 metre.

Meanwhile, the mobile sheave forms a vital part of crane hook assemblies, exhibiting vertical motion corresponding to the rope's movement. Employed to alleviate the force exerted on the rope, the mobile sheave necessitates only half the load weight as the downward force to hoist the load. However, lifting the load by 1 metre entails pulling the rope by 2 metres, effectively doubling the distance traversed. Notably, the pulling force's direction remains upward, aligning with the load's movement, thus maintaining a consistent force direction.

The composite sheave integrates multiple mobile and fixed sheaves to facilitate the lifting or lowering of heavy loads with minimal force. Comprising two mobile and two stationary sheaves, it can raise a load with a force equivalent to only one-fourth of its weight, under the assumption of negligible sheave friction and weightlessness of the hook assembly, including the mobile sheaves. Nonetheless, raising the load by 1 metre necessitates pulling the rope by 4 metres.

Figure 131: Example of a combination sheave.

Crane Tipping Force

The tipping force calculation formula provides an estimate of the force required to cause an object to tip over when subjected to a lever force at a certain angle.

A crane operator can use the the tipping force on a crane for several important reasons:

1. Safety: Understanding the tipping force helps ensure the crane operates within safe limits. Exceeding the tipping force could lead to the crane tipping over, causing damage, injury, or loss of life.

2. Stability: Knowing the tipping force allows the operator to assess the stability of the crane while lifting or moving loads. It helps in determining if the load is too heavy or if the crane's configuration needs adjustment to maintain stability.

3. Load Capacity: By calculating the tipping force, the operator can determine the maximum safe load the crane can handle under specific conditions. This information is crucial for preventing overloading, which could compromise the crane's structural integrity and safety.

4. Operational Planning: Tipping force calculations aid in planning lifts and selecting appropriate rigging configurations. It helps operators anticipate potential challenges and adjust their lifting techniques or equipment accordingly to ensure safe and efficient operations.

5. Compliance: Regulatory standards and industry guidelines often mandate adherence to specific tipping force limits. By knowing the tipping force, operators can ensure compliance with these regulations and standards, avoiding legal issues and penalties.

Calculating the tipping force of a crane involves considering various factors such as the crane's configuration, load weight, boom length, and the ground conditions. Here's a general approach to calculating crane tipping force:

1. Determine Load Weight: Measure or estimate the weight of the load being lifted. This is usually provided by the load specifications.

2. Determine Load Distance: Determine the horizontal distance from the crane's centre of rotation (slewing axis) to the centre of gravity of the load. This distance is crucial for calculating the moment arm.

3. Calculate Load Moment: Multiply the load weight by the load distance to obtain the load moment. This represents the turning effect of the load around the crane's centre of rotation.

Load Moment = Load Weight × Load Distance

1. Determine Counterweight Moment: If the crane is equipped with a counterweight, determine its weight and its distance from the crane's centre of rotation. Multiply these values to obtain the counterweight moment.

Counterweight Moment = Counterweight Weight × Counterweight Distance

1. Calculate Net Moment: Subtract the counterweight moment (if applicable) from the load moment to obtain the net moment acting on the crane.

Net Moment = Load Moment - Counterweight Moment

1. Determine Crane's Stability Margin: Consult the crane's load chart or stability chart to determine the maximum allowable net moment based on the crane's configuration, boom length, and load radius. This value is provided by the manufacturer and ensures safe crane operation.

2. Compare Net Moment to Stability Limit: Compare the calculated net moment to the crane's stability limit. If the net moment

exceeds the stability limit, there is a risk of tipping.

It's crucial to note that crane tipping force calculations should be performed by qualified personnel familiar with crane operation and safety practices. Additionally, factors such as wind speed, ground conditions, and dynamic loading should be considered for accurate tipping force assessment. Always adhere to manufacturer guidelines and safety regulations when operating cranes.

The following equation can be utilized to compute the tipping force of an object:

$$TF = \frac{m \times g \times \cos(x) \times b}{a+b}$$

Figure 132: Tipping force calculation formula.

Where:
- TF denotes the tipping force (measured in Newtons, N).
- m represents the mass of the object (in kilograms, kg).
- x signifies the angle of the lever applied to the object (in degrees, deg).
- b denotes the length of the lever arm below the centre of mass (in meters, m).
- a represents the length of the lever arm above the centre of mass (in meters, m).

As an example of its application:

Let's consider a mobile crane with a mass of 10,000 kg (m), and we want to calculate the tipping force (TF) when it's lifting a load with a lever arm configuration as follows:
- Lever arm below the centre of mass (b): 5 meters

- Lever arm above the centre of mass (a): 3 meters
- Angle of the lever applied to the crane (x): 30 degrees

Given these parameters, we can use the formula provided to calculate the tipping force:

$$TF = m \times g \times \cos(x) \times \frac{b}{a+b}$$

Where:

- $m = 10,000$ kg (mass of the crane)
- $g = 9.81$ m/s² (acceleration due to gravity, assumed to be constant)
- $x = 30$ degrees (angle of the lever)
- $b = 5$ meters (length of lever arm below the center of mass)
- $a = 3$ meters (length of lever arm above the center of mass)

Now, let's plug in these values into the formula:

$$TF = 10,000 \times 9.81 \times \cos(30) \times \frac{5}{3+5}$$

$$TF = 10,000 \times 9.81 \times \frac{\sqrt{3}}{2} \times \frac{5}{8}$$

$$TF = 10,000 \times 9.81 \times \frac{\sqrt{3} \times 5}{16}$$

$$TF \approx 8,517.72 \times \sqrt{3}$$

$$TF \approx 14,750.96 \text{ N}$$

Figure 133: Tipping force calculation example.

So, the tipping force exerted on the mobile crane under these conditions is approximately 14,750.96 Newtons.

Crane Tipping Load

The Crane Tipping Load formula is used to determine the maximum load that a crane can safely lift without tipping over. It helps crane operators and engineers assess the stability of a crane under various lifting conditions by considering factors such as the weight of the crane, the distance from the crane's centre of gravity to the tipping axis point, and the distance from the load's centre of gravity to the tipping axis point. This calculation is crucial for ensuring the safety of crane operations and preventing accidents caused by overloading or instability.

The following formula is utilized to determine the Crane Tipping Load:

$$TL = \frac{W \times D1}{D2}$$

Figure 134: Crane tipping load formula.

Where:
- TL represents the tipping load (measured in weight units such as pounds or kilograms).

- WW denotes the weight of the crane (in units such as pounds or kilograms).

- D1 signifies the distance from the centre of gravity of the crane to the tipping axis point.

- D2 denotes the distance from the centre of gravity of the load to the tipping axis point.

To calculate the crane tipping load, divide the distance from the centre of gravity of the crane to the tipping point by the distance from the centre of gravity of the load to the tipping point, and then multiply the result by the weight of the crane.

Let's consider an example to illustrate the calculation of the Crane Tipping Load (TL):

Given: Weight of the crane (W) = 20,000 kilograms Distance from the centre of gravity of the crane to the tipping axis point (D1) = 3 meters Distance from the centre of gravity of the load to the tipping axis point (D2) = 4 meters

Using the formula: TL = W × D1 / D2

Substituting the given values: TL = 20,000 kg × 3 m / 4 m

Calculating: TL = 15,000 kg

Therefore, the tipping load of the crane is 15,000 kilograms. This means that the crane can safely lift a load up to 15,000 kilograms without risking tipping over, considering the given distances and weight.

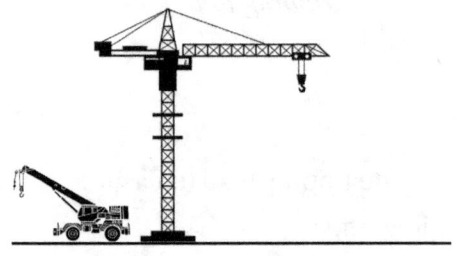

Chapter Twelve

References

Al-Hussein, M., Alkass, S., & Moselhi, O. (2001). An Algorithm for Mobile Crane Selection and Location on Construction Sites. *Construction Innovation*.

Arnott, W. (2020, 23/2/2024). Pick and Carry crane side slope deration.

Azami, R., Lei, Z., Hermann, U., & Zubick, T. (2022). A Predictive Analytics Framework for Mobile Crane Configuration Selection in Heavy Industrial Construction Projects. *Buildings*.

Breitsprecher, S. (2022, 18/2/2024). Spreader Bars vs. Lifting Beams: What's the Difference?

Certex. (2024). *Do you know the difference between WLL, SWL and MBL?*

Chant, C., & Goodman, D. (2005). *Pre-industrial cities and technology*. Routledge.

Economic Research Institute. (2024). *Mobile Crane Operator Salary*.

Fang, Y., Cho, Y., & Chen, J. (2016). A Framework for Real-Time Pro-Active Safety Assistance for Mobile Crane Lifting Operations. *Automation in Construction*.

Forest, D. (2024). *10 steps to safe and efficient tower crane erection*. Manitowoc.

Fullman, B. (2023, 22/2/2024). What Is a Crane Load Chart?

Hatton, L. (2024). *How to Determine the Center of Gravity of Any Load*.

Lagerev, I. A., Lagerev, A. V., & Tarichko, V. I. (2021). Modeling the Swing of Mobile Loader Cranes With Anchor Outriggers When Operating on Weak Soils. *E3s Web of Conferences*.

Maxim Crane Works. (2023, 23/2/2024). Crane Rigging Hooks: Different Types and Applications.

Mazzella Companies. (2024). *What Are the Different Types of Overhead Cranes?*

Mollo, J. (2021, 22/2/2024). How to Read a Crane Load Chart.

Ritchies Offsore Services. (2024). *Crane Calculation Termplate*.

Sacarlet Tech. (2022, 18/2/2024). Tower Cranes Wind Speed Lifting Guide.

Safe Work Australia. (2015). *Guide to Tower Cranes*.

Safe Work Australia. (2020). *Guide to Mobile Cranes*.

Salary Expert. (2024). *Tower Crane Operator*.

Skiba, R. (2020). Best practice standards and methodology for crane operator training—a global perspective.

Talbott, S. (2007). *Devices of the soul: battling for our selves in an age of machines*. " O'Reilly Media, Inc.".

talent.com. (2024). *Crane Operator average salary in United Kingdom, 2024*

Technomax. (2021, 18/2/2024). How Does A Level Luffing Crane Work?

Terex. (2005). *Rated Capacity Manual Model AT-20 - Book Part Number 16c1320-Hydraulic All Terrain Pick & Carry Crane*.

The Crane Industry Council of Australia. (2017). *CICA & CANZ Guidance Note: Crane Stability and Ground Pressure*.

WorkSafe Queensland. (2024). *Personnel and materials hoist - HP*.

Index

A

Accident prevention, 71, 89

Accuracy, 84–85, 127, 382, 441

Adaptability, 65, 333, 436

All-terrain crane, 334–335

Analysis, 109, 248

Assessment, 22–23, 79, 83, 106–107, 111, 120–121, 193, 295, 302–303, 318, 323, 347–349, 439, 481, 497

Audit, 123, 148

Awareness, 114, 120, 325, 369, 434–436

B

Barricades, 379

Best practices, 77, 120–121

Boom, 9, 34, 38–39, 42, 47–51, 53–55, 65, 77, 80–81, 84–85, 95–96, 125, 128–132, 135, 137, 140–146, 148–151, 153–155, 157–158, 163–170, 172–181, 184, 199, 272, 328, 334–335, 337–341, 343–346, 350, 352, 354, 365, 368–371, 381, 383–393, 396, 399–400, 404–405, 413–415, 426, 428, 440–441, 443, 445, 447–450, 479–480, 495–496

Bridge crane, 37, 283–288, 290–294, 297, 300–301, 303–304, 306–307

C

Capacity, 9, 26–27, 30–31, 34, 38, 42, 47–48, 56–59, 61, 66, 71, 73, 75–77, 81, 83–84, 87–88, 90, 95, 101, 105, 111, 116, 118, 120, 124, 127, 138, 140, 143, 145, 152–175, 177–181, 191, 193, 195, 205, 211, 216, 219–220, 223–224, 227–230, 235–236, 238, 248–249, 252, 263–264, 268–271, 273–276, 285–286, 288, 295–296, 298, 303–304, 313, 317, 328–329, 336, 339–340, 344–347, 352–355, 360–361, 365, 368–371, 374, 379, 382–391, 393, 399, 431–432, 439–444, 448–449, 464, 479–481, 486, 495, 502

Certification, 11, 34, 80, 155, 299, 465, 480

Chain, 20, 35, 38, 43, 83, 134, 284, 289, 293, 295, 301, 307, 313, 390, 405, 418, 426, 467

Collaboration, 98

Communication, 10, 13, 17, 19, 57, 77–78, 97, 102, 110–112, 115, 119–120, 122, 133, 142, 148–150, 194, 201–202, 209, 300, 305–306, 316–317, 319, 324–325, 327, 329, 348, 369–370, 380–381, 394, 402–404, 418–419, 425, 435, 437–438, 446

Communication channels, 78, 305, 316, 348, 380

Competency, 24–25

Compliance, 10–11, 24, 100, 104, 109, 111, 114, 118, 123, 126, 138, 146–148, 153, 155, 164, 194, 295, 297, 300, 306, 315–316, 328, 348–349, 369, 382, 400, 436–437, 439, 450, 495

Confined spaces, 44, 58, 62, 64, 66, 337

Construction, 12–16, 20, 22–23, 29, 53–73, 75–79, 85, 96, 99, 102, 104, 106–108, 111–115, 119, 136, 138–139, 142, 144, 147, 199, 287, 310–313, 333–337, 339, 375, 380, 390, 408–414, 430, 434, 464, 501

Controlling, 34, 86, 113, 150, 303

Controls, 26, 38, 51–52, 60, 63, 96, 100–102, 104, 106–107, 123–124, 127–131, 135, 141, 144–145, 149–150, 152, 204, 209, 211–214, 216, 226,

258, 261, 276–278, 289, 291–292, 302–303, 312, 316, 318–319, 322, 329–330, 340–341, 381, 395–399, 403, 405, 410–411, 419, 427

Coordination, 13, 34, 78, 82, 102, 112–113, 115, 139, 148, 213, 246, 255, 279, 324, 380, 402–403, 437

Crawler crane, 41, 48, 336–337, 352

D

Derrick, 9, 40, 53, 184–189, 191–193, 195, 198–203, 207, 209–211, 214–216, 218–222

Derrick crane, 40, 184–189, 191–193, 195, 198–203, 209–211, 214–216, 219–222

Documentation, 11, 105, 138, 148, 295, 297, 306, 327–328, 349, 369, 439

Downtime, 73, 410

E

Effectiveness, 107, 113, 122, 142, 400

Efficiency, 10, 67, 73

Electrical safety, 145, 318

Emergency procedures, 147, 316

Emergency stop, 61, 63, 73, 117, 122, 125, 128, 144, 147, 151–152, 290, 302, 311, 315, 317, 319, 322–323, 330, 340

Engineering, 46, 80, 318, 351, 375–376

Environmental factors, 76, 105, 382

Equipment, 26, 68, 100, 194, 205, 310, 316–327, 330, 334, 340, 342–343, 345, 348, 354–355, 361, 375, 379, 382–383, 390, 394–395, 399–404

Ergonomics, 288

Evacuation procedures, 317

Evaluation, 120, 145

Execution, 63, 103, 147, 172

Experience, 90, 371

Expertise, 91, 103, 111, 148

F

Fall arrest systems, 106

Fall protection, 106–107, 258, 317, 369

Feedback, 146, 398, 433

G

Gantry, 9, 53–54, 186, 226–227, 235, 253–254, 258–260, 295–297, 300, 302–303, 306–308, 332

Gantry crane, 9, 53, 226–227, 235, 253–254, 258–260, 295–297, 300, 302–303, 306–308

Ground conditions, 77, 83, 165, 181, 349–350, 352–353, 363, 385, 417, 437, 442, 445, 495

H

Hand signals, 76, 102, 110, 115, 149, 329, 380

Hazard identification, 193

Health, 22

Hoist, 9, 33–38, 50–52, 54, 88, 110, 130, 135, 139, 144, 150, 157–160, 170, 212, 289–293, 298, 301, 310–330, 389, 403, 405, 410, 418, 481, 493, 502

Hoisting, 36, 42, 44, 66, 84, 118, 126, 128, 135, 149, 152, 155, 158, 283–284, 288–289, 292, 301, 304, 316–317, 323, 329, 343, 394–395, 401–402, 493

Hook, 43, 57, 59–60, 65, 69, 81, 83, 124–125, 128, 130–132, 148, 167–170, 172–174, 229, 284, 287, 289, 292, 295, 301, 303–304, 307, 319, 321, 342, 356, 365–368, 381, 389–390, 393, 395, 399–400, 405, 416, 422, 440–441, 444, 447, 449–450, 452–458, 460–466, 481, 488–489, 493–494, 502

I
Innovation, 67, 501
Inspection, 13, 27, 34, 73–74, 80, 86, 95, 98–100, 104–105, 107, 109–113, 118, 122–124, 126, 129, 140–143, 145–146, 148, 152, 192, 194, 197, 203, 205–206, 217, 245–246, 248, 251, 255–258, 264–268, 279, 290, 295, 299–303, 307, 316–322, 324–326, 329, 347–350, 368, 370, 405–406, 431, 436–437, 439, 446, 451, 465

J
Jib crane, 53, 288

K
Knowledge, 91, 103, 111, 392, 480, 488

L
Licensing, 10–11, 21
Lifting, 452
Load, 9, 11, 13, 16–20, 25–26, 29–31, 33–36, 38–55, 57–62, 65–66, 69, 76, 83–85, 87–90, 95–97, 101, 105, 111–112, 116, 118, 120, 122, 124, 127–135, 137–138, 141–146, 148–175, 177–183, 185–186, 188–193, 195–197, 199–201, 203, 205, 210–225, 228–230, 232, 236, 242–244, 246–250, 252–255, 257, 261–266, 268–273, 275–279, 284, 286–299, 302–307, 313, 316–317, 327–329, 333–334, 337–342, 344–347, 349–361, 365–379, 382–396, 398–404, 409, 411, 416–418, 420–425, 429–432, 436–450, 452–462, 464–467, 469–473, 479–485, 487–489, 493–502
Load charts, 11, 26, 88, 124, 152–153, 155, 167, 170, 178, 180–181, 219, 269, 302, 328, 346, 368, 370, 384–387, 438, 442
Loader crane, 413, 502
Lockout/tagout, 330
Lubrication, 73, 105, 124, 448

M

Machinery, 12, 16–17, 36, 50, 73, 78, 143, 310, 317, 333, 354, 390, 482

Maintenance, 13, 39, 56, 73, 86, 93, 95, 97, 99–100, 104–105, 107, 109, 117–118, 121–123, 125–126, 135–136, 146–147, 229, 299–302, 310, 315–320, 322, 325–327, 330–331, 334, 339, 348, 370, 406, 419, 437, 446, 465

manoeuvrability, 62, 66, 75, 384

Manufacturer specifications, 80, 111, 124, 144–145, 147, 153, 297, 300, 302–303, 307–308, 347, 405

Materials, 9, 13, 27, 30, 33, 35, 39, 43, 46, 53–56, 60, 66, 72, 91, 95, 101, 106, 108, 110–112, 143, 159, 310–313, 315, 317–318, 324, 327–328, 330, 334, 342, 351–352, 354, 369, 390, 406, 408–409, 411, 427, 434, 482–483, 502

Mechanics, 376

Mobile, 9, 29–31, 33–35, 38–39, 41–42, 46, 48–50, 53, 56, 72–73, 78, 81–83, 94, 332–334, 337–342, 344–349, 351, 368–371, 373, 375, 378–379, 381–384, 388, 393, 395, 398–404, 429–434, 436–442, 444, 448–449, 493–494, 497–498, 501–502

Mobile crane, 9, 29–31, 33–34, 41–42, 46, 48, 50, 53, 56, 72–73, 78, 81–83, 332–334, 337–342, 344–349, 351, 368–371, 373, 375, 378–379, 381–383, 388, 393, 395, 398–404, 429–434, 436–442, 444, 497–498, 501–502

Monitoring, 9–10, 76, 87–89, 107, 109, 112, 114, 120–121, 128, 146, 306, 317, 323–324, 328, 345, 380, 394, 398, 400–401, 403, 446

N

Non-slewing, 9, 48, 429–430, 436, 438, 450

O

Operations, 10–11, 13, 15–17, 19, 21, 23, 25–27, 31, 33–39, 41, 43, 45–49, 51, 55, 57, 59–63, 65, 67, 69, 71, 73–79, 81, 83, 85, 87–93, 95–99, 101, 103, 105–107, 109–115, 117–125, 127, 129, 131, 133, 135, 137, 139, 141–145, 147–153, 155–157, 159–163, 165, 167, 169–175, 177, 179, 181–183, 185–187, 189, 191–195, 197–199, 201–203, 205, 207, 209, 211, 213, 215–217, 219–221, 223, 225, 227, 229, 231–233, 235–239, 241, 243, 245, 247–253, 255, 257, 259, 261, 263, 265, 267, 269, 271–273, 275, 277, 279–281, 285, 287, 289, 291–297, 299–301, 303–307, 309, 311, 313, 315–319, 321–323, 325–329, 331–337, 339–343, 345, 347–349, 351, 353–357, 359, 361, 363, 365, 367, 369–375, 377–379, 381–383, 385–387, 389–391, 393–395, 397–405, 407, 409, 411, 413, 415, 417, 419, 421, 423, 425–427, 431, 433, 435–439, 441–447, 449–451, 453, 455, 457, 459, 461, 463, 465, 467, 469, 471, 473, 475, 477, 480–481, 483, 485, 487, 489, 491, 493, 495, 497, 499, 501

Operator, 10–11, 13–17, 19–25, 27, 34–35, 38, 46–47, 51, 56–57, 60–63, 65, 72, 76–77, 79, 82, 84–86, 88–91, 93, 95–98, 102, 111–113, 115–127, 129–136, 139, 141–144, 146–154, 156, 158, 160, 163–164, 169–170, 172, 175, 177, 180, 194–196, 211–220, 232, 242–244, 256, 259, 261, 264, 271, 276–280, 290–292, 297–299, 305, 315, 327–329, 338, 340–341, 346, 351–352, 361, 369–370, 372–374, 378–381, 385–387, 391, 393–396, 398–404, 431, 433, 439, 442, 445–446, 448, 450, 479–480, 495, 501–502

Outrigger, 45–46, 72, 154–155, 164, 181, 200, 340, 343–346, 350–361, 363–365, 381, 384, 398, 405, 420, 430, 432, 480, 502

Overhead crane, 53–54, 283, 285–286, 297, 306, 481, 502

P

Pad, 13, 46, 137, 140, 344–345, 351–355, 357–363

Performance, 26–27, 68, 86, 105, 115, 123, 125, 127, 138, 141, 145–147, 153, 287, 305, 320, 324–325, 328, 374, 398, 400

Personal protective equipment, 318, 382

Personnel, 9, 34, 63, 74, 76, 83, 86–87, 89, 91, 93–94, 97–98, 100, 102–105, 107–108, 111–113, 115, 117, 119–122, 125, 127, 129, 138–139, 141–142, 145–148, 192, 194–198, 211, 216–218, 246–248, 250–251, 253–258, 265–266, 269, 276, 278–280, 282, 295, 297–300, 302–303, 305–307, 310–313, 315–318, 320–327, 329–330, 340, 347–349, 361, 369, 374, 379–380, 393, 399, 401–404, 406, 436–440, 444, 447, 497, 502

Physics, 13

Planning, 9, 45, 98, 103, 140, 192, 245, 294–295, 315, 347, 399, 415, 436, 444, 480–481, 488–489, 495

Portal, 9, 53, 184, 225–226, 228, 230, 238, 242, 245–246, 248–251, 253, 255, 257–258, 267, 269, 271, 276–279, 281–282

Portal crane, 225, 228, 230, 242, 255, 257–258, 267, 269, 271, 276–278, 281

Post-operational checks, 10

Pre-start checks, 438

Precision, 35, 39, 56, 61, 65, 130–131, 140, 170, 188–190, 211, 238–239, 284, 287, 294, 306, 333, 384, 399–401, 403–404

Preventive maintenance, 317, 326

Productivity, 61, 67, 127, 147, 294, 312, 323, 334, 402–403

R

Radio communication, 19

Regulations, 10–11, 76, 88, 111, 153, 155, 164–165, 297, 315, 320, 328, 368, 376, 386, 431, 434, 495, 497

Reliability, 84, 96, 106–107, 115, 145, 147, 296, 323–326, 438, 446

Reporting, 96, 125, 136, 148, 268, 325–326, 395

Rescue operations, 92

Review, 10, 102–103, 109, 113, 126, 148, 380, 415

Rigging, 34, 56–57, 75, 83, 111, 170–172, 200–201, 298–299, 302, 386, 389–390, 479–481, 495, 502

Risk assessment, 83, 318

Risk management, 108–109, 153

Risk mitigation, 109, 112

Root cause analysis, 109

Rough terrain crane, 335, 343–344, 387

S

Safety, 10, 12–13, 17–18, 20, 22, 24, 55, 60–61, 63, 65, 67–68, 71, 73–76, 80, 82–90, 94, 97–100, 102–107, 109–128, 131, 136, 138–148, 151–153, 155–156, 158, 164–165, 170, 181, 192, 195, 202–203, 205–206, 209, 211, 213, 216–217, 219, 223, 232, 242, 244–246, 248–253, 255–262, 264–267, 269, 271, 273, 276–280, 282, 289–290, 292, 294, 296–297, 299–300, 302, 304–307, 311–312, 314–330, 340, 345, 347–349, 351, 354–355, 368, 370, 372, 374–375, 377–379, 381–384, 387, 393, 395, 398–404, 406, 435–440, 444, 446, 451, 465, 480, 495, 497, 499, 501

Safety protocols, 13, 22, 88, 105, 112, 117, 119, 121–122, 139–140, 143, 145, 147–148, 211, 213, 219, 223, 278, 296, 319–321, 326, 370, 382–383, 399, 406, 438

Shackle, 368, 390, 405

Signage, 101, 110–111, 113, 118–119, 205, 209, 318, 379

Site layout, 100, 103

Skills, 480

Slewing, 9, 48–50, 61–63, 77–79, 93, 97, 118, 126, 128–129, 133, 149, 151–152, 155, 332–333, 338–344, 347, 368–370, 373, 375, 378–379, 381, 383–384, 388, 393–395, 398–404, 429–431, 436, 438, 442, 444, 450, 496

Sling, 43–45, 83, 132, 134, 295, 342, 368, 390, 405, 418, 440, 467, 470, 481

Stability, 30, 40–41, 43, 45–46, 51, 53, 55–56, 60, 62, 76, 79–81, 88, 111, 120, 125, 131, 136, 139–140, 142, 144–145, 153–155, 159, 164, 169, 171, 181, 284, 287, 303–304, 328, 333, 336, 340–341, 343–347, 349–351,

353–355, 370–374, 382–383, 385–386, 393–394, 400, 404, 431, 433, 436, 439–440, 442–444, 446, 480, 488–489, 495–497, 499, 502

Standards, 10, 24, 34, 63, 85–86, 88, 99, 104, 106, 109, 112, 123–124, 126, 146–148, 153, 202, 219, 223, 250, 296–297, 315, 371, 375–378, 395, 401–402, 418, 480, 495, 502

Supervision, 105, 132, 370

T

Technology, 89, 480, 501

Tower, 9, 29–30, 53–59, 61–88, 90–99, 106–112, 115–116, 118–121, 123, 127–129, 131–132, 134–142, 144–148, 150, 152–153, 156–157, 162, 164–170, 176, 179–180, 182, 310, 332, 501–502

Tower crane, 9, 29–30, 53–59, 61–88, 90–99, 106–112, 115–116, 118–121, 123, 128–129, 131–132, 134–142, 144–148, 150, 152, 156–157, 162, 164–170, 176, 179–180, 182, 501–502

Traffic management, 101, 114, 193

Training, 21, 34–35, 74, 82–83, 105, 107, 111, 122, 152, 164, 299, 315, 317–318, 370, 399, 465, 480

Truck-mounted, 9, 336

U

Understanding, 65, 81, 102–103, 109, 153, 156, 174, 182, 368, 379, 383–384, 400, 402, 419, 436–437, 480

V

Vehicle loading, 9, 336, 351, 408–409, 411, 419–422

Ventilation, 108

Versatility, 58, 61, 65, 67–68, 72, 333, 338–339

W

Warning lights, 124, 129, 290

Wear and tear, 105, 292, 321
Wire rope, 36, 43, 51, 124–125, 298, 301, 313, 391, 472, 475, 477
Working at heights, 82, 100, 106–107

www.ingramcontent.com/pod-product-compliance
Lightning Source LLC
Chambersburg PA
CBHW071850290426
44110CB00013B/1092